HISTORY AND INTERNATIONAL RELATIONS

HISTORY AND INTERNATIONAL RELATIONS

FROM THE ANCIENT WORLD TO THE 21ST CENTURY

Howard LeRoy Malchow

Bloomsbury Academic
An imprint of Bloomsbury Publishing Plc

B L O O M S B U R Y
LONDON · NEW DELHI · NEW YORK · SYDNEY

Bloomsbury Academic
An imprint of Bloomsbury Publishing Plc

50 Bedford Square
London
WC1B 3DP
UK

1385 Broadway
New York
NY 10018
USA

www.bloomsbury.com

BLOOMSBURY and the Diana logo are trademarks of Bloomsbury Publishing Plc

First published 2016

© Howard LeRoy Malchow, 2016

British Library Cataloguing-in-Publication Data
A catalogue record for this book is available from the British Library.

ISBN: HB: 978-1-4411-1574-4
PB: 978-1-4411-0625-4
ePDF: 978-1-4411-6400-1
ePub: 978-1-4411-9681-1

Library of Congress Cataloging-in-Publication Data
Malchow, Howard L.
History and international relations : from the ancient world
to the 21st century / Howard LeRoy Malchow.
pages cm
ISBN 978-1-4411-1574-4 (HB) – ISBN 978-1-4411-0625-4 (PB) – ISBN 978-1-4411-6400-1 (ePDF) –
ISBN 978-1-4411-9681-1 (ePub) 1. International relations–History. 2. International
relations–Philosophy. 3. International relations–Textbooks. 4. History–Methodology.
5. History–Philosophy. 6. World history–Textbooks. I. Title.
JZ1305.M3315 2015
327–dc23
2015006524

Typeset by Integra Software Services Pvt. Ltd.
Printed and bound in India

CONTENTS

Contents

LIST OF ILLUSTRATIONS

PREFACE

I must confess at the outset that previously my writing interests have been largely those of a historian of domestic, rather than international, relations, and of cultural and social, rather than political, phenomena; some International Relations (IR) scholars may regard that distance and late entry as a liability, and this book as a kind of impertinence. I, of course, prefer to think that it may offer the advantage of an outsider's perspective.

"Outsider" is not quite accurate. This text has been closely informed by my experience teaching an undergraduate introduction to IR. Moreover, my previous work and teaching profited greatly from transnational, postcolonial approaches to the formation of domestic identities, ideas, and practices, approaches that emphasize transnational hybridity and circularity. When some years ago I turned, as a research project, to the familiar subject of the Anglo-American special relationship, a topic generally approached as essentially one of politics and foreign policy and of the clubby relationship of political elites, what seemed to be missing often was the larger and deeper cultural context in which American and British political affairs were enmeshed. In a sense, the discipline of IR itself, in its origins and discourse, is a product of this special relationship; that is, it has a significantly Anglo-American, transatlantic character.

This exploration has led to two general conclusions about what a social science of IR might be or ought to be. The first is, unremarkably, that the study of politics generally, including the politics of foreign affairs, can almost always profit from a more serious engagement with social and cultural contexts—a commonplace in the discipline of History but, as will be clear below, a matter of some contestation among political theorists. Second, and perhaps more fundamental, is that IR has been too narrowly construed by both international historians and political scientists as relations among *states* within a system of states. Though such an assumption may have in the past been productive of interesting scholarship, there is growing reason to doubt its adequacy, either in explaining the past or, especially, in engaging the unfolding, borderless crises of our current era. In this book, I attempt to endorse the more holistic view, embraced by many "Constructivists," that the field needs to seek a larger understanding of international relations and the history of international relations in a global realm of shifting identities, values, ideologies, and economic regimes.

This book owes a great deal to my students and my colleagues at Tufts University and beyond. Special thanks are due to the patient and wise, if often skeptical, advice of Daniel Mulholland. Among other colleagues, thanks are due to David Ekbladh, Steve Marrone, and Vickie Sullivan for their useful comments. I am indebted to John

Fyler, master himself of lucid and thoughtful prose, for attempting to help me redress stylistic infelicities. Finally, special thanks are due to Erik Goldstein, past director of the flourishing IR program at Boston University, and long-time friend and colleague. Needless to say, what follows, however much improved by their kind advice, is my responsibility alone.

Somerville, Massachusetts

INTRODUCTION: HISTORY AND THE DISCIPLINE(S) OF INTERNATIONAL RELATIONS

The academic field of International Relations (IR) continues to grow in popularity as an undergraduate concentration. This is especially true at American universities where, often to the puzzlement—sometimes consternation—of teacher-scholars in the humanities and social sciences, IR departments and programs, separate or embedded as concentrations within older disciplines, have flourished even as their parent fields may have stagnated or declined. This growth is reflected in both the sheer numbers of students enrolled in IR courses (at some American universities, such as my own, IR is now far and away the largest "major"), but also in the growth of faculty engaged in IR research and writing, and in the institutionalization of the field—in journals and electronic mailing lists (listservs) devoted to its interests and in scholarly organizations to promote professional contact and dialogue.[1]

This textbook seeks to introduce, from the perspective of a practicing historian, IR's theory and practice to both undergraduate and graduate students of International History, as well as to students of IR and Political Science who may profit from a closer understanding of both the opportunities and the limitations of historical narrative and analysis. Its objective is to offer not just a general introduction to the discipline of IR, but to address ways in which History can inform and perhaps interrogate IR scholarship, as well as ways in which IR may inform History. We shall do this first by placing the field itself into its own historical contexts, relating both its institutional development and its central concerns and theories to the larger history of the times. That is, we shall "historicize" the discipline. We shall then examine a series of historical eras and events that have been highlighted in much IR scholarship as significant in defining the discipline and establishing its key concepts. We shall conclude with some observations about the current state of the special relationship between the disciplines of History and IR.

This is, of course, to beg the question whether IR is properly a *discipline* at all or whether it can best be understood as located within a larger parent field such as History (as diplomatic, international, global, or transnational history), as is the common orientation in Great Britain, or, as often in America, in Political Science (where IR is one of its major concentration fields). Or is it, as many IR programs in American universities declare, a composite discipline, an "interdisciplinary" or "multidisciplinary" discipline—with all the richness but also epistemological ambiguity that may suggest?

Questions also arise with respect to the various purposes served by IR as a scholarly field. Is it an interrogating *narrative* of past and present interstate conflict and conflict resolution (of, that is, war and peace)? Is it a social *science* that seeks to reduce the realm of myriad historical contingency to laws and probabilities? Is its implicit or explicit goal that of informing present and future policy? If so, whose policy? While any discipline as a scholarly enterprise requires objectivity, a stepping outside—as far as that may be possible—of one's cultural and historical conditioning, the "presentism" and policy orientation of much IR scholarship may pose special problems. Historians, closer to the sources upon which historical narrative is built, may be more sensitive than political scientists or historical sociologists to the dangers of employing history as simply a reservoir of examples for the construction and rationalization of theory. In this regard, historians themselves have, of course, not been free of malpractice, but their discipline is more attuned to the dangers of what may be called "Whig history" (using the past to justify the present) than many outside the field who seek to manipulate historical evidence.

As we begin, it may be well to bear in mind two adages that are both descriptive and cautionary. First, while History complicates, Political Science (or indeed social science generally) simplifies—either may be a virtue or a vice. Second, History, popular assumptions to the contrary, does *not* in fact repeat itself. As the ancient Greek philosopher Heraclitus observed, history is a flowing river where no man can step into the same water twice. This is not to deny that the "lessons of history" may be profitably examined, but to caution against a too-easy parallelism of past, present, and future.

History

Historical narrative as oral tradition is older than writing itself, and historical philosophy and analysis was no monopoly of the West—as the work of the late thirteenth, early fourteenth-century Persian Rashid al-din Tabib, a Jewish convert to Islam, or the late fourteenth-century Maghrebi Arab Ibn Khaldun illustrates. History as a scholarly discipline in the West, however, has its origins in the European Enlightenment, and assumed a legitimate place in university curricula and a professional presence in the nineteenth century. In Britain, while professorships in History had been appointed at Oxford and Cambridge from the early eighteenth century, History as a distinct examination field for undergraduates had to wait until the late Victorian period. In addition to an undergraduate History curriculum, American universities—more influenced by the professionalization of History in Germany—developed research programs, journals, professional organizations, and seminar-based postgraduate training by the late nineteenth century.

While this is not the place for a full narrative of the development of the discipline as an academic profession, it is relevant to our interests that History, as practiced in its formative years, was much influenced by its belles-lettristic origins, and by an interest in producing narratives of political power, war, and commanding personalities. Above all was the privileging of what German scholars of the era called *Außenpolitik*, the narrative and analysis of foreign affairs—generally from a nationalist perspective. Following from the eighteenth-century German philosopher Johann Gottfried Herder's observation that each people or *Volk* had its own unique culture and history, nineteenth-century historiography was above all a story of the rise and conflict of nations. German influences, again especially in the American academy, also pushed the field toward a more "scientific" and empirical character by insisting on the importance of objectivity and precision, to be arrived at through a close, disciplined attention to original archival documents. In the famous words of Leopold von Ranke (1795–1886), the task of the historian was, above all, to tell history "*wie es eigentlich gewesen*"—"as it really was," stripping away metaphysical and literary pretensions. It was Ranke as well who helped place diplomatic history at the heart of the nineteenth-century historian's enterprise through his own exploration of the detailed and voluminous archives of the sixteenth- and seventeenth-century Republic of Venice.

Some contemporary historians, critical of the uses to which some IR scholars may put historical "facts," argue that IR often seems to adopt uncritically the outmoded empiricism of nineteenth-century historiography, just as it privileges the *Außenpolitik* biases of that scholarship and its assumptions of the primacy of the (nation) state in its theory. Certainly "cutting-edge" History moved on in the early- and mid-twentieth century in ways that left the subjects of traditional historical exploration—diplomacy, war, Great Men, and Great Ideas—on the margins, if thriving in the genres of popular historical narrative, political biography, and the History Channel. While this criticism is no doubt unfair to those IR scholars who do care about and are informed by current historiographic issues and debates, as it is to many of those historians who continue to produce sophisticated work on warfare and diplomacy, certainly the "history" that matters to many IR scholars not trained in history can sometime seem dated and outside the profession's mainstream.

The modernist movement of History (from, roughly, the 1920s to the 1970s) into large areas of, usually domestic, social phenomena—and consequently a shift from an interest in the international narrative of war and politics to their domestic political and social contexts—involved a vast expansion of the historian's craft that saw historians absorb concepts and practices from many social science fields, from Anthropology and Sociology but also Psychology, Economics, and Demography. The rise of social history in the interwar period and, especially, in the 1960s, challenged the predominance of traditional political and biographical narrative, as well as the primacy of *Außenpolitik*: there was a shift from a view of social history as simply "history with the politics left out," as a source of narrative color, to one that demanded the integration of political, economic, and social/cultural understanding and thus centered questions of how social change constrained and shaped politics.

In this, the careful work of the historian of international relations, of diplomatic history as practiced in the archives, came to seem to many as less relevant and less interesting in an age defined by democracy and social conflict, and the retrieval of the history of those common people who had suffered from the "enormous condescension of posterity," in the words of the prominent social historian of the left, E. P. Thompson, in 1963.

Historical narratives, historical facts, and Edward Hallett Carr

Though History often borrowed heavily from the social sciences in its high modernist period—and we should bear in mind that more than most disciplines History contains a wide spectrum of practice—it remained in the minds of many social scientists from outside the field (and especially political science-trained IR scholars) an under-theorized realm of contingency ("one damn thing after another") and antiquarian detail. It might provide a useful warehouse of data, but the historian's reductionist project of historicizing all phenomena—that is, locating events and ideas in a particular and perhaps unique social/historical setting—inhibited his ability to construct larger views or pose meaningful questions and answers. This characterization, which continues to be repeated in some quarters of IR, of course oversimplifies and distorts the actual practice of many historians.

The lack of an explicit theoretical apparatus does not of course mean the absence of "theory," however unselfconsciously employed. Nevertheless, many social scientists rightly insist that historians are not always interested in understanding the limitations of the theoretical assumptions they may make, that they, or at least many of them, are more interested in constructing a narrative—telling a story—than in posing well-defined research questions, and that they are inclined to leave the search for "ultimate causes" to others. It is important, however, to understand that these issues have long been debated among historians themselves, especially since the advent of the new social history in the 1960s and, subsequently, its postmodernist critics.

From the ancient Greek historians on, at the center of most historical enquiry and of its epistemology (the study of the nature of historical knowledge) has been the issue of causation, itself embedded in the definition of history as change over time (whether the never-repeating river of Heraclitus, or cyclical or evolutionary change). Apart from "mere antiquarianism" (the discovery and presentation of detail for its own sake) that is regarded by most historians as allied with but properly outside the scholarly practice of History, even the simplest literary narrative engages at some level the problem of causation.

The definition and search for causes lies at the heart of much that has been written about the practice of history. The student interested in the application of History to the study of IR would do well to begin by familiarizing him- or herself with the issues raised in a classic of such historiography, Edward Hallett Carr's *What Is History?* Read by generations of undergraduate and sixth-form history students in Britain, Carr's essay has fallen out of usage in the United States, where his version of progressive modernism went out of fashion well before his death in 1982. Nevertheless, the text poses useful, instructive questions and caveats for those intending to practice or use history, from an academic sage who is also commonly regarded as a founder of the

Figure I.1 Edward Hallett Carr (1892–1982).

Source: National Portrait Gallery, London; photo Eliot and Fry.

Realist school of IR scholarship. In IR Cold War debate (and after), Realists are often identified with the ideological right, but Carr (Figure I.1) was a man of the left, a determined advocate of the wartime alliance with the Soviet Union who dedicated the rest of his long life to writing its early history (1917–29), a fourteen-volume study. This may sound like an antiquarian's love of detail, but in fact Carr was a great enemy of what he called a "fetishism of facts."

What Is History?, a series of lectures from 1961, has its critics—especially among postmodernists who find it insufficiently "intersubjective" and dated in its conception of "progress." While we can admit that it is certainly of its mid-twentieth-century modernist time, it is nevertheless also a text that continues to speak to us about how historians (and those who use history) ought to go about their business. The first chapter poses his central question—what is a fact, or more precisely, *what is a historical fact*? He means generally for all history writing, but one must note the special importance of the subject for IR, where there has long been a tendency on the one hand to accuse theory-averse historians of simply stringing facts together while on the other selectively to employ historical evidence in confirming "scientific" hypotheses and paradigms.

Though Carr sees History itself as a social science, he cautions (the warning is apt for both historians and political scientists) against cherry-picking—the selection and organization of some convenient "facts," and the suppression of others, to establish an argument. Selection of appropriate facts—whether in the creation of a simple narrative or an argument—being unavoidable in the writing of any history, he asserts that it is the historian's interpretation that converts a mere fact to an historical fact, and hence it is of critical importance to "know the historian" (his own historical context; his social milieu; his biases, convictions, and intentions) before one can judge the value of the history he writes. However much "objectivity" may be a laudable goal, it can only be imperfectly achieved; the historian himself can never stand outside his own history. Each generation writes out of and for its own time.

If we are all enmeshed in our own time, there can be no final, definitive history of the kind positivist nineteenth-century scholars sought to discover or create. Even the words we use have a meaning for us they may not have had in the past, or may not have in the future. Being well-versed in historical dialectic, Carr tells us that history, a flowing evolutionary process, is an unending dialogue between the facts and the historian, between the past and the present. If some historians attack political science for its present orientation, Carr reminds us that all history is itself illuminated by the (historian's own) present. *Good history* appreciates that theory and models of explanation are necessary (even when lightly or tentatively employed); *good social science* (i.e., both political science and historical sociology) dialogues with and adapts to historical fact. Where they differ is in the search in social and political science for basic laws, or at least hypotheses of basic laws. The historian, according to Carr in his third lecture, is interested in hypotheses as well, not to propose some general universal theory of history (the way now-unfashionable generalists like Arnold Toynbee attempted earlier in the twentieth century) but to help find what may be generalizable in a unique fact and which facts can help us understand long-term *processes* in history. In this, the historian is, above all, concerned with the problematic of historical *causation* (something Carr expands upon in subsequent lectures).

To understand causation is to learn from history about the present and from the present about history. But this does not mean that history's purpose is to confirm current moral judgments. Here Carr sounds like the IR Realist he was taken to be—leery of "hypothetical absolutes" like liberty, justice, or natural law. But if "learning from history" is a hard-headed, unidealistic affair, it is also extraordinarily difficult because of the myriad ways the world changes. Carr is therefore much concerned with the danger of misusing or misunderstanding history, reminding us that—he was a junior member of the British delegation at the Paris peace conference in 1919—"Everyone in the delegation believed that we could learn from the lessons of the Vienna Congress" (67). Of course they got it wrong.

Whatever caveats may be suggested by Carr's own location in time and place—and in the last few years there has been a fresh engagement with aspects of Carr's work—his advice about the practice of history generally and, in particular, the interpretation and uses of historical facts remains compelling and merits close attention by, especially, those students preparing to explore the disciplines of History and IR.

International Relations within the discipline of History: Diplomatic history

As the discipline History developed as a postgraduate-trained profession, there was a tendency toward specialization. By the beginning of the twentieth century, diplomatic history became increasingly separated as a field narrowly devoted to the study of the operation of foreign office bureaucracies and their political masters, through the intense examination of foreign office archives (the difficulty of access to this source made—and makes—recent or *contemporary* diplomatic history problematic) and correspondingly to the kinds of research questions that a preoccupation with the minutiae of such sources might suggest. Many historians came to consider diplomatic history as a kind of antiquarianism, in G. M. Young's famous dismissal, "the record of what one clerk said to another clerk." Like diplomacy itself, it seemed to many scholars too much a matter of form and process and too little of the larger social, and indeed political, contexts.

Generally speaking, the subfield of diplomatic history, as it was established in the early twentieth century, was a well- (if narrowly) defined narrative of state-to-state relations that viewed diplomacy as a by-and-large rational, self-contained activity, emphasizing (1) the study of formal negotiation within an early modern and modern structure of sovereign states, (2) the study of permanent bureaucracies and of a corps of officials sent abroad (the diplomatic profession), and (3) a Eurocentric—and in the case of diplomatic history in the United States often an American-centric—view.

The First World War provided a huge stimulus to the field of diplomatic history due to a contemporary need to unravel the complicated and secret nature of pre-war maneuvering, the (at least selective) opening of European foreign office archives after the war, and the general turn against pin-stripe-trousered diplomats for not preventing Armageddon. This led to a search for blame by liberal historians during and after the Paris peace negotiations in 1919. Moreover, the establishment of the League of Nations encouraged scholarly interest in the history of international law and arbitration. But the "failure" of the diplomats in 1914 also perforce heralded the diminution of the history of (inconsequential) diplomacy in the following decades at a time when social and ideological contexts came to demand a larger attention.

In the post-Second World War, mid-century revolution that saw the scholarly research and writing of history move from high political narrative to (usually domestic) social analysis and description—often informed by the allied disciplines of Sociology and Anthropology—a seemingly old-fashioned diplomatic history was in fact slow to take on the importance of domestic social contexts, or the behavioralist-inspired new work in Political Science. While it is true that some diplomatic historians made a tentative use of the new social history—in exploring for instance the social composition of foreign service elites—the epistemological narrowness of much traditional diplomatic history meant that it was increasingly "doubly marginalized" within the historical profession: as social-political history moved to study the dispossessed rather than elites, and as postmodernist cultural historians shifted focus away from politics and raised fundamental questions about the possibility of document-based objectivity.

As a result, diplomatic history became somewhat isolated; old departmental positions in the field went unreplaced, and there were relatively few new positions in the 1970s and 1980s. While there were some articulate voices for a new diplomatic history that was sensitive to both social and economic contexts, the history of foreign relations was by the late twentieth century something of a sidelined subfield. Ironically, the rise of a separate discipline of IR has served to confirm this relegation, while also validating diplomatic history as a reservoir of useful data.

Since the Second World War, the field of diplomatic history has followed two tracks: as a continuing "grand tradition" of a comparatively narrow historical subdiscipline, on the one hand, and on the other as an "international history" that continues to emphasize narrative, but through an interweaving of domestic and international politics, social milieus, and economic structures. The first track remains dedicated to a close examination of diplomacy as a largely self-contained activity—a negotiation event or the art of statecraft of a towering figure like Bismarck, with an emphasis on close description and, often, a deep suspicion of systems theory. If the reputation of this kind of tradition has long been on the decline among historians, by the end of the twentieth century the excesses of (especially Neorealist) IR theory inspired a revival in some quarters of diplomatic history as the history of an art that emphasizes contingency, personality, and unpredictability. A main thrust of international history has been to integrate international into national historical narratives by, for instance, presenting the United States as "America-in-the-world." In Britain, there has been a parallel, perhaps more pronounced, effort to incorporate its imperial past into domestic historical narrative, a perspective encouraged by its postcolonial, multicultural present.

The history of war and warfare

The subfield of military history is of course closely related to that of diplomacy—as war is often the consequence of the failure of diplomacy or the condition that requires diplomatic settlement. Moreover, war studies have traditionally shared with the history of diplomacy an interest in narrative and a focus on the behavior of rational actors—military leaders and strategists—somewhat removed from larger social and cultural contexts. Among historians at large, they have consequently also been regarded together as subdisciplines apart from the mainstream interests of the profession—though narratives of warfare continue to have a large presence in the genre of "great battles" popular history. Since the 1950s, this separation has been challenged, most notably, in work on "military revolutions" in early modern Europe—especially that of Michael Roberts (1956) and those like Geoffrey Parker (1988), who have followed him in attempting to place the study of war into a larger social and cultural history of, especially, the formation of the early modern state.

Historical studies of the origins and conduct of wars have long been consulted by political scientists, especially IR Realists, interested in distilling autonomous "laws of war." Like Stephen Van Evera (*Causes of War: Power and the Roots of Conflict*, 1999) or Stephen M. Walt (*Revolution and War*, 1996), they often make extensive use of historical narrative—generally of early modern and modern European conflict—and comparative methods, as in Daniel S. Geller and J. David Singer's "scientific study of international conflict" (1998) or the work of Claudio Cioffi-Revilla on "scales of conflict in long-range analysis" (1996). Though a political scientist, John Weltman, in his general narrative of the "evolution of war," has nonetheless echoed many historians in his skepticism about the search for "calculable laws of war," preferring to emphasize the particular "social, material, and intellectual context within which such conflicts occur" (Weltman, 1995, x–xi).

As a scholarly subfield, war studies cover a spectrum of approaches, from those that, like Thucydides' classic work, raise the widest historical and cultural issues, to narrower considerations of the grand strategy of, say, a Napoleon, down to highly specialized work on tactics and technologies. Military history has often been written, not by professional historians but by those with military training and experience, like the renowned early- and mid-twentieth-century British expert on military affairs, Captain Basil Henry Liddell-Hart (1895–1970), who never held a university post (other than as a visiting scholar), or the nineteenth-century American naval historian, Captain Alfred Thayer Mahan (1840–1914), who, like many of the modern specialists in war studies, both served on active duty and, subsequently, taught at a military academy. The field has often been located somewhere between academia and the world of the policy-oriented think tank: Mahan's work on the geopolitics of naval strategy was, as is well-known, influential not only in Theodore Roosevelt's White House but in pre-First World War Berlin, and Liddell-Hart was a passionate interwar advocate of tank warfare and the mechanization of the British cavalry.

The close connection between traditional military history and a somewhat discredited late nineteenth-century geopolitics encouraged a distaste for the field among many historians, as did a general low regard for the professional officer class during and after the First World War. In Britain, though a chair of military history was established at Oxford in 1909 and one in military studies at King's College, London, just after the First World War, the field waned until its revival at the beginning of the Cold War. The closeness of this subdiscipline to a Cold War and post-Cold War political science of "security studies" or "strategic studies" (a.k.a. International Strategic Studies [ISS]), subdisciplines marked by a Washington- or London-outward point of view, further discredited the field in the eyes of some historians, at least during the long Cold War. Subsequently, the field has been pushed to broaden its definition of "security" beyond a preoccupation with military affairs and beyond the state to include much that social and cultural historians might endorse—for instance, the concept of "human security" involving underdevelopment, disease, malnutrition, and gender issues.

The Cold War era nevertheless saw a revival of interdisciplinary interest in war, and scholars were often able to tap into government resources and government-supported think tanks. The salience of the nuclear arms problem in the 1950s and 1960s, and the importance of nuclear weapons technologies to both diplomatic and military affairs (Liddell-Hart turned late in his career to nuclear defense issues), fuelled a degree of institutionalization for war studies. In 1953, a Department of War Studies was established at King's College, London, to be followed by similar multidisciplinary programs elsewhere in the United Kingdom. On both sides of the ocean, the contemporary era has seen the emergence of scholars of widely regarded stature, like the military historian Sir Michael Eliot Howard, appointed Regius Professor of Modern History at Oxford University in 1980, or the prolific American political scientist and past president of the International Studies Association, Jack S. Levy. As one would expect, the study of war was most comfortably ensconced in the service academies where, by the end of the century, strategy and policy departments and chaired positions in strategic studies continued to proliferate.

More than is true of the subdiscipline of diplomatic history, modern military history can have a close affinity with certain social sciences. Studies of strategy and tactics may draw on Psychology and game theory while larger studies of war and society may be informed by Sociology and Anthropology. In the United States, the field of war studies was pioneered by historical sociologists at the University of Chicago in the interwar period as a part of the post-First World War liberal project to uncover the roots and character of mass violence (Quincy Wright's two-volume comparative historical analysis, *A Study of War*, the fruit of this collective effort, was published in 1942). And it is in the United States, as Cold War Superpower, where "strategic studies" has most flourished.

Military history can claim a deep and prestigious pedigree, beginning with (the perhaps mythical) General Sun Tzu's sixth-century BC text, *The Art of War*, or Thucydides' fifth-century BC classic, *The History of the Peloponnesian War*. It often has a theoretical affinity for the work of Niccolò Machiavelli (who wrote a book on *The Art of War*) and Thomas Hobbes, and owns a major figure in the philosophy of war in Carl von Clausewitz. Nevertheless, the field still struggles somewhat for legitimacy among professional historians, if not among IR scholars (especially Realists) who see it as closely related to their central concern with power and state security.

Political Science

Disciplinary histories are perhaps inevitably prone to present a field as more unitary and progressive in its evolution than the facts allow. Political Science is no exception, and consequently there has been some debate of late over how best to approach its history—through the development of its "internal discourse" or by locating it in specific historical moments, focusing on its emerging self-identity in academia, the purposes it has served to advance beyond the university, and the differences that might be observed through cross-country, cross-cultural comparisons.

The fact that the largely Anglo-American discipline of IR has been marked by contrasts and tensions between (a British) historicism and (an American) scientism, though these differences can be exaggerated, derives at least in part from the development of Political Science in the United States as a distinct social science discipline, and its putative ownership of IR as a subdiscipline self-consciously aligned with the deductive, positivist tradition of the natural sciences rather than the humanist orientation of history and political thought.

As a distinct institutionalized field of professional, academic study, Political Science began to emerge in the United States at the end of the nineteenth century from the "service role" of courses in Government as instructors of undergraduates in citizenship and public service. Influenced by the German field of *Staatswissenschaft* (the science or study of the state), the first school of Political Science in the United States was that at Columbia University, opened in 1880. An American Academy of Political and Social Science was founded in 1889, and an American Political Science Association (APSA) in 1903—followed shortly by the emerging discipline's major journal, the *American Political Science Review* (1906). From its origins, Political Science was closely tied to political history, and before the First World War was often combined with History at American universities. There were on occasion joint meetings of the American Historical Association (AHA) (founded in 1884) and APSA. The field that emerged reflected disparate traditions of Western political history and Western political philosophy, beginning with the ancient Greeks, on the one hand, and on the other a historical-comparative politics that traced a route from early Enlightenment thinkers like Montesquieu to the work of late nineteenth- and early twentieth-century liberal scholars of comparative political systems like the British historian and politician James Bryce.

In Britain, the study of "politics" remained close to its humanist, historical, and philosophical roots at Cambridge and Oxford, and universities were slow to establish it as a single honors field. There was no APSA equivalent until 1950. In America, however, academic programs in "political science" proliferated after the First World War, with the programs at Harvard and Chicago rising to special prominence; the discipline as a separate social science flourished, though marked often by a sharp tension between those who wished to emphasize political thought (the older tradition) and those social scientists, as at the University of Chicago, who pushed for a methodology drawn from Sociology, Psychology, and the natural sciences. In part this was a battle for legitimacy *as a discipline*, and a corresponding need to justify an institutional and epistemological separation from History and Philosophy in order to secure a professional presence and career field in the American university. After the Second World War, there was a significant growth in APSA membership and in the number of university departments, while the field as a predictive social science moved further away from History and historical Sociology in its research objectives and methods. The "behavioral revolution" (the scientific study through quantitative analysis of observable determinants of human action), encouraged by the Ford Foundation, was adopted by many in American Political Science, a trend that was not followed in the British universities.

History and International Relations

The behavioralist approach had a commanding presence in American Political Science in the 1950s and 1960s. The discipline remained however a (somewhat uneasy) marriage of traditions—as expressed in its official designation of the separate fields of "political philosophy" (as a history of ideas) and "comparative politics." While behavioralism was subsequently challenged by other scientistic approaches drawn from, say, cognitive psychology (dealing with the internal mental processes that may shape motivation and choice) or structuralism (the view that individual action is determined by the constraints of external systems or structures), the scientific method it demanded, "parsimonious" theory built on hypotheses of laws of behavior tested by empirical evidence, remains dominant.

Like Sociology, which had also grown out of an historicist past, Political Science as a social science was by nature present-oriented, and, to a much greater degree than History, rested on assumptions of the predictive value of its scientific analyses. To the degree that IR was lodged as a subfield of Political Science and draws many (perhaps most) of its practitioners from that parent, it too has typically been seen as a predictive discipline that aspires to contribute to present and future governmental policy. IR also illustrates something of Political Science's uncomfortable double identity in its own division between those who privilege canonical texts (Thucydides, Machiavelli, Hobbes), as do the Classical Realists, and those who deal in the scientific analysis of systems or the cognitive psychology of actors.

International Relations

The study of international affairs as a special field emerged after the First World War in multidisciplinary graduate programs established at a number of universities in both Britain and the United States. After the Second World War, American schools of international affairs, however, rapidly proliferated due to the expansion of universities generally, the availability of émigré European academics like Hans Morgenthau, the opening of professional opportunities in both expanding government agencies (like the CIA) and policy-center institutions (like the government-funded RAND corporation), and generally a sense that the United States had emerged from its isolationist tradition to embrace its hegemonic role as the "defender of the free world." The curriculum these schools advanced was largely that of Politics and Sociology, with Economics and History in somewhat marginal roles. A core group of these professional schools (at Columbia, Georgetown, Tufts, Johns Hopkins, and Princeton), with support from the Ford Foundation, formed a kind of collaborative network from the late 1970s, and, joined by a number of other schools, established the Association of Professional Schools of International Affairs in 1989.

Though at the *undergraduate* level the study of IR may be pursued entirely within the disciplines of either History (as international history, history of diplomacy, military history, etc.) or Political Science (as a subfield specialization), there has been since the late 1970s an accelerating trend, in America at any rate, toward establishing administratively separate programs or departments that offer the subject as a distinct undergraduate concentration—located, usually, within the Social Sciences. Faculty, however, are likely to be recruited from those with a postgraduate training in either History or (more commonly) Political Science since there are relatively few Ph.D. programs in IR as a separate, distinct discipline. Moreover, many undergraduate programs are entirely staffed by "borrowed" faculty from Political Science, Economics, Sociology, History, and other appropriate fields, and often such programs do not hire and tenure new faculty as would a traditional department, or offer postgraduate training in the field. IR's heavy dependence on the recruitment of faculty from its component disciplines means that it exists in a kind of epistemological borderland as a liminal discipline, or indeed a multiplicity of disciplines. A recent survey of IR faculty in the United States (Maliniak et al., 2011) indicates that IR scholarship, even when practiced largely by those with primary training in Political Science, spans considerable, and increasing, theoretical diversity.

The myriad interests and methodologies of both History- and Political Science-trained IR scholars complicate any attempt to characterize the field. At the same time, such diversity within their parent disciplines may enhance the chance of historians and political scientists finding common ground, as bridges multiply and boundaries weaken.

Gordon Alexander Craig, "milieu et moment," and a larger diplomatic history

In February of 1983, the then president of the AHA, Gordon Alexander Craig (1913–2005), published his inaugural lecture in the discipline's leading American journal, the *American Historical Review*. Craig was the most prominent American scholar of German political and military history, as well as an eminent diplomatic historian. His lecture was both an examination of the limitations of the traditional history of diplomacy and a plea for closer cooperation and understanding between the disciplines of History and Political Science. Though in his work and teaching on diplomacy and Cold War security Craig encouraged collaboration and drew on the social sciences, he was by training and preference essentially a humanist with a love of nineteenth-century literature and an interest in locating foreign relations within particular political cultures.

The AHA address was a balanced piece that both admitted the weaknesses of much traditional diplomatic history and defended the field generally against the "condescension and apathy" of much of the historical profession. Good diplomatic history, according to Craig in an earlier, somewhat autobiographical piece, involved "more than sitting in a library for a while and then writing a monograph about some aspect of foreign affairs" (Craig, 1979). It meant acquiring a "habit of mind" informed by an understanding of the nature of the diplomatic process, the traditions and practices of diplomacy in a particular era, and constraints imposed on diplomats by the national and international contexts of a particular problem. Being a German historian with a close regard for Clausewitz, he was also sensitive to the relationship between diplomacy and "that other more drastic instrument of policy," the art of war.

In the address, Craig notes that traditional diplomatic historians had come in for sharp criticism by other historians for isolating their work from larger social and intellectual forces. They were challenged to expand their view to include the ideological element in foreign relations as well as domestic political contexts—including the growing importance of public opinion and the media—though with his deep knowledge of how independently Bismarck had operated, Craig was skeptical of the importance of these latter elements of *Innenpolitik* (domestic political constraints) before the First World War. His advice sounds a generous note of sympathy with at least some political science theorizing—the need to understand the "modalities" of international relations, attempts at "system-building," the relationship between force and statecraft, and the need for analysis as well as description. Historians, he cautioned, had to get over their distrust of theory and their tendency to insist on the uniqueness of the event (his own textbook, in collaboration with the political scientist Alexander George, *Force and Statecraft*, became a well-established, widely used narrative text that went through many editions). At the same time, however, Craig argued that political scientists could profit from the historian's concern to situate events in what he calls their *milieu et moment* (their place and time)—something that would greatly complicate the way political scientists sometimes select and interpret historical events to suit their theories.

What both Carr and Craig suggest is that, in the attempt to understand international relations, History and Political Science may be, as Jack Levy has written, the "ends of a continuum" (Levy, 2001, 40). There is, in their view, a middle ground between what some historians deplore as the theoretical rigidity of the social sciences (and their misuse of history) and, on the other hand, the "mere description" and event narration that some political scientists see as characteristic of the discipline of History. Historians often feel that the further one gets from primary sources, the more speculative and dubious the history. Political scientists argue, with some justice, that historians have difficulty stepping away from the archives in order to simplify and generalize. What was needed was a creative interplay between fact and theory, between History and Political Science, between a history of generalizable fact and a political science of *middle-range theory* that is sensitive to historical contexts in its dialogue with the past.

In this book, our task is to draw attention to History's perspective and methods—in part this will involve understanding its skeptical critique of the perspective, purposes, and methods of much of the IR scholarship of nonhistorians, while encouraging ways in which each can learn from the other. Such observations and advice as Carr and Craig offered of course reflect their own times, when there seemed to be a clear divide between the kind of scholarship each of the two disciplines pursued. Neither Carr nor Craig could have anticipated the late twentieth-century "cultural turn" in postmodern historical studies or the rise of a vigorous "Constructivist" challenge in IR (see Chapter 2), both of which have raised serious issues with the way either discipline goes about its business—with the way historians attempt to construct narrative and Political Science-trained IR scholars attempt to think about the kinds of empirical evidence most useful in the construction of theory.

The "historical turn" and the future of IR

In recent years, the discipline of IR has seen the previously dominant—at least in the United States—school of Neorealism thrown on the defensive in the face of a new "historical turn" in IR scholarship. Not one of the major assumptions and definitions of Neorealist systems logic (see Chapter 2)—the unitary state, state sovereignty, system anarchy, or rational expectations—remains unchallenged. Some scholars grounded in History like Richard Ned Lebow or Marc Trachtenberg would argue that IR's pretentions as an objective social *science* have always been suspect, embedded as the field is in its own social- and power-legitimating contexts and always prone to reading too much structure into diverse historical reality. The prominent British scholars Barry Buzan and Richard Little provocatively suggested at the turn of the present millennium that IR as a whole (by which they meant the American-dominated, Political Science-informed field) has simply "failed as an intellectual project." IR programs may be proliferating, but the discipline's "big names" are virtually unknown outside the field, it has generated no significant public interest or debate outside academia, and is so dependent on other disciplines like History, Economics, and Sociology that its own claim to status is "weak" (Buzan and Little, 2001, 21). Moreover, its Eurocentrism (i.e., its Western origin and bias) is increasingly glaring and inhibitive in a dawning post-US era, while its promise as a predictive social science has, twenty-five years on, not yet recovered from the embarrassingly unpredicted and sudden end of the Cold War. Can an "historical turn" or return save and revitalize the discipline, or is it an historical artifact of the mid- and late twentieth-century Cold War era doomed to ever-greater specialization and fragmentation?

Of course, History itself as a discipline has only recently emerged from a divisive late twentieth-century debate—"the History wars"—between traditional historians and radical historicists, between positivism and a postmodern deconstructionism, which contested the discipline's ability to mount any coherent narrative that was not artificial and subjective. Though radical deconstructionism has receded in the discipline, the historical turn in IR cannot be a return to simple uncomplicated archive-based narrative. It must perforce take on at some level the understanding that narrative is subjective story-telling and that "grand narratives" are always located in the present.

Students and practitioners must grasp the fact that the field lives through dialogue and contestation across boundaries, and that it is not *a* discipline but a congeries of disciplines, of History, Philosophy, Political Science, Sociology, Anthropology, Economics, and Psychology. IR's ability to evolve may depend to a significant extent on the robust back and forth of its multidisciplinarity. For instance, with the post-Cold War waning of "systems theory" there has been renewed interest in what social and cultural history may have to offer IR. What is called *normative analysis*—how norms or values arise, how they shape and constrain the behavior of individuals and groups, including states—may offer keys (beyond simple rational calculation) to why states respond to security threats in different ways, with aggression, conciliation, or defensive cooperation.

While the growth of IR has been a striking phenomenon of the American academy since the mid-twentieth century, and to a lesser degree of British universities where in some sense the field was born, other regions of Europe, the Americas, Africa, or Asia—indeed most of the world at large—have been slow to embrace IR as an academic discipline, and where it does have a presence it is heavily influenced by what many would consider a form of American scholarly hegemony. That a discipline—both its theory, culled from Western modes of state behavior, and its practice, as a policy-generating resource—may be so closely implicated in the interests of a particular Great Power may pose a significant problem for a supposedly objective, scholarly, and universal field of study. The contemporary student of IR must bear in mind the special challenges posed by a discipline that many beyond the West characterize as, if not exclusively then largely, dominated by the view from Washington DC.

Recommended readings

There is a growing critical literature on E. H. Carr. See Charles Jones, *E. H. Carr and International Relations: A Duty to Lie* (1998), and Jonathan Haslam, *The Vices of Integrity: E. H. Carr, 1892–1982* (1999). Michael Cox (ed.), *E. H. Carr: A Critical Appraisal* (2000), is a collection of essays on various aspects of Carr's work.

For the history, art, and theory of diplomacy, see Richard Langhorne and Keith Hamilton (eds.), *The Practice of Diplomacy: Its Evolution, Theory, and Administration* (1994), and Langhorne and Christer Jonsson (eds.), *Diplomacy* (3 vols., 2004). Also Michael Graham Fry, Erik Goldstein, and Richard Langhorne (eds.), *Guide to Diplomacy and International Relations* (2002). Diplomatic history, like military history, has its journals like *Diplomacy and Statecraft* (UK) and *Diplomatic History* (US), while there are more specialized periodicals like the *Journal of Cold War Studies* or *Cold War History*. For Gordon Craig's reflections on the need for an interdisciplinary approach in diplomatic history, see "The Historian and the Study of International Relations," *American Historical Review* 88 (1983), 1–11. For a more recent and more conservative view of the "grand tradition" of diplomatic history, see Karl W. Schweizer and Matt J. Schumann, "The Revitalization of Diplomatic History: Renewed Reflections," *Diplomacy and Statecraft* 19 (2008), 149–86.

A number of specialized and popular journals deal with war studies in general and more narrow aspects of military history. The ongoing issue of how warfare may be culturally determined can be followed in Victor David Hanson, *Carnage and Culture: Landmark Battles in the Rise of Western Power* (2001), and John A. Lynn, *Battle: A History of Combat and Culture* (2003). For one ambitious social-scientific study of warfare, see David S. Geller and J. David Singer, *Nations at War: A Scientific Study of International Conflict* (1998). Dale C. Copeland considers how the study of warfare might serve in the construction of Realist theory in *The Origins of Major War* (2000). For a general history of security and strategic studies, see Barry Buzan and Lene Hansen, *The Evolution of International Security Studies* (2009).

On the origins and development of Political Science in the United States down to the 1960s, see Albert Somit and Joseph Tanenhaus, *The Development of Political Science: From Burgess to Behavioralism* (1967). Other still useful older sources include Richard Jensen, "History and the Political Scientist," in Seymour Martin Lipset (ed.), *Politics and the Social Sciences* (1969), 1–28, and J. Austin Ranney (ed.), *Essays on the Behavioral Study of Politics* (1962). More recent analysis and narrative can be found in, for example, John S. Dryzek and Stephen T. Leonard, "History and Discipline in Political Science," *American Political Science Review* 82 (1988), 1245–60; James Farr, John Druzek, and Stephen T. Leonard (eds.), *Political Science in History: Research Programs and Political Traditions* (1995); and David Easton, Michael Stein, and John G. Gunnell (eds.), *Regime and Discipline: Democracy and the Development of Political Science* (1995). For the postwar field in the United Kingdom, see Wyn Grant, *The Development of a Discipline: The History of the Political Studies Association* (2010).

The character of IR as an especially American academic discipline, and its close identification with American Political Science, was set out by Stanley Hoffmann in "An American Social Science: International Relations," *Daedalus* 106 (1977), 41–59. For the perspective from Europe, see Ole Waever, "The Sociology of a Not So International Discipline: American and European Developments in International Relations," *International Organization* 52 (Autumn 1998), 687–727. For a somewhat optimistic collection of essays on cross-border relations between History and Political Science in IR scholarship, see Colin Elman and Miriam Fendius Elman (eds.), *Bridges and Boundaries: Historians, Political Scientists and the Study of International Relations* (2001).

Calls for a "return to history" can be found in Christopher Thorne, "International Relations and the Promptings of History," *Review of International Studies* 9 (1983); Marc Trachtenberg, *The Craft of International History: A Guide to Method* (2006); and Hidemi Suganami, "Narrative Explanation and International Relations: Back to Basics," *Millennium* 37 (2008), 327–56. For the view from historical Sociology, see John M. Hobson and George Lawson, "What Is History in International Relations?" *Millennium* 37 (2008), 415–35.

The large question of where IR as an interdisciplinary social science might be headed has become a much-debated topic. See, for example, Barry Buzan and Richard Little, "Why International Relations has Failed as an Intellectual Project and What to Do About It," *Millennium* 30 (2001), 19–39, or Jan Klabbers, "The Bridge Crack'd: A Critical Look at Interdisciplinary Relations," *International Relations* 23 (2009), 119–25. The special problem of historical approaches in IR is treated in Colin Elman and Miriam Findus Elman, "The Role of History in International Relations," *Millennium* 37 (2008), 357–64; Michael Cox, Tim Dunne, and Ken Booth, "Empires, Systems and States: Great Transformations in International Politics," *Review of International Studies* 27 [Special Issue] (2001), 1–16; Nick Vaughan-Williams, "International Relations and the 'Problem of History'," *Millennium* 34 (2005), 115–36; and Geoffrey Roberts, "History, Theory and the Narrative Turn in IR," *Review of International Studies* 32 (2006), 703–14.

PART I
INTERNATIONAL RELATIONS:
THE HISTORY OF A DISCIPLINE

Students of History are by nature and training prone to put any phenomenon—a social fact, an idea or ideology, a personality, a political act, an economic decision, or even a whole academic discipline—into its own formative historical (i.e., cultural and temporal) contexts, what Gordon Craig called its *milieu et moment*. As we shall see, this can be a useful approach, and one that gives historians good ground from which to challenge what they may regard as the more hubristic claims of ahistorical, deductive IR theory. Such "historicism," of course, if taken to its logical extreme— though few practicing historians would do so—may threaten to reduce all thought and action to exceedingly complex forms of material determinism, a kind of chaos theory of social and political life. This is especially disliked by some historians of ideas who argue that a "sociology of knowledge" approach reduces the universality of great ideas and the debates they have sparked down through the ages. Something of the same tension prevails in Political Science, where those scholars of a great tradition or canon of political thought find little common ground with either behavioralism, which risks treating ideas only as functional choices, or systems theory, which may relegate the thought and action of the individual "unit" to an inferior and inconsequential level.

In fact, to argue that thoughts and actions are enmeshed in their historical contexts need not necessarily deny a degree of autonomy to the individual actor—the degree being the issue. Most historians of change find themselves exploring just that territory defined by the tension between the constraints that the past imposes and the propelling forces for change, between the inertia or stasis of the system and the agents of movement and innovation; in the life of a scholarly discipline, between the hold of certain theories or paradigms and the social-historical forces—including ideas—that unsettle them. In attempting to understand the emergence and development of the discipline of IR, we shall therefore attempt to employ the perspective of both the historian and the sociologist, without losing sight of the autonomous power of ideas to shape the development of the discipline's "discourse."

There are two ways one may consider the passage from one commanding theory (i.e., a convenient explanatory abstraction) to another in the discipline of IR or in any other social science. The first is to view the field as one in which knowledge evolves the way positivists used to regard progress in the natural sciences, in a linear, if often dialectic, fashion. Here progressive change is the result of building from one (proved and elaborated or disproved and discarded) theory to another, from serially generated hypotheses. This *internal discursive approach* views the discipline of IR through its successive Great Debates. One may feel that this is the way social science *should* operate, and yet it risks isolating intellectual change from larger constraints and forces. Another approach follows the logic of Thomas Kuhn's work on scientific revolutions (Kuhn, 1962), and will regard a theory as "working," that is satisfying the discipline's needs and generating ever-diminishingly productive research agendas until the burden of defending it against contrary evidence or in the face of a significant alteration in its social-cultural context becomes so great that it suddenly fails to satisfy—that is, it fails to secure research grant money or is marginalized in introductory textbooks.

The historian, often the same historian, can find him- or herself on either side of this problem. Many who, like Carr, value the idea of progressive, evolutionary change are also (like Carr) committed to the view that intellectual fashions, even in the sciences, are to some degree the product of their times. That is, they are to this extent *contextualists* who are suspicious of viewing presently dominant ideas as the logical and positive outcome of past struggles with error (a variety of Whig history) and thus are unlikely to regard any theory as simply the outcome of a long intellectual vetting process.

Here we shall present the history of IR as a discipline, and the major debates of the field *in their times*, not with an eye to dismissing all theoretical constructions as so much history, but to give us a better means of understanding why certain theories gained power and acceptance when they did, and how it is that one idea or set of ideas may have compelling force in a certain environment and lose its hold on the scholarly imagination in another.

Recommended readings

There is a growing literature on what one scholar calls IR's new "subfield" of the study of the "history, identity, and self-legitimation" of the discipline. See Gerard Holden, "Who Contextualizes the Contextualizers? Disciplinary History and the Discourse about IR Discourse," *Review of International Studies* 28 (2002), 253–70. For a contextualizer's point of view, see Chris Brown's *Understanding International Relations* (2001), ch. 2. Brian C. Schmidt, *The Political Discourse of Anarchy* (1998), on the other hand, argues for a narrower "internal discursive" approach.

For a critique from a sociological perspective of the Kuhnian understanding of paradigm breaks in IR theory, see P. T. Jackson and D. H. Nexon, "Paradigmatic Faults in International-Relations Theory," *International Studies Quarterly* 53, 4 (December 2009), 907–30.

CHAPTER 1
THE DISCIPLINE OF INTERNATIONAL RELATIONS FROM THE FIRST WORLD WAR TO THE EARLY COLD WAR

The "great debates" tradition

Introductory textbooks and courses commonly present the history or field of international relations (IR) as a series of "great debates." There is considerable practical advantage in this approach. For students it reduces the plethora of IR theory and practice to a more easily assimilable main story. It is congenial both to many historians who are trained to think in terms of narrative and evolutionary development, and to many political scientists who view the field as a social *science* advancing by a process of hypothesis and counter hypothesis. In a larger sense, it confirms the boundaries of the discipline and gives it manageable intellectual coherence and an organizing principle. Moreover, a vigorous debate will itself promote research agendas (either to substantiate a provocative thesis or to demonstrate its weaknesses), and thus the discipline is moved along and focused, even if a majority of IR practitioners follow other lines of analysis. We must, however, also be sensitive to the way the great debate approach advances a too tidy construction of the field as a series of binary confrontations. In the last decade or so, the great debate tradition has been subjected to increasing criticism for its oversimplifications and misleading juxtapositions of somewhat artificially constructed "schools" of thought, and what some regard as its ulterior purposes. It has been suggested that it exaggerates the power and influence of a "dominant" theory or method, suppressing the great variety of IR work, and that it misleadingly suggests progression from one commanding paradigm to another when in fact the field is much more multidirectional, and "defeated" approaches often retain much vitality and traction.

That IR is, as a social science, somewhat unique in its need severely to reduce and order its intellectual life in this manner may also suggest a degree of self-consciousness and defensiveness about its intellectual location and justification. Certainly the widely popularized representation of "the First Great Debate"—that supposedly between (naive) "Idealism" and (hardheaded) "Realism"—as a foundational moment for IR promotes the image of a useful "science" being born. And at the end of our story, in the current, early twenty-first-century era of fragmentation and contestation, of the emergence of a host of challenges to mainstream IR theory and practice, the great debate tradition offers, in the absence of any satisfying unified theory, a linear structure of sorts to which the discipline may cling. Some would argue, however, that it is likely that the tradition of great debates will simply collapse under the weight of its own pretensions. One IR scholar caustically observed at the end of the last century, "[n]ot only were these great debates little more than propaganda, pressed into service by academics looking to legitimize their profession, but the explanation for the winners and losers is wrongly attributed to changes 'out there' in the world of politics" (Dunne, 1998, 349).

The conventional approach that locates the birth of the discipline in a supposed confrontation in the 1930s and 1940s between Idealism and Realism has also been challenged by an American political scientist, Brian C. Schmidt, who argued, first, that the academic origins of IR, narrowly construed, are to be found in the earlier development of late nineteenth-century American Political Science, and, second, that "a critical internal discursive history" of these ideas can tell us more than can any attempt to "contextualize" (i.e., to historicize) them (Schmidt, 1998). This of course stirs a number of long-familiar feuds—over assumptions of American intellectual hegemony, the discipline's relation to American Political Science, and, especially, the relation between ideas and their social, cultural, and historical contexts. Contextualizing phenomena is of course what most historians do. It is engrained in our epistemology, and is arguably what we best bring to the table, assuming—unlike Schmidt—that IR is, and ought to be, interdisciplinary. Most, if not all, historians would probably agree that to narrow our understanding of the field to (part of) its internal discursive tradition, much less to assume that that tradition is essentially to be found within and constrained by that of American Political Science, severely reduces the real and potential pluralism of our understanding of the relations of states, peoples, and cultures.

In our unapologetic attempt here to historicize the development of IR, it will of course be necessary to contextualize those conflicting discourses that the discipline as a whole seems to privilege as significant markers. At the very least the great debate tradition allows us to enter the discipline as historians, to examine and perhaps contest the ways in which a significant part of the field has represented itself. The great debates may be somewhat dubious constructs, but nevertheless they represent much of what practitioners of IR regard as the red meat of their chosen field, and, as even one European critic (Ole Waever) admits, there is simply "no other established means of telling the history of the discipline" (Waever, 1998, 715).

The foundation years

> The division of history into periods is not a fact, but a necessary
> hypothesis or tool of thought … dependent for its validity on interpretation.
> (E. H. Carr, *What Is History?*, 76)

While some would argue, accurately enough, that the scholarly origins of a field of IR reaches back into the late nineteenth century, in the Anglo-American establishment of politics as an academic discipline and in the teaching of international jurisprudence, and that many of those scholars who were prominent in interwar IR discourse had begun publishing their work in these fields well before 1919, nevertheless it is useful to begin a narrative of the *institutional* foundation of what was self-consciously styled "International Relations" in the aftermath of the Great War.

The first academic chair in IR was established in 1919 at the University of Wales at Aberystwyth (and named the next year the Woodrow Wilson Professor of International Politics). It was founded by a wealthy Welsh businessman, a pacifist, "in memory of the fallen students of our University for the study of those related problems of law and politics, of ethics and economics, which are raised by the prospect of a League of Nations and for the true understanding of civilizations other than our own" (John, 1972, 86). Other chairs followed at the universities of Oxford, London, and Edinburgh. By the 1930s, such positions and programs were being encouraged elsewhere by an International Studies Conference (under the League's Institute of Intellectual Co-operation), though the field took deepest root in the Anglo-American world where it was nourished often by the same concerned citizens who had promoted the "democratic control" of foreign policy and the idea of a League of Nations.

In America, as in Britain, popular reaction against the unprecedented scale of slaughter during the war and the failure of traditional diplomacy to prevent it—indeed the complicity as many saw it of traditional diplomacy in bringing it about—provided a strong motivation among some, often wealthy men of liberal conscience, to endow institutions that would work to ensure that the next generation's New Diplomacy might see, as President Wilson had demanded, "not a balance of power, but a community of power." The progressive Foreign Policy Association (founded in New York in 1918) aimed to inform the general public, while the more elitist Council on Foreign Relations, like its counterpart in Britain, Chatham House (the Royal Institute of International Affairs), was established in 1923 along lines agreed upon at a meeting of British and American scholarly "experts" at the Paris Peace Conference. The new Social Science Research Council, initiated the same year by political scientists to bring scholars together on issues of "public concern," soon came to include sociologists, anthropologists, economists, psychologists, *and* historians (coining, it is said, the first use of the term "interdisciplinary") and set up among its various permanent committees one dealing with IR. At Tufts University in Massachusetts, Austen Barclay Fletcher left, on his death in 1923, a substantial legacy for a new school of "law and diplomacy" (somewhat belatedly established in 1933) where graduate education would emphasize a "fundamental and thorough knowledge" of international law. In 1924, plans were launched at Johns Hopkins University to establish a School of International Relations (it was named for Wilson's ambassador to Britain, Walter Hines Page, and opened in 1930) to support research in foreign relations. In 1928, an interdisciplinary Committee on International Relations was founded at the University of Chicago, which became a major center for IR thought and teaching through the interwar years and beyond (the Political Science department at Chicago was especially oriented toward a "scientific approach" to politics).

The new field drew heavily from those scholars, like Quincy Wright (who helped found Chicago's Committee on International Relations), who had expertise in international law—reflecting the general surge of interest in international jurisprudence that followed the establishment of the League of Nations and the Permanent Court of International Justice. Many of the founding IR scholars were liberals[1] with a concern and hope that the international anarchy of the prewar world might be to some degree cooperatively reformed, ordered, and regulated. Beyond those with an academic interest in international law, the field attracted many with foreign service experience, either career diplomats like E. H. Carr or those who had done temporary service as experts, like the historian Charles Webster (1886–1961), the second holder of the Wilson Chair at Aberystwyth.

Historians were prominent among the founders of the discipline in the 1920s and 1930s. Often these had a strong interest in the "national" ethnicities of pre- and postwar Europe or in international law and, significantly, had served as advisors before and during the Paris Peace Conference in 1919—marking the first time that the foreign and intelligence services heavily recruited university dons in preparation for a major international conference. Such experience itself may have helped coalesce an interest subsequently in organizing a discipline and educational institutions that would both generate practical knowledge for public policy debate and give scholars, many of whom felt shoved aside or ignored in Paris, a greater influence.

When Quincy Wright published (in the midst of the Second World War) the results of his long-running historical, social, and psychological investigation into the causes and nature of war, he prefaced it with the observation that it had been "begun in the hopeful atmosphere of Locarno [1925]" and addressed it to "those who are opposed to war-in-general, probably a majority of the human race" (Wright, 1942, I, 3). The fact that many of the British and American academics who worked to establish IR programs, research projects, and journals in the 1920s and 1930s were committed to international organizations like the World Court at the Hague, the International Labor Organization, and the League of Nations and were often prominent in movements to promote peace and international cooperation makes it tempting to characterize the discipline in its foundation years as "idealist" or, in Carr's well-known language, "utopian."

And yet we should hesitate to accept a reading of this era as simply one of wooly wishful thinking that ended inevitably in appeasement, war, and the collapse of Idealism and of the League as an effective instrument of international cooperation. If the idea of a First Great Debate, retrospectively established by Realists after the Second World War, is set aside, we can perhaps get a clearer view of the institutional and theoretical origins of the discipline as it emerged in both Britain and the United States. While many of its founders were no doubt inspired by "the spirit of Locarno" and the prospect of an end to all war through new international institutions, the discipline as a whole can hardly be said to have been based on Quaker pacifism or an anticipation of the "perpetual peace" of the philosopher Immanuel Kant. Drawing on a long history of thought and some practice, IR scholars in the interwar years were engaged in exploring quite concrete issues of how force might be applied by the international community to achieve "collective security," how international law should be developed by postwar international institutions, and how sovereign states related to a newly democratic (it was hoped) society of nations. It would be wrong historically to ignore, as the great debate tradition does, the considerable divergence of liberal opinion on issues such as the use of force or the need to address the grievances of what Carr called the "revisionist" powers. Interwar IR scholarship suggests a host of little and large debates growing out of the problematic of adapting international law to contemporary circumstances.

As a scholarly enterprise, interwar IR meant bringing to the fore the long history of international jurisprudence, especially the early seventeenth-century work of Hugo Grotius and those following in this tradition. International law, especially appealing to historians of ideas and institutions, defines one of the early and enduring "schools" of IR scholarship. Thrown on the defensive no doubt by the failure of the League and the weakness of the judicial institutions established to give it voice, it was neither displaced nor much diminished by the clash with American Realism. Indeed, as Morgenthau was crafting his arguments for an IR social science based on the concepts of power, security, and the state in a world defined by international anarchy, others were building legal briefs for the International War Crimes trials at Nuremberg and Tokyo and working out the re-establishment of the World Court under the aegis of the United Nations (UN). Not only does international law continue to provide a deep subfield in IR studies (reinvigorated perhaps at the end of the twentieth century by the Balkan War Crimes tribunal), with a close connection to Liberal Institutionalism (see Chapter 2), it itself—in spite of the tendency of the great debate tradition to create simplified antagonistic binaries—encompasses a spectrum of assumptions and approaches from the admittedly idealistic to "realist" explorations of how sovereign states come to cooperate out of self-interest.

International law and the liberal canon

The foundation of IR as a scholarly discipline in the 1920s was accompanied by a search through the history of political and legal thought for appropriate historical texts. For many this project was informed by the need to establish the intellectual credentials of international law and arbitration, shaped and promoted by (largely Anglo-American) progressive political movements of the previous half-century that—following the arbitration of the United States' *Alabama* claims against Britain in 1871—had lobbied for peaceful solutions to conflict between states. The important early modern thinkers in this canon included Francisco de Vitoria (1492?–1546), an early sixteenth-century Spanish Dominican who had studied with humanists in Paris and whose lectures at Salamanca, influenced by the thirteenth-century scholar Thomas Aquinas, tried to find justification for the Spanish conquest of the Americas in natural law rather than in the argument that savages could not possess territory or in any special authority granted by the Pope; significantly, he does not attempt to employ the argument of Christian Crusade that had been used to justify the *Reconquista* of the Iberian peninsula. Alberico Gentili (1552–1608) was an Italian jurist from Perugia who, as a Protestant, fled Italy in 1577, ultimately taking a position teaching civil law at Oxford. Both a scholar and a practicing advocate, he specialized in international cases like that of the Spanish ambassador accused of plotting against Elizabeth I. *De Jure Belli* (*Of the Law of War*, 1589) was influential in applying the concepts of domestic civil law to international cases.

Both Vitoria and Gentili influenced the work of Hugo Grotius (1583–1645), the central figure in the European international law tradition. He rose to prominence when, acting as advocate for Dutch merchants, he argued against Portuguese, Spanish, and English monopoly interests in the Far East. His major work on war and international law, *De Jure Belli ac Pacis* (*Of the Law of War and Peace*, 1625), written during the Thirty Years War, asserted that natural law (derived from the Roman *Ius Gentium*, dealing with foreign peoples) constrained the acts of rulers; war only had a legitimate basis if resorted to with sufficient cause: that is, in self-defense, to remedy injury and to punish wrong. Simple aggrandizement was an insufficient motive. Rather than the anarchy that Thomas Hobbes would theorize, Grotius posited a *society* of states whose practices are determined not only by expediency but also at some level by a shared sense of common practice among nations—as in commercial and maritime law. Grotius was also concerned with the rules that should govern the *conduct* of war. By mutual interest, conflict was, or ought to be, limited by certain rules and conventions.

In the era that succeeded the end of the Thirty Years War and the peace of Westphalia (1648), European scholars further developed the lawyerly ideas of Grotius. The key figure of this era was Samuel von Pufendorf (1632–94), whose reading of Grotius and Hobbes at university led him to question the Hobbesian idea of the anarchic state of nature and to explore issues of international jurisprudence. His *De Jure Naturae et Gentium* (*Of the Law of Nature and Nations*, 1672) takes up the problem of the concept of the just war, arguing that states, like individuals in society, have a moral character. After Pufendorf, this tradition of speculation about the law of nations in an era of frequent warfare was carried on most prominently by Emer de Vattel (1714–67), a characteristic philosopher of the eighteenth-century European concept of a balancing system of states. His *Droit des Gens* (*The Law of Nations*, 1758) accepted the formal equality of sovereign states and the principle of domestic noninterference. As for Grotius and Pufendorf, for Vattel the sovereign state lies at the heart of a system in which warfare is a common reality. But unlike Machiavelli or Hobbes, he presents it as, potentially at least, an ethical system, in which the doctrine of balance of power that ensures its equilibrium also has a moral character in countering the hubris and arrogance of nations seeking to impose their will on others.

In the IR foundation years of the post-Great War era, the Carnegie Endowment for International Peace funded the publication of the works of Hugo Grotius, especially, but also of Vitoria, Gentili, Pufendorf, Vattel, and others. There is a large literature on each of these seminal thinkers—and an even larger literature if the earlier (Ancient and Medieval) work on the concept of "natural law" and a "just war" is included. For the historian of international thought and international relations, such sources may be approached in two ways. They can be seen as part of a linear European tradition that directly constitutes the basis of a major subfield in IR. Such a history-of-thought approach often deals chronologically with the intellectual debt each great thinker owes to his predecessors and his own contribution to the evolving canon. But, as we have suggested, most historians would also want to think horizontally, as it were, by locating the ideas characteristic of each scholar (they were often also practicing lawyers) in the context of his times.

International law was by and large a tradition dominated by a search for definition and application of basic principles and shaped by a pragmatic need for interstate conflict resolution and for a justification, through law rather than monarch's whim, of legitimate state violence. It reflected, in other words, the close reasoning of lawyers and a desire to bring a degree of order and process to an otherwise anarchic system, rather than an overtly pacifist or utopian idealism. For this latter project—promoted by relatively few interwar IR scholars—the tradition of a search for a universal moral order reached back to the medieval Church, especially Thomas Aquinas and his attempt to define what might be a just war, while the search for a moral order *based in reason rather than theology* might include the Abbé Saint-Pierre's *Project for Making Perpetual Peace in Europe* (1713) and the German philosopher Immanuel Kant's call during the era of the French Revolution for a cosmopolitan organization of republican states (*Perpetual Peace*, 1795).

Establishing the discipline

Generally speaking, whether driven by the pragmatism of international lawyers or the idealism of moral reformers and pacifists (some of whom were no doubt also international lawyers), the discipline was dominated in the 1920s and early 1930s by a focus on the problematic of war (and its prevention), the growing interdependence of states, and the need for institutions and formal processes that would not so much replace the sovereign state as preserve and shield it—in part by modifying the juridical concept of sovereignty itself. The First World War had seen the defeat of the multiethnic empires of Austria, Russia, and the Ottomans in Europe and the Near East, and consequently the number of sovereign nation-states enrolled in the world system expanded as it would do again due to decolonization after the Second World War. The new discipline of IR was to a significant degree shaped around issues of how their interests and their fragile sovereignty might collectively be secured from the arbitrariness of Great Powers.

If a common thread runs through much of the scholarship of the time, it is that IR was a project for bringing order out of anarchy through international institutions that would challenge a system where historically states had pursued their interests through balancing alliances and hegemonic power-grabs. For the most part, these were not utopian one-world-government idealists, however, but scholars who thought in terms of the legitimacy of the (democratic) nation-state as a universal given. The characteristic IR scholars of the era were trained in history and/or the law with an interest in international jurisprudence, and sought to channel conflict between sovereign states away from the resolution of disputes by war (which many regarded, not as Carl von Clausewitz's "politics by other means," but as a pathology or atavism) into legal processes—replicating the way the sovereign state itself had achieved a "monopoly of violence" domestically. Many were also liberals, influenced by the near-millennial view of some nineteenth-century political economists that free trade would create world interdependence and thus encourage universal peace. But while a few no doubt looked to the kind of idealized future imagined by H. G. Wells, for most the League of Nations was not a proto-universal state but a collectivity or society of states, based on the rational expectation that the force of mutual interest could be brought to bear in promoting security, prosperity, and perhaps social justice—rather as some today regard the European Union.

The interwar era, "liberal idealism," and its critics

It is important to understand that "Idealism" as a supposedly dominant aspect of interwar IR practice and theory was neither monolithic nor without its realist critics well before "Realism" emerged as a coherent alternative at the hands of Carr, Morgenthau, and others. In the first place, "idealism" is a somewhat misleading label that jumbles together what we might call both hard and soft liberalism, on the one hand, those scholars who advocated some form of collective force or threat of force as a guarantee of the security of democratic states and, on the other, those who looked to a future where, with the breakup of autocratic empires, democratization would lead to some version of a "democratic peace" and obviate the need for the munitions, armies, and navies that undemocratic elites had promoted to entrench their own status. Similarly, there were those liberals who looked to international law (however enforced) and institutions and those who assumed that free trade, and transnational intercourse generally, would lead to a progressive evolution of a more pacific international society. The debates *among* liberal internationalists are not insignificant. International institutionalists had long debated whether an international body like the League ought to be composed of sovereign states or be democratically representative (through the direct election of delegates). International lawyers argued over the purview of international courts, for instance whether their jurisdiction should stop at national borders or whether private citizens should have access to these remedies. The Galician-born and London School of Economics (LSE)-trained international jurist Hersch Lauterpracht (1897–1960), elected to the Whewell Chair of International Law at Cambridge in 1937 and later a judge on the International Court of Justice, argued forcefully in 1933 (in *The Function of Law in the International Community*) that attempts to extend the jurisdiction and authority of international law would inevitably encounter numerous and probably insuperable limits.

Finally, the view that IR in the interwar period can be simply characterized as "Idealist," an approach that Realism displaced and relegated to the scrap-heap of history, has obscured the importance of interwar theoretical rethinking, in both Britain and the United States, of the idea of sovereignty and of "state monism," a reaction not only to the need to justify the new international institutions of the era but a further scholarly exploration of what, before and during the First World War, had widely been seen as one of the dangers of "Prussianism." "Pluralists" like Harold Laski, it has been argued, significantly anticipate both the important work of Robert Keohane and Joseph Nye (see Chapter 2) in the 1970s, which emphasized interdependence and the transnational and the critique of sovereignty that became a prominent feature of the reaction against Realism and Neorealism by the end of the twentieth century.

Beyond, liberal idealism in international relations—of whatever variety—was challenged throughout the era by those skeptics who feared that law and institutions would be inadequate in the face of rogue states, atavistic elites, the machinations of capitalist arms manufacturers and merchants, or the eruption of the irrational, not least among democratic populations themselves. The pessimism of José Ortega y Gasset (1883–1955) or Oswald Spengler (1880–1936), drawing on the specter of mass society, international Bolshevism, and the decline of European culture, was a powerful counter to the optimism of the liberal IR establishment. Moreover, the prospect of decolonization and an emergent global democratic system brought to the fore the problematic of the Eurocentrism of liberal theorists and the prospect that other civilizational values, revealed by a new Anthropology, might be less conducive to liberal nostrums. The history of the discipline also needs to give more attention to the central contests of the era between liberalism and the illiberal internationalisms offered by Marxism and Fascism. To some degree, these have been marginalized because the grand narrative has been about what constituted IR in the Anglo-American academy where, unlike on the Continent, overt ideology was subordinate to policy-oriented pragmatism.

Marxists had little interest in the state, other than as a vehicle for advancing class interests, and consequently was held by many post-Second World War Realists, for whom the reified state and state system lay at the heart of the discipline, to have little to contribute to the field (there are of course other reasons why Cold War Realism might have dismissed the contributions of Marxist theory). Yet Marxist analysis constituted a major response to bourgeois liberal idealism and institutionalism. In the language of IR, it centered issues of *international system* (as a class system), *transnationalism* (as a revolutionary phenomenon), and the role of *war*, in which the domestic was linked to the international—Lenin having observed that the world required not liberal peace (which Trotsky dismissed as the dream of bourgeois Quaker pacifists) but civil war everywhere. Revolutionary Marxism, through the Comintern, also therefore endorsed the violation of what Realists came to regard as a key feature of the modern state system, established as their narrative has it, by the Westphalian settlement—the domestic sovereignty of the state.

Fascism certainly *did* have "a theory of the state" and any larger discussion of interwar IR theory in this era should engage fascist ideology as, like Marxism, offering a major critique of liberal idealism and institutionalism, if only because it is—as Bolshevism was in the early 1920s project of recreating an international liberal order—a ghost at the table. That little can be found (unless one considers Carl Schmitt a proto-fascist as well as a proto-Realist) in the literature of IR as a discipline on fascist internationalism, the fascist concept of the (unitary and corporate) state, fascist geopolitical theory, or fascist centering of war and power is all the more curious in that many of the central tenets of classical Cold War Realism—the unitary state in a Hobbesian anarchic system, the inherent drive for power in human nature, or a functional approach to war and the threat of war that is stripped of moral concern— are clearly resonant with elements of interwar fascist thought, while so-called "Offensive Realism" has recently refurbished geopolitical arguments that would have been familiar to "Hitler's geographer," Karl Haushofer. That little is made of such resonances, or of fascist or Marxist theorizing about international relations, of course reflects the taboo status of overtly fascist ideology after the Second World War and the ostracizing of Marxists in at least the American academy in the 1940s and 1950s.

Idealism, Realism, and a First Great Debate?

Recent scholarship has raised serious issues with the great debates approach generally and with the idea of a founding First Great Debate in particular. It has been cogently argued that the idea of a contest between Idealism and Realism out of which Realism emerged as the dominant organizing principle for a new discipline was in effect a "foundational myth," an "invented tradition," or at best a "half-truth" that ignores the critical pluralism of interwar liberal thought, exaggerates the pacifism of the leading interwar scholars, misrepresents the long-established field of international law as well as the idea of collective security as idealist or utopian, and for the sake of realist polemic severely truncates the long historical development of Liberal Internationalism by focusing on the era of the League, while endowing Realism and its rational-calculating, power-balancing Realpolitik with a long historical genealogy. It also, in the context of the early Cold War, in effect relocates the narrative of a new, more rigorously and scientifically defined "discipline" from Britain, where the debate between liberal internationalism and imperialism had a history reaching back to the early nineteenth century, to an America newly cognizant of its world role—that is, from one declining world hegemon to a rising one. The First Great Debate may be understood not only as defining and delimiting the field of IR as a new social science but as a strategy that relocated it to a postwar *American* realm.

Before Carr

It is fair to say that for many, perhaps most, of its academic practitioners the emerging interwar discipline of IR was more about praxis than theory. That is, in the eyes of its key founders and advocates, it was a policy-oriented field largely defined by the purpose of bringing about constructive, progressive, and rational changes in the way governments pursued foreign policy. The proliferation of chaired positions in the interwar years reflects the interest of founders in advancing their ideas about the practical reform of international politics. Of course, founders were sometimes disappointed (as founders are prone to be) in the actual appointments made and the directions some scholars' work took the new discipline. At Aberystwyth, the appointment of E. H. Carr to the professorship in 1936, and his provocative inaugural lecture, which condemned pacifism (as a flight from responsibility) and utopianism (as an intellectual's pastime) in favor of taking things as they were rather than as one wished them to be, sparked a violent reaction from the founder who rightly judged that, unlike the first two holders of the chair, Carr would be dismissive not only of the League as an institution but of the League idea—the possibility of engineering or enforcing a new international regime based on cooperation rather than competition among nation-states. Nor did the later appointment of Hans Morgenthau at Chicago prove congenial to either the Wilsonian idealism or the pluralist approach to World Politics of many of his colleagues there.

If the rise of fascism and its ideology of power, the outbreak of war in Asia, Africa, and Spain, and the perceived failure of the Versailles settlement and of the League and international law to instill a higher morality in foreign relations led to some uncomfortable re-evaluation within the discipline, these debates were for the most part about means rather than ends. The grounds for a deeper and more pessimistic critique of the Enlightenment assumptions of the improvability of mankind that may have been embedded in interwar IR were however already available in the relatively new field of social Psychology as well as more familiarly in traditional conservative readings of history or the sterner morality of Calvinist theology.

Outside the discipline, there had from the beginning been plenty of skepticism about both means and—less overtly—ends, among, say, British imperialists or American isolationists, but these dismissive voices had not by and large engaged in a deeper consideration of theory. An important exception was the more philosophical work of a Yale-educated Protestant American theologian, Reinhold Niebuhr (1892–1971)—an important precursor of post-Second World War American Realism—who in 1932 published a work, *Moral Man and Immoral Society*, which cast doubt on the liberal international lawyers' idea of progress through international institutions, and which anticipates some of the critique that Carr and Morgenthau would later level.

A sharp distinction, Niebuhr claimed, had always to be drawn between the behavior of *individuals* and that of "national, racial, and economic" *social groups*: individuals could call upon religious resources for social living in countering the self-regard that was emblematic of original sin, but "those elements in man's collective behavior which belong to the order of nature and can never be brought completely under the dominion of reason or conscience" meant that among nations "conflict is inevitable, and in this conflict power must be challenged by power." This distinction "justifies and necessitates political policies which a purely individualistic ethic must always find embarrassing." An ability to coerce was necessary for peace, while the League's moral suasion was irrelevant (and impotent) (xi–xiii).

While Niebuhr can be read as echoing the hard liberalism of those who advocated collective security through the threat of force, there was little in his views that would encourage confidence in the ultimate goals that defined interwar IR. Nor does he share their sense that history was a narrative of progress. From the beginning of mankind to the present, "[t]ypes of power have changed … but the essential facts have remained unchanged." "All through history" power had necessarily sacrificed justice to peace within communities (employing evil for the sake of good) while destroying peace between communities. History, as a realm of perennial conflict, demonstrated that it was not true, as liberals claimed, that only kings made war, or, as Marxist historicists claimed, that the modern capitalist system was to blame. History showed that international society was "in a perpetual state of war," and that the idea of a future of "perpetual peace and brotherhood" was an unrealizable "dream" (8–16).

Though he was, domestically, a progressive social activist in the interwar period, Niebuhr's pessimistic view of the international sphere became increasingly pronounced and by the end of the war he was regarded as the founder of a particular version of "Christian Realism" that was marked in the following decade by a vigorous opposition to Marxism and the Soviet threat. Embracing the need for nuclear weapons, Niebuhr, though no admirer of John Foster Dulles, became a darling of the Cold War anticommunism of the 1950s.

George Kennan is credited with the observation that "Niebuhr is the father of us all." Niebuhr's critique of utopianism, his emphasis on the ineradicable fact of human nature (i.e., original sin) and the need for power (not only defined as military might) to counter power in international relations, as well as his somewhat ahistorical and highly tendentious recourse to the "facts" of history in establishing his case, make him a harbinger of the more formal theories of Realism that mark the post-Second World War period, though his grounding in the Christian teaching of St. Augustine ("to the end of history the peace of the world, as Augustine observed, must be gained by strife" [167]) and his belief in absolute moral values (the distinction between moral force and immoral force) may in fact align him more closely with the vision of Herbert Butterfield and the English School (see Chapter 2).

The discipline of IR and E. H. Carr's Twenty Years' Crisis

Whether or not Carr's well-known text *The Twenty Years' Crisis*, written in the year of the Munich crisis and subsequently revised, should be seen as the first salvo in a war against Idealism in IR from the camp of a soon-to-be dominant Realism, it is unquestionably a significant piece of the history of the discipline—if only because it transcends its time and place, and indeed much of its own internal argument, to become part of the foundational narrative of the field. In fact, Carr himself subsequently had little interest or played much of a role in the development of the discipline.

Born in 1892, two months before Gladstone's last government was formed, and dying ninety years later under Margaret Thatcher, Carr had a long life as, first, a career officer in the British foreign service, then a professor of IR, a journalist-advocate of the Soviet alliance during the Second World War, and, following the war, a prolific doyen of the early history of the Soviet Union. It was, it has been argued, his disappointment in Paris in 1919 at what he came to regard as Woodrow Wilson's cynical rhetoric and program (designed, he believed, to weaken the rival power of America's imperial allies), which propelled him away from liberal idealism. This skepticism, as with many others in his generation, was encouraged by his reading of John Maynard Keynes' famous diatribe against the conference and its treaty. By the time of his appointment to the chair in Aberystwyth in 1936, he had also become fascinated with Russia and the Soviet experiment.

Carr's text was a sustained attack on what he termed the "utopianism" of progressive, liberal advocates of an IR based on the ideals of cooperation enshrined in the idea of the League. Informed by his reading of Karl Mannheim's work on the sociology of knowledge and his *Ideology and Utopia* in particular, as well as Niebuhr's *Moral Man and Immoral Society*, he presented the idealism of the liberal West in the years since Versailles as grand statements of moral principle that were either the cynical rationalizations of status quo states or the product of bourgeois wishful thinking conditioned by its social, economic, and psychological contexts. Carr was especially contemptuous of a previous holder of the Aberystwyth chair, Sir Alfred Zimmern—a classics scholar who as an advisor to the British Foreign Office had helped draft proposals for a League of Nations in 1918 and was in the interwar era perhaps the most eminent liberal internationalist, a dedicated advocate of cooperative institutions (though no great believer in the "pipe dream" of the international lawyers) who wrote two books on the study (1931) and teaching (1938) of IR.

Using internationalists like Zimmern as straw men, Carr argued that direct negotiations among the great powers, between status quo states and those states that demanded a revision of the treaties, were likely to be more productive than either moralistic lecturing or hopes that a new culture of internationalism would make power politics a thing of the past. Written in the context of the Munich agreements, Carr's 1939 text could be regarded as pro-appeasement (subsequent editions elided his praise for the Munich process). But the postwar American Realist reading of Carr's text passes lightly over both his apparent endorsement of Munich and, more significantly, his analysis of the weaknesses of the realist case. While he spent most of the book demolishing liberal idealism, in his sixth chapter he turns his caustic attention to its opposite. Realism per se could not provide a universal calculus for IR since the presumed rationality upon which it was based was also the product of social conditioning, material interest, culture, and history, though there had been great realists like Machiavelli or Marx who had been able to so liberate themselves from their times and condition that they could identify universal truths.

As the revisionist scholar Charles Jones observed some time ago in his extended analysis of "the trouble with Carr," *The Twenty Years' Crisis* is more polemic than a "scientific" work seeking to re-establish IR on a new basis of a "hard and ruthless analysis" of power. It goes about its demolition through dichotomy and dialectic and in the end adopts a kind of synthesis of idealism and realism (a third way) that has been largely ignored by those American IR theorists who later saw the book as a foundation text. As regards the *use* to which Carr was put in forging a new Realist discipline, other revisionist scholars have argued persuasively that since interwar "idealism" as a unitary school of IR thought or practice never existed but was crafted by Carr out of a variety of discourses (one would have been hard pressed to find anyone in the interwar era who labeled himself an idealist), the whole concept of a First Great Debate speaks more to the need of American Realism to establish its own identity through construction of a mythic "other." Without needing to go that far, we may nonetheless acknowledge as historians that Realism's core narrative has all the marks of Whig history—the selective use of the past to confirm the present. Whig history, as defined and described in a famous extended essay of 1931 by Herbert Butterfield, is history through the eyes of the victor—only in this case Realism's self-identification as winner is also something of a fiction.

An American discipline defined: Morgenthau and the uses of history

It is uncertain whether Carr's famous text really should be considered the foundation stone of a new discipline grounded in a "realist" approach to IR. Carr's assault on utopianism was aimed as much at idealist attitudes in society as a whole as at IR theory and academic practice. Unlike the Classical Realists who followed, his analysis does not hinge on human nature nor is it "systematized" the way Morgenthau would do in offering his "six principles" of state behavior. Moreover, there were, beyond Niebuhr, other realist (if not Realist) voices in the interwar period among the community of IR scholars—such as the political scientist and historian Frederick Schuman (1904–81) who taught first at Chicago and then at Williams College, and published a study, *International Politics*, in 1933, which anticipates post-Second World War Realism in its argument that "power is sought as an end in itself in international politics" (Schmidt, 2005, 531).

Another interwar realist in the American academy with a claim to some influence, Nicholas John Spykman (1893–1943), was a (Dutch) European transplanted to the United States whose early work had been on social theory but who, by the early 1930s, had embraced the field of IR and published articles on its teaching and its methodology. As Sterling Professor of International Studies at Yale (where a graduate Institute of International Studies was founded in 1935), his later work reflects his conversion to the tradition of geopolitics established by Mahan and the turn-of-the-century British imperial geostrategist Halford Mackinder. Spykman's work, culminating (before his early death) in his wartime publications on America's future, explored themes that resonate with Morgenthau: he was a critic of the League's unrealistic project of getting great powers voluntarily to limit their own strength, and an advocate of sustaining America's global role after the defeat of the Axis powers. He argued however that security meant not relying on alliances to "balance" against threats (any equilibrium was inherently unstable) but in ensuring a unilaterally superior position of power through global rather than regional strategies ("Eurasia" being now as critical to American security as the Western hemisphere had once been) and perpetual preparation for war. While after the end of the Cold War some of the proponents of what is called "Offensive

Realism" have returned to elements of Spykman's geopolitics and to his call for power maximization, his work, where it is remembered at all, is regarded by international historians as, like much of the literature of what is now called Classical Realism, resting on a highly questionable selection and interpretation of historical evidence and overly influenced by a dated genre of late British Empire geostrategic thought.

There is, however, little doubt about the centrality and importance of Hans Morgenthau (1904–80; Figure 1.1), whose *Politics Among Nations: The Struggle for Power and Peace* (1948) quickly achieved a presence in the field due to the particular *milieu et moment*, its wide-ranging erudition, and the way it went to the heart of the discipline's principles and methods.

Like Spykman, who came to America following the Great War, Morgenthau was also an intellectual émigré—fleeing, like Hannah Arendt and many others, the Nazi regime. A German Jew, he studied law at Munich under a left-wing scholar of jurisprudence, but with a parallel interest in diplomatic history and international law, spending some time at the Graduate Institute of International Studies in Geneva before taking

Figure 1.1 Hans Joachim Morgenthau (1904–80).

Source: National Portrait Gallery, Washington DC; S/NPG.82.64; photo Philippe Halsman.

up his legal practice in Frankfurt-am-Main. His first book, on international law (1929), reflected his Weimar tutelage (how to adapt legal ideals to social and political reality). With Hitler's appointment as Chancellor in 1933, the writing was on the wall, and the young Morgenthau abandoned his practice and took a teaching position in Geneva and subsequently Madrid before leaving for America in 1937. In the States, he was something of an academic nomad before finally taking a position at the University of Chicago in 1943. Significantly, Morgenthau's intellectual journey away from the progressive tradition in international law arguably had more to do with the domestic than the international; that is, it had less to do with a loss of faith in the League of Nations than his personal experience of the collapse of Weimar social democracy in the face of Nazi power.

Morgenthau's first American publication, *Scientific Man vs. Power Politics* (1946), worked against the grain of the liberal IR and Political Science establishment at Chicago, arguing that "scientific" (i.e., rationalist, progressive) reforms were unlikely to prevail without the application of *moral force*, an argument that was borrowed from Niebuhr but also colored by America's wartime crusade against fascism. Developing what he called a "practical realism," *Politics Among Nations* followed in 1948 and was intended as a guidebook for (especially American) statesmen that conceived of politics in terms of interests and power rather than ideals and suasion.

The book opened with the admonition that "International politics, like all politics, is a struggle for *power*." By power he meant "man's control over the minds and actions of other men," and therefore power was not merely a matter of a state's material ability to win a war. Power and the perception of strength created a "psychological relation between those who exercise it and over whom it is exercised." Moreover, the struggle for power was "universal in time and space … throughout historic time, regardless of social, economic, and political conditions …" Morgenthau regards the social science of IR as the analysis of how this constant—a universal drive embedded in human nature (what he also calls "elemental bio-psychological drives")—plays out in a Hobbesian, that is violent and anarchic, world of sovereign states attempting to ensure their security. In such a universe of self-interest and the lust for power, "no rules of international law are binding" (13–17, 244). To confirm his case, Morgenthau, like the so-called Classical Realists who follow him, has frequent recourse to European history that he sifts for examples that are congenial to his thesis that the drive for power and the balancing of power are constants that constitute the "reality" of international life through time and across different cultures and environments.

Realism's canon of historical texts

For historians, the use of historical texts to confirm present-day theory is always likely to be somewhat problematic. There is a danger that events and ideas will be wrenched out of context. Moreover, there is an implied ahistoricism in the assumption of comparability across the vastness of historical time and the variety of historical cultures. The problem is more acute, for a supposedly international (i.e., global) social science, when the historical texts are all drawn from the familiar canon of "European civilization."

Many IR scholars in the interwar and early Cold War period were themselves trained as historians or (given the education common among the middle and upper classes at the time) were at least familiar with European political philosophy and European historical narrative. This is as true of Realists and proto-realists like Niebuhr, Carr, Schuman, Spykman, and Morgenthau, or among the English School realists, Herbert Butterfield, Martin Wight, or Hedley Bull, as it is of the international lawyers and liberal institutionalists. The Realists however especially draw from a few core texts to reinforce Morgenthau's assumptions about human nature and his hypotheses about the behavior of states. There is also arguably a significant difference in how history is perceived and used. Where liberal internationalists tend to see historical events and ideas as so many steps along the road, as signposts and precedents upon which those who follow build toward an evolving progressive future, Realists see canonical texts as confirming the timelessness of their laws of nature and behavior.

These principal texts would include, especially, *The History of the Peloponnesian War* by Thucydides (ca. 460–395 BCE). The most accessible and useful of the ancient texts (Greek philosophy rarely considers interstate relations, though Aristotle held war to be natural to man), the *Peloponnesian War* is frequently cited by Realists for its supposed insight into the problems of power and leadership, especially the so-called "security dilemma" whereby the achieving of sufficient power to protect the state (as in the Athenian empire) may promote aggression against it by others (Sparta and its allies). Thucydides' long text has also been mined for aphorisms that suggest a universality of human nature and condition, with special attention often given to the Melian Dialogue: "the powerful do what they will, the weak suffer what they must."

If Thucydides' marvelous—though unique—history provides a kind of confirmation for elements of Realist theory, Niccolò Machiavelli (1469–1527) is central to the Realist understanding of the modern (or proto-modern) state, the pursuit of power as a mark of *virtù* or manly spirit, and the necessarily amoral ethics of inter-(city)state relations. *The Prince* (1531, posthumous) urged the ruler to devote himself to the art of war as an instrument in getting and keeping power. It is apparently concerned with *la verità effettuale* (things as they really are rather than as they should be), with ends rather than means, and is based on experience (Machiavelli was an official and sometime diplomat for the Republic of Florence) rather than moralists' platitudes and good intentions. Realists are especially fond of quoting his observation (a reference to Savonarola, the messianic friar who led the Republic after the overthrow of the powerful Medici family in 1494) that "unarmed prophets" inevitably come to grief. Most important is the concept of *necessità* (political necessity). Machiavelli is seen as the originator of the doctrine of "reason of state" (*ragion di stato, raison d'état*) as a realm beyond private morality, and of "situational ethics." Those Realists who take the work as a simple guide to conduct claim that his insights are grounded in the actual diplomacy and warfare of the renaissance city-state that, by a stretch, can be seen as the prototype of the modern sovereign nation-state.

The third, and perhaps most important, in Realism's trinity of canonical writers is Thomas Hobbes (1588–1679). *The Leviathan* (1651) was written during the English Civil War while Hobbes was in exile in Paris at the court of Charles II (as he later became). Hobbes, who likely knew his Machiavelli and had himself translated Thucydides into English, famously identified the state of nature as a state of war, and viewed human nature as self-interested, unconstrained by higher law, and characterized by "a perpetual and restless desire of power after power, that ceaseth only in death." The natural social condition is one of violent chaos, and while individuals can combine to escape this anarchy by devolving authority to a sovereign, the state, lacking any higher authority, is condemned to perpetual conflict: peace for Hobbes is only a period of recuperation before the next war, and, as with Machiavelli, foreign policy is perforce conducted in a moral and legal vacuum.

For the Realist, Thucydides, Machiavelli, and Hobbes speak to each other and to contemporary Realist theory across the centuries because the issues they address (human nature, the pursuit of power, and the anarchic character of the international realm) are timeless. This conception of timelessness concerns many historians. In the first place, the discovery that passages from Thucydides, Machiavelli, or Hobbes seem to corroborate Realist theory is hardly surprising when their theories were extrapolated from those same texts. More worrisome for those trained in historical methods and the use of historical evidence is the danger of *anachronism* whenever an event or text is taken out of its original setting and applied more broadly, or described in terms that have meaning for us (like "liberal" or "conservative") that would have been meaningless in its own time. Conal Condren, a political scientist, some years ago noted five kinds of anachronism: *judgmental* (a biased view of the past based on one's own values), *descriptive* (labeling a past event or person in terms appropriate to another time), *discursive* (using a construct or discourse specific to one era to analyze an historical event from another), *structural* (confusing or ignoring horizontal or hierarchical relationships among phenomena), and *sequential* (assuming linear, developmental relationships between events or ideas because they follow one another in time).

The influential British historians of ideas, John A. Pocock (b. 1924) and his younger colleague Quentin Skinner (b. 1940), have been critical of the tendency among scholars of political thought to detach their subjects from their historical milieus and "rhetorical practices" and interpret them according to modern categories and concepts. Machiavelli and Hobbes have proven especially fruitful for their project of rethinking our approach to the classics of political thought. Others, and especially those informed by postmodern theory, argue that the ideas in these texts are dependent on then current social norms and interconnected meanings, and that norms, meanings, and purposes are constantly being reconstructed; that human nature, that is human psychology, is a product of social construction, not a static given. Moreover, there is always a danger of assuming language itself has the same meaning across time, as, for instance, with the word "sovereignty"—not in the sixteenth century an abstract concept but the tangible honor of kings.

Morgenthau's use of history

> Historians, says Namier in a deliberately paradoxical phrase …, 'imagine the past and remember the future.' (E. H. Carr, *What Is History?*, 162–3)

Morgenthau's method—deducing the behavior of states from universal constants like the drive for power, and then confirming his deductions through wide-ranging historical example—presumes a theory of history that regards the past as directly analogous to the present—different players, but the same game, as it were. This not only allows him to use the historical narrative of different times and cultures as a convenient repository of evidence, but to treat the patterns thus created as a guide to the future. There is therefore a certain paradox that historians encounter in coming to grips with Morgenthau's work.

On the one hand, he takes history seriously. His world is the familiar one of European war, peace, and diplomacy, and of classic texts drawn from a well-established canon stretching from the ancient Greeks to the modern era. On the other hand, his use of this history begs serious questions. Though Morgenthau himself came to admit that historical "facts," including those culled from canonical texts, derive from a particular social milieu, he pointedly resisted contextualizing Thucydides, Machiavelli, or Hobbes. He was ready to argue that Idealism drew from a special context, but hesitated to see the eternal verities of Realism as relational. Moreover, the Realist use of historical evidence runs the dangers summarized by Thomas Smith in his study of History and IR: *selection-bias* ("cherry-picking"), *anecdotalism, ahistoricism* (assuming that a phenomenon in one period is necessarily comparable to an apparently similar one in another culture or period), and arguing with a *precision* that goes beyond what the incomplete historical evidence may allow (Smith, 1999, 3–4).

The concern here would arise not only from the tendency of Realists (and others) to choose and arrange vignettes of historical evidence to suit their assumptions and argument (a common problem with the deductive approach in the social sciences), but that Morgenthau's text reflects the education in European philosophy, history, law, and diplomacy that one might expect from a literate, middle-class German of the early twentieth century, well-schooled in Enlightenment thought, Bismarck's Realpolitik, Nietzsche's cultural pessimism, and Weber's sociology. Without going so far as to reduce Morgenthau's interesting, indeed often compelling, argument simply to his own conditioning and experience, we can at least raise the problem of how far the historian (in this case the political scientist) manages to step outside of his own history. Morgenthau himself would later admit that the familiar concept of the balance of power, rather than a structural mechanism, was a metaphor that was directly derived from the European Enlightenment's assumption of natural order and equilibrium.

Morgenthau's legacy for the discipline

Though *Politics Among Nations* became a standard textbook for decades, going through several editions, the claim that Morgenthau's work *established* the modern discipline of IR is somewhat inflated. It has, however, at least this justification: in the interwar period the field had been dominated by debates over policy and practice; after Morgenthau, over theory and method. In the decades that followed publication of *Politics Among Nations*, it is significant how much IR research and writing was inspired by a need to comment and elaborate upon Morgenthau's insights, explore areas he had not treated, or critique his theory and method through alternative approaches. If it is not quite true that after Morgenthau *Realism* became *the* dominant approach in IR scholarship, it certainly influenced a wide range of IR practitioners. John H. Herz (1908–2005), for instance, another German Jewish intellectual émigré who, like Morgenthau, had fled (in 1938) first to Geneva and the Graduate Institute of International Studies before making his way to America and a position in Political Science at Howard University, began his work also from within the progressive liberal international law tradition, and was part of the US delegation at the Nuremberg trials. The book he published in 1951, however, *Political Realism and Political Idealism*, was an attempt to find a middle way (a liberal realism) that engages and expands upon Morgenthau's insights, developing the idea of the "security dilemma" and the anarchic nature of the interstate system, while preserving a role for international law and institutions in limiting the exercise of power.

Morgenthau's work prospered because it engaged issues that must be central to an intellectual discipline—what exactly is it about, what are its underlying principles, what questions might be asked of them, and how might such questions be answered? For Morgenthau the guiding principle in IR as a social science was the recognition that "politics, like society in general, is governed by objective laws that have their roots in human nature" (quoted by Gilpin, 1984, 292). Realists, following Morgenthau, center power and the will to power—as a fundamental aspect of human nature—in their extrapolation of the laws of state behavior. These laws involve definitions of power (as material resources or, as Morgenthau held, as a "relational" concept that extended to the effectiveness of diplomacy and subjective issues of "prestige"), strategies for acquiring power, the use (management) of power to attain various ends, and the extent to which rationality might dictate limits to the acquisition of power. If Realism emerged in the post-Second World War era as a seemingly more coherent and social-scientific school than other varieties of IR discourse, it is in part owing to the ways in which Morgenthau drew attention to basic assumptions (his "six principles") and methodology. That is, he redefined the field *as a discipline* rather than a rather loose coterie of historians, political scientists, foreign policy specialists, and international lawyers. Even a critic like Stanley Hoffman admitted that "[i]f our discipline has any founding father, it is Morgenthau" (Hoffmann, 1977, 6).

That Morgenthau's work had the impact it did is owing only in part to the ways in which he was able to focus purpose and method; it also owes much to the historical and contemporary political contexts of his central argument that international relations were about *power*—the drive for power and the need for power. If early IR as Liberal Internationalism had been significantly enabled and amplified by the popular sense that the Great War had been an unnecessary war, Morgenthau's realism drew its force from a popular perception that the Second World War had been a necessary war, a good war, and a war for the security, indeed the survival, of the state itself, and that the great failure of the 1930s had been in the lack of power or will to "stand up to the dictators." During the war and for a generation afterward (and more), the "lessons of Munich"—chiefly that negotiating without coercive power was a highway to failure—were widely invoked and established as a kind of self-evident common sense.

More specifically, Morgenthau's text is situated in a critical period of wide debate about America's role in the postwar world (as guarantor of a new world order—a role it had politically, if not economically, renounced after 1919), its hegemonic relation to both the defeated powers and its exhausted wartime allies, and the uncertain character of the successor to the League, the UN. Most importantly, Morgenthau's argument that history demonstrated that only power could speak to power is located in *the early Cold War* (an "intellectual matrix event" according to Thomas Smith [1999, 32]) and a public rhetoric that drew parallels between Nazism and Communism, as illiberal ideologies that only understood force and threatened state security externally through war and internally through subversion. "Containment" was not primarily about negotiation or détente (a.k.a. appeasement). It was about military power balancing military power, and guile (i.e., covert intelligence and propaganda) balancing guile.

The era of the early Cold War, from roughly 1946 to the resolution of the Cuban missile crisis in 1962, was fraught with confrontation between the United States and its former ally the Soviet Union. It saw a shift from the multipower politics familiar through much of history to a superpower bipolar world that seemed, in the beginning at least, dangerously and inherently unstable. Though Morgenthau's work looks back to the familiar multi-polar world before nuclear weapons (both superpower bipolarity and the existential threat of the hydrogen bomb would arguably undermine aspects of his theory and its applicability) and he has little to say about international economics other than as a part of state power, there was much in his work that spoke to the early Cold War era: security (survival) as the primary "interest" of nations, the need for power balancing, and lessons of history that strongly suggested that Liberal Internationalism was unlikely to much redress the inherent anarchy of international politics. This echoed, rationalized, and attempted to inform the American policy shift toward global leadership and "containment" of the Soviet Union.

The early Cold War also saw a significant expansion of the number of institutions and academic programs, mostly in the United States, that were dedicated to the purpose of generating policy advice in a world now clearly distinguished by American hegemony. A new School of Advanced International Study was founded during the war (in 1943, and absorbed into Johns Hopkins University in 1950). In 1951, Columbia, under General Eisenhower as university president, established an Institute of War and Peace Studies, and the next year MIT set up a Center for International Studies. Meanwhile, Cold War think tanks like the RAND Corporation (established in 1948 by the US Air Force) offered increasing support for research and analysis.

To recapitulate, for Classical Realists international relations are, as history confirms and the greatest of early modern political thinkers aver, the province of expediency and power. Politics at both the domestic and international levels are about power (whether for aggrandizement or security). The state is a unitary, sovereign entity (like a person, though without a moral sense) and is likely to pursue "reasons of state" with a predictable logic whatever the domestic character of the regime may be. In this sense the state becomes an "anthropomorphic unit" (i.e., it acts as though it were a rational human individual). Many Realists argue that the key to understanding the past and future of international politics lies in the idea of a natural tendency to equilibrium through a balance of power (as opposed to an artificial equilibrium engineered by idealist interstate or suprastate legal processes and institutions). They share a pessimistic view of human nature as consistent over time and place, argue that this psychological drive infuses the character of states, and believe that, consequently, conflict and the threat of conflict has been, is, and will be endemic in international relations.

In its postwar context, Realism was crafted to suit the problem facing American statesmen—how to draw America into world affairs in spite of its long tradition of isolationism. In a sense the discipline of IR was recrafted around this purpose, one reason perhaps why it has not prospered elsewhere. One well-known critic argued that IR had reached a dead end as an academic discipline, in part by becoming an American prescriptive, policy-oriented, Washington-outward-in-perspective field (Hoffmann, 1977). Moreover, the Realist reliance on historical example and on classic texts of political thought means that its theory is especially prone to constructing a somewhat simplistic genealogy or historical lineage for its concepts—in what might be called the "Plato to NATO" line of argument. In the eyes of many historians, this risks the error of assuming that past thinkers are "necessarily trying to write like us, for us and about our problems." Some of these texts and authors are simply too familiar—that is, we think we can get inside their heads, their meaning, when all of our knowledge of history since their time, and the inevitable comparisons and qualifications that understanding suggests, gets in the way. As Conal Condren put it, we can't "know" the eighteenth-century Mozart precisely because we know Wagner (Condren, 1997, 47–9, 56).

Recommended readings

For a general overview of IR theory, see Paul R. Viotti and Mark K. Kauppi, *International Relations Theory: Realism, Pluralism, Globalism, and Beyond* (3rd edn., 1999); Chris Brown, *Understanding International Relations* (3rd edn., 2005), or Scott Burchill et al., *Theories of International Relations* (4th edn., 2009). Torbjörn L. Knutsen offers an approach sensitive to historical contexts in *A History of International Relations Theory* (2nd edn., 1997). Thomas W. Smith's *History and International Relations* (1999) is an indispensable guide to the complicated relationship between IR theory and its historical or ahistorical methodologies.

Literature critical of the great debate tradition continues to grow. Begin with Lucian M. Ashworth, "Did the Realist-Idealist Great Debate Really Happen? A Revisionist History of International Relations," *International Relations* 16 (2002), 33–51. Also see Cameron G. Thies, "Progress, History and Identity in International Relations Theory: The Case of the Idealist-Realist Debate," *European Journal of International Relations* 8 (2002), 147–85; Joel Quirk and Darshan Vigneswaran, "The Construction of an Edifice: The Story of a First Great Debate," *Review of International Studies* 31 (2005), 89–107; Robert Vitalis, "Birth of a Discipline," in David Long and Brian Schmidt (eds.), *Imperialism and Internationalism in the Discipline of International Relations* (2005), 159–81; and Lucian M. Ashworth, "Where are the Idealists in Interwar International Relations?" *Review of International Studies* 32 (2006), 291–308. A sense of the variety of thought concealed by the label "interwar Idealism" can be found in David Long and Peter Wilson (eds.), *Thinkers of the Twenty Years' Crisis* (1995). For an overview of the subdiscipline of international law history, see Ingo J. Hueck, "The Discipline of the History of International Law," *Journal of the History of International Law* 3 (2001), 194–217. For an historicist exploration of the profession of international law, see Martii Koskenniemi, *The Gentle Civilizer of Nations: The Rise and Fall of International Law 1870–1960* (2001).

Robin W. Lovin, *Reinhold Niebuhr and Christian Realism* (1995) is useful on Niebuhr, while James Arnt Aune, "Reinhold Niebuhr and the Rhetoric of Christian Realism," in Francis A. Beer and Robert Hariman (eds.), *Post-Realism: The Rhetorical Turn in International Relations* (1996), 75–94, provides a postmodern analysis of Niebuhr's Cold War rhetoric. Also see Vibeke Schou Tjalve, *Realist Strategies of Republican Peace: Niebuhr, Morgenthau, and the Politics of Patriotic Dissent* (2008).

For relatively recent scholarly re-evaluations of E. H. Carr, see Cox's "E. H. Carr and the Crisis of Twentieth-Century Liberalism: Reflection and Lessons," *Millennium* 38 (2010), 523–33, and Peter Wilson, "Radicalism for a Conservative Purpose: The Peculiar Realism of E. H. Carr," *Millennium* 30 (2001), 123–36. Mark Mazower, *No Enchanted Palace: The End of Empire and the Ideological Origins of the United Nations* (2009), has recently sought to retrieve interwar utopianism, and Alfred Zimmern, from Carr's polemic. What is now called Classical Realism and the central concept of power and power balancing has generated a large critical literature. See, for instance, Brian C. Schmidt, "Competing Realist Conceptions of Power," *Millennium* 33 (2005), 523–49; James Der Derian offered a general critique in the 1980s, which he adapted for his essay "Hans Morgenthau: The Limits and Influence of 'Realism'," in Der Derian (ed.), *International Theory: Critical Investigations* (1995), 70–84. On

Morgenthau's own intellectual development, see Christoph Frei, *Hans J. Morgenthau: An Intellectual Biography* (2001), and Greg Russell, *Hans J. Morgenthau and the Ethics of American Statecraft* (1990). For the use of historical evidence in IR, see, in addition to Condren, Markus Kornprobst, "Comparing Apples and Oranges? Leading and Misleading Uses of Historical Analogies," *Millennium* 36 (2007), 29–49.

CHAPTER 2
AFTER MORGENTHAU: SCIENTIFIC REALISM AND ITS CRITICS

IR, scientism, and a bipolar world

By the time Morgenthau published his study of *Politics Among Nations* in 1948, the familiar world of multipolar IR he had known as a maturing interwar scholar was shifting rapidly to the bipolar global politics of two superpowers—something that seemed confirmed by the Soviet atomic bomb test the next year. That America would replace the global hegemony of the British Empire and Commonwealth with its own had been obvious from about 1943. The "Arsenal of Democracy" was able to far surpass the productive capacity of both allies and enemies, dominate financial markets and indeed the new postwar reconstructed global financial system, and maintain high standards of living at home while much of the rest of the world was impoverished and exhausted. Its (albeit short-lived) monopoly of nuclear war technology conferred both real and symbolic power. The applied science of its vast array of exported consumer goods and its military-industrial weaponry, promoted by huge budgets for defense and world policing, confirmed, like the skyscrapers of Manhattan and the modernist embassies the United States began to build around the globe, a reading of America as the very locus of a modernity of power, wealth, and science.

In this mid-century anticommunist Cold War era, a new "scientific thinking" permeated the social sciences in America—and especially Political Science—in part as an answer to the intellectual left. In this, an Austrian émigré philosopher of science at the London School of Economics, Karl Popper (1902–94), played a significant role. Popper had argued that what distinguished good scientific theory (and by extension good social scientific theory) from inadequate or nonscientific theory was the "falsifiability" of its hypotheses. In his work attacking "historicism" (and especially Marxist historicism), Popper denied the validity of theories of historical necessity and progress because the "laws" upon which they were based were not susceptible of disproof. The most tangible manifestation of the new scientism in American Political Science was the so-called "behavioralist revolution" that privileged a supposedly scientific analysis of the observable and quantifiable over the *normative* (assumptions about social norms or values). Behavioralism also eschewed the left-ideology of historical materialism for a supposedly value-free mathematical analysis of social and political data. These two phenomena, the hegemonic position (beyond the Soviet system) of the United States and the valorization of science and the scientific method in the American social sciences, had a profound impact on the development of IR theory and practice—at least in the United States.

Morgenthau had written in *Politics Among Nations* of the need to discover through a "scientific inquiry" the laws that governed international politics, and held that theory ought to be explicit in IR research. However, he arguably had in mind "science" in the sense of the German word *Wissenschaft*, that is, any general understanding or academic learning based on rigorous research, rather than more narrowly the method and theory of the natural sciences. He would argue in later years when he felt much bothered by the growing scientism (or "scientification" as he said) of the discipline that the "contingent element" in history made precision and predictability—the hallmarks of natural science—impossible in the study of politics, echoing one of the major reservations that historians have about much IR theory. For Morgenthau and for Classical Realists generally, the *practice* of international politics, that is, diplomacy, was as much an art and a skill as a science, while the central concern of Realist *theory*, power (and especially the perception of power), could not be measured the way natural scientists measured material phenomena. In fact, Morgenthau considered his own "orientation" to be that of a historian and would come to rail against fashionable abstract theory. By 1970, he would advance a distinctly historicist, contextualist critique of political theory in general as *Standortgebunden*, or tied to a particular social-historical situation (Morgenthau, 1970, 40–7).

Morgenthau's objective in the late 1940s had been to encourage American statesmen to take up the challenge of global leadership rather than retreat once again into isolationism. He was of course pushing at an open door, as the pursuit of "containment" in Europe, the Middle East, and Asia through US aid for the government forces in the Greek civil war (1946–9), the Marshall Plan (1948–52), the Berlin Airlift (1948–9), the creation of the North Atlantic Treaty Organization (1949), and, most dramatically, the Korean War (1950–3) signaled. But the early Cold War of global superpower confrontation complicated as well as confirmed Realism's analysis, informed as it had been by the multipolarity of the European sovereign state system whereby ambitious Great Powers had, since at least the days of Richelieu, been "balanced" against by others. Realists attached much importance to the role of the mechanism of the *balance of power* in an essentially anarchic sovereign state system that through war and shifting alliances had tended to promote a rough equilibrium unfriendly to power-hungry, would-be-universal hegemons. This balancing was however a complex affair in which the arts of diplomacy as well as the hammer and anvil of war were constantly making and remaking combinations of small and great powers. The new Cold War bipolarity confirmed the idea of balance but as a static state of perpetual confrontation, marked less by the balancing strategies of small sovereign powers than by a nuclear stalemate and a kind of "bandwagoning" whereby lesser states (not in a full sense "sovereign") aligned themselves with, and under the nuclear umbrella of, a superpower.

There were other important differences as well. For one, the old European balance of power system had ordinarily not involved an *existential threat* to the sovereign state

(Poland being the great exception), while in the Cold War it was otherwise. Second, while Realists might dwell on the importance of the sovereign state system and the security dilemmas and balances of power that it engendered, the Cold War was also about ideology. As a factor both in foreign policy decision-making and in fears of domestic "subversion," ideology blurred the line between interstate and intrastate politics, and led some to talk about a return to something like the pre-Westphalian horrors of the wars of religion. Moreover, the prospect of a swift nuclear holocaust made the era one of heightened anxiety among both decision-makers and the public at large—a mass psychology of living with the dread of nuclear weapons that one British critic famously called "bomb culture."

This then was an era that knew neither the diplomatic minuets of eighteenth-century Europe nor the "managed" Cold War of 1970s *détente*. It was unclear whether a regional conflict of containment might spiral out of control, whether nuclear strategies then in formulation and shifting with each development of delivery and targeting technology—of joint use, or theater use, or a Strangelovian massive preemptive first use—might make the triggering of a general, world-destroying nuclear exchange more or less likely, by design or accident. The hydrogen bomb as *threat* might (through what came to be called Mutually Assured Destruction [MAD]) keep the system precariously balanced, but not its actual use. The balance of power could no longer be adjusted by the *practice* of Great Power warfare.

The key to understanding the impact of this early, and dangerous, phase of the Cold War on the discipline of IR lies in part in the psychological need it instilled for plausibly scientific calculation and predictive theory. If Classical Realism emphasized subrational "human nature" and its primordial drive for power, scientific Realism offered a politics of rational calculation and constrained choice.

Behavioralism, American Political Science, and systems analysis

We have seen that IR as an academic field began as a broad church, enfolding historians of diplomacy and foreign policy, political scientists of varied interests, Weberian sociologists, and scholars of international jurisprudence and institutions. This inclusivity, however, inevitably highlighted the heterogeneous nature of its definitions, assumptions, and methodologies. In other words, it was in some eyes not a "discipline" at all, in the sense of a social science with a core of formal theory (however contested) and exacting practice in an era when other social sciences were engaged in a rapidly evolving professionalization. If some Realists like Morgenthau had stopped well short of seeing the field as analogous to the natural sciences, by the 1950s others voiced increasing concern that IR theory, such as it was, was inadequate if IR were to be more than a set of "lessons" drawn haphazardly from history and political thought.

The prominence of Morgenthau's work inevitably generated criticism, not only from Liberal Internationalists and some historians but from political scientists concerned about his unscientific—that is, unverifiable—assumptions about, especially, human nature or psychology and about his methodology (his selection of historical examples). In the 1950s and early 1960s, many scholars in American Political Science departments embraced a more scientific approach to theory, what constitutes a "system," and the quantification of behavioral variables. This in turn influenced a new generation of postwar IR scholars trained in these departments.

A political scientist at the University of Chicago, Morton Kaplan, led the way with an assault on the "vague and unsatisfactory … tautological … inaccurate" definitions of power politics that his colleague at Chicago, Morgenthau, and E. H. Carr before him, seemed to be using. This was the opening of what would later be called (by Kaplan himself) the "New [that is, Second] Great Debate"—one between traditionalism and science. Instead of loose, unscientific, and undisprovable theorizing, Kaplan proposed in *System and Process in International Politics* (1957) a "conceptual scheme"—an ambitious project to explore the structural characteristics of international systems (including the balance of power system), through "modeling" a large number of plausible factors affecting the behavior of states in different types of systems. These models would make possible the testing of hypotheses about structure and process, and, ultimately (very ultimately, his critics said, given the vast array of possible variables) the construction of a general theory of international politics. Along the way, behavioral psychology, mathematical modeling, and game theory would be of more use than historical case studies.

Kaplan's early "systems analysis" was an ambitious attempt to theorize systemic structures that would be universally applicable—that is, they would function similarly whatever their historical locus. Historians, Kaplan suggested, lacked any useful theory by which their facts could be recognized as significant variables or how these might relate to other variables. Moreover, their "system of reference" was constantly shifting as their narratives progressed. Kaplan anticipated challenges by those he called the "traditional opponents of scientific method"—historians, notably, but also those from his own discipline who followed a tradition of political philosophy.

The behavioralist approach to IR, with its assumption that with enough data there could be a rational, mathematical, and predictive calculation of motivation and conduct, its increasingly complicated taxonomies, and the seeming distance between its abstracted models and messy reality, did more than Morgenthau's Realism had done to encourage a rapidly widening gulf between the work of most historians of international relations and that of political scientists trained in the new scientism. Theirs was an approach that often seemed contemptuously to dispense with the "impressionistic" insights of History and the traditional canon of political thought, preferring, as Kaplan put it, "more sophisticated techniques" and "newer methods." Kaplan had, nevertheless, put his finger on weaknesses in much early Realist work—loose definitions and unverifiable assumptions, and its casual use of historical case studies—even if his own solutions might appear obsessively abstracted.

The key challenge in Kaplan's scheme was of course the gargantuan task of isolating variables that were both significant and quantifiable for analysis and testing. Historians, often uncomfortable in any event with the complex statistical procedures necessary for multivariate analysis and suspicious of their application to the kind of partial, second-hand, and uninterrogatable data with which they often dealt, might reasonably argue that a deep understanding of historical contexts and practices, rather than *a priori* theory or mathematical manipulation, was required to understand how a system worked—that there was, in fact, some virtue in the "impressions" of a careful, deeply informed and focused historian who knew the textures of the culture he or she studied. Moreover, the idea of "testing" a plausible hypothesis through close statistical analysis made more sense for the natural sciences than for the social world of human interaction where cultural values, ideals, and symbols resisted such methods of understanding. It was feared that the behavioralist method would in fact narrow and skew IR's intellectual reach. For instance, to treat "power" as a quantifiable, material phenomenon would lead to a preoccupation with its military, geopolitical, and perhaps economic manifestations, with armies, technologies of war, and materiel (things that could be counted and compared), rather than larger, less tangible psychological and subjective issues of the symbols of power and prestige. Many were in fact simply put off by the density of Kaplan's jargon, as well as by his ahistorical concept of structure. Historians were especially concerned that, though functional analysis of a system might capture its working at a point in time, it could say little about a system's tendency to change, its evolving character. This would remain a major issue over the following decades.

Others, however, who were sympathetic to the project of a more scientific, theory-based "systems analysis" approach were nevertheless daunted by the prospect of dealing with all the variables that the mind could invent. Kenneth Waltz (1924–2013) was Kaplan's near-contemporary at Columbia. Two years after Kaplan's book appeared, Waltz published *Man, the State, and War: A Theoretical Analysis* (1959). It set out as well to engage problems of analysis posed by Morgenthau's method but also to clarify somewhat the confused undifferentiated welter of potential causal factors that many felt was a problem in Kaplan's analysis. Man's nature (or psychology, or evilness) might lead to war, but it could hardly be used as an analytical tool to help explain why sometimes there was war and sometimes peace. It was, Waltz argued, in any event but one kind of factor in the *first image*, or level of analysis, of international relations, and since human nature could not be changed, "one shifts attention to that which can: social political institutions." A host of domestic influences were at work shaping the internal structure of the state, the political institution with which IR scholars mostly dealt, and plausibly influencing its behavior in the system of states. This realm of differently constituted state regimes, and the many factors at work within them—their democratic or autocratic structure, their dominant political ideologies, their economic condition, their social structure, the influence of groups, public opinion, and so forth—embodied the *second image*, or level of analysis. But there were apparent limits to the determining effect of the internal nature of states. Contrary to the hopes of Liberal Idealists anticipating a "democratic peace," both representative democracies *and* atavistic empires had gone enthusiastically to war in 1914. A third level of analysis, the *third image* involving the international system itself, and an understanding of its essential anarchy and the constraints it might impose upon state actors, was necessary for predicting the force of the two other groups of factors. By sorting potential factors into distinct levels of analysis and implying a hierarchy of importance in his three images, Waltz both thinned some of the tangled underbrush in Kaplan (he also wrote simpler, more forceful prose) and pointed the way to the leaner Neorealism he would develop in the 1970s.

The work of Kaplan and Waltz, and of others in the mid-century American academy committed to a "scientific Realism," confirm that the social-scientism—the behavioralism and systems analysis—that was powerfully shaping the practice of American Political Science was also laying claim to the hitherto undertheorized discipline of IR. This colonization of IR by an emerging dominant school within American Political Science drew articulate and critical reaction: from Stanley Hoffmann at Harvard, another intellectual émigré who was trained as a historian of French politics; and also from British scholars grounded in the discipline of international history. Often these responses to the new scientific Realism (later, "structural Realism" or "Neorealism") admitted the need for more rigor and perhaps for theory appropriate to the field, but resisted both the narrowing effect of behavioralism and what seemed to some to be the American co-optation of an international discipline.

Hoffmann's first assault (he called it a "wrecking operation") came in a 1959 article that admitted the need for more rigor. IR was loosely multidisciplinary, he observed, but "a flea market is not a discipline." Morgenthau's Realism failed, however, not because his theory was unverifiable, but because "it sees the world as a static field in which power relations reproduce themselves in timeless monotony," and was itself an idealization of the eighteenth- and nineteenth-century golden age of European diplomacy. The systems theory envisioned by scientific Realists like Kaplan was, however, not the answer. It would result in an even more artificial model of a closed system inappropriate for the decentralized international milieu and in what could only be called a kind of "methodological Byzantinism." The attempt to produce a precise analysis of myriad imprecise variables would lead to a false sense of precision that could neither explain nor predict the real world of international politics. Kaplan, however, had taken "a huge misstep in the right direction"—toward systematic empirical analysis—but the search would be a "long road" (Hoffmann, 1959).

The English School

The long road to useful IR theory was one that many British scholars of international history and politics were prone to consider less a highway than a maze or a cul-de-sac. Many of these, including those who considered themselves realists (if not exactly Realists), were from the first sharply critical of the American academy's obsession with measurement, with, that is, a science of quantifiable international behavior (so like Americans to want to count everything).

There was, as we have seen, a long tradition in the older British universities that politics, including international politics, was best approached through philosophy and history, and the discipline of IR in Britain reflected this bias. It is true that the LSE had long swum against the Oxbridge tide in its social science curriculum, and that the significant postwar expansion of the university system saw the new universities often raise the sciences and social sciences, especially Sociology, to prominence in their curricula. The social sciences in Britain, however, as on the European Continent, were heavily influenced by historical materialism (Marxism) or the historical sociology of Max Weber, and thus were often as resistant to the American-led behavioral revolution as were their colleagues in the humanities.

Nevertheless, IR in Britain (like the country generally in the years after Suez) was going through a period of self-examination and reevaluation. Those British scholars who accepted the primacy of the state, interests of state, and an international system of anarchy as definitional also felt some need to firm up IR theory and practice, but not necessarily in the directions that Morgenthau or, even less, Kaplan, suggested. In 1958–9, a group of scholars organized, with financial help from the American Rockefeller Foundation, a British Committee on the Theory of International Politics. This would form the nucleus of what would later be called (by one of its critics) an *English School* of IR theory and practice, offering an alternative to the scientism of the American academy. They are generally regarded as British-style Realists, though some question this designation given the school's deep interest in human agency and issues of moral obligation and normative behavior. The leading organizer was the well-known historian Herbert Butterfield (1900–79), Master of Peterhouse, Cambridge. Among others were Hedley Bull (1932–85), an Anglo-Australian lecturer in international relations at the LSE who had studied politics at Oxford, and Martin Wight (1913–72), who had read history at Oxford and also taught at the LSE. Like Niebuhr, Wight and Butterfield came to the study of history and the history of international relations as Christian moralists.

Wight's journey into postwar IR is perhaps instructive. He had been a pacifist supporter of the League of Nations and was a conscientious objector during the Second World War. A prewar researcher at Chatham House under the direction of the historian Arnold Toynbee, Wight returned there in 1946 and published *Power Politics*, a tract that expressed his disillusionment with the international law idealism of the failed League as well as his doubts about the prospects for the new UN. His teaching, grounded in history and the "Western tradition," was influential in British IR though he did not live to write a large general study.

By 1960, Wight was calling for more serious attention to the "intellectual and moral poverty," as he saw it, of the discipline—concerns that were later published (in 1966) in a much-read essay: "Why Is There No International Theory?" He points to the inadequate "small-scale" political theory of the sovereign state and to limiting traditions of international law, and was concerned that most of the classic works of political thought were unfortunately ignored because they did not *directly* treat issues of relations between states. Though like the scientific Realists he also felt that Marxism had little to offer in understanding interstate relations, he dismissed the American scientist answer as being ahistorical and rigid and called instead for a more carefully designed methodology of comparative historical case studies. History was likely to do the job "with more judiciousness and modesty" and with a closer attention to actual experience (Wight, 1966, 32). Wight was a Realist in the sense that he was pessimistic about the prospects of progress toward a more moral and ordered international system, and acknowledged the inadequacy of Liberal Internationalism and international law, while the philosophic utopian tradition (as with Kant) too easily slid into what he called a "grand theodicy." But systems analysis Realism was wrong to reject the importance of the values and ideals of statesmen in motivating state behavior or in its unwillingness to search beyond the "natural" sovereign state in a system of anarchy. There were, Wight argued, historical varieties of state systems.

In 1966, Hedley Bull also attacked what he considered an obsessive American scientism, that is, behavioralism and systems analysis. This gave rise to a sharp exchange that Kaplan regarded as a new Great Debate between science and traditionalism, though to label Bull simply as a "traditionalist" misrepresents his considerable insight. Bull's *The Anarchical Society* (1977) remains a major riposte to the scientific Realism of both Kaplan and Waltz. He accepts the importance of the balance of power, but rather than seeing it as a simple, automatic mechanism driven by the structural constraints of the anarchic system, he presents it as "conscious and shared practice." Dismissing the Hobbesian idea of an unsocialized anarchy of isolated individual states, he argues that there can be an anarchic *society* of states, that is, independent units motivated by state interests but that operate under certain rules of the game that are not the result of the constraints of the system but of cultural conditioning—as with the ancient Greeks or the European nations in the eighteenth and nineteenth centuries (Bull, 1966, 1977).

In Bull, "power" remains central to IR, but as a social attribute shaped by norms and historically constructed mutual expectations. That states pursue national interests provides little guidance about state behavior unless we know how interests are conceived—not in terms only of security, but also, say, of prosperity—and through what ideological and cultural lenses. The English School subsequently came to stand for the importance of "normative" behavior (of individuals, states, and indeed societies of states) in the analysis of international relations—best understood by returning to specific historical, perhaps civilizational contexts. While the English School's affirmation of historical perspectives and historical methods was central in their answer to American scientism, it should be noted that neither Wight nor Bull was much informed by the new social history of their era—itself much influenced by the social sciences of Sociology, Anthropology, and Economics, and by techniques of statistical quantification.

Bull and other early English School scholars like the ex-foreign service officer Adam Watson (1914–2007), an undergraduate student of Butterfield, remained largely within the postwar Realist (if not Neorealist) understanding that the sovereign state pursuing tangible interests in an anarchic system lay at the heart of the discipline. Watson would argue (in 1991), however, that history taught that hierarchy was as important as sovereign equality in understanding the pendulum-swing between periods of hegemonic empire and those of a balanced international politics. The English School founders also saw virtue in the traditional field of diplomatic history, in reading peace negotiations as important processes mirroring and creating international order, and in the classics of political philosophy, properly and closely considered, which enshrine norms of their times. They did not however endorse the special importance of Grotian international law (or the UN), and found Kantian idealism even less useful (order among states, in their view, not requiring a legal code, international organizations, or a higher morality).

Like Classical Realism, the English School has enjoyed a resurgence of interest among IR scholars (not all of them British) since the end of the Cold War. It offers an approach that preserves elements of political Realism while emphasizing a culturally conditioned and constructed (rather than systemic) international order. There are elements here that resonate with the "constructivist" critique (see below) of Realist and especially Neorealist theory, and these have been emphasized and further developed by some later English School scholars like Barry Buzan, Burton professor of International Relations at the LSE until 2012, and Richard Little, at the University of Bristol. Sharp divisions however continue to arise over the alternative concepts of "international society" (of states) and a (cosmopolitan) "world society," and over a "pluralist" approach that continues to center the state and the international institutions it creates versus an often activist "solidarist" approach that centers human rights in the constitution of international/world norms.

Finally, in the sharp exchanges between Bull and the scientific Realists one might detect an Anglo-American context beyond the debate's discourse. Bull suggests, in his assault on *American* theory, that IR should not be studied solely from the perspective of the powerful—one reason why the English School has some attraction outside the United States and Europe. That he himself wrote from the vantage point of a citizen of a declining power in the shadow of postwar American hegemony is of some relevance. As Robert Cox (2009, 321) has observed, "It is much easier for the scholars of a *former* empire to adopt the historical perspective of the rise and decline of empires, than it is for the scientifically tuned minds of citizens at the centre of the day's hegemony … ." The two political cultures drew from different world views and histories—those of, on the one hand, a formal empire, and, on the other, a new hegemon prone piously to denying its own "imperialism" while promoting a global politics-cum-political economy that was an extension of its Cold War ethos. The English School's sensitivity to the role of history, culture, and hierarchy in assessing the nature of the system of international relations can be said to draw, at least at some level, on British experience— of a sustained hegemonic empire as a valid, reoccurring type of political organization rather than, as American structural Realists would argue, an unstable and unnatural phenomenon. Or seeing the Commonwealth of Nations as a "society" of independent states. The competitive Hobbesian anarchy posited by Waltz's mature Neorealism or John Mearsheimer's later Offensive Realism (see below) did not seem to prevail in the realm of British, Canadian, Australian, and New Zealand affairs any more than it helped to understand the post-Second World War development of the European Community and Union.

From the Cuban Missile Crisis to a "managed" Cold War

The uneasily balanced Cold War came close to slipping into the Hot War of a general nuclear exchange in the fall of 1962. At the time most analysts would have looked to divided Berlin, where the Soviet and American occupiers directly faced each other, as the likeliest trigger for a nuclear Armageddon. Castro's Cuban Revolution of 1959, and the threat that it would inspire other left-wing insurgencies in Latin America, may have caused deep concern in Washington, but it was not, however, considered a high security threat for the United States itself. This changed with the discovery of the secret placement of Russian nuclear missiles on the island. The motives behind this remarkable Kremlin decision may have been partly domestic—which of course raises the issue of whether systems analysis, by ignoring what Waltz had called "second image" factors, could be a reliable guide to predicting the behavior of states.

It is clear that the Cuban missile crisis (see Chapter 9) is a critical watershed. It brought home to policymakers and analysts, IR scholars, and the public at large the enormous and not entirely calculable risks involved in the push-and-shove confrontation of superpower "balancing" in the nuclear age. In the long run, it encouraged a search for a "managed" Cold War not of confrontation but of accommodation, very much along the lines of Classical Realism's model of how diplomacy from a position of strength is meant to work. Among IR scholars, the crisis in October 1962 produced contrasting readings on a number of levels. Some Realists (though not Hans Morgenthau) saw the successful American threat of the use of force, but in the context of firm negotiation, as confirmation of their own school of thought, while structural Realists might believe that MAD, though nuclear powers were taken to the brink, nevertheless had worked to guarantee (and illustrate) "system stability." Among others it encouraged a postmortem examination of the behavioral aspects of "decision-making" highlighted at the various stages of the Crisis, and to elaborate explorations of game-playing psychology.

Among much of the general public, however, such academic exercises and analyses were beside the point. The Crisis had been one of unprecedented anxiety and its resolution an emotional release. It changed the public environment for future American and European policy (for many Europeans it brought home the dangers they faced of utter annihilation should the superpowers resort to even a limited nuclear exchange). Among some Realists like Morgenthau or the English School scholars, the issue of nuclear warfare had all along been an unresolved moral question, one that pushed Morgenthau, Niebuhr, and Kennan at least to reconsider ideas about international organization that they had previously considered idealistic. Such reevaluation of Cold War Realism's tenets was further encouraged by Morgenthau's disapproval of American involvement in the Vietnam War. Realists, like other IR scholars, were deeply divided over America's reassumption of the French colonial war in Vietnam. Some like Morgenthau were opposed on grounds of morality as well as expediency, while others doubted the importance of the region to the security of the West and found the calculation of costs and benefits—especially as the conflict engendered deep division at home—ultimately unpersuasive. At least in the short run Cold War Realism was undermined and fractured by the Vietnam War.

It has been argued (by Alan Gilbert) that Morgenthau's writings during the 1960s, when he was most engaged with opposition to the war in Vietnam, mark a watershed from a reductive Realism to one that affirms the common good and is sensitive to moral issues involved in the exercise of power (Gilbert, 1999). Morgenthau had already come to doubt that there could be any ethical use of nuclear weapons and argued for their control by the UN or some other international body. In *Power Among Nations*, he had suggested that an international moral consensus was necessary to sustain a genuine balance of power and that, while states might pursue a Machiavellian approach to fulfill their objectives, those objectives (like the struggle against Nazism) had a moral dimension. By 1970, Morgenthau also came to rethink the nature of superpower hegemony, not in terms of global balance but as demonstrating the "impotence of power," whereby lesser satellite allies were "parasitic" on the superpower host and dragged it into unwanted or ill-advised conflict. "Power" that could destroy the world was in practice unusable and irrelevant.

The return of Liberal Internationalism and Institutionalism

It can be argued that the First and Second Great Debates encouraged a too-close concern with Realism (either classical or scientistic) at the expense of other approaches to IR theory and practice. While histories of the discipline inevitably focus on varieties of Realist discourse throughout the Cold War era and often assume that they commanded a dominant position in the field, it is probably true that, even in the United States, Realist research and publications, however generously defined, accounted for only about a third of the work being done by IR scholars. Realism not only did not bury Idealism or Liberal Internationalism, it remained itself on the defensive over its own methodological and theoretical shortcomings.

One way of retrieving the role of a "liberal" alternative in this era is to draw lines of continuity from the days of the League to the quotidian operations of the UN. Sometimes, as with the British historian of diplomacy Charles Webster, there were direct, personal continuities—Webster was an ardent supporter of international organization and had attended both the last meeting of the League and the first of the UN General Assembly and Security Council in 1946. While it may be true that the UN was a hybrid of idealist and realist conception, any hope that the Security Council would serve as a kind of (Classical Realist) Concert of the Great Powers to arbitrate disputes had quickly been dashed by Cold War polarization. This, however, had the effect of actually enhancing the somewhat secondary, internationalist aspects of the organization enshrined in those bodies that had continued from the League days—like the International Labor Organization or the Health Organization (refounded as the World Health Organization in 1948)—or in new bodies such as the United Nations Scientific, Education, and Cultural Organization (UNESCO, 1945) or the United Nations Children's Fund (UNICEF, 1946). Moreover, the UN's Universal Declaration of Human Rights (1948) seemingly endorsed a continuity of liberal idealism and the rule of international law, as did the war crimes tribunals at Nuremberg and Tokyo.

Another approach might place Liberal Internationalism's revival in the historical context of the growing transnational character of world affairs that followed the transformative experiences of the Second World War. The reestablishment (outside of the Soviet sphere) of an international financial order, following the Bretton Woods conference of 1944, was marked by new international organizations like the International Monetary Fund and the World Bank and the increasing globalization of trade and manufacturing generally, while the growth of global communications and media networks (Marshall McLuhan's "global village") threatened the boundaries of the closed nation-state, long taken for granted by traditional international history and enshrined in much Realist IR theory.

There is not, of course, a simple opposition of Realist and Idealist traditions. If there are varieties of Realism, there are also different kinds of Liberal Internationalism drawing from quite distinct objectives, historical contexts, and theoretical traditions. Some of these, like "liberal institutionalism" (which emphasizes the growing role of international organizations), though perhaps assuming an increasing interdependence of states, may share with Realism an acceptance of the state and the state system as the basis from which their analysis builds—international institutions, however much they may develop an autonomous character, originating out of decision-makers' calculations of their utility. Others, like "World System" theorists (see Chapter 3) or those who argue generally for the importance of transhistorical phenomena in a globalized world (social, economic, or cultural networks and identities within and beyond the state), are much less committed to key statist assumptions. Since the 1970s, there has been a growth of interest in "normative theory," which, following lines previously addressed by the English School, explored the emergence of an international or transnational sense of community. The debate over the slaughter in Vietnam and the use of modern technologies of war (napalm, land mines, or agent orange) against a local population indistinguishable from "the enemy" raised issues anew about the ethics of force and concepts of international justice. Finally, the long tradition of a "utopian," or Kantian, approach, which has resurfaced as a major issue for debate after the end of the Cold War (see Chapter 10), itself can be broken down into at least two traditions, that of a visionary and cosmopolitan world government, and that which anticipates the "democratic peace" that would ultimately follow from a federation of democratic states that preserve a large degree of sovereignty.

The new Liberal Institutionalism was promoted most prominently by the work of the American political scientists Robert Keohane and Joseph Nye, both students of Stanley Hoffmann at Harvard. The new journal they edited, *International Organization*, and two books, *Transnational Relations and World Politics* (1972), an edited collection of the essays from this journal, and *Power and Interdependence* (1977), had a significant impact in the 1970s. According to one Realist scholar, the 1972 book "transformed the American discipline" (Gilpin, 1987, xi). The second focused more closely on the theoretical implications of what they called the "complex interdependence" of states, a system in which force might be of "low salience" and issues other than security might determine behavior. Though this approach was to some extent shoved aside by the reformulation of structural Realism by Waltz in 1979, it remains a coherent and tenacious subdiscipline, and one that has enjoyed a significant revival in the post-Cold War era. Keohane and Nye argued that since much "intersocietal intercourse" with significant political importance takes place without governmental involvement, as in trade and the media, states cannot be assumed to be the only—or in some instances even the chief—actors in world politics. This growing prevalence of transnational actors (multinational corporations or political, ethnic, or religious movements across national boundaries) and international processes (the growing density of international organizational activity) in the modern world required that Realist state-centric theory be reconsidered. The state remained, of course, but its power might lie in nonmilitary sources of influence, in, for instance, international institutions constructed to advance common interests, and be constrained and determined, not by the international state system, but by changes in the world economic environment. This was the decade that saw the unraveling of the US-dominated Bretton Woods global financial system and OPEC's oil embargo.

Neoliberal Institutionalists, therefore, focus on international "regimes," like that envisioned by the General Agreement on Tariffs and Trade (GATT, 1948; subsequently [1995] the World Trade Organization), which reflect state interests other than that of "security," as defined by a plurality of national and transnational groups. They often draw from the allied social science disciplines of Sociology and Anthropology (especially from ideas of social networks) and from the newly developing field of International Political Economy (see Chapter 3). To some extent, these ideas were not new. Early (interwar) work of the British scholar Harold J. Laski (1893–1950) had questioned the idea of the sovereign unitary state by emphasizing its "pluralist" nature, that is, the variety of corporate interests at work both within and beyond the formal boundaries of the state. In the 1970s, some American Liberal Institutionalists looked back to Laski in their questioning of the assumptions of Realist theory, or (unusual among American Political Scientists, but perhaps not to students of Stanley Hoffmann) to the work of the prolific French intellectual Raymond Aron (1905–83) and his own concept of "transnational society" (Aron, 1966). Keohane and Nye set out to answer the "level of analysis problem" to which Waltz had drawn attention in 1959 by (1) broadening the conception of "actors" to include transnational actors and (2) breaking down the "hard shell" of the nation-state, though some would claim that they did not go far enough in this direction.

Neorealism

The difficulties posed by Morgenthau's Classical Realism, the complications of multivariable analysis facing scientistic Realists, and the challenge from the Neoliberal Institutionalists led in the 1970s to attempts by many American Realists to defend or rethink their theories. One prominent response came from Robert Gilpin, a political scientist with an interest in Economics as well as IR. As a classical, state-centric Realist, Gilpin (who also describes himself as a "soft realist" [Gilpin, 2005, 361]) nevertheless found the Neoliberal emphasis on transnational actors like multinational corporations especially instructive and called for a new paradigm that would integrate the transnational and the state—as suggested by the way the postwar "Pax Americana" had facilitated the spread of global economic liberalism. His 1975 study, *U.S. Power and the Multinational Corporation*, explored what would become a fresh area, or subdiscipline, that took form over the decade as International Political Economy. He confirmed his, at least American, leadership in this field in 1987 with a book on *The Political Economy of International Relations*.

Gilpin's work, including an influential study of war and world politics in 1981, was attractive to some historians but did little however to resolve the manifold problems of analysis facing scientistic Realism. The work of rethinking the theoretical basis of IR that "came to trump all others" (including Gilpin) was Kenneth Waltz's second major work, *Theory of International Politics*, which appeared at the end of the decade (1979) and laid the basis for a major revival of American Realism (as "Neorealism"), but with an intellectual cost—a narrowing of IR theory to issues of the structure of the interstate system and a further alienation of many historians from the field as practiced in the United States. Scoffing at "the myth of interdependence," Waltz's Neorealism served as a provocative foil for Neoliberalism (which in these exchanges itself became more scientistic), the English School, and latterly the important post-Cold War, postmodern challenge of Constructivism.

Waltz announced his intention to explain long-term continuities in international relations ("the striking sameness in the quality of international life through the millennia") that persisted "even as actors vary," by constructing a theory of international politics that would remedy the defects of present theories. He attacked Morgenthau's Realism for its "reductionism" in favoring agency (with its emphasis on human nature) over structure, and denied that the first concern of states was to maximize their power. Rather it was to "maintain their positions in the system." Citing *Occam's razor* (if two hypotheses have equal explanatory power, the simpler theory is to be preferred to the more complex), he also sought to save scientific Realism from the awkwardness of Kaplan's overly complex modeling ("more of a taxonomy than a theory") by focusing on the paramount importance of the "third image," that is, the interstate system, using severely trimmed down, "parsimonious," deductive theory to posit the laws governing international relations. He endorsed the scientific method of posing hypotheses that could be proved or disproved, if not through experiment as in the natural sciences, then through observation of state interaction throughout history. Waltz aimed to produce a theory shorn of inessential variables that could establish the significant *constraints on state behavior* that were generated by the prevailing *anarchic structure* within which *unitary sovereign states* perforce had to operate.

This approach made for a leaner, pared down theory, but one that was inherently ahistorical (though historical data might be selectively used to confirm its hypotheses). This rejection of historicism was enshrined in its assumptions about (1) the systemic constraints on actors to pursue rational calculation (unmitigated by cultural and social factors) and (2) an interstate regime that had remained unchanged in its basic characteristics since the sovereign state had emerged in the seventeenth century. The idea of a stable, rather than evolving, system drew to some degree from the influential work of the historian of science, Thomas Kuhn (1922–96), who had famously argued that science did not proceed in a uniformly progressive way, but moved from one "paradigm" to another in a series of sharp breaks. For Waltz, history was only useful insofar as it could establish the long-term fixed continuity of the structure (or paradigm) within which modern international relations continued to operate. In this the interstate system was not unlike the capitalist economic system identified by nineteenth-century political economists, with their iron laws of market-driven behavior and consequences.

Like Gilpin, Waltz had been attracted as an undergraduate and early graduate student to the field of Economics. But what Waltz took from this was a reading of economics at the *microeconomic* level, whereby individuals and firms make rational choices within a system defined by market forces—or failed. His theory of IR would similarly view the state as a "unit" constrained, whatever its internal character, to respond in predictable ways, most importantly involving (1) "balancing" against threats and (2) imitation of successful states, which thus assured the prevalence of "like units," that is, states of very different composition behaving in similar ways. The principal motive was that of survival (or "security") in a system of fierce and dangerous interstate competition. States that did not seek sufficient power to balance against threats put their security—the highest priority of a state—at risk. States adapt to their structural environment, or go to the wall.

By treating the state as the equivalent of a generalizable "economic man," Waltz moved, not as Gilpin had done to accommodate the Neoliberal attempt to break down the hard shell of the state, but further to *reify* (i.e., invest a concept or symbol with a concrete reality) it into an object whose course of action could be as calculable as a billiard ball's. The aim of his Neorealism is to show how the global system creates the parameters for international relations, the implication being that the theory can then predict *probable* outcomes better than a history that is preoccupied with the uniqueness of the event or a historical Sociology dominated by the concept of progressive development. At the same time, Waltz emphasized that his theory was not about predicting *specific* outcomes, the reaction of individual states at any moment in time to the constraints of the system. This led some to observe that it was a convenient theory that appeared to let him both have his cake and eat it.

Waltz's theory was indeed elegantly parsimonious and, at a certain level of abstraction, logically persuasive and defensible. It offered a scientific method that dispensed with "historical contingency": "Nations change in form and purpose; technological advances are made; weaponry is radically transformed; alliances are forged and disrupted. These are changes *within* systems" (Waltz, 1979, 67). His theory did away with both the need for an argument based in human nature and for a search for myriad second-image factors. The problem, especially for many historians, however, was the level of abstraction that it called for, and its relegation to areas of secondary importance much of what historians (and many Classical Realists) consider of interest in explaining international politics—personalities, ideas, or social and cultural conditions. By taking the position that, so far as theory was concerned, it did not matter whether states actually behaved as predicted in the short term or in any particular set of circumstances (since errant states would ultimately "pay" for their wrong choices), Waltz's closed system might satisfy logically, but some claimed lacked much predictive power. Nevertheless, it was a theory that resonated with, and therefore drew strength from, the context from which it itself emerged—that of a bipolar, stable, and apparently managed Cold War.

Neorealist theory as laid out by Waltz endorses equilibrium; "balance" is an integral aspect of the system, whether or not any particular state wishes to balance with others. Morgenthau saw balancing in terms of wise statesmanship; the English School in terms of normative behavior and "shared practice." For Waltz it is simply a dictate of the system. Even nonconformist or rogue states (like the early USSR) *inevitably adapt to the system* whatever their ideological character in order to ensure their survival. There is, therefore, a systemic *tendency to stability*, and the bipolar superpower system demonstrated even greater equilibrium than the European multipower system of the past. Both American and Russian policy (at least from the vantage point of 1970s *détente*) had, whatever the nature of their outdated early Cold War rhetoric, adapted to working within this structure.

The end of the Cold War

Almost as soon as Waltz's theory appeared in print, the "managed," stable Cold War appeared to lurch back into a reprise of its earlier confrontational and threatening mode. The geriatric leadership in Moscow occupied Afghanistan. More accurate missiles (the Soviet SS20s) and advances in multiple warhead technology threatened to undermine the slow progress toward nuclear arms control, as did the North Atlantic Treaty Organization's (NATO) deployment in 1982 of short-range nuclear missiles in Europe. In the United States, where concern for human rights in eastern Europe and support for the "Refuseniks" in Russia (as well as a traditional chauvinism) had created strong dissent in Congress to *détente*, the end-of-the-decade negotiations for a second strategic arms limitation treaty (SALT II) ran into trouble and, though observed by the United States until 1986, was not ratified. Ronald Reagan's Strategic Defense Initiative in 1983 appeared to undermine the Anti-Ballistic Missile treaty negotiated in the early 1970s, and his own rhetoric ("an Empire of Evil") seemed to invoke the moral posturing of American anticommunism in the 1950s. Rather than embracing bipolar stasis as a necessary consequence of systemic equilibrium, hardliners in the Reagan administration (Machiavellian Realists perhaps but not Waltzian Realists) seemed determined to undermine the continued viability of their opponent through a costly competitive new arms race. When the Soviet Union *did* collapse at the end of the 1980s, hardliners took the credit, though the role of increased defense costs in causing this is highly debatable.

What is clear however is that Waltzian Neorealism had difficulty explaining either the turn to a more rebarbative Cold War in the early 1980s or the sudden collapse of the bipolar structure in 1989. In 1979, Waltz had written that "despite some outdated rhetoric from the doughtiest of cold warriors, American aims have shifted from changing the system to maintaining the system and working within it ... This profound change in the definition of the American mission marks the maturation of the bipolar world." Of course, Waltz had hedged the issue of whether his theory could predict specific outcomes, and in an aside he had claimed that though "the system appears robust ... [it was] unlikely to last as long as its predecessor [the 300-year-old European multi-polar system]" (Waltz, 1979, 162, 303). Nevertheless in 1989, Waltz's system theory did not offer much guidance to understanding how and when an apparently stable paradigm might shift to a new one. The end of the Cold War was a crisis for Neorealist thought.

Historians and Neorealism

Though Waltz's theory of structural Realism dominated much (American) IR discourse in the 1980s, attracting a large following almost exclusively among IR practitioners trained in Political Science, from the beginning it in fact also generated a vigorous negative critique—especially among historians of international politics, some of whom, like Paul W. Schroeder, a specialist in eighteenth- and nineteenth-century European diplomacy, believed that embracing Waltz's abstract theorizing meant the death of good history. He argued that IR political scientists often misused history in constructing their theories—not the "garden variety of bad history often found in works of political science" that stemmed from an inadequate understanding of the original historical data, usually taken from secondary sources, but (echoing Carr) a failure to understand that the historical "facts" they use were selected and often indeed constructed by historians, and often represent "acts of purposive agency," not "constrained behavior." Schroeder objected that not only structural analysis but game theory and statistical-mathematical calculation "along the lines of econometrics" was not so much a question of a misfit between History and Political Science "as one of no real connection at all" (Schroeder, 1997, 71, 73).

Others, like the historian and political scientist Marc Trachtenberg, are prepared to argue that while Political Science in general and even abstracted structural Realism can be of some use in explaining historical behavior, in revealing long-term continuities in the real world, it is probably fair to say that Neorealism has failed to persuade most international historians of its promised "pay off" in the analysis of the past. Their concern centers on the ahistoricism of Waltz's deductive approach and the way it appeared to strait-jacket the discipline. Neorealist parsimony meant a rejection of the social, ideological, and cultural factors that determine the nature of a regime and that *along with structural constraints* are necessary for a full (and useful) historical analysis. As Stanley Hoffmann had earlier observed, Waltz's theory is "conceptually so rigorous as to leave out much of the reality he wants to account for" (Hoffmann, 1977, 15), while R. B. J. Walker has claimed that structuralism, and its "longing for timeless categories," is more interested in identifying rules than in explaining or recognizing *change over time*—the historian's prime objective (Walker, 1989, 322–3). Martha Finnemore, a political scientist, complained that rather than generating interests and constraining actors a system is instead constituted by them; that it itself is inside, not outside, history (Finnemore, 1996, 14).

Many critics in fact complained that the best close "fit" with Neorealist structuralism was the classical economic theory that apparently inspired it. As William Fox wrote (1985, 10): "World politics is not...like classical economics. It does no good to imagine a nation-state single-mindedly pursuing something called 'power' the way...economic man is presumed to be single-mindedly pursuing something called 'wealth.'" There are at least two issues imbedded here. One involves structural Realism's dependence, like classical political economic theory, on a "rationalist model" of behavior, a problem for both cognitive psychologists and those historians who believe that the assumptions of "rational choice" theory obscure the fact that in the real world behavior is culturally, emotionally, and historically constructed. It also begs larger questions about a discourse that slides from individual rationality to that of the state (or other collective group). Both Neorealism and Neoliberal Institutionalism highlight the instrumental rationality of actors and focus on decisions and choice in ways that may be ahistorical.

Finally, some observed that ironically Neorealism was itself engaged in establishing a kind of normative behavior. As Joseph Nye once commented (1988, 235–6), Waltz's works "can best be read as exhortations to policymakers and fellow citizens about how they *ought* to respond to the structure of power rather than as accurate accounts of how...powers behave." Such a perspective has special relevance when one moves from scientistic theory-construction to the realm of policy; from the ivory tower to the think tank and the hard Realist world of, say, the foreign policy analyst eager to have a voice in Washington.

Post-Cold War Realism

The decade or so after the fall of the Soviet Union was a period of serious reflection for IR theory generally, and especially among the Neorealists whose approach had been significantly geared to understanding and applying the lessons of superpower Cold War confrontation. By the mid-1990s, many scholars, not only historians but some from within the political science IR community, were prepared to argue that Waltzian Neorealism was fatally flawed—perhaps already dead on its feet. There was a return in some quarters to the Realism of early Morgenthau, reborn as a *Neoclassical Realism*, which saved some aspects of Neorealism's structural approach and retained the state as the central analytical concept but opened the way to reintroducing domestic factors affecting state behavior. There was "an imperfect 'transmission belt' between systemic incentives and constraints, on the one hand, and the actual diplomatic, military, and foreign economic policies states select, on the other" (Lobell et al., 2009, 4).

More aggressively, a University of Chicago political scientist, John J. Mearsheimer, proposed a harder Realism, *Offensive Realism*, as a response to the probable return of a multipolar global politics. Seeing history as an "empirical database," Mearsheimer attacked Waltz's concept of equilibrium and "status-quo bias" in which states seek to preserve their autonomy by securing just enough power to meet threats to their security but not so much that the security dilemma kicked in. He theorizes rather that states pursue *as much power as they possibly can achieve*, and argues that the world will likely return to the familiar geopolitics of competitive national power-grabbing—whether in the new Asia or old Europe (Mearsheimer, 2001a). His predictions that Europe would slough off the interdependence culture of the European Union and return to nation-state geopolitical competition was, however, a prediction too far for not only many international historians but some of his colleagues in the Realist community. These doubters coalesced around versions of *Defensive Realism* (Mearsheimer's term for Waltzian analysis) and argue for a less pessimistic reading of the near future.

Though Realism has emerged from its post-Cold War crisis of doubt with many articulate advocates like Jonathan Haslam who are prepared to argue for its continued value (*No Virtue Like Necessity*, 2002), its fragmentation proceeded apace. One critic (Snyder, 2002, 149–50) observed that there were at least two varieties of structural realism, probably three kinds of offensive realism, and several types of defensive realism, in addition to neoclassical, contingent, specific, and generalist realism. At the same time, Realists of all varieties were subjected from beyond by the rise of alternative, often radical "postmodern" and "poststructural" concepts in IR (as in the humanities and social sciences generally), terms enclosing a number of theoretical shifts that question the utility, indeed viability, of any definition of state and system.

Radical perspectives and critiques

According to the poststructuralist critic Nicholas Onuf, writing at the end of the Cold War, a Third Great Debate was taking shape out of an assault generally on aspects of scientistic (i.e., positivist) IR theory—on the search for "laws" of state behavior, described by one critic as "onto-theological" assumptions rather than proven hypotheses (Der Derian, 1995, 373), on the assumed central role of the state and the rational logic of its behavior, on the casual fixing of identity and meaning in what was actually a shifting, discordant, and increasingly no longer Western-defined world, and on the ways in which Waltzian "like-units" concealed significant and fluid differences in the subjectively constructed character of the nation-state (Onuf, 1989).

Concepts familiar to other social sciences since at least the late 1970s—identity-formation, intersubjectivity and reflexivity, and "discourse"—were, like the long-familiar problematic of "agency," deployed in the postmodernist, poststructuralist assault on mainstream IR scholarship. The language of Realism was itself subjected to analysis through a deconstruction of its "rhetorical performances"—the ways in which its self-representation as a science and its textual strategies served as a hegemonic discourse to privilege a Western form of international order. One scholar, James Der Derian (who had been an American student of Hedley Bull at Oxford), argued that Realism, with its mythic, imagined beginnings, was itself a symptom of a general condition of late modernity (Der Derian, 1995, 279). Another, Yosef Lapid, held that Neorealism's ontology (the study of basic categories of being) of undifferentiated, like-unit states was deeply flawed because states, especially after *nationalism* became normative, were not concrete entities but variable states of mind, subjective identities, and were constructed through performance and discourse (Lapid, 1996). Leading the attack were, often, postmodern feminists and social and cultural Constructivists, who shared a concern with how identities and interests (including state interests) are formed; Realists, they claimed, generally simply accept them as given.

Constructivism

In the 1990s and 2000s *Constructivism*—the term was apparently coined by Nicholas Onuf—gnawed away at the foundations of much political science theorizing about IR, an increasingly "divided discipline," but did not, its critics claim, manage to generate a unified body of theory upon which a sound alternative might be raised. In fact, the general concept that the phenomena of IR theory do not exist as concrete givens but are socially and culturally "constructed" and reconstructed, not once but continually, encouraged quite different angles of approach. Some, like Alexander Wendt, accept that states are the principal actors in an international system and state identities and interests are integral to the structure of the state system, but regard their construction as *intersubjective* (i.e., constituted by interaction among persons or groups or states and between them and the system of states) rather than simply determined and fixed by the system. For Wendt, a fundamental principle of Constructivist social theory is that people (and states) act toward others on the basis of meanings they project onto them: that is, for instance, they act differently toward those perceived as enemies than they do toward friends. In a well-known article of 1992, "Anarchy is what states make of it," he observed that identities were "inherently relational." Others place the concept of individual and group *identity* foremost and regard the state and state system as less important than the social and cultural construction of, say, a nationalist sense of belonging. Still others, like Richard K. Ashley, would dispense with the entire enterprise of state-system analysis.

Some Constructivists hold that since meaning (understanding) is constantly being socially, experientially reconstructed (either domestically or internationally), there can be no absolute and fixed understanding of terms like sovereignty or power, and thus no fixed "system." The calculus of political science using these concepts is built therefore on shifting sands. For scholars like John Ruggie, a core Constructivist research concern is how world views, civilizational constructs, and intersubjective identities shape interests and international outcomes. There is a need to understand more about system *transformation* (which involves how collective intentions and aspirations may change) rather than simply accepting a system or structure as a given—bringing human consciousness, what Ruggie calls shifting "ideational factors," back into the study of international life (Ruggie, 1998, 857–8, 878–9). If human society comprised "webs of meaning and signification," the same is true of societies, or systems, of states; the European state system from which Realists have abstracted their views was "socially constructed" through specific historical experience, geography, and the cognitive dimension of its social life, its collective *mentality*. Most historians, for their part, probably sympathize with some aspects of a "cultural theory of international relations" while remaining leery of its often hyper-intellectualized engagement with ontology.

At the extreme end, some philosophical postmodernists hold that reality, shifting or not, is ultimately unknowable. The very terms and concepts we use simply represent the way our minds work—as, for example, in the idea of "sovereignty," central to both the Classical Realist and Neorealist models. The concept of (domestic) sovereignty versus (international) anarchy is, from this point of view, merely another oppositional dichotomy that says more about the binary ways in which we construct reality than reality itself. Carried to an extreme, this line of analysis, however, seems equally destructive of the narrative of History as it is of the positivist rationalism of Political Science. While historians may be able to learn something from examination of hidden "discourses" and "languages" of IR, a nihilistic postmodernism that simply dissolves analysis and narrative is on the far edges of scholarship and, some think, has, by the twenty-first century, run into its own cul-de-sac.

If Constructivism has not, as Ruggie admitted in 1998, "been well received in the mainstream of the discipline," it nonetheless provided a significant challenge (that of demolition) to the modernist, materialist assumptions of a rather tired Realist, and especially Neorealist, agenda. The use of Constructivist concepts of identity and normative behavior in IR scholarship has trickled into most areas of inquiry—even in "security studies," once a nearly exclusively Realist terrain.

The feminist challenge

Feminist IR offers another radical critique, related to the postmodernist and Constructivist challenge ("identity" and the ways gender differences are socially constructed have been central concerns in contemporary feminist theory). Like them it has moved from the margins into—or nearly into—mainstream IR discourse. A distinctive feminist approach to IR has of course been available since the pacifist revulsion against the First World War, when it was associated with Liberal Idealism generally as offering, say, a mother's perspective as a nurturing, caring, inclusive alternative to an international politics of masculine violence and competition. As such it may have advanced a dubious psychology that was caricatured by hard-headed realists, but some version of this gendered binary (war is masculine, peace is feminine) remains embedded in the progressive politics of "peace and justice" studies.

Postmodern Feminism has however become an altogether more complex and scholarly enterprise. In the past twenty years, it has emerged as a body of theory and method that offers an increasingly coherent and productive perspective—with a close affinity with other areas of radical critique that draw from Sociology, Anthropology, and Psychology and focus on behavioral norms and identity. Some years ago, most IR textbooks (and perhaps many IR introductory courses) treated feminism, if at all, as something of an afterthought. In the language of feminist critique, it was "silenced" in an overwhelmingly male-dominated, masculine/Realist discipline. This has for some time been changing. Feminist IR began to find traction as the Realist and Neorealist paradigms appeared to falter; in 1988, the scholarly journal *Millennium* (founded at the LSE as a voice, often, for those critical of American Political Science IR) published a special issue devoted to women. The late- and post-Cold War of the 1980s and early 1990s saw the emergence of a significant body of feminist-informed IR scholarship and the rise to prominence in the academy of IR feminists like J. Ann Tickner (president of the International Studies Association in 2006–7), Christine Sylvester, and V. Spike Peterson. These scholars have promoted the careers of a successor generation of feminist IR scholars, and important aspects of feminist IR theory can no longer be ignored by mainstream practitioners. The "arrival" of feminist IR was celebrated in 2011 in a substantial five-volume compendium of scholarship on the concepts of *Feminist International Relations*, and there is increasing attention paid to ways in which feminism may suggest productive research agendas and methodologies.

Feminist IR reflects the post-Cold War shift in the discipline away from questions of power, sovereignty, and a balanced world order to areas of human rights and "human security," peacekeeping, norms of international law, and nonstate actors. It also importantly scrutinizes the ways in which the key factors in IR analysis are "gendered" (following Joan Scott's insistence in 1986 that gender was "a useful [and necessary] category of historical analysis"). Areas of feminist scholarship include often a reinterpretation of the classic texts of IR—focusing on *masculinist structures of thought* buried in, for instance, ideas of sovereign authority (as inviolable) or the nature of power. This extends to *absences* in classic political and philosophic texts, to, say, Rousseau's exclusion of women from his idea of the general will or the way Kant relegates women to subordinate status in the ideal republics of his perpetual peace. The feminist perspective also highlights the use of women or femininity in classical IR texts to characterize the antithesis of rationality or to justify a masculine concern with security, as in Machiavelli's dismissal of women as the ruination of the state and his image of *Fortuna* as an unpredictable temptress contrasted with manly *virtù*, or Hobbes's invocation of women as vulnerable in a state of nature because unlike men they must care for the weak. Some feminists also place an emphasis on communitarianism and socialization rather than anarchic individualism and competitiveness in the analysis of state systems.

Feminist IR generally embraces a multidisciplinary approach, challenging the idea that IR can be "purely political" or state-centric, and has taken an interest in how gender relations relate to International Political Economy or Liberal Institutionalism. Drawing from psychological theory, it emphasizes (like Constructivism) the importance of subjectivities, that is, self- and mutually constituted identities, both in state interaction and for the IR scholar herself—whose work ought to be "self-reflective." It shares with critical theory (see Chapter 3) a commitment to change and often insists upon a close connection between scholarship and activism. Critics of feminist approaches (and there has been considerable resistance) would respond that subjectivity and activism are not conducive to "objective" analysis, and that there remains a problem of "audience"—of feminists writing for other feminists.

While it is not yet the case that the perspective and concerns of feminist IR have been smoothly integrated into the theory and practice of the discipline, they are far more likely to be taken seriously than in the past (especially perhaps by historians). In some areas of critical analysis, like that of the problematic of sovereignty, the postmodern questioning of the scientific Enlightenment project, and the exposure of the Eurocentric bias of the discipline and how that might be addressed by the inclusion of the voices of, say, Third World women, feminist scholars have made a significant contribution.

Recommended readings

For a suggestive general, historicizing critique of both Classical and Neorealism, see Stefano Guzzini, *Realism in International Relations and International Political Economy: The Continuing Story of a Death Foretold* (1998).

There is a considerable literature by and on the English School. A brief introduction is provided by Andrew Linklater, "The English School," in Burchill and Linklater (eds.), *Theories of International Relations* (2005), 84–109. Also see Timothy J. Dunne, *Inventing International Society: A History of the English School* (1998), and a special forum in *Review of International Studies* 27 (2001). On the English School and the uses of History, see Joao Marques de Almeida, "Challenging Realism by Returning to History: The British Committee's Contribution to IR 40 Years On," *International Relations* 17 (2003), 273–302, and Edward Keene, "The English School and British Historians," *Millennium* 37 (2008), 381–93.

For a general introduction to postwar Liberalism in IR, see Scott Burchill, "Liberalism," in Burchill and Linklater (eds.), *Theories of International Relations* (2005), 55–83. For the Neorealist–Neoliberal debate, see Robert Jervis, "Realism, Neoliberalism, and Cooperation: Understanding the Debate," *International Security* 24 (1999), 42–63, and a special issue of *Millennium* 38, 3 (May 2010). Gilpin's adaptation of Classical Realism is treated by William C. Wohlforth, "Gilpinian Realism and International Relations," *International Relations* 25 (2011), 499–511, and Wolfgang Danspeckgruber (ed.), *Robert Gilpin and International Relations: Reflections* (2012).

Waltz's Neorealism has been the subject of an extensive literature. A large collection of critical essays on aspects of structuralism in IR can be found in the two issues of *International Relations* devoted to Waltz and IR theory, 23, 2 (June 2009) and 23, 3 (September 2009). For a post-Cold War critique from the latter-day English School perspective, see Buzan and Little, *The Logic of Anarchy: Neorealism to Structural Realism* (1993). For the Neoclassical perspective, see Steven E. Lobell, Norrin M. Ripsman, and Jeffrey W. Taliaferro (eds.), *Neoclassical Realism, the State, and Foreign Policy* (2009). Mearsheimer's "Offensive Realism" is addressed in Glenn H. Snyder, "Mearsheimer's World—Offensive Realism and the Struggle for Security: A Review Essay," *International Security* 27 (2002), 149–73, while Brian C. Schmidt provides a discussion of a key issue in all varieties of pre- and post-Cold War Realism in "Competing Realist Conceptions of Power," *Millennium* 33 (2005), 523–49. On the problem of rational choice in Realist theory, see Miles Kahler, "Rationality in International Relations," *International Organization* 52 (Autumn 1998), 919–41; Stephen Walt, "Rigor or Rigor Mortis: Rational Choice and Security Studies," *International Security* 23 (1999), 5–48, and Lisa Martin's response, "The Contributions of Rational Choice: A Defense of Pluralism," *International Security* 24 (Fall 1999), 74–83. Also suggestive in its use of sociological theory in critiquing structuralism from a normative standpoint is Martha Finnemore's *National Interests in International Society* (1996). For a more general consideration of normative theory, see Molly Cochran, *Normative Theory in International Relations: A Pragmatic Approach* (1999).

For the early (1980s) poststructuralist, antipositivist position, see Nicholas Onuf's "The Third Debate: On the Prospects of International Theory in a Post-Positivist Era," *International Studies Quarterly* 33 (1989), 235–54. Subsequently, the Constructivist field evolved considerably and claimed a deeper provenance, leading some scholars (see Timothy Dunne, "The Social Construction of International Society," *European Journal of International Relations* 1 [1995], 367–89), to speak of "proto-constructivists" (Carr) and "classical constructivists" (Bull), as well as "neoconstructivists." Christian Rees-Smit's chapter, "Constructivism," in Burchill and Linklater (eds.), *Theories of International Relations* (2005), 188–212 is a useful introduction, as is Nicholas Onuf, "Constructivism: A User's Manual," in Kubálková et al. (eds.), *International Relations in a Constructed World* (1998). Also see Onuf's major work, *World of Our Making* (1989), Yosef Lapid and Friedrich Kratochwil (eds.), *The Return of Culture and Identity Theory* (1996), Alexander Wendt's *Social Theory of International Relations* (1999), and Stefano Guzzini, *Power, Realism and Constructivism* (2013). For an example of John Ruggie's approach, see "Territoriality and Beyond: Problematizing Modernity in International Relations," *International Organization* 47 (1993), 139–74, and "What Makes the World Hang Together? Neo-Utilitarianism and the Social Constructivist Challenge," *International Organization* 52 (1998), 855–85. For other aspects of postmodernism and poststructuralism in IR debate, with a focus on issues of "discourse," see Francis A. Beer and Robert Hariman (eds.), *Post-Realism: The Rhetorical Turn in International Relations* (1996). A thorough-going defense of structural Realism against the Constructivist critique can be found in Stacie E. Goddard and Daniel H. Nexon,

"Paradigm Lost? Reassessing Theory of International Politics," *European Journal of International Relations* 11 (2005), 9–61.

Useful general studies of the feminist approach in IR can be found in Christine Sylvester, *Feminist Theory and International Relations in a Postmodern Era* (1994), V. Spike Peterson, *Gendered States: Feminist (Re)Visions of International Relations Theory* (1992), and Brooke A. Ackerly, Maria Stern, and Jaqui True (eds.), *Feminist Methodologies for International Relations* (2006). Also J. Ann Tickner's recent collection from her own extensive contributions since 1988, *A Feminist Voyage Through International Relations* (2014).

CHAPTER 3
THE OTHER SOCIAL SCIENCES
AND THE STATE

Though we have thus far centered the relationship between History and Political Science, the fields of Sociology, Anthropology, Psychology, and Economics have been often, if selectively, used to confirm, elaborate, or critique IR theory. How historians of international relations might draw upon these fields cannot however be addressed without also understanding that the "other" social sciences are themselves shaped by the evolution of both internal discursive traditions and external historical contexts and fashions, as well as being within their broad boundaries marked by a wide plurality of theory and practice. While it is certainly beyond the scope of this text closely to scrutinize the historical evolution of each of these allied disciplines, this chapter offers some necessarily sketchy observations, from the historian's point of view, on their character and usefulness.

Sociology and Anthropology

As we have seen, historians, for the most part, have been reluctant to buy into IR system theory generally and especially into an ahistorical concept of the reified billiard ball state. They are more likely to see and write about sovereign states (or nations, or peoples) as historically dynamic and socially and politically plural. They are also reluctant to accept that the constraints imposed from above by an anarchic system simply trump those operating from below through a host of domestic social, economic, and psychological factors. Historians by the early twentieth century increasingly regarded the state as led and populated by individuals with complex identities and loyalties and corporately composed of groups and interests, some of which were also transnational in character and not definable or containable by the nation-state. The turn toward social history encouraged significant borrowing from the field of both Marxist and Weberian Sociology and from subsequent trends in sociological and anthropological thought and practice. Historians came, in particular, to see the nation-state—its definition as well as its ownership—as an inherently contested realm.

For the modernist Carr (1961, 84), there was, or ought to have been, a reflexive symbiosis between History and Sociology: "the more sociological history becomes, and the more historical sociology becomes, the better for both." There has however been some of the same tension between History and Sociology as between History and Political Science, with History (almost by definition) being at least as interested in change over time as in horizontal analysis of the systemic and functional laws of operation of a society at a moment in time. Sociology itself, as it took shape as a modern academic discipline, was of course originally deeply invested in historical, that is, developmental, thinking. "Historical Sociology" is now a subdiscipline in the field, but a historical, evolutionary, and progressive approach was central to all nineteenth-century social and social-biological thought. Both Sociology and cultural or social Anthropology (the border between the two is somewhat artificial) saw a significant post-First World War shift in theory and practice. Large schemas incorporating the historical processes of growth in social organization from ancient (or primitive) to modern (or complex) fell out of fashion in favor of a narrower in-depth study of the functioning of more or less closed social systems, privileging statistical analysis and description over broad speculation about change over time, the synchronic over the diachronic, and the domestic over the intercultural.

Historical Sociology from Weber to Mann

The founding father of much of what is now regarded as classical Sociology, the German scholar and liberal Max Weber (1864–1920), stands in an important but complex relation to the disciplines of both History and IR. Weber invoked broad cultural comparisons (of Western and Eastern civilizations) and deep historical perspectives (on the growth of rational modernity in Europe), through the use of universals and generalized definitions of state and power.

Weber began as a historian, but concerned (in the German philosophical tradition) with the relationship between the particular and the general. Furthering history as a social *science* required constructing generalized or "ideal types" for analysis from historical data (as in traditional vs. rational-legal forms of authority). These were convenient conceptual constructions imposed on particular phenomena in order to lend them significance. Defining the modern state as characterized by its monopoly of the legitimate domestic means of violence, Weber emphasized the *process* of state-building seen in the historical conflict in early modern Europe between patrimonial rulers and new elites (educated clergy and laymen as well as landlords, merchants, and financiers) over control of administration in the context of an unfolding dynamic market economy. In reaction against the economistic determinism of Marx, however, Weber was concerned also with concepts such as honor and status in this competition for power, and generally with the role of ideas and values—how do certain ideas become social forces?

Weber sought to uncover social meanings through the method of *Verstehen* (understanding) that examined social actions from within, that is, from the viewpoint or mentality of an actor who is located in a set of social practice. He speculated on intangible factors like *prestige* (as a form of power) and *nationalism* (to be sought in the memories of people and their sense of destiny), or the almost mystical character of leadership in the concept of *charisma*.

Aspects of Weber's thought, however, his broad historical-philosophical speculations about the origins and character of modernity through the growth of secular rationality and the end of "enchantment," and especially his reproduction of common nineteenth-century prejudices about the modernizing West and the cyclic, traditional East, fell out of fashion among many mid-twentieth-century practicing sociologists, less concerned with questions of origin, civilizational comparisons, or temporal change and more with the (often statistical, behavioral) analysis of function and differentiation in an observable ongoing social system—in, that is, the special domestic rather than the universal and historical. Some historians followed this particularizing trend while others continued to find Weber's broad canvass useful and suggestive. By the end of the twentieth century, aspects of Weber's *historical* sociology in fact enjoyed a revival among some sociologists and historians. In IR, this neo-Weberian historicism leant itself to the Constructivist critique of Realism and Neorealism.

Aspects of classical Weberian sociology were also important in the founding of IR Realism. In the 1930s and 1940s, both Carr and Morgenthau found aspects of his thought especially congenial: "All ideas aimed at abolishing the dominance of men over men are 'Utopian'" (Weber, quoted in Hobson and Seabrooke, 2001, 242). Well read in German scholarship, they drew on what they took to be Weber's idea of the autonomous modern state and the centrality of power (including prestige) in establishing its domestic authority through the monopoly of the legitimate means of violence and, though less overtly developed in Weber, of power as a universal aspect of any international system. If however "all political structures use force," Weber (1958 [written before 1914]) also observed that "they differ in the manner in which and the extent to which they use or threaten to use it ... These differences play a specific role in determining the form and destiny of political communities." This may suggest—at least to some neo-Weberians—a normative approach to the role of states in an international system and their differentiation rather than the like-unit sameness of states of Neorealist theory.

Another founding figure in classical late nineteenth-century historical Sociology, the French scholar Emile Durkheim (1858–1917), has also exercised some influence among twentieth-century social historians, but has been of rather less interest than Weber in IR scholarship until relatively recently. Durkheim thought like Weber that the disciplines of History and Sociology "naturally tend to veer toward one another," though he promoted the positivist scientific method, believing that only a close study of social data could lead to understanding the social system and that that system determined behavior (functionalism). He was concerned with how communities operate within a social system and how the social bonds that enable them to hang together may erode and dissolve. He famously posited *anomie* (alienation) as characteristic of modern urban industrial life.

There has been recent interest in how elements of Durkheim's thought, especially ways in which the growth of functional differentiation and the concept of "dynamic density," might be useful in shifting from Waltz's ahistorical, micro-economic view of international system to a concept of an evolving "world society" (Buzan and Albert, 2010). Waltz, it is argued, drew upon Durkheim's theory of differentiation (in his construction of separate images) but without its necessarily social and historical contexts. Durkheim's approach to what constitutes social data has also interested those who have sought to challenge Realism and Neorealism via normative analysis. For Durkheim, social data involved more than the material condition of individuals and classes, but also their linguistic practices, moral norms, religious beliefs, and so forth, constituting a *collective conscience*.

Classical sociological thought was broad-scoped in generalization and in its use of historical processes to understand social differentiation in ways that were attractive to many social historians, but less obviously useful to many IR scholars. The problem in mobilizing Weber or Durkheim for IR analysis is that neither presents a clear theory of *international* social development. Weber's interest in the state did not extend to how one society (or state) affects change in, or is affected by other societies (states). Part of this *problem of the state* in social theory was, however, addressed in the revival of historical Sociology in the late twentieth century. Aimed at a familiar lacunae of Marxist theory, this "bringing the state back in" addressed how the international might impact the domestic character of states, but left open the further debate over state "agency"—how states might structure the international system. This is something that a "second wave" of neo-historical Sociology has subsequently pursued.

Neo-historical Sociology

The reaction against wide-ranging historical Sociology, as that against universal and civilizational histories, can be at least partly explained by the further specialization of professional disciplines and the corresponding decline of the philosopher-scholar whose broad speculations and historical allusions, analogies, and parallels came to seem both unscientific and hubristic. When historical Sociology reemerged after the 1960s, it was less expansive, stripped of its at least overt nineteenth-century Eurocentrism, and in part driven by a renewed interest generally in the state in sociological theory. The work of Theda Skocpol at Harvard on comparative revolutions focused on the material (socioeconomic and administrative-military) resources of the state and especially on the ways successful social revolutions (in France, Russia, and China) seemed to result in strengthened national states better able to survive in the world system. This encouraged an agenda largely ignored in IR theory—seeing the state not as a closed, functional unit in a static system, but as a shifting amalgam of coercive institutions attempting to create domestic order as well as (and in order to) survive internationally, and which also may affect the character of other states within the system: "the key to successful structural analysis lies in a focus on *state organizations* and their relations both to international environments and to domestic classes and economic conditions" (Skocpol, 1979, 291 [emphasis in original]). Charles Tilly (1929–2008), a social historian of the left whose work was informed by sociological theory, in the 1970s also turned like Skocpol to the problem of the state, and especially the rise of European states from the medieval to the modern era. With an interest in what he has called "the *big structures, large processes, huge comparisons*"—that is, "*where sociology meets history*" (1992, xi [emphasis in original]), Tilly addressed, in *The Formation of National States* (1975), the question of which of the various kinds of early modern state eventually were best adapted to survive in the modern state system and why. A later work, *Coercion, Capital, and European States* (1990), moved away from Marxist economic argument to focus, as had Skocpol, on the coercive power of the military—in tandem with capital—within different kinds of state structures. Tilly argued for complexly varied state units interacting with the system.

Tilly and Skocpol's work has important implications for IR theory. Their attempts to reassert the importance of the origin and differential nature of states in understanding both the processes by which domestic order and legitimacy was achieved (an old Weberian concern) and the relation between the domestic and the international (in intrastate conflict generally and specifically in revolutionary movements) were of interest to some IR scholars. Their materialist approach however sidelined Weber's own interest in the role of ideas and norms and by the 1990s their state-centric focus and especially their preoccupation with the resources of administrative-military factors increasingly set them apart from both "second-wave" historical sociologists like John M. Hobson who are interested in bringing normative behavior and ethical enquiry back in, as well as some postmodernists who wish to subvert, that is, deconstruct, the very concepts of state, state sovereignty, and state system.

The historical sociologist who perhaps has most directly addressed issues embedded in IR theory is Michael Mann. A transatlantic scholar (with degrees from Oxford in both History and Sociology), Mann takes on, in his work on *The Sources of Social Power* (1986 and 1993), a key issue in IR, and especially Realist, theory—the concept of power. He moves beyond Weber's European-bound civilizational comparisons as well as those of historical sociologists like Skocpol and Tilly who narrowed their definitions to one aspect—state-enabling, material, especially military, power. For Mann, power is of many kinds. His *social* power project is hugely ambitious, with a historical scope reaching from the beginning of human history to the modern world. With regard to the interdisciplinarity of History and Sociology, he argues that, while it is delusional to try to achieve a general, universal theory of historical social change, there is a need to study history not only because "most of the key questions of sociology concern processes occurring through time" but also, echoing Carr, that History itself is "impoverished" without sociological theory—otherwise historians "imprison themselves in the commonsense notions of their own society" (Mann, 1986, vii). He especially questions the unthinking application of modern notions of class or the state to earlier historical periods. History, he says, does not repeat itself, it develops.

Power, for Mann, cannot be defined simply as a characteristic of the sovereign state but more broadly as "organized power networks" operating both below and beyond what IR theory often regards as the "unitary" state. "Societies are not unitary. They are not social systems (closed or open); they are not totalities" (Mann, 1986, 1–2). The ability to use physical force (military or state police power) both in asserting the legitimate monopoly of violence domestically and in the defense of the state internationally is generally held in IR theory to define the sovereign state. However in reality, according to Mann, most states have not in fact possessed a domestic monopoly of organized force, and international relations are often characterized by a peaceful stratification. The wider international society is not clearly determined by crude military power, but may involve other forms. "Power" derives from multiple sources—military, ideological (the social organization of knowledge, social norms, shared aesthetic and ritual practices), economic, and political (Weber's bureaucratic, institutional state). *These networks overlap and intertwine*—for instance, in the way military power (a military "revolution") may be enabled by economic change, which in turn may allow an elite to create economic and ideological power.

Mann himself denied that his work on power and on the interaction of social forces with the international system should be characterized as "Realist." It challenges much Realist and Neorealist theory of the unitary state—states crystallize in several different forms and power networks may operate across international space—as well as the idea of an anarchic system of states. States inhabit "a multipower-actor civilization," a community of shared norms and perceptions (i.e., statesmen have social identities of class and community that go beyond issues of security to define conceptions of state interest and morality in a much more complex, multilayered way). According to Stephen Hobden, Mann "offers a serious challenge to international relations theory" by attempting to integrate domestic and international analysis, providing a theory of historical change in the international system, and arguing that none of the sources of power are individually determining factors (Hobden, 1998, 117–41).

In 1998 the International Studies Association invited work that straddled IR and historical Sociology. By the end of the following decade, it could be maintained that historical Sociology was "at the heart of international theory" (Curtis and Koivisto, 2010, 434). Skocpol's and Tilly's focus on the state or Mann's complicating of Realism's understanding of power brought Sociology back into a dialogue with IR. But from the 1990s, a "second wave" (including Constructivists, Gramscian Marxists, and latter-day English School scholars) has focused less on the state and its resources and more on issues of system change, cultural hegemony, and the play of transnational social networks and ideological values—agendas that were sharpened by the abrupt end of the Cold War and the debate over an emerging "global society."

Such perspectives have been especially influential in the new global or world history, a school that emerged in the 1970s. Inaugurated, or at least most prominently advocated by the University of Chicago historian William McNeill, who developed a comparative but non-Western-centric approach to the multiple sources of world culture (Indian, Chinese, Middle Eastern, Greco-Roman) and the increasing *interconnectedness* of spatially and culturally disparate societies since ancient times. It has since become a "cross-cultural, comparative and global" subdiscipline institutionalized (at least in the United States) since 1982 in the World History

Association and a *Journal of World History*. The relevance of World History for IR lies not only in the ways it may question IR's traditionally Euro- or Western-centric character, but, more specifically, in the attention it draws to a contemporarily evolving world society that is characterized by a significant degree of awareness of mutuality and interconnection—as in the rapidly evolving field of global human rights.

For their part, some Constructivist and latter-day English School scholars like Barry Buzan have transposed elements of Weber, Durkheim, and neo-Weberian historical Sociology in their own analysis of the history of world society as a dynamic system (or systems) of unlike units (imperial, hegemonic, independent, dependent, autocratic, democratic), and different environments (zones of peace, zones of conflict), focusing less on systemic constraints than on what historical Sociology (especially the work of Charles Tilly) has to offer about classifying different types of political units and identifying processes of change over time. This is a sociologically driven retreat from severe Neorealist theoretical parsimony that has been welcomed, especially by those international historians who have also been receptive to contributions from cultural or social Anthropology.

There has, then, been a "sociological turn" as well as a "historical turn" in IR. Historical Sociology has offered a corrective to the ahistorical nature of, especially, Neorealism, and has therefore been attractive to some historians, though many remain skeptical of ambitious, historically wide-ranging schemas like Mann's. Like political scientists, sociologists may also lack training in historical methodology and make use of the secondary work of historians as data for grand theory in ways that may not be sensitive to the limitations of this work for global generalization.

Anthropology

The social science of Anthropology developed from its ethnological roots in the Enlightenment as part of the project to create a global taxonomy of peoples. In the nineteenth century, it readily assimilated a Darwinian perspective—hierarchical and evolutionary—that informed early approaches to the study of cultures (often colonized, non-Western people), civilizations, and "races," and of the relationship generally of the West to the Rest.

By the early twentieth century, though physical Anthropology with its racial and eugenicist associations retained a certain popularity, there was an intellectual reaction in the Anglo-American academic world against much of this primitive-to-modern paradigm by those wishing for a more scientific exploration of other cultures. Anthropology was reoriented away from grand evolutionary theorizing toward a more empirically based, "scientific" field, represented in Britain as "social Anthropology," closely associated with its great promoter at the LSE, Bronislaw Malinowski (1884–1942), and subsequently with the "structural functionalist" A. R. Radcliffe-Brown (1881–1955) at University College London and, after the Second World War, E. E. Evans-Pritchard (1902–73) at Oxford. In the United States, the field came to be known as "cultural Anthropology," closely associated with the German-born founder of the first doctoral program in Anthropology at Columbia University, Franz Boas (1858–1942). Subsequently, the discipline on both sides of the Atlantic promoted field research that was purged as far as possible of prior concepts of developmental history based on comparisons with the West. In microstudies freed from notions of a hierarchy of cultures, these interwar approaches promoted cultural relativism, objective observation, and functional analysis. The search for "uncontaminated" extant societies, however, tended to wash history out of the discipline, as did its structuralist implications, and reduce its apparent usefulness to IR scholarship, which, if interested at all in the non-West, privileged those aspects of other societies and their histories that most resembled the Western state system.

With its focus on the operation of symbol, myth, rhetoric, and ritual, social or cultural Anthropology did offer, however, much of interest to some postwar political scientists, especially those concerned with the familiar problem of just how *legitimacy* is established in political societies—as did Anthropology's methodology grounded in the close case study. Early on, some social historians also borrowed heavily from anthropological work, especially the concept of the social construction of identities and "mentalities," in their analysis of Europe's own past. This was most apparent in the *Annales school* (after a French journal devoted to social and economic history), pioneered by Marc Bloch (1886–1944), a medievalist, and Lucien Febvre (1878–1956), a historian of early modern Europe. Though much Annales scholarship involved close local studies, the work of the *annaliste* historian Fernand Braudel (1902–85) explored the broadest civilizational realms, emphasizing the unity of the transnational region of the Mediterranean basin and epochal geo-cultural time spans, the *longue dureé*. Braudel exercised a significant influence on many scholars looking to expand international history and politics beyond IR's preoccupation with the Westphalian state—from the neo-Marxist historical sociologist Immanuel Wallerstein (b. 1930) and his "world system" work in the 1970s and 1980s to the renewed interest in "civilizations" in the post-Cold War 1990s. The IR subfield of the politics of environmentalism also owes something to Braudel.

The French anthropologist Claude Lévi-Strauss (1908–2009) promoted a structuralism that was less about social structure than the fundamental structures of the human mind and how specific cultural practices relate to "systems of signification." While Straussian ideas, and subsequently postmodernism generally, had a large, debated presence in academia and beyond, they were however virtually ignored by Cold War IR. Structuralist Neorealism drew more directly from the materialist philosophy of classical economic than anthropological theory and had little interest in the "deep structures" of the human mind. By the 1970s and 1980s, however, "identity" construction came to fashionably penetrate even the Anglo-American historical discipline, especially in concepts of the nation and nationalism—as in Eric Hobsbawm and Terrence Ranger's *The Invention of Tradition* or Benedict Anderson's *Imagined Communities*, both published in 1983. The construction of identity posed a potential challenge to an IR scholarship largely grounded in the analysis of the material resources of the state and the nature of a state system of sovereign units. If Mann explored the complex nature of power and its grounding in social, as well as economic and military, character, social or cultural Anthropology suggests that not only the nature of power but the *perception* of power and the manner of its *use* ought to be central concerns for both international historians and IR theorists.

If social historians and some political scientists found the insights of anthropological thought richly suggestive, mainstream IR scholars were, at least until the Constructivist challenge, only marginally interested if at all. This is in part due to the centrality of the state in IR theory. Anthropology, though it might speak to nation *building*, seemed to contribute little overtly toward a theorization of state *behavior*. This changed in the 1990s when historical Sociology, Anthropology, and cultural History proved increasingly attractive to those who, amid the crisis in Realist thought, moved from the search for laws governing the operation of a static state system to consideration of increasingly global processes of cultural formation (the "politics of identity") that developed traction after the end of the Cold War, the Balkan wars of the 1990s, and 9/11. The late twentieth-century Constructivism of critics like Wendt and Ruggie or the neo-English School work of Buzan encouraged a renewed interest in how norms are constituted and how states and state systems may evolve and be codetermined. Buzan and Mathias Albert (2010, 316) have gone so far as to assert that "anthropology and sociology are closer in form to IR than political science and economics." Anthropological insight has provided a useful perspective on a host of key issues and debates in IR and international history—on, for instance, the causes and practice of war as well as conflict resolution, on the "democratic peace" (see Chapter 10), and on changing global society generally (Snyder, 2002).

Anthropology has assumed a larger role in the collectivity of disciplines that inform IR as a social science. This is especially true for latter-day English School and Constructivist scholars, but it also may contribute, like the discipline of Psychology, to the pragmatic need of, say, security studies to "get inside" the mind of decision-makers from other cultures or other states.

Economics and political economy

The discipline of Economics traces its origins to eighteenth-century Scottish, English, and French Enlightenment thinkers, though in Britain the first university chairs (in Political Economy) date from the early to mid-nineteenth century. Classical political economy involved both the identification of the iron laws constraining *individual* behavior in the marketplace and a normative discourse about the policies *governments* should take to maximize the production of wealth—that is, the ideal relationship between state and economy. Economics as an academic social science with a set of analytical techniques (econometrics), however, did not properly take shape until the late nineteenth century with the statistical-mathematical analysis associated with the "marginal revolution" of William Stanley Jevons and Alfred Marshall. In the United States, professionalization can roughly be dated to the

1880s and the 1890s with the creation of the American Economic Association in 1885 and the elaboration of university programs for research and graduate studies. In pre-First World War universities, however, Economics was still commonly partnered with Political Science.

As with Sociology, Economics as a university discipline turned away from large historical and political philosophizing in favor of narrower statistical analysis—though economic *history* flourished in the interwar period (the Economic History Society was founded at the LSE in 1926 and the *Economic History Review* the next year) and provided a reservoir of comparative data on trade cycles and financial crises. Though some self-consciously interdisciplinary IR programs were constructed, as at Chicago, to include coursework in Economics, the field remained somewhat outside the main areas of IR interest. Traditional international and diplomatic history tended to relegate economic issues to the specialist area of the negotiation of trade and tariff regimes rather than drawing the discipline into a dialogue about methodology and theory. As in Britain, this neglect also reflected the common separation of (lower status) trade ministries from (high status) foreign affairs ministries. Marxist economics of course vigorously held to a global and historical view, focusing on transnational class relations within a globalizing capitalism rather than the economic relations of states—the later exception being neo-Marxist interest in the Third World postcolonial state and in resistance movements against the capitalist world system.

Classical political economy had been preoccupied, at least until late in the nineteenth century, with production rather than markets (i.e., with largely domestic factors surrounding industrialization), and regarded the state, the key object of interest in IR, in largely negative terms as either irrelevant or, more often, dangerous to healthy economic growth. The extended debate over the economic consequences of the Versailles settlement, the Soviet command-economy experiment, the Great Depression, the Fascist assertion of economic autarky, and the growth of "welfare capitalism" in the democracies, however, led to a renewed ferment of interest in the extended state and its economic planning—and to John Maynard Keynes' reconstruction of a political economy that stressed full employment, a critical regulatory role for the state, and an international financial regime that would facilitate this. Keynesianism's macroeconomics came to dominate (political-) economic thought in much of the postwar West, even if Keynes ultimately failed to convince the US Treasury of the need for a technocratic, depoliticized global financial regime.

The Bretton Woods Conference (1944) and the subsequent American-driven restructuring of the post-Second World War global trade and financial system in a Cold War context in fact highly politicized the export of American-style capitalism as an aspect of Western state security, with the new International Monetary Fund (IMF) symbolically located in Washington DC. This encouraged the movement of international economics from the periphery toward center stage in IR theorizing and practice. It drew attention to the ways in which the free trade regimes endorsed by a classical political economy that was theoretically opposed to the state both served the interests of and were indeed constructed by hegemonic states like Britain and latterly the United States—a phenomenon emphasized by Karl Polanyi (1886–1964) at the domestic level in his influential study of the creation of a market economy in preindustrial Britain, *The Great Transformation* (1944), and subsequently employed by historians like John Gallagher and Ronald Robinson in their 1953 reevaluation of supposedly sovereign relations between hegemonic Britain and lesser states in Latin America in the era of empire. The concept of "free-trade imperialism" led directly to *dependency theory* and its concern with the actual effects of the extension of a free market economy globally.

If twentieth-century social historians both drew heavily on economic analysis in their narration of domestic social change and attempted to place the development of economic thought into its historical and social-political contexts, international historians—with the exception of the Marxists and later world system theorists—have nevertheless tended to restrict their use of Economics to the analysis of one of many factors in nation-state competition and of the material resources of the state as it sought security or hegemony. As we have seen, however, both Neorealism and Neoliberalism draw heavily on different aspects of economic theory. Waltzian analysis posits a system that is modeled on that of classical nineteenth-century political economy, where the behavior of "economic man" (the equivalent of Waltz's like-unit states) was characterized by rational, utilitarian choice in the pursuit of material goals within the constraints of the (market) system. Neoliberals, for their part, drew not on the constraining factors of microeconomics but on the *idealism* of nineteenth-century liberal political economy and its (utopian) belief that free-trade capitalism would inevitably lead to benign global interdependence through mutually beneficial exchange, the undermining of autocratic elites, and a democratic peace. Where Waltz envisioned a static world of anarchic conflict that paralleled the pessimistic Malthusian origins of the "iron laws" of political economy, the Neoliberals drew on the optimism of Cobdenite liberalism's free-trade belief in peaceful "progress" through the proliferation of global economic networks. This optimism was significantly reanimated after the end of the Cold War when Neoliberal scholarship embraced in the 1990s a positive reading of the force of globalization in a no-longer confrontational and bipolar world.

Economic dependency rather than interdependency however colored the perspective and predictions of many scholars to the left of the Neoliberals. Wallerstein's world system theory was a reworking of Marxist and Leninist analysis that saw the historical evolution from the sixteenth century of a global system distinguished by the exploitation of the non-Western periphery by the Western center. It was influential or at least widely discussed in the 1970s and 1980s, but failed to win much ground within IR—in part due to Wallerstein's lack of interest in the state and the state system, and in part to the highly contestable character of his chronology and Eurocentrism.

A field, oriented generally toward the left in contrast with the new right's embrace of neoclassical libertarian economics, did emerge however within or alongside IR scholarship, largely in critical response to both Neorealism and Neoliberalism. *International Political Economy* quickly developed in the United States as an orientation within Political Science rather than Economics ("once the political scientists arrived on the scene, economists for the most part abdicated" [B. J. Cohen, 2007, 205]), and both authors of the most commonly used international political economy (IPE) textbook, *The Politics of International Economic Relations* (7th edn., 2010) are political scientists. In Britain, by contrast, the field was more autonomous and grew by the 1990s into a quasi-discipline rather than a subdiscipline, with its own journals (the *Review of International Political Economy* from 1994 and *New Political Economy* from 1996), research agendas, and academic appointments.

History, IR, and IPE

In 1985, William Olson and Nicholas Onuf (1985, 10) observed that "the most notable development of the last decade has been the institutionalization of a new field of International Relations called international political economy". They distinguished the IPE phenomenon, often oriented toward the liberal-left, from what seemed the other rapidly developing field of the time, Security Studies, often associated with neoconservative Realpolitik and a narrow preoccupation with military power. Both areas of research and writing have flourished since then, with some security studies scholars significantly expanding their field of reference especially to economic analysis. IPE has never quite managed, however, to establish itself as a unified discipline, divided as it is by its distinct British and American origins and orientations and by uncertainty perhaps over just what it is or ought to be about. Although IPE began—in the ferment that surrounded the collapse of the Bretton Woods regime and the rise of OPEC—as an array of differing theoretical approaches on issues such as transnational relations and the relation of domestic structures to the international economy, the American manifestation, inspired by the work of Keohane and Nye on interdependence, and Gilpin, who defined IPE as the intersection of the pursuit of wealth and the pursuit of power, was state-centric and empirical. A prominent IPE scholar in the American school, the Stanford political scientist Stephen Krasner, has written influentially on "international regimes" and the state sovereignty problematic.

Institutionalized in an International Political Economy Society (founded in 2007), American IPE remains more or less wedded to liberal economic theory and quantitative methodology. The British version, on the other hand, is more "holistic" in its approach and owes much to the work of Robert W. Cox and Susan Strange (1923–98), both of whom had a background in History rather than Economics or Political Science. Strange, a Burton Professor of International Relations at the LSE, organized as early as 1971 an International Political Economy Group within the British International Studies Association, resented the pigeon-holing of IPE within Political Science by the Americans, and argued that the field ought to be more open, multidisciplinary, less wedded to "scientific" methodology, and oriented toward engagement with social issues globally. She was especially critical of what she regarded as the limitations of American state-centered analysis, believing that economic power could be exercised in many ways, as in global structures of credit. Cox, who has written on "world order" from a neo-Gramscian and Critical Theory perspective (see below), encouraged a "historicist" approach that emphasized ways in which evolving modes of production and their social and cultural complexes operate on and beyond the state, and indeed "beyond [state-centered] International Relations theory" (Cox, 1981). The openness of the British school of IPE to areas of inquiry beyond the politics of IR (and beyond neoclassical Economics), especially its interest in normative, ethical issues, has encouraged some sympathetic resonance with other scholars (especially feminists) critical of mainstream IR.

Both versions of IPE were responses to the perceived loss of American economic and political hegemony in the 1970s, and were occupied with questions, familiar to political economy, of the relation between the modern, supposedly sovereign state and developing *global* markets. Like much of the early literature on globalization, IPE in its early form often assumed a tension between the state (and state system) and the multinational, transnational economy, though it also explored, as have some economists more generally, the role of "civil society" both within states and transnationally that emphasized normative issues—especially characteristic of British IPE and of those economists more generally who are critical of the classical model of an abstracted self-interested "economic man." Such scholars endorse the "socialization of economics," arguing that the "economic" is inevitably embedded in the historical, the social, and the cultural. At the same time, the social *science* of economics was, as in other disciplines, subjected to a deconstructive assault by postmodernists who saw in mathematical models and statistical tests "figures of speech—metaphors, analogies, and appeals to authority" (McCloskey, 1985, xvii), and emphasized the *rhetoric* of scientism and consequently issues of intention and audience.

The post-Cold War crisis of Neo- or structural Realism has encouraged a wider and more complex application of economic analysis in IR. Jettisoning or at least questioning Waltz's restrictive microeconomic assumptions about state behavior has allowed some Realists (and others) to return to "second-image" issues—the ways in which domestic economic interests and lobbies, themselves responding to both local and world economic forces, have historically influenced foreign policy at the state level and may shape international regimes beyond the state. At the same time, IPE scholars have returned to the political in political economy in part as a response to the rise of the restructured, postwelfare, "competition state" and its neoclassical approach to the global market and its regulation. Finally, following the shifting debate over the nature of (thick or thin) globalization, some recent IPE scholars have debated ways in which the global economy is heterogeneous rather than uniform and consequently the ways in which its creation and maintenance are historical-political and local processes.

In its analysis of the contemporary, post-Cold War economy, IPE has encouraged a historical dimension in, for instance, the connections that may exist between the United States' New Deal domestic regulatory experience (for instance, the creation of the Securities and Exchange Commission in 1934) and the international regulation of financial services. More widely, an historical approach has suggested instructive parallels with the "first era" of globalization—that of the British empire in the nineteenth century—which raises larger issues about how properly to historicize economic practice and economic thought in IR. If IPE itself was in part born out of a sense that American economic hegemony was waning by the 1970s, the global financial crises of 2001 and 2007 and the rise of China as a global economic player have inspired a return to issues of the state, the nature and limitations of the twenty-first-century global regulatory regime, and America's (doubtful) role as chief enforcer.

Marxism: World order, civil society, and world system theory

If some IPE scholars have returned to the state, as have some historical sociologists, many have not. This would include not only classical Marxist scholars who continue to insist that political structures are simply derived from their underlying economic foundations and tend, with the spread of capitalism throughout the globe, to become homogeneous and irrelevant, but those neo-Marxist revisionists who have advanced Gramscian concepts of a hegemonic world order, critical theory, and world system theory.

As we have seen, the Marxist tradition has generally had little traction in mainstream American IR, though more presence across the Atlantic. In part this was because American IR, and especially Neorealist system theory, was less interested in the origins or ultimate (in)stability of the system than in analyzing its character—and consequently had little use for Marxist teleology (its assumption of evolution toward an ultimate resolution of contradictions). Since the 1980s, however, Marxist and post-Marxist analysis has become rather less marginal as the problem of change (or paradigm shift) in IR system theory became a post-Cold War issue. One response was that of Fred Halliday (1946–2010), then professor of International Relations at the LSE, who argued for the significance of "moments of rupture and transition" in world politics by moving *revolutions* in world history and especially the international dimensions of revolutionary aspiration and accomplishment to the center of IR rather than viewing them merely as interregnums of breakdown in the state and the state system. Revolutions have had "international consequences," he argues, important for the "reassessment of international relations"—for the ways great powers act, the alliances they create, and the way the international system of states has itself been repeatedly reconstituted (Halliday, 1999). Other Marxist critics of IR theory have insisted on an historicist approach to the globalization debate itself and the ways international historians and political science IR have exaggerated the autonomy of states and state and interstate political structures and institutions. At the very least, the state and its international system need to be reassessed as the shifting products not only of material power but of both ideology and social-economic foundations that are dynamic rather than static.

Neo-Gramscianism

The early twentieth-century Italian Marxist Antonio Gramsci (1891–1937), in his posthumously published *Prison Notebooks*, drew attention to the *cultural hegemony* rather than the coercive economic and political power of the bourgeoisie in capitalist society, and how this served to forestall the development of working-class consciousness and thus thwarted the social and political revolution that Marx anticipated. From the 1960s, there has been a revival of interest in Gramsci's thought and its wider application beyond class relations within the liberal nation-state to the international sphere. Constructivist scholars like Robert Cox or Stephen Gill propose to incorporate elements of Gramsci's thought into an alternative to IR positivism and its focus on the material factors of state power. Instead of privileging the crude material power of individual states or combinations of states, they would focus on the importance of the *legitimacy* that enables states, international institutions, and regulatory international regimes. In other words, they would emphasize the quasi-consensual nature of successive "world orders" (whether the *Pax Britannica* or the neoliberal *Pax Americana*) and the "political architecture" of global capitalism (the IMF or the World Trade Organization [WTO]) that enables a hegemon like the United States to shape and maintain the global order.

Inevitably, there are those who claim that Gramsci has been rather selectively appropriated for IR and IPE, and that the Italian socialist's work itself must be contextualized within a specifically Italian postunification debate over the nature of the state. Nevertheless, it might be observed that Italian political traditions have been central to IR thought since the Renaissance, and as Cox (1983, 164) has observed Gramsci himself cited Machiavelli (that power was a centaur—half man, half beast; half consent, half coercion) in his attempt to understand hegemony as a form of power. Neo-Gramscianism, as deployed, may help us as historians to envision *how* the international system as both a political and a capitalist regime came into being—by focusing on the issue of agency—and how it is held together.

Critical theory

The so-called critical theory as a revisionist critique of capitalism had its origin before the Second World War in the work of the German sociologist and philosopher, Max Horkheimer (1895–1973), who sought to understand the totality of society in its historical dimension, incorporating all the major social sciences. The project, grounded in an Enlightenment sensibility and ambition, subsequently led to the critical exploration of modern capitalism in democratic societies. The German philosopher Jürgen Habermas, exploring the historical problem of human freedom, began with the Marxist dialectic but employed Kantian morality to move from issues of production to "communication" in the pursuit of an essentially liberal idealist program of reform grounded in rational discourse in the public sphere, consensus, and "moral learning."

If Habermas's thought was a response to the way the Cold War threatened freedom of thought and expression, the application of critical theory to IR (especially in the work of Richard Ashley) was an attack on the foundations of Neorealism and arose in reaction to Waltz's elevation of system above ideas, values, and morality. According to critical theory, the state and its "civil society" (which cannot be understood outside of discourse and ideology) are necessarily intimately related. As one early British advocate said, critical theory "provides the basis for reintegration of International Relations into the broader traditions and concerns of social and political theory" (Hoffman, 1987, 244). Another, American, scholar put it this way: "the normative purpose of critical theory is to facilitate the extension of moral and political community in international affairs" and to deal with issues of exclusion and inclusion that concerned Habermas (Linklater, 1992, 93).

Critical theory, which interrogates the origins and liability to change of the structural character of the present system, has had some impact on the margins of IR—especially among feminist scholars and Constructivists—in focusing on civil society as a socially constructed phenomenon that operates both within states and transnationally. It is characteristically seen, however, as the creation of a European scholarly academy more attuned to the revisionist debates of contemporary Marxist— or "post-Marxist"—philosophy than is the more pragmatic Anglo-American world. Many trained in American Political Science may find the applicability to IR of Gramscian cultural hegemony or Habermasian critical theory to be tenuous or obscure at best while being suspicious of their promotion of an activist left agenda of reform. Moreover, some historians as well, though appreciating the ways in which these theories are grounded in *historical* materialism and a questioning of the unhistoricized and reified state as the central analytical object in IR, nevertheless regard them as unhelpful in the creation of a useful international historical narrative or in escaping the Euro- or Western-centrism that is all too characteristic of IR generally.

World system theory

Varieties of "world system" scholarship, on the other hand, are especially attractive to some world or international historians (there is a World System History Group) because the concept is generally, if not invariably, approached historically. World system theory is "transdisciplinary" and can of course involve significantly different ways of approaching the historical record—as a reservoir of examples for *comparative* analysis, establishing *continuity* over time (including the discovery of cyclical patterns in world history), or defending an evolutionary perspective. Its chronologies often embrace much longer epochs and a greater variety of global cultures and (resistance) movements than either Gramscian concern with industrial and postindustrial capitalist class relations or Habermasian philosophizing about a specifically liberal European tradition of free discourse in the modern, democratic public sphere. Though all versions of world system theory emphasize the importance of social and economic structures, they can take very different forms, from McNeill's long-historical multicivilizational perspective to Robert Gilpin's present-oriented and essentially liberal and state-determined global political economy or the historical-materialist version of world system as globalized Western capitalism promoted by Wallerstein.

The revisionist Marxist argument of Wallerstein's *The Modern World System* (Vol. 1, 1974, and continuing) largely ignores the state in the establishment and maintenance of the transnational, global capitalist system that privileged and continues to privilege the capitalist metropolitan core and impoverish a dependent and semi-dependent periphery. Wallerstein's theory was much debated in the 1970s and 1980s. On the one hand, there was concern that his large generalizations suppressed significant local social and historical-cultural contexts and variation—ironically he shares with Waltz a structuralist-functionalist approach that is disinclined to credit domestic factors—while Marxist scholars were skeptical of his shift from (class) relations of production to those of exchange (trade) and the fact that his global capitalist world system did not recognize fundamental differences between the capitalist and noncapitalist world (either the precollapse Soviet Union or contemporary China). Historians challenged his location of the birth of capitalism in the sixteenth-century expansion of European trade (rather than in domestic social relations of both an earlier and later nature) or the Eurocentrism of his insistence on an enduring center/periphery model—though the dependency theory that his thesis both absorbed and encouraged developed a significant following among scholars of the underdeveloped world. And of course his privileging (as a Marxist) of economic relations above all other sources of power has also been problematic for many.

Psychology

The social science discipline of Psychology (including social and cultural psychology, cognitive psychology, and even bio- and evolutionary psychology, as well as the theories upon which varieties of psychoanalysis are based) has long been of interest to some international historians and IR scholars for the ways it may promise to advance our understanding of the behavior of individual decision-makers and the collective behavior of, say, bureaucracies, crowds, armies, revolutionary or terrorist cadres, regimes, and civilizations. If Economics, or at least classical economic theory, endorses models of rational choice within a constraining system, Psychology is often concerned with the analysis of irrational or subrational influences on behavior—with special relevance for the problem of how, for example, alliances function, arms races accelerate, and decisions to go to war are reached.

Revulsion in Europe and America against the First World War, and the spread of Freudian theory and jargon into not only scholarship but popular discourse, gave a special impetus to attempts to "psychologize" guilty leaders. The interwar years saw a fashion for psycho-biography and the application of, especially, Freudian theory to understanding historical figures, though much of this work was subsequently denigrated by many professional historians as "arm-chair theorizing" from insufficient or dubious evidence and unjustifiable inference. The then unprecedented violence of the Great War also led to attempts to explore collective behavior, that is, the practice of war itself, as a psychopathology of (especially male) aggression. This line of analysis remained an important theme on the pacifist and liberal-idealist left, as well as in second-wave feminist analysis, well into the era of the Cold War, with its scarcely veiled sexual innuendo of nuclear penetration, jet-engine thrust, bang for the buck, and missile envy.

Studies of war available to IR scholars have often been grounded in theories of the innate proclivity to violence of *individual* human kind ("human nature"), or, for feminist scholarship, *masculine* human kind. The rise of fascism and its celebration of (state as well as individual) aggression, and the horrific extent of mass murder in Stalin's purges and gulags or Hitler's death camps, led to an extension of the interwar literature on the pathology of aggression to types of state regimes in, especially, the psycho-analysis of "totalitarianism," most notably in Hannah Arendt's influential postwar work. At the same time, the successful establishment of a revolutionary regime in the Soviet Union (and later in China and Cuba) drew some liberal historians and political scientists to the study of the collective psychology of religious and political zealots, past and present, their ascetic mentality, and the disciplined organized movements they vanguarded. Much of this work drew directly from social psychological studies of group behavior.

Though psychological analysis of violent men, revolutionary cadres, states, and even civilizations was often shaped and informed by a liberal, individualist, and rationalist critique of *abnormal* zealotry and violence, what came to be known as the "Freudian Left" also explored, from a Marxist perspective, aspects of the liberal West. This was not the pathology of antiliberal movements or rogue regimes but of liberal capitalism itself, specifically the repressed character of the Western bourgeoisie. Investing civilizations with a psychological-cum-social-cum-economic character, building on Freud's own speculations about the sources of "civilization" and extending this to the class-bound culture of the industrialized world—most explicitly in Herbert Marcuse's text, *Eros and Civilization* (1955)—the Freudian Left enjoyed, like neo-Gramscian ideas in the 1960s, some vogue in revisionist Marxist scholarship; E. H. Carr observed in 1961 that "Freud compliments, and does not contradict the work of Marx" (Carr, 1961, 185). It did not, however, attract much interest among the scholarly IR community, especially in the United States.

Some prominent postwar historians have also taken the application of psychology and psychotherapy beyond biography to the study, generally, of culture and especially the construction of domestic prejudice and its connections with international aggression and imperialism, notably Peter Gay in his trilogy on *The Bourgeois Experience* in nineteenth-century Europe or Sander L. Gilman and G. L. Mosse on the psychosexual aspects of nationalism, racism, and fascism. Others, however, have been highly skeptical of the civilizational application of cultural psychology as highly speculative, ultimately unverifiable, and of doubtful use in predictive analysis.

Within IR scholarship, generally, it is the narrower, practical applications of psychological research and method that have exercised considerable influence. The Second World War saw academic and clinical Psychology coopted by combatant states into war planning and propaganda. Afterward, in 1950s America, psychological themes and theory were widely embraced in the ideological propaganda struggle with Moscow, while the state department looked to cognitive psychology to decode and anticipate secretive Kremlin thought processes. Psychological warfare and psychology-informed crisis management had "arrived" as fashionable aspects of security planning. This application occurred at two levels: that of the dynamics of the system itself (how, for instance, conflict may unintentionally or unpredictably spiral or escalate) and, more commonly, that of individual (interpersonal) behavior. Here, for instance, there emerged a body of thought that argued for the importance of *perception* (i.e., *mis*perception) of situations and opponents and how this may derive as much or more from one's own cognitive state as from the external realities of a crisis or the interests of states. The political scientist Robert Jervis, in his important *Perception and Misperception in International Politics* (1976), argued that history itself, that is, the "not entirely conscious" learning from history, could contribute to erroneous expectations on the part of "rational" actors (Jervis, 1976, chapter 6).

Social Psychology versus Cognitive Psychology?

Social Psychology—a bridge between the disciplines of Sociology and Psychology—deals with the way individual behavior may be affected by social groups, with norms (values that shape behavior) resulting from the internalization of social practices. This subfield is generally congenial to international historians concerned with cultural factors. For instance, social psychology's "identification theory" can be used to help understand issues of national identity, patriotism, and "national character," and the way these may contribute to the tenacity and coherence (and thus to the security) of the state. As one scholar has written, "Power politics create a state, but its endurance is guaranteed only if the psychological nation is built" (Bloom, 1990, 56). Some Constructivist and latter-day English School scholars like Buzan or Ole Waever and the "Copenhagen School" have sought to bring social psychology into IR by focusing on issues of *societal security* (and the perception of an "identity community" within and beyond the state) as an alternative to Realism's preoccupation with state security, especially in cases where state and society are not congruent (as in multiethnic states or the European Union).

Cognitive Psychology, on the other hand, addresses the IR scholar's interest in "the cognitive maps" of individual decision-makers and how these—rather than social relations per se—may channel, modify, or restrain rationality. Borrowed, to some extent, from the bargaining strategies of the world of commerce and finance, Cognitive Psychology has been attractive both to some political historians (writing, for instance, on a major event like the Cuban missile crisis) and to political analysts and advisors searching for an applicable tool to shape and evaluate current and future policy. During the Cold War, cognitive psychology was increasingly applied to strategic and tactical analysis through varieties of scientific "game theory" (in war or crisis simulation) in the Pentagon and CIA. Game theory, with its focus on bargaining and risk-taking, originated among economists attempting to study interacting decisions in a conflicted environment (as in the classic study by John von Neumann and Oskar Morgenstern, *The Theory of Games and Economic Behavior*, 1944 and 1953), but was taken up in the 1950s and 1960s, especially by American scholars of international affairs like Thomas Schelling (an economist), Kenneth Boulding (also an economist by training), and Anatol Rapoport (a mathematical psychologist).

Game theory may be congenial to Realism's concern with states and their decision-makers as actors (players) in *conflict*, but can also be applied to understanding issues inherent in *cooperation* (viewed as problems of complicated strategies of reciprocity and the rational calculation of "payoffs"—as in the famous "Prisoners' Dilemma," originally proposed at the RAND corporation in 1950). As with any other "science" of abstracted actors and system constraints, game theory can lead to the use of quite complex mathematical formulas that many historians view as far removed from the reality they wish to illuminate. Even with computerized modeling, "*n*-number" games are so complicated as to defeat the idea of practical application, while two-player games, popularized in the bipolar Cold War, would seem inappropriate for the analysis of multipolar politics.

Critics of the application of Cognitive Psychology to IR range from some Neorealists who argue that system constraints ultimately determine *successful* decision-making, whatever the psychology of players may be, while others (not only historians) have pointed out that foreign policy decisions are generally made within bureaucratic organizations that may restrain individual decision-makers, and that foreign policy is not simply the result of coping rationally or irrationally with contingencies and crises, but is constrained by, sometimes constructed by, underlying ideologies and domestic institutions and practices. Nevertheless, the application of psychological theory generally to the politics of international relations achieved momentum in the post-Cuban crisis 1960s, as can be seen in two 1965 collections of essays edited by Herbert C. Kelman and by Gerald Sperrazo, and became something of a subdiscipline by the late 1970s. Some argued that the application of psychological insight was especially valuable in situations of "information overload" and unanticipated crises requiring speedy reaction (both characteristic of the modern world of instantaneous communication and ballistic missiles), where the decision-maker's "belief system" or "cognitive map" might play a larger role than simple rational calculation. Some, like Glen H. Snyder and Paul Diesing, sought to apply the fruits of game theory and cognitive modeling to our understanding of past crises, a highly selective historical exercise that searched for common linkages, in this case, from the Fashoda incident in 1898 to Cuba in 1962. Typically, historians could be expected to object that, beyond the common complaint of selection bias, this kind of political science analysis generally runs the risk of lifting past events out of context and drawing strained and perhaps misleading parallels. Moreover, what may be questionable history is also uncertain science: the analysis is shaped by known outcomes and is not empirically falsifiable.

The chief problematic for historians lies in the inherently ahistorical character of much psychological analysis. On the one hand, bio- or Cognitive Psychology, by emphasizing the human mind's "hard-wiring," seems to reject, or at least to minimize, the importance of historical context and social conditioning. The same is by and large true of evolutionary Psychology, which locates the formation of behavioral responses in an atavistic, primitive, prehistoric, perhaps even prehuman, past. On the other hand, though *Social* Psychology would seem to offer more of interest to the historian, the location of individuals (whether persons or groups or states) within a social context does not necessarily ensure a developmental, historical vision and is commonly in danger of generalizing across time and across different cultures from locally specific, usually Western, research to the general sphere of global international relations among cultures with quite different social milieus and practices.

Recommended readings

A general treatment of historical Sociology can be found in Philip Abrams, *Historical Sociology* (1982). Also, Stephen Hobden, *International Relations and Historical Sociology: Breaking Down Boundaries* (1998), and Hobden and John M. Hobson (eds.), *Historical Sociology of International Relations* (2002). For a complaint that emphasizes the limitations of classical social theory for IR, see Justin Rosenberg, "Why Is There No International Historical Sociology?" *European Journal of International Relations* 12 (2006), 307–40. For a recent exploration of how Durkheim's classic work on differentiation might be brought into IR, see Barry Buzan and Mathias Albert, "Differentiation: A Sociological Approach to International Relations Theory," *European Journal of International Relations* 16 (2010), 315–37.

Theda Skocpol's argument for "bringing the state back in" can be found in her contribution to P. B. Evans, D. Rueschemeyer, and T. Skocpol (eds.), *Bringing the State Back In* (1985), 3–42, as well as in her earlier book *States and Social Revolutions* (1979). Also see Fred Halliday, *Rethinking International Relations* (1994). Critique of Mann's contributions to IR from a number of perspectives can be found in a special section of *Millennium* 34 (2006), 476–550. For the world society perspective, see Mathias Albert, Lothar Brock, and Klaus Dieter Wolf (eds.), *Civilizing World Politics: Society and Community Beyond the State* (2000). Richard Little and Barry Buzan have addressed the conjunction of World History, IR, and Historical Sociology in their work on *International Systems in World History: Remaking the Study of International Relations* (2000).

John Monaghan and Peter Just, *Social and Cultural Anthropology: A Very Short Introduction* (2000), offer a convenient entry into this social science, as do Paul A. Erickson and Liam D. Murphy, *A History of Anthropological Thought* (3rd edn., 2009). While Alan Barnard, *History and Theory in Anthropology* (2000), Carol Lowery Delaney, *Investigating Culture* (2nd edn., 2011), and Jeremy MacClancy, *Anthropology in the Public Arena: Historical and Contemporary Contexts* (2013) present valuable general insights, of special interest in the application of Anthropology to IR are Myron J. Aronoff and Jan Kubik, *Anthropology and Political Science: A Convergent Approach* (2012), and Jonathan Xavier Inda and Renato Rosaldo (eds.), *The Anthropology of Globalization* (2008).

General introductions to IPE can be found in Matthew Watson, *Foundations of International Political Economy* (2005), and Benjamin J. Cohen, *International Political Economy: An Intellectual History* (2008). For important contributions to early IPE scholarship, see the work of Robert Gilpin and Susan Strange, especially her *Casino Capitalism* (1986) and *States and Markets* (1988). For trends in later IPE, see the special issue of *New Political Economy* 4, 1 (1999), and, a decade later, the special issue of the *Review of Political Economy* 16, 1 (2009).

For an example of the application of IPE to issues of international security, see Kevin Narizny, *The Political Economy of Grand Strategy* (2007). Randall D. Germain (ed.), *Globalization and Its Critics: Perspectives from Political Economy* (2000), offers a critique from a variety of perspectives of IPE's relation to the scholarship on globalization. On the need to historicize IPE, see Louise Amoore et al., "Paths to a Historicized International Political Economy," *Review of International Political Economy* 7 (2000), 53–71. Robert Cox has attempted to find bridges between IPE, Gramsci, and critical theory's concept of civil society in "Beyond Empire and Terror: Critical Reflections on the Political Economy of World Order," *New Political Economy* 9 (2004), 307–23.

An overview of the issues raised in addressing IR from a Marxist or neo-Marxist perspective can be found in Andrew Linklater's essay, "Marxism," in Burchell (ed.), *Theories of International Relations* (2005), 110–36. Also see John Maclean, "Marxism and International Relations: A Strange Case of Mutual Neglect," *Millennium* 17 (1988), 295–319, for the lack of interest before the late 1980s and 1990s. For the application of neo-Gramscian concepts in IR, see Robert W. Cox, *Production, Power and World Order* (1987) and *Approaches to World Order* (1996), and Stephen Gill, *Gramsci, Historical Materialism and International Relations* (1993). A critique of the appropriation of Gramsci's thought in IR can be found in Randall D. Germain and Michael Kenny, "Engaging Gramsci: International Relations Theory and the New Gramscians," *Review of International Studies* 24 (1998), 3–21. Also see Richard Bellamy and Darrow Schecter, *Gramsci and the Italian State* (1993). For critical theory, see Linklater, "The Question of the Next Stage in International Relations Theory: A Critical-Theoretical Point of View," *Millennium* 21 (1992), 77–100, and Richard Devetak, "Critical Theory," in Burchill and Linklater (eds.), *Theories of International Relations* (2005 [3rd edn.]), 137–60.

For a sampling of historical approaches to the transdisciplinary concept of world system, see Robert A. Denemark et al. (eds.), *World System History* (2000). Wallerstein's world system thesis has been subjected to sustained criticism. See, for instance, Robert Brenner's Marxist critique, "The Origins of Capitalist Development: A Critique of Neo-Smithian Marxism," *New Left Review* 104 (1977), 25–92, or Theda Skocpol, "Wallerstein's World Capitalist System: A Theoretical and Historical Critique," *American Journal of Sociology* 82 (1977), 1075–90, for early responses, or, for example, Gurminder K. Bhambra, "Talking among Themselves? Weberian and Marxist Historical Sociologies as Dialogues without 'Others'," *Millennium* 39 (2011), 667–81, for a recent critique of Wallerstein's Eurocentrism (and that of the discipline of historical Sociology generally).

There is a considerable literature applying psychological theory to IR, from the psychologizing of historical decision-makers to the reevaluation of past top-level diplomacy (as in Judith M. Hughes, *Emotion and High Politics: Personal Relations at the Summit in Late Nineteenth Century Britain and Germany* [1983]), the use of social-psychological concepts (e.g., see Tobias Theiler, "Societal Security and Social Psychology," *Review of International Studies* 29 [2003], 249–68), or the use of cognitive psychology to map future outcomes via game theory. For example, see Thomas Schelling, "What Is

Game Theory?" in James C. Charlesworth (ed.), *Contemporary Political Analysis* (1967). For the "Freudian Left" and its amalgamation of Psychology and Marxism, see Paul A. Robinson, *The Freudian Left: Wilhem Reich, Geza Roheim, Herbert Marcuse* (1969). A general critique of the use of Psychology and psychotherapy by historians can be found in Jacques Barzun's *Clio and the Doctors: Psycho-History, Quanto-History and History* (1974), but for a more balanced view, see Thomas A. Kohut, "Psychohistory as History," *American Historical Review* 91 (1986), 336–54.

PART II
INTERNATIONAL RELATIONS AND
INTERNATIONAL HISTORY

A major objective of this book is to illustrate the need for an understanding of how the behavior of international actors—states, groups, and individuals—may be shaped by their history and culture. This is, most historians would argue, especially necessary when one moves from the abstract realm of theory, generally, and system analysis, in particular, to the exploration of specific actions in specific places and times. There may be a danger, as many have charged, that such historicizing favors the particular and unique over the generalizable, but neither does forcing history into a theoretical straightjacket necessarily serve the interest of a larger predictive social science of International Relations (IR) across time and place.

In this section, we shall examine, not as a continuous narrative but as highlighted "moments," the history of war, peace, and foreign relations from the ancient world to the post-Cold War present, emphasizing the ways historical events, eras, and texts have been used in constructing and rationalizing IR's master narrative of the (Western) origins of the "modern" form and practice of interstate/international relations. We shall highlight key concepts, like those of sovereignty and the unitary state, which historians often find more complexly problematic than is often the case in mainstream IR literature. Along the way, we shall interrogate the several schools of IR theory treated in Part I with regard specifically to how they employ historical evidence and interpret canonical texts.

Admittedly, the material treated in this section is selective, though embedded in a loosely chronological narrative. It is also drawn largely, if not exclusively, from the history of relations among Western regimes. This may seem perverse since we have criticized the discipline for its Eurocentric biases. The purpose of this section, however, is not to corroborate and further IR's Eurocentrism but to engage the themes that have been central to its construction, while bearing in mind the constant need for a comparative approach sensitive to the ways in which other cultures and polities may challenge as well as confirm IR theory and its grand narrative.

As we have seen, in the discipline of IR the state is generally taken to constitute the chief unit of analysis, inter*national* relations signifying inter*state* relations. This of course begs a number of questions that may be more salient to an international historian than, often, to a political scientist. Some transregional or world historians are committed to the exploration of layers of cultural, social, intellectual, and economic connection and conflict, not only as important conditioning factors in understanding the politics of international behavior, but as phenomena unbound by the state or the romantic understanding of an essentialized territorial nation. There is, then, the fundamental question of just what we mean by "state." The modern construct, larger than a face-to-face "knowable community," which involves a (at least theorized) monopoly of violence within its borders and which acknowledges no superior authority beyond, is an abstraction that emerged in Europe by the sixteenth and seventeenth centuries. But states by some definition, perhaps with indefinite shifting borders, with mixed or feudal ideas of sovereignty, encompassing a single city or a vast empire can of course be found much earlier and beyond Europe. IR realists, it might be argued, have had it both ways: insisting on the importance of the post-Westphalian European state yet drawing on history for examples of analogous societies like the Greek city-state or the Chinese "warring states" that seem to anticipate the modern system while regarding other polities—empires or feudal systems—as negative evidence of what a modern state is not. Historians are often skeptical of "using" the past in this way, of understanding it in terms of how it resembles or differs from the modern rather than trying first at least to understand it *on its own terms*.

Part II of this text begins with the ancient world (Chapter 4). Of interest are the ways IR scholarship has drawn upon ancient history and thought (from prehistory to late antiquity) in establishing and affirming central concepts in the discipline. At the center of this chapter is the reading of Thucydides' *History of the Peloponnesian War* and of fifth-century Greek city-states that has become central to Realist interpretation. Chapter 5 will then address another foundational text in IR, Machiavelli's *The Prince*, and another competitive small state system, that of fifteenth- and early sixteenth-century Italy, an era characterized, we are told, by war, secularization, "situational ethics," and *ragion di stato*. Rather, however, than seeing Machiavelli only as a precursor of modern politics, as is common in IR literature, we shall first locate him at the end of a period that has proven problematic for the discipline of IR. Scholars who have emphasized seemingly modern aspects of the ancient Greeks and the fifteenth-century Italian city-states often see in medieval Europe only confusion and ambiguity over the key concepts of sovereignty and state. This chapter will argue that IR would be better served by a more serious consideration of the medieval period (not only in Europe), including Byzantine, Venetian, and Muslim diplomacy, and, more generally, a searching for continuities as well as discontinuities between the medieval and early modern Mediterranean.

Chapter 6 will address the emergence of large territorial sovereign states and then reconsider the importance ascribed in IR scholarship to the Westphalian settlement of 1648, before assessing the war, diplomacy, and global expansion of the ancien regime, its bureaucratic, fiscal-military character, and the importance IR scholarship ascribes to the eighteenth-century concept of antihegemonic balancing. Chapter 7 explores how the revolutionary concept of the nation and of *popular* sovereignty— issues that are underplayed in much IR scholarship—may constitute a paradigm shift more significant than Westphalia, unleashing social and ideological forces that served to complicate and destabilize a system of limited objectives, rational (Newtonian) expectations, and enlightened balance. It will focus on the nineteenth-century idea of a European system of *nation*-states, contextualizing Great Power relations in the large social-historical realm of urban-industrialization and middle-class "public opinion" within which it is played out.

The final two chapters take us from one climacteric to another—from the rapid erosion of European dominance following the Great War to the collapse of the Cold War. Chapter 8 addresses the consequences of the World Wars and decolonization for the practice of international relations—the multiplication of nations, the definitional problems of sovereignty and self-determination, as well as the emergence of a *pax Americana*. Chapter 9 lays out the coevolution of the bipolar global system and the discipline of IR, in many respects handmaiden to American hegemony, concluding with the shattering of this "system" and the "return of history" in the Balkans and elsewhere.

CHAPTER 4
THE ANCIENT WORLD

Where and *when* might the narrative and analysis of IR properly begin? One's answer to those deceptively simple questions depends of course on what is meant by IR. If the field is essentially the study of the formal, that is political, interaction of nation-states within the modern state system, about, that is, the diplomacy, alliance strategies, perceptions of power and security, and resort to warfare of recognizably modern polities, then the IR narrative will inevitably privilege the post-Westphalia, globalizing West. If the field is somewhat more generally construed to be about how any regime or "state"—unitary or otherwise, ancient, medieval, or modern—has interacted with others, then the chronological and spatial hinterland of the discipline opens to include Western and non-Western polities of whatever era that have left significant record of their character and their pursuit of security or empire. But we are also sensitive to a third definition: if IR is still more broadly construed so as to include the interaction of *peoples* across political boundaries, with an emphasis on the transcultural and the transregional or the evolution of "civilizational" norms and practices, then questions of "where" and "when" float free from a focused narrative of the state per se. This latter sense of IR as the study of the ebb and flow of the myriad interactions of humankind (the political being but one, perhaps subordinate, kind of interaction) may be especially attractive to many world historians, some world systems theorists, and some Constructivists, but so opens the disciplinary field of IR across temporal and spatial boundaries that most policy-oriented political scientists, as well as some international historians, would find it too loosely focused (as well as too speculative) to be of much practical use.

As we move more or less chronologically from the ancient world to what follows, we shall shadow mainstream political IR's historical quest to understand the past in terms of the development of latter-day state institutions, systems, diplomacy, and norms—but at the same time keeping in view the larger world and other roads not taken. A chief goal in this chapter is to question IR's sometimes superficial or at least casual "reading" of the ancient past with the deeper (or at least more complicated) understanding found in the work of historical-archeological, linguistic, and literary specialists.

States, empires, and the origins of diplomacy in the ancient Near East

European philosophers of the seventeenth century—most notably Thomas Hobbes and, with differing conclusions, John Locke—famously speculated that the state's origins lay in human nature and the fearful need for self-preservation (they themselves of course had experienced an especially tumultuous and violent era). The historian or historical sociologist would of course argue that such speculation is of little practical use in arriving at a scholarly understanding of either the origin or the great diversity of types of "sovereign" authority in the prehistoric and ancient world. For them the story begins with vast human migrations after the last ice age—migration and "ethnogenesis" were also important at the end of antiquity—and the domestication of grain that led to the coalescence of agricultural communities in the fertile areas of the Near East (Mesopotamia) and China (the millet- and rice-growing river basins). In the most productive regions, settled communities produced surpluses that encouraged not only the development of trade networks but the emergence of surplus-extracting elites and, ultimately, the evolution of larger than local polities, bureaucracies, and, importantly, the record-keeping necessary for tax gathering, trade, and law-giving. Whether the evolution of the prehistoric state as a coercive institution had most to do with defense (self-preservation) or the enrichment of an elite may be debated. We cannot, in any event, get very close to the prehistoric millennia before the ancient Greeks offer their written thoughts on war and politics in language we think we can understand and to which we can relate.

In IR theory, an issue of great contention has been the idea of interstate anarchy. Adam Watson argued (1992) that the earliest identifiable state system—that of Sumerian city-states in fourth-millennium BC Mesopotamia—may have been a competitive small-state anarchy but one that originated within the framework of a common culture, and that these states—or statelets—were part of a shifting society in which from time to time one or the other would emerge with hegemonic authority. Others would opt for an even longer time frame; Buzan and Little, while admitting that Sumer sees "the first fully-fledged international system," draw attention to a variety of yet earlier "pre-international systems" (Buzan and Little, 2000).

The Sumerian "anarchy"—which in IR scholarship anticipates the competitive city-state systems of the ancient Greeks or the fifth-to-third-century BC "warring states" system in ancient China—gave way in the Mesopotamian area to Babylonian hegemony from the time of Hammurabi's successful wars, public works, centralized bureaucracy, tax-gathering system, and law code in the mid-eighteenth century BC. The Babylonian "empire" (or hegemony) sought to abolish internecine warfare where its authority ran and presumably offered merchants and others certain advantages of security and opportunity. There were also relations of a sort with other nascent empires—the Egyptians and the Hittites. Realist and Neorealist IR theory suggests that there should be evidence of balancing against an over-powerful state, but in both the Babylonian and early Assyrian cases (as with other ancient empires), what we see is often a kind of "bandwagoning" where lesser polities become tributary client states rather than grouping together in opposition. This pattern may be a problem for much state and state-system theory in IR unless empires are taken out of the equation as somehow anomalous.

According to one IR text on "balancing" in biblical times, the first significantly imperial power (should it be called a state?) emerged with the Assyrian kings who managed to succeed to the hegemony of their Babylonian precursors by the ninth century BC, and then to consolidate shifting hegemony into a more tangible empire a century or so later. An expansionist king of this latter period, Ashurnasirpal II, used the hubristic titles "king of the world," "subjugator of the unsubmissive," and ruler of "the total sum of all humanity" (Kaufman and Wohlforth, 2007, 27). Though the Assyrian empire may have become an example of "clear unipolarity," some historians, rather than seeing in it simple tyrannical authority enabled by naked and brutal military power, would argue that behind the overblown rhetoric was, as with the Babylonians, a kind of *pax Assyrica* that brought tangible benefits to communities under its sway and operated through a clientage system that involved some local autonomy. Like other ancient empires, however, Assyria was dependent on tribute to sustain its armies and court, and its collapse—and the fall of Nineveh in the late seventh century BC—can be attributed to "imperial overstretch" as these over-taxed tributary sources fell away or dried up.

Ancient texts are of course thin on the exact nature of these regimes—we are dependent on biblical tales, epics, monument inscriptions, the cuneiform clay tablets of merchants, tax gatherers, and occasionally law-givers, and later classical-era Greek and Roman historians. The historical record becomes more tangible with the Persian Empire—in large part because the ancient Greeks wrote about them. The Greek record naturally enough emphasizes the tyrannical or despotic nature of a Persian system with which Greeks were alternatively in vassalage or at war. Watson, however, sees the Persian system as one where authority was loosely expressed through what he calls "hegemonial diplomacy" and only occasionally dependent on force. In IR terms, this introduces the concept of a kind of sovereignty (of the Persian overlord, or king of kings) that may have been largely nominal or rhetorical, and a system that operated through give and take between the imperial and the local and that enfolded or exerted a heavy influence upon a variety of ancient cultures.

Though this chapter and those that follow will address aspects of the history of distinct eras that most engage the main schools of IR theory and the central concepts of sovereignty, state, and state-system, these are not our sole concern. International historians, including especially historians of war and diplomacy, rightly consider themselves to be practitioners of IR within their own narrative and analytical traditions and not merely generators of data for the use of sociological, economic, or political science. The chronology of the ancient world is significantly constructed around narrative moments of warfare and conquest—from Marathon and Thermopylae to Gaugamela, from Canae to Pydna and Actium. There is a long and continuing literature on military strategy and tactics, the social and organizational character of ancient armies and navies, and technological innovations that seem to constitute a succession of "military revolutions." Of interest is where these (sometimes admittedly antiquarian) interests may further a more general social-scientific understanding.

We shall be especially concerned to address an important tradition—the "history of diplomacy" as the history of international relations in the most literal sense. There are two somewhat related aspects of many such scholarly explorations that may be problematic. The first, less common in recent historiography, is the tendency to compartmentalize diplomatic institutions and procedures away from their larger social and political contexts and to assume that diplomacy is definitionally comparable in its purposes and routines from regime to regime or era to era. Of course, approaches that do factor in particular contexts, of, say, regime type, social structure, or the normative values of elites, may often reflect the historian's own acculturated assumptions about the type of diplomacy to be expected from a type of regime—the coercive demands of a militarized Persia or the arbitrative debate of a "democratic" Greek polis. This kind of *a priori* stereotyping is especially a danger in the construction of social scientific theory.

The second problem may be suggested by approaches, quite common in the field, which construe the task of the historian to be that of identifying those elements of past practice that most anticipate the familiar modern diplomacy of resident, credentialed ambassadors, protected by diplomatic immunity and answerable to sovereign political and bureaucratic institutions of the nation-state. This search for origins encourages a history that is both linear and highly selective, and that can advance a sense that diplomacy from the ancient world to the modern is a matter of evolution from the confused and primitive to the instrumentally rational and sophisticated. A good history of diplomatic practice in fact needs to be sensitive to both how diplomacy relates to/draws from specific social and political milieus, and how it may anticipate/lead to modern usage. An allied issue might be how the processes and institutions of one society or state may influence others—the ways in which, for instance, highly developed Venetian diplomatic practice inspired emulation among other late medieval and renaissance European states.

The definition of "diplomacy" is more ambiguous than many assume. This may be a special concern when dealing with the ancient world. Our modern understanding of diplomacy as negotiation is a bad fit for forms of ancient state-to-state contact, where bellicose rhetoric and subordinating ritual may convey meanings and purposes beyond the settlement of disputes and the cementing of alliances. Diplomatic relationships, ancient or modern, are often not among equals (Bismarck once observed that in every alliance there was a rider and a horse), and practices in the ancient world may not be what they seem—or, rather, what we, in the twenty-first century, might take them to be. The Greek envoy familiar to us from Thucydides' *History*, who has come to present a case before a public assembly, is often in fact simply a herald of decisions already taken—even assuming that the ritual of public argument is not itself a Thucydidean dramatic fiction.

In the ancient world, as in the modern, diplomacy had many purposes: the arranging of dynastic marriages, the exchange of "gifts" among nominally equal sovereigns, and explicitly defensive or offensive alliances. More often communication between (unequal) regimes was in the form of demands, ritualistically and formally asserted—for retributive justice, tribute, and obeisance—preliminary to the use of force or subsequent to a military victory. Negotiation and arbitration of grievances were not unknown in the ancient world, but were not common in a system where hegemons (or would-be hegemons) expected clientage and tribute and where the first resort was likely to be force or the ritualized display of force. Clientage and tribute, however much this was a diplomacy among unequals, nevertheless could call for relations that might involve envoys bearing credentials, complicated forms of protocol, and written treaties.

A diplomacy that required trained scribes, archives, familiarity with the requirements of protocol and court ritual, and, above all, access to a common written language for communication emerged in the Near East from the third millennium BC, closely associated with the development of urban culture and writing itself. The Semitic Akkadian language became what one scholar calls "the international diplomatic language, adopted by kings as powerful and different as the Egyptian, the Babylonian, the Hurrian, the Hittite or the Elamite" (Lafont, 2001, 43). The cuneiform clay tablets that are a distinguishing and prolific feature of the ancient Mesopotamian world provided a resource not only for the conduct of diplomacy but for law-giving and tax collection, as well as for the quotidian affairs of ancient commerce, of trade and inventory. Significantly—and not for the last time in the history of diplomacy—concepts and practices, it has been argued, "flowed along the trade routes together with merchants, envoys and goods" (R. Cohen, 2001, 35).

The Sumerian city-states of third-millennium Mesopotamia provide not only the earliest examples of diplomatic negotiation but the formulas found in oaths of alliance, as in "friend with friends and enemy with enemies," which appear long after and among other Near Eastern societies. By the second millennium, according to some recent scholarship a kind of golden age of ancient diplomacy marked by great kings of roughly equal status, this system had become ritualized and improved—to be transmitted down to the Persian empire and east to India.

Though the ancient Greeks had their own indigenous customs—most notably that of the public herald delivering oral argument or the common Hellenic prohibition of the exchange of gifts—it can be argued that the sacralization of treaties through religious oaths and recurring forms of covenanting language common in the ancient Near East indicates the spread of a "Great Tradition" of diplomacy—out of Akkadian Mesopotamia, via Persia, to the wider world. Others would endorse the diffusion of Near Eastern forms and practice, but see a significant break in the tradition with Alexander's conquests, the Hellenization of the Near East, and the consequent disappearance of "cuneiform culture," while the Romans of the late Republic and Empire significantly subordinated diplomacy to the arbitrary rule of force.

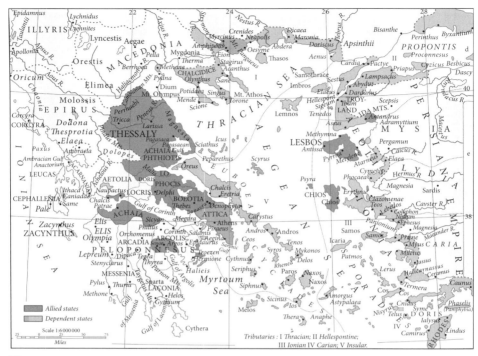

Figure 4.1 Thucydides' Greece.

Source: *Encyclopedia Britannica*, 1911.

Father of the discipline? The Greeks, the *polis*, and Thucydides

The vast Persian "world empire" constituted, it has been argued, a kind of multicultural, international society that not only enveloped myriad vassal or client states but exerted influence beyond its tribute-paying periphery. The question emerges as to the degree and the kind of influence this political culture exercised on other systems, and especially on the ancient Hellenic world of competitive city-states—sometime vassals, sometime resisters to the Persian imperium. The Greek *poleis* themselves (Figure 4.1), in contrast to their would-be Persian overlords, constituted a much less culturally diverse interstate system of their own—a "society," however anarchic, that was linked by language, pan-Hellenic institutions, and culturally defined rules of diplomacy, war, and peace that both emulate and contrast with those of the wider Near East.

The Greeks of the classical age have been, in the Western tradition generally and in a dominant version of the IR historical narrative, represented not only as the originators of modern political thought, but as precursors of modern interstate political practice in an anarchic, competitive state system. Though few scholars would argue today that slave-holding, patriarchal fifth-century Athens was exactly an avatar of modern democracy or that the *pax Romana* that followed was in any real sense a model for nineteenth-century British liberal imperialism, the writing of the ancient Greeks and the surviving Roman canon are variously made to rationalize later European practice. In the eighteenth and nineteenth centuries, an education in the Classics was accorded high status among just those Western elites who determined foreign policy and staffed diplomatic missions.

The Hellenic city-state system

On the northwestern periphery of the expanding, competing, and alternating Near Eastern imperial systems, ancient Greek culture evolved by the eighth and seventh centuries BC into something of its familiar pan-Hellenic character throughout the Aegean region—from the Peloponnese and Attica through Thrace, the Ionian islands and the Anatolian shore and hinterland. A region of independent city-states, sometimes allied, sometimes at war, emerged with a distinctive military organization on land (the citizen hoplite) and at sea (the highly maneuverable oar-driven trireme) and, especially, a political culture that makes ancient Greece interesting for the discipline of IR.

What we know of Greek diplomacy draws mostly from relations *within* the Greek city-state system, that is among those poleis that differed in historical character and territorial ambition perhaps, but shared a common language, culture, and the presumption (if not always the reality) of independence. These traditions of inter-polis relations, then, may have extended to dealings with far-flung independent Greek colonies such as those in Sicily, but were not necessarily extendable to the barbarian outsider; nor were they exactly appropriate for the business of dealing with the asymmetrical relations imposed by a hegemonic empire such as Persia. Moreover, it must remain an open question how much of the Greek way was borrowed in some form from their Near Eastern neighbors and how much was indigenous. Where Greeks employed special envoys, these were expected to be unmolested and free to travel, like the credentialed ambassadors of Near Eastern states. They were, however, almost never empowered to negotiate. Nor did they bear written instructions, but conveyed oral messages—arguments—that rationalized and announced the beginning of conflict or presented compelling reasons for an alliance that was often not between equals.

Frequent intra-Greek warfare, the competitive city-state system, the era of defensive existential conflict with Persia, and the somewhat kaleidoscopic nature of fifth-century BC Greek alliances (leagues), whether among rough equals or, as increasingly with Athens, between a growing hegemon and lesser poleis, meant that diplomacy was a commonplace feature of Greek life. It included the concepts of state neutrality and third-party arbitration, and, unique perhaps to the Greek world, the use of what we would call consular officials (*proxenoi*), resident citizens of a polis who might formally represent the interests of other cities. The making of foreign policy, if we may call it that, devolved upon the deliberative assembly of citizens of freemen—in some more aristocratic poleis a narrower part of the male population than in other more democratic cities. Hence, as Andrew Wolpert has argued (2001), it is important to realize that the internal politics (social values, family traditions, demagogic ambitions) of the polis might constrain policy as much as the power-balancing, security dictates of the anarchic state system.

Though the misfortune of internal conflict (*stasis* or discord) within the polis is a pronounced theme, interstate conflict received, outside of Thucydides, almost no attention in Greek literature. Ancient Greek philosophy has little to say about state system and interstate relations, and can offer little *direct* contribution to the construction of IR theory. Although Clinias the Cretan in Plato's *Laws* is made to say that all cities were engaged in lifelong war against all, that aggression real or anticipated was "natural" between city-states, one can take Plato's Clinias (and Cretans were held to be notorious liars) to be representative of a primitive archaic period in dialogue with a more rational Athenian of the golden age. While Aristotle's *Politics* (ca. 350 BC) is indeed concerned with the city-state as civic community, where authority might lie in this polity, and the obligations of the freeman class of citizens, there is no engagement with any larger idea of what might constitute a sovereign territorial state or with the polis's relations with other states. While some IR scholars, especially those of a Constructivist-cultural bent, might argue that indirectly much can be gleaned about Hellenic international custom and politics from Greek philosophy, moral teaching, and drama, IR scholars have generally limited themselves to a literal reading of the one ancient Greek source that most directly addresses themes of interstate relations, of the hubris and reality of the politics of war and peace in the modern-seeming anarchic city-state system of fifth-century BC Greece—Thucydides' monumental *History of the Peloponnesian War*.

Before we consider this famous text and its use and abuse by IR scholars, it is well to remember that there are substantial reasons why one should be suspicious of any too-close parallel between the world of the Greek polis and the modern state, or between the apparent anarchy of inter-polis rivalry of the fifth century BC and the secular, competitively anarchic state-system of post-Westphalia Europe. In the first place, the size of the political unit alone probably makes a difference: in the Greek city-state, the "knowable community" of citizens was a face-to-face world, unlike either the large dynastic territorial polities that come to dominate the European system after the Renaissance or Benedict Anderson's "imagined community" of the modern nation-state. Nor can fifth-century Greeks be assumed to be proto-modern in their mentalities; the past really is a different country, and subjectivities and identities in this small-state, custom-bound, and clannish world were certainly different from ours. As with many rural and small-town folk, theirs was a shame-and-honor culture, and they were motivated by passions largely (if not wholly) alien to our cosmopolitan age. They certainly lacked the modern notion of the autonomous, self-sovereign individual.

Thucydides' History of the Peloponnesian War

The ancient Greek city-states, though culturally distinct from the Near East in language, writing, and political life, were—especially in the Ionian north and in Anatolia—

inevitably drawn into a somewhat fluid relationship as, often, tribute-paying clients of the vast Persian empire founded by the Achaemenid dynast Cyrus the Great in the mid-sixth century and subsequently extended by Darius the Great from the Black Sea and central Asia to Egypt and northern Libya. By the end of the sixth century, concern by Darius and after him his son Xerxes I to bring the somewhat anarchic western Aegean more firmly under Persian control, combined with a growing collective sense of independent identity among the Greeks—inspired in part no doubt by the Persian insistence on overlordship—led to revolts against Persian claims, first among the Ionians. By the early fifth century, a spreading Hellenic resistance took the form of defensive alliances of poleis organized by, especially, the Athenians and the Spartans—though some Greek city-states remained neutral or loyal to the Persian overlord. The Persian Wars (500–448) saw Athens, with its sea-borne prowess, mold an alliance system (the Delian League) into something resembling an empire that threatened the independence of lesser poleis (in 454 Pericles moved the League's treasury from Delos to Athens, highly symbolic of Athenian hegemony). This especially concerned Athens' chief competitor, custom-bound, conservative Sparta. As the Persian threat retreated, a period of haphazard warfare followed between the Athenian and Spartan alliances. A peace was arranged in 447, which held until 431 when Sparta and Athens were drawn again into a long-lasting struggle (the Peloponnesian War of Thucydides' *History*) that persisted, except for the brief Peace of Nicias from 421 to 415, until the defeat of Athens in 404.

The Western historical tradition of this era of the Persian War and of the struggle of the Greek poleis for dominance in the Aegean has of course absorbed the perspective of the Greeks who wrote about it—Herodotus, Thucydides, and Xenophon among others—and has been transmitted through the ages as a defining moment in the birth of Western civilization and Western values, providing various lessons of heroic resistance to tyranny and the hubris of empire. From the Persian perspective, one can imagine that the Greek revolt was somewhat marginal to larger imperial interests in the Near East, central Asia, and Egypt. Certainly, the peculiar Greek political system—alternatively chaotic and organized, anarchic and hegemonic, democratic and aristocratic—hardly provided a model for contemporary emulation or concern beyond the quarrelsome Greeks themselves. The classic era of the polis ended by the third century BC with Macedonian conquest, Alexander's universal ambition, and, ultimately, Roman military and bureaucratic administration.

Thucydides (ca. 460–395 BC), an Athenian citizen and general, chronicled as a contemporary the war between Athens and Sparta and their allies that recommenced in 431; his narrative, presumably reworked and rearranged over the long years of conflict, stops short (in 411) of the final defeat of Athens in 404. It is both a history of his generation, of his times, and a rational analysis (in the sense that he had no use for oracles and divine intervention) based on eyewitness testimony, he assures us, and overtly grounded in a sage reading of human nature. It combines extensive and widely varied narrative detail with a search for causes on many levels, and thus rises above a mere chronicle to an often modern-seeming level of historiography. It is also a literary epic, a dramatic narrative of tragic proportions, that like a work of literature suppresses, compresses, arranges, and perhaps invents "facts" that are nevertheless true to the reality as he sees it and the cautionary themes he seeks to establish. He means to produce a work, he tells us, that will be a "possession for all time."

Thucydides' story is of an Athens that overstretched itself, tightening its control of its lesser allies and attempting to extend its power through overseas domination of Greek settlement colonies like those of Sicily—independent city-states rather than imperial possessions. It is a narrative with an underlying moral lesson: ultimately, through its hubris and cupidity, Athens catastrophically failed not only to sustain an imperial hegemony, but even to preserve its own independence. In the common IR reading, however, the Thucydidean text is a prescient exploration of timeless phenomena, and illustrative, as Kenneth Waltz (1979, 66) says, of "the striking sameness of the quality of international life throughout the millennia." It is commonly found on the reading lists of twenty-first-century war colleges.

The text[1]

Typically, in English translation Thucydides' *History* runs to some 600 pages of closely printed text. It is an elaborate chronicle and "inquiry" that aims not only to narrate the unfolding events but to use a close narration to search out the true causes of the war (and perhaps of war itself). It is full of digression and enriched by the vivid recreation of the speech of leaders, spokesmen for political faction, and, especially, city-state envoys. Like Greek diplomacy, it is based on oral testimony rather than written documents. It is characterized by a narrative voice that, while informed by the author's own closeness to the unfolding events, is impersonal in tone—giving a crafted sense of immediacy while seeking to be analytically objective and above the fray.

Generationally, Thucydides is located between the other two Greek golden age founders of the art of historical narration, the earlier "father of history," Herodotus (ca. 484–425 BC), who created a large, sometimes fanciful narrative of the era and peoples of the Persian wars based on a wealth of testimony and hearsay, and the later soldier–historian–philosopher Xenophon of Athens (ca. 430–354 BC) whose *Hellenica* was a continuation of Thucydides' work. What distinguishes Thucydides, and establishes him as the first historian in a modern sense is his concern to ground his work, as he says, on only the most verifiable evidence and to sort out essential (underlying, primary) causes from immediate pretexts and secondary factors.

Thucydides did not simply narrate the Peloponnesian war, he made it into a single and analyzable *subject*. These twenty-seven years constitute of course only a fragment of centuries of rivalry and conflict among the Greek poleis, starting long before 431 and unresolved long after 411 (or 404). The *History* thus pursues a strategy that narrows the chronology and the field of action in order better to focus its analysis— and its blame. Much of what the discipline of IR has seized upon in the work in fact comes from the author's determination to center the problem of Athens.

In the First Book, Thucydides introduces the subject with some brief background about the Persian war and the drawing of many of the Greek poleis into two factions around Sparta and Athens ("the one supreme on land, the other on the sea"), and his "Athenocentric" analysis is established early on in his important observation that "What made war inevitable was the growth of Athenian power and the fear which this caused in Sparta" (I, 23). Athens, as its power grew, was able to turn a collaborative defensive league into an Athenian hegemony or empire, to take over the fleets of its "allies" and make them pay monetary contributions to a treasury now under absolute Athenian control, and to extract a brutal retribution from those states that threatened disloyalty. But with its strength came its nemesis—in the form of an anxious coalition of weaker poleis that looked to Sparta to humble an overambitious Athens. The war is set in motion by the Athenians taking the side of the Corcyreans in their dispute with the Corinthians, who then appeal for justice to Sparta. The Spartans vote that Athens has violated the sense of its treaty by attempting to extend its power throughout Hellas (I, 88).

The second lesson commonly drawn from Thucydides' text centers on those passages where the Athenians themselves appear to rationalize their power and the brutal discipline they impose and to preserve it with a kind of Realpolitik, might-makes-right amorality: as the Athenian envoys to Sparta explained, "We have done nothing … contrary to human nature in accepting an empire … It has always been a rule that the weak should be subject to the strong" (I, 76). This line of reasoning is endorsed in Book III by the demagogic foe of Pericles, Cleon, who (approvingly) calls a spade a spade: "What you [the citizens of Athens] do not realize is that your empire is a tyranny exercised over subjects who do not like it … your leadership depends on superior strength and not on any goodwill of others" (III, 37). Finally, the most-quoted passage that appears to reference and endorse human nature itself in justifying the exercise of political power comes from the Melian Dialogue of Book V. The Athenian envoys lecture a polis that is threatening neutrality (and which will in due course be brutally punished with death and enslavement even after unconditionally surrendering): the Melians, who had appealed for fair play and just dealing, are told that "practical people" will recognize that "the strong do what they have the power to do and the weak accept what they have to accept … it is a general and necessary law of nature to rule whatever one can" (V, 89–90, 105). It remains of course an issue whether such passages should be read as Thucydides' own realist observation (the assumption of much IR interpretation). They are of course put in the mouths of envoys and could just as plausibly be taken for the kind of mis-reasoning and amorality that led to and made inevitable the catastrophe that will overtake Athens.

There is, certainly, much else in Thucydides' text that appears to be mainly about violations of civic morality (i.e., about the domestic locus of misperception and ill-judgment in foreign relations)—the self-interest of demagogues, the cupidity of a foolish public that listens to them, and the inevitable consequences of hubris and loss of virtue. The central issue in Books VI and VII is the tragic result of the ill-advised Athenian expedition to conquer Syracuse in Sicily, and the horror and pathos of (unnecessary) war itself—the sacking of temples, the waste of treasure, the slaughter of children, and the rage of vengeance.

Thucydides and the discipline of IR: Issues and critique

> We should stop trying to bend [Thucydides] to our will by making him speak to debates about which he would understand little and care even less. We should stop treating him as a mirror for our own assumptions, convictions, and biases. We should stop competing for his imprimatur. And, perhaps most importantly of all, we should stop trying to reduce his subtle and sophisticated work to a series of simplistic banalities. (Welch, 2003, 302)

Thucydides' *History* has long provided IR scholars (especially Realists) with corroborative evidence for some basic concepts in the discipline: the role of human nature in international affairs and the exercise of power, the so-called "security dilemma" (whereby the stronger a state becomes to ensure its security, the more likely other states will be compelled to take defensive measures against it) and the related "balance of power" mechanism, common it is often argued to an anarchic system of sovereign states (and seen in Corinth's traditional role as shifting balancer within the Greek system). A few examples of its *practice*, however, hardly establish that balance of power was understood by the ancient Greeks as a *doctrine*.

Thucydides' own presentation and voice are beguilingly rational and unadorned, probingly analytical, and his method seemingly empirical and modern. He is accessible (in modern translation) to nonspecialist scholars, a high-status source ready for appropriation without the burden of having to get inside the mind and culture that produced him. This is, of course, just where historians—particularly those with some close knowledge of the culture, history, and languages of the ancient world—begin to have doubts. The easy appropriation of Thucydides (as "the father of realism") and of his text (as uncomplicated description and analysis, easily transferable to our times) begs some very large and significant questions about Thucydides' method and his purposes, as well as even more substantial issues about the comparability of his world of the ancient polis and ours. The first issue that arises, however, is whether IR scholars who are not classicists and perhaps not historians, and who are dependent on modern (usually English) translations, are likely to fall into the error of assuming Thucydides' modernity because the texts they use have been crafted precisely to make an ancient source speak to us in our own vernacular.

Translations that casually employ modern terms or assume parallel modern meanings encourage the kind of ahistorical assumptions that we find in some IR analysis. One example is the tendency to make the polis into the equivalent of the modern nation-state. Rex Warner in the still-popular 1954 Penguin translation commonly uses the terms "nation," "national honor," and "nationality"—probably imported from the late Victorian translation of Richard Crawley. There is of course some parallel in the ancient Greek for the modern concept of patriotism, but hardly of "nationalism," the resonance of which is significantly anachronistic.

It has been forcefully argued by Arthur Eckstein that "important realist conclusions drawn from Thucydides rest on the habitual use of careless translations"—most significantly, the impression that Thucydides offers (in Book I, 23) a deterministic, system-level version of the "power transition" crisis in explaining the inevitability of the Athens-Sparta war: "immediate cause," he claims, is a translator's invention, nor does "inevitable" exist in the Greek (Eckstein, 2003, 757, 760). As Robert Gilpin subsequently observed, such corrections suggest that "Thucydides was not so absolute in his claims as many of us now think" (Gilpin, 2005, 367). He does not, that is, offer the kind of parsimonious theory of the "real" cause of the war that Neorealists imagined that they found in the text, but rather a complex, sometimes contradictory "layered" explanation.

For historians who are trained to scrutinize primary sources for bias and allow for their contexts, there is a further problem—the tendency, because he is our only detailed source, to take Thucydides' work as simple evidence rather than a highly politicized argument. Even accepting the proposition that the Thucydides we think we know is a reliable observer of the international and domestic politics of his times—at least from the perspective of an Athenian citizen of a certain class—we are left with a host of issues. Any work of history of course selects, arranges, and in the narrative telling molds reality. The important set speeches that dialogically establish Thucydides' narrative are hardly real-time transcriptions, but recreations, perhaps based on memory and reportage but artfully shaped and sharpened for effect and purpose. Some scholars have emphasized the artfulness of a work that seems a straightforward narrative and analysis, the fact that Thucydides is likely to have added and subtracted, redrafted and amended, and improved his text over the lifetime he took writing it, and the ways in which it may be read as a *tragedy* paralleling the themes of hubris and nemesis central to Greek drama.

Then there is the question whether those passages that contemporary IR scholars assume Thucydides the Realist endorses in fact reflect his own views of human nature and Realpolitik, or whether, as a closer reading of the text would certainly suggest, they are meant to convey only the not-necessarily prescient views and actions of those whom he blames for the catastrophe of war and defeat, ironically presented. Does this make a difference? It does, if the underlying message, as some scholars now would suggest, is not the inescapability of system constraints or human nature but the terrible consequences of the violation of civilizational norms and communal values. The *History* is, as the classicist scholar M. I. Finley (1972, 32) observed some time ago, "in the last analysis a moralist's work," and there is a need to read it in the context of fifth-century Greek moral discourse involving the vice of excess and the need for a golden mean.

These questions should warn us, as historians, that there is likely to be considerable danger in assuming that Thucydides can speak to us directly, that his text is simply drawn from the empirical facts rather than reflecting a specific kind of fifth-century Greek "rhetorical universe" (Garst, 1989, 7). One cannot simply cite the Melian

Debate, fished out of Book V, as evidence of universal verities without considering its textual purpose—not so much reportage as a "sophistical piece, thinly disguised" (Finley, 1977, 12) to allow Thucydides to display abstract ideas about empire, justice, freedom, and slavery.

Some scholars would now claim that Thucydides' ultimate goal was not *historical* truth per se but an *abstracted* truth concerning men's behavior, and that his methods—such as his opposed dialogues—are ahistorical literary devices. Thucydides was likely to have been influenced by the fifth-century Sophists and their concern with the effects of self-interest and greed. To understand Thucydides we need, some would argue, to understand the moral ideals associated with a "Greek" identity, an ethnos, and the basis on which such constructions rested: a shared oral and written literature (especially Homer), pan-Hellenic institutions (the Olympic games, the Delphic oracle), and customary practices (oaths, rules of proper behavior, rules of warfare). The problem of identity, a prominent Constructivist concern, complicates the Realist insistence that the formal anarchy of the political system or human nature offer a sufficient explanation for war. Though Thucydides may privilege the fear of expanding Athenian power as the "most genuine" cause, a variety of "explanations" for a conflict that was not inevitable can be found in the text, from the way in which powerful states may be dragged into conflict by lesser allies to the consequences of moral failure and the violation of norms, and the essentially contingent and domestic factors—the sudden appearance of plague and the death of Pericles, the tendency of some Athenian politicians to try to please the demos or crowd, the greed, corruption, and foolishness of individuals.

At the beginning of the present century, a collection of essays by IR scholars concerned to defend the discipline's appropriation of Thucydides' text as, especially for Realists, a help in understanding "our contemporary condition," was given the title *Thucydides' Theory of International Relations: A Lasting Possession* (ed. L. S. Gustafson, 2000, 1). Apart from the somewhat dubious assertion that the Greek historian had in any conscious sense a *theory* of international relations, the claim that it was a "lasting possession" unintentionally no doubt raises a concern about ownership and how such a property is employed and for what ends. Certainly historians as well write from within the present. But the central question for us is whether the interpretations of those IR scholars of politics and political thought who have used Thucydides' text have been fully informed by the rich social and cultural history of his time and place. *The History of the Peloponnesian War* is a magnificent and enduring monument to its author's historical sensibility and to the search for truth in the Athenian philosophical and literary golden age. Whether modern IR theorists and practitioners are justified in turning it into a foundational text for their own discipline may turn on their understanding of the (deep) differences as well as (perhaps superficial) similarities of that age and ours. Some of the few IR scholars trained in classical history and languages—like Arthur M. Eckstein—would still endorse some, rather qualified, version of the view that Thucydides is in fact the father of the discipline and a Realist. Others have been highly skeptical.

After the fifth-century Greeks: Late antiquity and empire

While Thucydides' Greece has long been of great interest to IR scholars, the Hellenistic period and Alexander's empire, the expansionist politics of the Romans, or the diplomacy of their Eastern successors at Byzantium have not drawn anything like the same interest within the discipline and in the construction of IR theory. As we have seen, the centrality of Thucydides to IR discourse is largely due to the way in which dominant schools of thought in the discipline, Realism and Neorealism, have sought corroboration in this classic text for their theories about human nature or the structural constraints of a competitive state system.

Ancient empires, however, have generated some interest among other schools of thought—especially the English School, where questions were raised about formal and informal hegemony, common through history, and how it emerges and persists, why, that is, "balancing" is so often unsuccessful. It may also be that European—especially British—scholars may relate to issues of imperial politics and identity more readily than American IR scholars who find empire to be alien to their understanding of the modern world and are loathe to draw parallels between historical empires and the kind of hegemony represented by the United States in the twentieth and twenty-first centuries. Nevertheless, IR interest has grown considerably since Michael Doyle's *Empires* (1986) initiated a debate about different kinds of hegemony. There has been considerable reconsideration about what the study of the empires of late Antiquity around the Mediterranean and in the Near East, but also of Asia, may bring to the discipline. This is no doubt pleasing to international and world historians and to those who feel that the overwhelming post-Westphalia, European focus of much IR scholarship stands in great need of a wider field of view and a deeper chronology.

The classic period of the system of autonomous Greek city-states gave way by the fourth and third centuries to Macedonian domination based on military prowess and, ultimately, some emulation of the Persians: when Alexander (356–322 BC) defeated Darius III in 332, he proclaimed himself King of Kings and adopted Persian dress, inaugurating a period that saw a degree of cultural hybridization in the East, a Persianization of expansionist Greeks and a Hellenization of the Persian empire. Alexander's universal empire however was hardly a unitary state—but rather exhibited a very great deal of variation in governing practices and local custom. And after his death it quickly fragmented into a number of military-dynastic regimes that engaged in diplomatic relations and intermittent warfare. While these multiple, successor states coexisted in what some IR scholars might regard as another type of anarchic competitive system, and arguably shared certain elements of Hellenic culture, they proved to be both internally unstable and vulnerable to the expanding Roman Republic and Empire.

The rise of Rome beyond Italy began with the two defensive, existential wars with Carthage in the West in the third century BC. The decisive defeat of Carthage allowed the Republic opportunistically to extend its control and influence in the eastern Mediterranean, beginning with the Greeks—often reluctantly as a means of keeping other powers at bay, or at least assuring that there would be buffer states, clients of Rome, between them. In considering how the history of the expansive Roman Republic and Empire might bear on important debates and concepts in the discipline of IR, a number of interpretive questions arise. The first is whether one can speak of interstate relations in the Roman period as comparable in any sense to that of the classic Greek city-state system, that is, whether relations rested on some idea of the at least formal equality of states and on underlying assumptions about diplomatic conventions, the sanctity of treaties, and the construction of alliances. Only in the early Republic, from the fifth to the third century, when Rome sought to achieve primacy in Italy through diplomacy (it concluded some 150 treaties by 246 BC), as well as through war and intimidation, can one speak of the familiar relationships of a competitive state system. Thereafter, Rome of the late Republic and early Empire by and large used its disciplined military superiority in the first instance and its diplomacy to settle things afterward. As the Greek-born historian of the Republic, Polybius (ca. 200–118 BC), observed, "The Romans rely on force in all their undertakings" (quoted by Campbell, 2001, 1). Significantly, perhaps, there are no surviving Roman treatises on diplomatic method though many about generalship and military organization.

The second question to arise over the Roman Empire—and indeed for most hegemonic *qua* imperial systems down to that of the Soviet Union—is whether we should, for the purposes of IR narration and analysis, regard the Roman world as a sovereign unity interacting diplomatically with other empires and peoples, or as *itself* a kind of international system. Much depends no doubt on which particular period during the long era of Roman dominium one has in view. Does one regard "Rome" as a civilizational whole or as a plethora of parts more or less knit together by military force, continual local negotiation, and state-sponsored or autonomous migration? In the historiography of Rome, it is of course an old debate about how Roman the Empire might have been, even in the high tide of its *pax*, its aqueducts, its military roads, its trade, or its exported social system.

Diplomacy and Rome's Mediterranean system

Though there may have been evidence of the interstate practice of balancing in the early period (as in Hiero II of Syracuse's siding with Carthage against Rome during the First Punic War), this appears to disappear as Rome's preeminent authority spreads and the diplomatic traditions of the Greek city-state system are put to other uses. Unlike among the Greeks, the "Roman peace" came to denote, as "a pivotal concept in Roman foreign policy," not merely the cessation of war (and Rome was in a more or less perpetual state of war somewhere), but order and Roman domination. The treaties of the late Roman Republic commonly required that the other party provide conscripts of soldiers to serve in the Roman army. Rome also came to offer a form of common citizenship to those beyond Italy that was not based on the Greek understanding of a shared ethnicity.

An instructive example of Roman difference can be found in the Republic's practice of receiving surrender "to the faith, to the power, and to the jurisdiction" of the Romans—a ritual that had become common practice in the Mediterranean world by the second century BC. Though this has provided ground for some debate between a Constructivist approach that emphasize the "normative and moral" aspects of a customary ritual sanctioned by religious oath and a Realist one that sees *deditio* as simply a convenient practice imposed at the discretion of the Roman commander, there can be little doubt that it represents a diplomacy of diktat rather than negotiation.

By the time of the Emperor Augustus the anarchic independent states system of the Mediterranean basin had been largely abolished, though on the wider stage Rome interacted with other empires to the East via a diplomacy familiar to the ancient world that involved emissaries (messengers and negotiators, though not resident ambassadors) normally protected by a code of safe conduct, the exchange of gifts, and due regard for protocol. Though the forms of diplomacy might draw on Hellenic precedent—as in the use of the formula "friends of friends and enemies of enemies"—the object was not alliance in the Greek tradition. Foreign policy was at the whim of the emperor rather than being, as under the Republic, formally vested in the people via the senate; its character was less defensive and reactive and more imperious. As one scholar has said, "even the pretence of reciprocity had gone" (Campbell, 2001, 13). "Negotiation" was generally conducted in Latin.

Though varieties of Realists, interested in the role of offensive power in interstate affairs, and some Constructivists, interested in identity and concepts of moral order, have of late been taking more interest in the Roman period, liberal idealist and international law traditions have long drawn on aspects of Roman history, on the Roman Republic's continuation of Greek concepts of public participation and obligation and, especially, on the Roman idea of international law—itself influenced by the Greek (Stoic) idea of a natural moral order. The Roman concept of a "natural law" for dealing with foreign peoples has cast a long shadow into the medieval and early modern era, through Aquinas to seventeenth-century scholars like Grotius. Tutored in the Greek philosophers, and especially the Stoics, Cicero (106–43 BC) equated natural law (*ius naturale*) with the law of nations (*ius gentium*). He argued that war could only be just if it was defensive—if Rome were threatened with invasion, if its ambassadors were violated, if treaties were broken, or if an ally gave support to an enemy. Moreover, the Roman Republican concept of the just war as a defensive war, assuming that this had force in public opinion, has been taken by some IR scholars to argue against the Realist view that the Roman system simply affirmed the role of force in international affairs—to which Arthur Eckstein, a self-proclaimed Offensive Realist, has responded that "one may doubt that the populace … , or the soldiers of Caesar in Gaul, read much philosophy" (Eckstein, 2010, 321).

Antiquity and IR schools of thought

IR as social science and political practice, deeply engaged with current global affairs and committed often to present and future policy analysis, is not, understandably, necessarily much interested in history for its own sake. Some IR scholars, of course, are, and some of these are trained historians. To the extent, however, that IR scholars from fields other than history are much interested in historical narrative—often in fishing expeditions to discover practices, systems, and events useful in corroborating contemporary theory, they are not often much concerned with historical methods of research, much less with the idea of the "total history" of a time and place and of the danger of plucking an isolatable historical fact out of a dense, interconnected, multilayered web. This, of course, is not a problem unique to other disciplines that "use" historical material. Civilizational history, comparative history, and world history have often been criticized for loose generalizations about comparability across vast stretches of time and geography.

Realism and the ancient world

Hans Morgenthau, with his prewar European education in Western political thought, was prepared to find in Thucydides aspects of "timeless" truth and a riposte to progressive contemporary liberal idealism. Realism, grounded in human nature, the urge to power, and the search for security, found ample confirmation in passages such as the Melian Dialogue. Classical Realists have, however, been sharply criticized for a historical method that is both highly selective and tends to assume and imply that the "voice" in these passages is that of Thucydides himself. The result, one critic has recently said, is to reduce this rich and complicated work to "a handful of banal axioms" (Klusmeyer, 2011, 4). Nevertheless, many moderate Realists like Robert Gilpin have continued to find the *History* intriguing and instructive: "everything … can be found in *The History* of Thucydides"; "I have been greatly influenced by Thucydides," "Thucydides viewed mankind as driven by … honour, security and wealth … they will produce similar results throughout history" (Gilpin, 2005, 366–7). Even a sharp critic of structural Realist readings of Thucydides, Richard Ned Lebow, can claim with the Classical Realists that "while human practices vary enormously across time and cultures, human nature does not" (Lebow, 2005, 553–4).

Great historians of the Western tradition have of course been as prone as latter-day IR scholars to invoke human nature in the narration and analysis of distant times. Edward Gibbon, in the first volume (in 1776) of his magisterial *Decline and Fall of the Roman Empire*, tells us that "the knowledge of human nature, and of the sure operation of its fierce and unrestrained passions, might, on some occasions, supply the want of historical materials" (Gibbon, 1909, I, 256). For the modern historian, however, the issue of human nature as a determinant in history is an open one. On the one hand, there is the lively current debate over socio-biology and the ways in which humans may be "hard-wired"; on the other, many historians will feel that as a causal factor the concept is always open to misuse and can be an excuse for not probing more deeply into those social, economic, and cultural contexts that frame and perhaps shape our natures.

While Waltzian structuralists emphasized the constraints of an anarchic competitive state system rather than eternal human drives in theorizing interstate relations, they readily found parallels to the working of the modern Westphalian system in the Athenian security dilemma and Greek balancing. This reasoning by analogy has been challenged by those historians and Constructivists who insist that any reading of Thucydides requires a focus on values and cultural aspects peculiar to his time and place, on difference rather than similarity. Nevertheless, a somewhat ahistorical reading of fifth-century Greece persists in the discipline.

The search for confirmation of a Realist reading of the European state system in fact led beyond fifth-century Greece to parallel universes, as it were, of roughly the same time in ancient China of the "warring states" period (ca. fifth-to-third century BC) and in South Asia of the post-Vedic period (ca. sixth-to-third century BC). In addition to an apparent example of an anarchic state system, the Indian case provided Realists with a Mauryan court text, Kautilya's *Arthashastra* (translated as "the Book of the State" or "The Science of Politics"), that advises how a wise ruler should manage his foreign relations: rulers should seek to augment their power and consider any neighbor with power a potential enemy; moreover, it recognizes a process of balancing, whereby a third party may be considered a *madhyama*, or mediatory force. Such readings determined to find parallels with European thought and practice have, however, been challenged by some South Asian scholars who observe, for instance, that the Hindu ideal of harmony was not that of a balance of opposing parts but of an ordered hierarchy. The Chinese Warring States era has provided a more developed example of Realism's search for confirming parallels.

China had long been largely excluded from IR discourse about the growth and character of modern state systems. The dominant political ideology of the Chinese Empire was that China was the center of a universal system where it presided over submissive, tribute-paying suzerain and barbarian states. It operated, that is, according to rules quite different from those of the West as represented in Realist thought. The Westphalian notion of territorial sovereignty and autonomous states, and of the international recognition of formal equality among states was largely unknown in the East where participants were not formally equal and the authority of the emperor in theory extended beyond any territorial boundary of the kingdom; interests of state were less important than "virtuous rule," and ritual and personalized relations mattered more than international law. To locate China in IR structural theorizing about an anarchic system of sovereign states, one had to look at it *before the imperial system became entrenched.*

In terms familiar to European historians, the warring states period in China's history has been described as marked by the disintegration of "feudalism," constant warfare between emergent territorial states, and conditions of international anarchy marked by the tactics of balance of power—a world finally displaced by successful attempts at universal domination under a new dynasty that escaped from balancing by buying off lesser powers and making them dependent. And so the limited warfare of the multiple states period gave way to total war in the period of imperial hegemony, where competing states were not merely thwarted but turned into client states or exterminated. Qin fought a series of wars from 230 to 221 BC (roughly parallel to the rise of the Roman Republic in the West) in which all opposing states were crushed one by one and annexed. Subsequently, imperial authority was entrenched by a developing bureaucracy and by court "legalists" who came to celebrate the ideal of autocratic rule.

While the period of Warring States itself can be made to conform to Realist theory, its denouement poses some awkward questions. Qin's innovations should have resulted in other states emulating them in order to survive. They did not. The theory of balance of power (as a transhistorical, universal phenomenon) was ultimately unsuccessful in China, and thus did not there become any more normative than within the Roman imperium. According to David Kang, it is a concept that in the Asian case is "profoundly and fundamentally wrong" (Kang, 2007, 199). China should have represented an existential threat to its neighbors, yet rather than balancing against it by forming alliances, they (from Japan to Siam) chose to bandwagon with the Chinese empire militarily, politically, diplomatically, and commercially. Being a client state offered greater rewards than the risk of warfare against it. The Chinese empire, a remarkably stable and long-lasting system, presents a case where the prevailing theory endorsed formal hierarchy while allowing a degree of informal equality among states—the opposite of the formal equality and informal hierarchy of the European system.

Nevertheless, Realist IR scholarship has made much of the similarities to Thucydides' Greece and post-Westphalia Europe it claims to have discovered in these extra-European cases. On the one hand, one can applaud IR's attempt to reach beyond Western experience for historical confirmation of what had been widely regarded as Eurocentric theory; on the other, many historians, specialists in early China and South Asia, remain highly skeptical of a methodology that selected relatively brief eras, focused on elements that appear to be similar to European usage, avoided aspects that had no obvious parallel, and in both China and India largely ignored or avoided analysis of the much longer-lived successor imperial systems and the ways in which *they* might compare with Western or Near Eastern practice.

Finally, one might note that the Offensive Realism espoused by Mearsheimer and others after the end of the Cold War has returned to the "warring states" period of *Greek* history, not for confirmation of Waltzian balancing and the defensive security dilemma but for evidence of the insatiable lust for power and of the role of brute force in history. This has led some Offensive Realists to look beyond the anarchic competitive small-state systems of Greece, India, and China, to the empires that displaced them for evidence of just how eras of balanced interstate anarchy end in violent suppression and military conquest—as with Rome, the Qin and Han dynasties in China, and the Mauryan rulers in India.

The English School

Attacking Realist readings of Thucydides has long been something of a cottage industry, beginning with the critique offered by the English School of Realism's highly selective use of some and not other classical texts, its lack of interest in or suppression of the extent to which the fifth-century "anarchic" Greek world also constituted an

Hellenic society, and, finally, its lack of interest in the larger histories of the empires of the ancient Near East and Mediterranean.

The attempt by Realists and Neorealists to take the competitive world of Thucydides' warring city-states as evidence for their theories of human nature and systemic anarchy was challenged by Wight and Bull, who argued that beneath the apparent anarchy of the alternatively allying and warring Greek poleis there was a "nascent international society" or cohering political culture constructed of language, myth, philosophy, pan-Hellenic institutions, and historical practice. These admittedly warring states pursued among themselves (and occasionally with their Persian overlords) a common system of diplomacy and negotiation marked by the concept of *dike* (justice or reasonable settlement). English School scholars also sought to employ a wider canvas, as in Adam Watson's *The Evolution of International Society* (1992), which began with "the Ancient States System" of the Near East. Subsequently, scholars like Barry Buzan, working in the English School tradition and informed by historical Sociology and the flourishing world history and world systems projects, devote more space and narrative interest to both the ancient (even prehistoric) and medieval periods of Western and non-Western societies. They argue that an exclusive focus on Thucydides and his era serves to attenuate IR theory that ought to embrace the larger field of interstate relationships, and especially that of empires, before, during, and long after the Hellenic fifth century.

Constructivism, postmodernism, and feminism

The English School's concern with extending the discipline's search for relevant meaning to texts other than those passages in Thucydides that directly addressed the politics of war and alliance and especially its interest in the cultural aspects of what might constitute a "society" of states informed the Constructivist challenge of the 1990s and subsequently. Postmodern Constructivist analysis searches between the lines and under the overt political meaning of texts for norm-forming contexts (of identity, religion, language, customary social practices, and rituals) in which the bickering of the separate poleis are situated—drawing attention to how Thucydides himself locates the war and its conduct not in a *system* of amoral anarchy or the *necessity* of security, but in the violation of moral norms.

Some scholars like Richard Ned Lebow would set aside questions such as "Is Thucydides' text as an empirical history 'true'?" as unanswerable, and explore instead its internal construction as rhetoric. Lebow has emphasized ways in which issues of honor and legitimacy, rather than simple calculations of security and power, frame the concept of hegemony and suffuse the warring world described in the *History*. Similarly, Jean Bethke Elshtain, echoing the postmodern perspective of James Der Derian's influential mid-1990s collection of essays on international theory, argued that there is a need to "unravel its complex rhetorical universe" by "reading" the *History* "against the grain" to understand how it employs a "culture of argument" located less in the universal rationalism of Realist analysis than in the conventions of Greek rhetoric and debate (Elshtain, 1995, 346).

Elshtain was also a feminist scholar, interested in the many ways in which gender may be used as a "prism" to cast light on our understanding of texts like that of Thucydides. Questioning the "democratic" character of fifth-century Athens as an idealized construction that ignores the rule "by force" of women (who were excluded from the masculine realm of public debate) and slaves, feminist scholars suggest there is a normative association between the arbitrary role of power in the domestic and the external Hellenic spheres. By the time of the Peloponnesian war, another scholar has argued, the Greek system was "suffused by formal and informal relations of supremacy and subjugation" (Kokaz, 2001, 92). Though feminist scholarship has been credited with attempting, like the Constructivists generally, to bring the historical study of culture and mentality back into arid, parsimonious, pared down IR political theory, some historians have been concerned that analytical categories (gender) and concepts (gendered identities) may not travel well, and, especially in the hands of scholars not trained in the languages and culture of the ancient world, end by telling us more about our own late twentieth- and early twenty-first century than Thucydides' era.

Liberal Internationalism

The idea advanced by some Constructivists that the anarchic ancient Greek world can be better understood as a unity with a moral foundation marks a radically different approach to the sovereign state and state system endorsed in Realist theory. Rather, it resonates with another tradition in IR discourse that traces its roots back to the classical world of fourth-century BC Greek philosophy and late Republican Roman legal argument. The natural law/international law school has commonly located its origins in classical Greek philosophical discourse that culminated in the Stoics of the early third century BC and their influence on Cicero (especially in the *Republic* of 51 BC). Whereas Realists have traditionally seen the Greece of Thucydides as a precursor of the modern state system that was supplanted by universal empires of less interest, the International Law tradition sees continuity and *development* from Greece through the Roman period to the medieval world and beyond. The Roman concepts of *ius naturale* and *ius gentium* and of a just war serve to shift our attention from political structure and practice as the ultimate objects of IR study to the important evolution of powerful ideas, legal traditions, and universal institutions on which a liberal reading of the current and future world system may rest.

***

In the last analysis, the ancient world and classical Greece in particular can be made to offer historical "evidence" for many conflicting, indeed contradictory, schools of IR thought.

But the central problematic remains of a too-easy application of what we think we know about the ancient to the contemporary world. Varieties of Realism may be most implicated in drawing comfortable analogies, but a scholar with a sharp eye for cultural readings and a Constructivist inclination like Lebow can similarly strain to find "lessons" in ancient Greece that might instruct contemporary American foreign policy (for instance, in Lebow, 2005, 581). This may be a temptation endemic to a discipline established and sustained as a policy-oriented field. Neither political scientists nor historians can resist, apparently, drawing across millennia the thinnest lines of comparative analysis, as when Eckstein tells us that we can learn from the Athenian "power-transition crisis" about the origins of the First World War (Eckstein, 2003, 759). Nor can feminist scholarship escape the same charge of straining for analogous readings.

In the West we have been conditioned since the Renaissance to consider the classic texts of the Greeks and Romans as essentially modern, speaking to us in language and with a mentality that we can take on board as very like our own. This is a dangerous assumption, and one that is directly related to the methodology of IR as a political and social science that attempts to pare down the complexity and contingency of history in order to arrive at the essence of a phenomenon, across cultures and times. This is what it means when we say that Thucydides' city-state system is "like" that of China's Warring States or Mauryan India or Westphalian Europe. There may indeed be gains to be had from this method of analysis, but at what cost?

Recommended readings

For the incorporation of the larger ancient world into the discipline of IR, see Adam Watson, *The Evolution of International Society* (1992), chs. 2–4; Barry Buzan and Richard Little, *International Systems in World History: Remaking the Study of International Relations* (2000), Parts II and III; and, for a very long-term, indeed prehistoric, analysis, see essays in Robert A. Denemark et al. (eds.), *World System History: The Social Science of Long-Term Change* (2000). For ancient diplomatic history, see the special issue of *Diplomacy & Statecraft* 12, 1 (2001).

There is a very substantial literature in classical studies on Thucydides: the prominent scholar, M. I. Finley, provided a generation ago a balanced introduction to Thucydides in the Penguin edition of 1972 (1–32). Also see his still-relevant 1959 work, *The Greek Historians* (1977 edn.) and his "Myth, Memory and History," *History and Theory* 4 (1965), 281–302. More recently, there is the large corpus of work by Donald Kagan. Lawrence Tritle's *A New History of the Peloponnesian War* (2010) stays close to Thucydides while adding psychological themes of warfare and a reading of classical Greek plays. For a study that spans scholarly research in classics, history, and IR, see Greg Crane's *Thucydides and the Ancient Simplicity: The Limits of Political Realism* (1998).

Critiques of the ways in which Thucydides has been used in IR abound. See, for example, Daniel Garst, "Thucydides and Neorealism," *International Studies Quarterly* 33, 1 (March 1989), 3–28; and Jonathan Monten, "Thucydides and Modern Realism," *International Studies Quarterly* 50 (2006), 3–26. In 2001, the *Review of International Studies* (27) published a number of articles that provide a turn-of-the century snapshot of contested readings of Thucydides. Also see, among many others, Richard Ned Lebow,

"Thucydides the Constructivist," *American Political Science Review* 95 (2001), 547–60; Arthur M. Eckstein, "Thucydides, the Outbreak of the Peloponnesian War, and the Foundation of International Systems Theory," *International History Review* 25 (2003), 757–74; and Stefan Dolgert, "Thucydides, Amended: Religion, Narrative, and IR Theory in the Peloponnesian Crisis," *Review of International Studies* 38 (2012), 1–22.

For ancient India and Kautilya, see Gerge Modelski, "Kautilya: Foreign Policy and International System in the Ancient Hindu World," *American Political Science Review* 63 (1964), 549–60; and William J. Brenner, "The Forest and the King of Beasts: Hierarchy and Opposition in Ancient India (ca. 600–232 B.C.)," in Stuart J. Kaufman, Richard Little, and William C. Wohlforth (eds.), *The Balance of Power in World History* (2007), 99–120. Among the substantial literature on China in the Warring States period and after, see Victoria Tin-bor Hui, *War and State Formation in Ancient China and Early Modern Europe* (2005), and Yongjin Zhang, "System, Empire and State in Chinese International Relations," *Review of International Studies* 27 (2001), 43–64.

The general problem of how to regard the empires of late antiquity in IR historiography can be approached through the comparative Oxford Studies in Early Empire: W. Scheidel (ed.), *Rome and China: Comparative Perspectives on Ancient World Empires* (2010), and I. Morris (ed.), *The Dynamics of Ancient Empires: State Power from Assyria to Byzantium* (2010). For various topics of interest in the interstate relations of ancient Rome, Republic and Empire, see Claude Eilers (ed.), *Diplomats and Diplomacy in the Roman World* (2009); Christian Baldus, "*Vestigia Pacis.* The Roman Peace Treaty: Structure or Event?" in Randall Lesaffer (ed.), *Peace Treaties and International Law in European History* (2004), 103–46; Arthur M. Eckstein, "Intra-Greek Balancing, the Mediterranean Crisis of c.201–200 B.C., and the Rise of Rome," and Daniel Deudney, "'A Republic for Expansion': The Roman Constitution and Empire and Balance-of-Power Theory," in Stuart J. Kaufman, Richard Little, and William C. Wohlforth (eds.), *The Balance of Power in World History* (2007), 71–98 and 148–75. On the subject of international law in antiquity, see, for instance, David Boucher, *The Limits of Ethics in International Relations* (2009), Ch. 1.

CHAPTER 5
TOWARD THE MACHIAVELLIAN MOMENT: IR's MIDDLE AGES

The Middle Ages have not been fruitful of concepts important in constructing IR theory, except in the negative sense of providing a foil for the Westphalian paradigm break from "medieval" to "modern," from multiple and confused feudal jurisdictions and *domestic* anarchy to the sovereign state's monopoly of violence and *international* anarchy, from theological schemas of the universal and ideal to the rational calculation of Realpolitik. Such unexamined views can reflect a somewhat dated historiography. While some contemporary medieval historians now question our conventional understanding of "feudalism," IR textbooks continue to reify this concept as a definitional reality that sets the medieval era apart from the modern and its sovereign state system. At the same time, many IR scholars continue to employ rather uncritically the long-familiar parallel image of the Renaissance as uniquely characterized by secular ambition, rationality, and the disintegration of the normative values of medieval Christendom. Machiavelli's work, canonical in both the history of political thought and in IR, is commonly regarded, especially by Realists, as illustrative of just this sea change—that is, its interpretation depends often on the binary of medieval and modern.

Chronologies are important but often abused or ignored. In the shorthand language of the textbook, "medieval" is invoked for a vast expanse of time and a variety of significantly distinct places with shifting boundaries and fluid societies (the myth of unprogressive medieval stasis has long since been abandoned by most specialists in the field). While "modern" awkwardly enough can comprise 500 years of early modern to postmodern, the medieval runs to a thousand years. At the very least, in order to deploy "medieval" evidence in IR, one would have to distinguish an early medieval of migrations and Christianization growing out of late antiquity from the medieval of the Carolingian empire and its successor regimes, the coalescing Western high medieval marked by the rediscovery of Roman law, vassalage, and conflicting universal jurisdictions of empire and church, an altered medieval of "bastard feudalism" that sees the growth of a monied society of payments rather than service, a stressed medieval of demographic and political crisis and the rise of dynastic, territorial kingdoms, and a late medieval that overlaps and may share much with what we call the humanist early Renaissance. At what point does Florence cease to be "medieval" and become "modern?"

Nor is the medieval in Italy the medieval of the Western kingdoms, the Eastern marches, the Scandinavian north, Byzantium, or Islam.

This chapter will not attempt an inclusive narrative of the long Middle Ages, nor a synopsis of the current state of the voluminous social, political, and intellectual historiography of the medieval millennium. Appropriate to our purpose, it will however treat a selection of themes and events that have been, or should be, of special interest to IR scholars—both international historians and political scientists—as a way of approaching the substance and location of the most familiar name in political theory, Niccolò Machiavelli.

Universal empire, universal church, and feudalism: The medieval problematic

By and large the view from within IR of the medieval period has been that of Realists concerned to establish a paradigm break (in mentality as well as system) that inaugurates the modern world of interstate relations, though some would argue that the medieval era, while lacking modern concepts of sovereign authority or the state as a unitary actor, nevertheless can easily enough be made to confirm the timelessness of human nature's lust for power and conquest. But for the most part, IR is content to bypass the era.

In the standard view, the enfeeblement and collapse of the Roman imperium in the West, the successive migrations of Germanic and other peoples, and the rise of the Roman Church as a repository of (canon) law and moral authority resulted in great confusion over the locus of legitimate power and the definition of authority. After the recreation of the Western empire in 800 under Charlemagne as the secular sword of the Church, the medieval realm, with a more settled and Christianized polity, was nevertheless torn between imperial ambition and a bureaucratized Church eager to defend and expand its authority. Though the fortunes of the empire or papacy waxed and waned, the contestation for theoretical and practical supremacy and the replication of imperial/papal contestation over issues of moral sanction and punishments, taxation, and investiture remained unresolved until the rise of territorial, dynastic regimes led to the emergence of the early modern state and the effective end of claims of universal imperial *or* papal authority. This contest penetrated to the most local level of social and political life, further confused and complicated by the impact of hereditary vassalage (a.k.a. feudalism) on landholding and military rights and obligations. Conflict was endemic at every level, among royal dynasts, regional nobles, and local vassals, and such recourse to arms often had a certain legitimacy according to the feudal code, however much the Church might attempt to interpose its "peace of God" or to displace local violence to the suppression of heresy, the evangelizing of the eastern marches, or the crusading project in the Middle East. The problem of violence is a common theme in medieval thought— echoed often in the defense of the universal authority of the emperor as maintainer (in theory) of a general peace.

The practice of violence and the ideology surrounding its suppression does provide IR an opening for appropriate focus and analysis. But for much "scientific" IR theory the problem posed by the medieval world is the apparent lack of a single identifiable and generalizable *unit* for conflict analysis, and no clear "theory of the state" seems available or possible from medieval practice. International historians, on the other hand, are less inhibited and are likely to see in the long era developments (of trade and the origins of market capitalism, revolutions in warfare, and the decline of dependency) that fitfully and unevenly but cumulatively build toward the early modern. Machiavelli's warring city-states or the post-Westphalia territorial dynastic state do not spring fully armed out of a rupture with the medieval past. As one Constructivist IR scholar critical of the "myth" of a sharp disjunction between feudal and early modern says, "the early-modern period grew out of processes that had already been underway … Continuities have come to seem at least as important as ruptures" (Walker, 1993, 89). This was also the message of Joseph Strayer's (1970, 9) study of the medieval origins of the modern state: "Sovereignty existed long before it could be described in theory."

The most striking issue that IR scholarship faces in the medieval era is the ambiguity of sovereignty. While in the East Byzantium was the self-conscious inheritor of the Roman imperium, headed by an emperor who in his person combined territorial rule and leadership of the (Eastern) church, in the West there emerged two theoretically universal, supra-territorial, institutions often in competition: the Church presided over by the sacerdotal figure of the pope, and, after Charlemagne, the Holy Roman Empire, presided over by a quasi-elective member of the Salian, then Hohenstaufen, and finally Habsburg dynasties. Each claimed extensive, often conflicting, jurisdictions.

The medieval pope was both a territorial and spiritual magnate, usually resident in Rome, at the head of an extensive bureaucracy, including a far-ranging system of special envoys or legates (papal nuncios and other ranks) at the top but also officials at every level of the royal administration of finance and justice in the various kingdoms of Western Christendom, since most regimes (until the late medieval growth in secularly trained lawyers) were dependent on literate clergymen. A "twelfth-century renaissance," born of prosperity and marked by the growth in the number of educated clergymen and the rediscovery of Roman law—transmitted through the early Byzantine emperor Justinian's *Corpus Iuris Civilis*—empowered the Church in its tug of war with secular authority in the settlement of disputes over succession, the administration of justice, the appointment of bishops and abbots (power-brokers themselves often), and the collection of revenue. Moreover, the largest international relations project of the medieval period, the several Crusades, was organized by the papacy for reasons that did not involve merely the recovery of Jerusalem, but also the assertion of its own moral and political authority. The popes themselves, endowed with territorial rights in Italy, were often drawn from the families of powerful Italian proprietary magnates, confusing any line one might try to draw between the secular and the religious. Finally, the canon law of the church that governed domestic as well as larger issues was a form of *international law* in the medieval period, presided over by trained lawyers and an elaborate system of church courts with ability to *appeal back to Rome* (which therefore could function as a kind of higher authority compromising the anarchic sovereignty of states).

The German emperors claimed to have inherited in the West the authority exercised by the Eastern Roman emperor, but such inflated claims struggled (as an aspiration largely) in the face of both obstinate local resistance and papal politics—Henry IV's humiliating submission to Pope Gregory VII at Canossa in 1077 had a long-lasting effect in undermining the authority of the Western emperor. Nevertheless, his assertion of secular overlordship vis-à-vis the lesser kingdoms of central Europe throughout the medieval period was a potent one, confirmed through an aggressive diplomacy and often backed by the force of arms. If by the late medieval period the emperor may no longer have hoped to exercise Justinian's authority over either Church or Empire, he remained a major player in war and negotiation. Indeed, by the end of the medieval period the "decline" in the Holy Roman Emperor's authority appeared to be dramatically reversed by the Habsburg super-emperor, Charles V—who could command financial and military resources from America-enriched Spain, rich Burgundy, the textile and trading wealth of the low countries, and the traditional fiefdoms of central and eastern Europe. In 1527, Charles' Spanish army shocked Christendom by sacking Rome and holding the Pope himself hostage. While the modern concept of *balance of power* can plausibly be seen operating from time to time in the late medieval period, especially among the Italian city-states, it was only fitfully effective. In the 1520s, a powerful alliance arrayed itself against Charles on the Italian peninsula (France, Milan, Venice, Florence, and the Pope himself as secular magnate of the Papal States), but it was swept away by the wealth and military prowess of the Emperor.

Feudalism

The territorial sovereignty of the medieval kingdom was thus complicated and limited, in theory, by the Empire and the Church, and by the normative values of Christendom. The reality was of course violent contestation for power at every level. Sovereignty, it has long been argued, was also strongly qualified by the institution of "feudalism"—most advanced in just that part of Western Europe that would produce the first recognizably modern, territorial nation-states.

"Feudalism" (of twentieth-century scholarly coinage) refers to the system by which a warrior nobility—and those knightly vassals beneath them—held land from their liege lord (an emperor, king, or great or lesser noble) in exchange for service—or later, monetary fees. As such, and especially as vassalage became hereditary and powerful territorial lords built castles and gathered armed men loyal to them alone, it limited the autonomous authority of the emperor or monarch by essentially privatizing the realm, leading to the alienation of much of what would in the modern period be considered the defining prerogatives of the sovereign—the administration of justice, the collection of revenue, and the organization of military force. The medieval kingdom was, then, composed of often competing regional and local magnates upon whom had been devolved by the crown the privileges of governance, who held courts of their own and commanded the primary allegiance of knights and other vassals, down to the village level. A powerful king of course might reassert his authority but civil war was endemic. Conversely, however, the claim to feudal right might also form the ostensible basis for the *extension* of dynastic territorial power—as in William the Conqueror's pope-blessed seizure of the throne of England. "Feudalism" has also of course long been deployed, especially by Marxists and Weberians, in a much more general sense—as that stage of development before the growth of a marketized economy ushered in a world of individualism and instrumental rationality.

For our purposes, the question arises, do the universal claims of pope and emperor above and the clear absence of a "legitimate monopoly of violence" below so compromise the sovereignty of a medieval monarch that one is justified in excluding the period from serious consideration in the theory and practice of IR? Historians might answer in various ways. First, one can always trace aspects of "modern" interstate relations in embryonic form. England and France evolved a form of sovereignty (albeit incomplete) well before the early modern period, as the concept of territorial rule shifted from nonexclusive to exclusive. Second, if one sets aside Realist or Neorealist definitions as too constricting, there might be something to learn from an examination of just how *diplomacy* at whatever level operated within "European international society" however fragmented, overlapping, and confused the political realm may appear. Third, the long medieval era begs questions about the interplay of power and normative values—in say the history of the Crusades—which speaks to general issues of the construction of regimes and the nature of warfare. Finally, the "confused" feudal era might itself resonate with, and help shed light on, the ambiguities and fictions of modern sovereignty. Some scholars, for instance, talk about the European Union ushering in a "new medievalism" in its apparent modification of the absolute sovereignty of its members. As one study of the search for a theory of IR asserts, the medieval period "has been virtually ignored by scholars," even though "all the elements of international relations as we understand them—autonomous actors, violence and war, system solidarity and culture, and supranational organization—were in fact present and were topics of great moment to scholars of the period" (Ferguson and Mansbach, 1988, 49–50).

R. B. J. Walker, motivated perhaps by our own turn-of-the-century debates over globalization, has drawn attention to the ways in which much IR theory presumes a distinction between "inside" and "outside," between the domestic and the international, drawing attention to the spatial and temporal specificity of the (especially early modern) need to construct such a psychological as well as political boundary against the universal claims of empire and papacy (Walker, 1993). Though the central issue in IR theory is generally taken to be the invention of the abstracted unitary sovereign state, the idea of inside/outside clearly has a far wider application, and may be one way of drawing the medieval world into the conversation. How do the Crusades or the Reconquista generate, as well as illustrate, civilizational boundaries? How might inside versus outside relate to "domestic" strategies pursued by the papacy from the eleventh century on in, say, defining heretics and Jews as outside the body of Christ, or in the use of excommunication as a political threat in its contest—and negotiation—with secular competitors? Because early feudal dynastic regimes lacked a clear, territorial delimitation, the problem of what was properly inside the nexus of feudal obligation and subordination and what outside was constantly litigated and fought over, a continually contested issue of claim and counterclaim involving feudal and dynastic rights of territorial inheritance. But the long medieval period also saw an uneven process of resolution—whereby the late medieval kingdom in the West began to take on a firmer bordered territorial exclusionary and inclusionary character.

Medieval "military revolutions"?

There is a subfield of IR and international history that is concerned with technologies and practices of war. The long medieval era saw a variety of military innovations—the shift from late Roman infantry tactics to those of a lightly armed cavalry, from the heavily armored knight (with stirrups and lance) of the high medieval era to the late medieval crossbow and pike of peasant and mercenary armies. Gunpowder and artillery were important for overcoming the castle defenses of over-mighty feudal barons and the walls of Italian cities, and allowed kings, at least if they had fiscal resources, more easily to organize warfare for reasons of state. More centrally of interest in the discipline should be the ways in which these changes depend upon—and encourage—the kinds of social, economic, and intellectual changes that directly affect the character of the state. The end of the warrior class of knights with their local power base and locally sourced retinues meant the end of the feudal state, as did the growth of fiscal resources in the western kingdoms and Italian city-states that increased due to the important spread, from the eleventh century, of more efficient agriculture, wider commerce, and the beginnings of modern banking. Much of what is "modern" in the early modern era built upon centuries of change during the long medieval period, just as much that was "feudal" in mentality (in warfare as in politics) in the Middle Ages survived well into the early modern era.

Diplomacy in the Middle Ages

Though the modern concept of the unitary sovereign state can hardly be said to exist in much of the medieval period in Europe, or in the Mediterranean Muslim world, there was a tradition of envoys and negotiation inherited from late antiquity in both East and West. "Diplomacy" of one kind or another was a commonplace phenomenon not only among territorial regimes in the West, among the Italian city-states, between the Church and the Western Empire, the Church and the Eastern Empire, or the

Eastern and Western Empires, but between these and their lesser clients, between, especially, the Eastern Empire and a host of non-European polities, including both Muslim and "barbarian." Though we generally assume that diplomacy properly refers to interstate relations, in the politics of the feudal-era arbitrative negotiation can be found at every level of corporate political and social life: between barons and king, or commune and king or parliament and king or bishops and abbots and royal regimes over a host of complicated disputes involving customary obligations, land tenure, or the applicability of secular or canon law. Where there was conflict or the threat of violence, there was negotiation—within as well as outside the state. As the historian Jeremy Black (2010, 24) has recently observed, "there is a need for an appreciation of the dynamic aspects of medieval diplomacy."

Diplomacy was employed for a variety of purposes—from simple communication, gift-exchange, dynastic marriages, and espionage to large issues of church and state or practical affairs of trade. Most courts had relations of a sort—formal or informal—with potential allies and enemies. Resident ambassadors however were uncommon, and formal contact was usually done by means of special envoys. Relationships between sovereigns or between feudal suzerains and their vassals or between kings, territorial bishops, and the papal court were ritualized and commonplace. Moreover, there was an expanding corps, so to speak, of literate intermediaries (generally clergymen) scurrying back and forth across Europe—*papal nuncios* at all the important royal courts, many of which sent their own representatives to Rome (as *procuratores*), a developed bureaucracy in Rome devoted to negotiation and diplomacy, elaborate archives (organized at the Papal Chancery from the early thirteenth century), and canon lawyers specializing in relations with secular powers and pushing forward the expanding realm of canon law.

The Papacy engaged in near-continual diplomacy, both within the disparate parts of the Church itself, and with secular powers, as in the early eighth-century Donation of Sutri (728), an agreement between Pope Gregory II and the king of the Lombards that saw additions to what would become the Papal States—territory directly under the control of the pope. The fraught relationship between Church and Empire, the shifting factionalized politics of the Italian peninsula, and, with the Crusades, longer-range diplomacy, along with a growing litigiousness—the discovery and invention of ancient treaties and "donations," the sharp practices of legal contestation and interpretation— mean that the high and late Middle Ages are full of diplomatic activity. The long investiture struggle was itself addressed in the Concordat of Worms in 1122, a treaty between Pope Calixtus II and the Holy Roman Emperor Henry V, while subsequently the give and take of war and politics in the Italian peninsula produced a number of negotiated agreements like that of the first Treaty of Constance between Emperor Frederick I and Pope Eugene III in 1153, the 28-clause Peace of Venice in 1177 between Frederick I and Pope Alexander III following the imperial defeat at the battle of Legnano, or the Treaty of San Germano (of 1230) between Frederick II and Pope Gregory IX that saw the Papal States and papal possessions in Sicily returned to the pope's control.

"Europe" (i.e., western "Christendom") was itself an expanding system: by force of arms (as with the Teutonic knights in the east or the Reconquista in Iberia) and conversion, as well as (at least until the Black Death of the mid- and late fourteenth century) the outward push of its growing population and its agriculture. Nor was western Christendom ever a tightly enclosed realm. Archaeology has revealed an active long-distance commerce outside these shifting borderlands from the earliest medieval era—scatters of Byzantine coins and trade goods from the eastern Mediterranean, the Near East, and beyond emerge from grave sites in Scandinavia, Anglo-Saxon England, or the north of France. The Crusades as well meant a sustained contact with non-European peoples in the Middle East for several hundred years.

Warfare, trade, and the growth of commerce in the medieval period had a complicated effect on international (i.e., interstate and intercivilizational) relations. The growing merchant and financial class was uniquely positioned to know and care about "foreign" affairs—to have contacts beyond the territory of town, region, or feudal/monarchical state, and to depend on "contracts of exchange" that are in effect private treaties. Merchant banking, and trade generally, flourished from the thirteenth century, and was especially active in the northern Italian cities, though prominent banking houses were established in the transalpine empire and the low countries as well. By the fifteenth century, the *Medici* family in Florence or the *Fuggers* in imperial Augsburg were well-positioned to exercise political and diplomatic influence within and beyond the borders of their cities, while those medieval Italian city-states that most prospered from and organized international trade and finance (Genoa and Venice) pursued trade, war, and diplomacy beyond Christendom itself.

The peculiarities of diplomacy, broadly considered, in a medieval world where negotiating entities might be commercial or financial families and other corporate interests (like the Hanseatic League), city-states and territorial sovereigns, dynasts who were liege-lords to some and vassals to others, and the nominally universal institutions of Church and Empire, weave a dense and complexly overlapping tapestry. Rather than seeing this as a static and confused "pre-sovereignty" era with little to offer, IR scholars might profitably seek to identify change-producing processes at work inside the medieval system, including the spreading emulation of *models* of negotiation provided by the Italian city-states—and their own debt to that of the thousand-year empire in the east.

Byzantium

If the European Middle Ages have been neglected in the discipline of IR, the history of the Eastern Roman Empire, which in some form spans the entire era from late antiquity to early modern, has been practically invisible. This is surprising and unfortunate because the history of Byzantium has much to tell us about warfare, statecraft, and diplomacy across civilizational lines, and because there are tangible connections—competitive and emulative—between East and West, as during the era of the Crusades and the rise of Venetian power in the eastern Mediterranean. The neglect is not difficult to understand. Byzantium, as an imperial theocracy, stands outside the standard narrative of the secular development of the Western state and state system. Erased by the rise of the Ottomans, it seemingly leads nowhere in the evolution of "modern" practice. Its intellectual legacy—except as a conduit to the medieval West of Roman law—is obscure. Though the early Byzantine scholar and historian Procopius knew Thucydides' *History* (by then over a thousand years old) and in emulation chronicled the wars of Justinian the Great and his renowned general Belisarius, Justinian himself suppressed the Academy at Athens as a pagan institution. There is no apparent line of intellectual descent through Byzantium to Machiavelli and Hobbes (neither of whom cared to acknowledge Byzantine legacies).

Like the European Middle Ages, the Byzantine era comprises very different periods, from the early attempts to reclaim the Roman imperium in the Mediterranean and Near East, to long eras of consolidation and defense on land and at sea in eastern Europe, the Black Sea region, Anatolia, the Middle East, and the eastern Mediterranean. Though it may be argued that the thousand-year Byzantine state—its culture and imperial ideology—evidences a surprising degree of "socio-economic, political, institutional and ideological" continuity (Haldon, 1999, 1), the long decline and retreat (in both Europe and Asia) led to important shifts in military tactics and diplomatic tradition. By the end, the reduction of the Empire to Constantinople (the greatest city in the world), its immediate hinterland, and a few islands and enclaves in the eastern Mediterranean meant that the Eastern Romans had in a threatening world to live on their wits, that is, on their diplomacy. In this they were not unlike their Italian city-state neighbors to the west, and the diplomacy they developed, quite different in character from that of their Roman progenitor, was a diplomacy not of conquest but of defense, of balancing, bribery, and intricate "duplicity." In other words, there are grounds to see late Byzantium as proto-modern, in this regard at least.

At its height, Byzantium had been insistently imperial in its assertion of universal authority, but its fortunes rose and fell, and it often operated in a way that reflected its essentially defensive need to guard diverse borders—from the Danube to the Black Sea, Persia, the Middle East, Africa, or Sicily. Byzantine rulers could expect to be at war somewhere more often than not, and needed treaty arrangements to hold other areas stable—Justinian the Great in 562 concluded a "fifty-year" multiclause peace treaty with the Sassanid Persians, and copies survive in both Persian and Greek.

Byzantium over the centuries survived by adapting its military traditions (for instance, turning from the heavy infantry tactics of its Roman past to relying, like the Hun it apparently emulated, on horsemen armed with short bows). But as its powers waned and its enemies grew in number, it came to rely even more on persuasion in recruiting allies and inducing its enemies to fight each other. The advice of every Byzantine military manual was that the commander is, when at all possible, to avoid battle. The Byzantine system required, that is, an elaborate form of diplomacy and intelligence gathering, involving a calculated combination of military pressure and financial subsidy, as well as religious and cultural proselytizing and the politique display of its wealth and splendor. As early as the mid-fifth century, Theodosius II managed to buy off Attila with 6,000 pounds of gold and annual payments—deflecting the Hun horde from the Balkans to the west. Treaties with the Bulgars in the eighth and early ninth centuries repressed and diverted dangerous conflict to the north, and allowed the Empire to concentrate its military defenses elsewhere. Not that such devices were ever permanent solutions. Negotiations to end harassment from the Kievan Rus' in the ninth and tenth centuries were—as is true of much medieval diplomacy between East and West—only intermittently effective in creating breathing periods between outbreaks of violent conflict. The Peace of Nicephorus, a series of negotiations in the early ninth century, attempted to sort out the awkward issue of imperial title and territorial jurisdictions (in the Adriatic) between the Eastern Emperor and Charlemagne.

The long Byzantine tradition of diplomacy, described by one recent scholar as "hard-headed, well-informed and practical" (Black, 2010, 35), with Christian and non-Christian, extended beyond immediate military objectives of offense and defense. It reached out for long-distance relations, as in the mission to the Mongolian khaganates in the late sixth century. The 911 treaty with the Kievan Rus', a complicated document drawn up in both languages, anticipates the trade treaties later negotiated with the Italian republics of Venice and Genoa. Trade and military alliance were often intertwined, as in the treaty with Venice in 1082, which offered Venetian merchants access in exchange for military aid against the Mediterranean expansion of the Normans.

The eleventh century also saw the Anatolian incursion by the expanding Seljuk Muslims, a warrior mass movement less amenable to diplomacy. The spread of Islam by Arab conquest in Syria and Africa from the late seventh century, and the imperial defeat by the Seljuk Turks at the battle of Manzikert (1071), however, shifted Byzantine diplomacy to the pressing business of reestablishing alliances in a Middle East fragmented by Muslim expansion and Monophysite Christian resistance to Byzantine theology and taxation. Subsequently, the Crusades inaugurated an era of complicated diplomacy between the Eastern Empire, the papacy and the Western Empire, and the Latin kingdoms in the Levant.

The fortunes and forms of Byzantine diplomacy shifted according to its changing military capabilities and eroding territorial position through these long centuries, though there is always a danger of regarding the Eastern Empire as a unitary state with rational and continuous strategies for survival. There were no "professional" diplomats or central administration of foreign affairs (there was however a "Barbarians' Bureau" for protocol, record-keeping, and translation). Byzantium however established an enduring tradition, known to the West, of diplomatic sophistication, a "culture of strategic statecraft," that was passed on in handbooks like that of ca. 948 during the reign of Constantine VII Porphyrogenitus (the first Western tract on diplomacy, the *Ambaxiator Brevilogus*, by a French cleric, dates from 1436). Moreover, amid the confusion of its politics and its multiple ethnicities, the Eastern Empire apparently maintained a significant and defining degree of self-regard as *the* oikoumene, the civilized universal, rather as the contemporary Chinese dynasties considered themselves the center of the world. But this normative ideology/theology did not prevent them pursuing—indeed it may have encouraged them to pursue—diplomatic conversation with inferior polities and peoples, crafting a diplomacy, as the historian Dmitri Obolensky says, that was "an intricate science and a fine art, in which military pressure, political intelligence, economic cajolery, and religious propaganda" were fused (quoted in Watson, 1992, 109). We should hesitate to dismiss, as a recent textbook of IR theory does, Byzantine diplomacy as "religiously informed" and thus lacking in "theory and abstract analysis" (Knutsen, 1997, 18), or claim baldly as another scholar has recently done, that modern diplomacy was simply "born in northern Italy" (Russell, 2005, 233).

The Muslim world and the Crusades

Byzantium's storied location and identity as both Eastern and Western, European and Asian, Mediterranean and Near Eastern raises the question of the degree to which one might conceive of a global, or at least transregional, transcivilizational Middle Ages. Within IR discourse this line could be pursued as an exploration of structural constraints and incentives—as in the ways somewhat amorphous large, pre-state polities of conquest and conversion might evolve along similar lines, toward, for instance, forms of feudal derogation and fragmentation or alternatively in the invention (or emulation) of techniques of central administration, taxation, and military organization, or the ways in which warrior leadership becomes sedentary, hereditary, and dynastic. Alternatively, a comparative history of medieval religious identities might involve a fruitful exploration of similarities and differences in the construction of a sense of a community (an oikoumene, ecumene, ummah) of the faithful across ethnic and territorial boundaries, and in a "cultural, religious, and ideational" worldview "as a foundation of truth and the 'good life'" (Tadjbakhsh, 2010, 174).

The idea of a global Middle Ages comes into sharper focus with the history, often ignored in IR scholarship, of the evolution beyond the West but contiguous to it of Muslim polities—Arab, Turkic, or Persian, fluid empires and settled states—in the medieval and late medieval period, and how they drew from Byzantine practice and experience, established their own unique political ethos, or interacted with and perhaps influenced medieval Western political and intellectual life, from Andalucía to the Crusader kingdoms and Constantinople. While the complicated narrative of Western relations with Islam in the medieval period is beyond the scope of this text, we should briefly consider ways in which IR might profit from some understanding of the parallel development of an Islamic system, if one can call it such, in the era before the early modern expansion of European empires.

Certainly aspects of the medieval Islamic realm, in both its inherent dynastic character and its overarching civilizational/religious self-conceptualization, strongly resonate with Western and Byzantine Christian politics. The idea of the *Dar al-Islam* (the house of Islam), the worldwide *Ummah* or community, was developed by medieval Islamic scholars as a single sphere (a "Civilization" like Christendom) knit together by the Koran—both as a source of rules of behavior, but also as a language, Arabic, that was the literal word of God. The fact that Islamic regimes were often successors to Byzantine practice raises the issue of the influence Byzantium may have exercised—though one can also argue for some degree of influence in the other direction, as with the eighth- and ninth-century outbreak of iconoclasm in Constantinople. And some might argue that the pope's late eleventh-century call for a Crusade to retake Jerusalem suggests the Islamic idea of jihad.

By the High Middle Ages, conquest and conversion had created a vast and differentiated Islamic world from Spain and Africa to Persia and India, the religious, cultural, and political unity of which was, as in Christendom, much more an ideal than a reality. Islam was divided into significantly different sects from early on; politically and culturally the Islamic centers that were coalescing into the great if loosely constituted Ummayad and Abbasid caliphates or the Mughal Empire in India were to some degree hybrid affairs adapting many traditions from a host of diverse peoples. Some Islamic scholars focus on the rapid development of difference within the larger Ummah from the ninth century onward, a great variation based on sectarian difference, the mixture of ethnicities, different economic systems, and differences in the way authority is legitimized. But in the last analysis, the medieval Dar al-Islam (and the persistence of the concept into the modern era) suggests that, in spite of inter-Islamic conflict and the anarchic instability of regimes, the Islamic ideal of the universal Ummah was more tenacious and tangible than the corresponding Western ideal of a universal Christendom. A recent scholar taking a Constructivist approach has emphasized divergence in Islamic and Western IR, and the obstacles to the development of a Western definition of the sovereign state that are inherent in Islamic legal theory (Tadjbakhsh, 2010).

Generally, Islamic empires/states differ from the medieval West (if not from Byzantium) in the degree of autonomy they allowed to communities of other religions within the Dar al-Islam and their willingness to negotiate with infidel rulers outside it. Beyond was the Dar al-Harb (or realm of war) and the Dar al-Suhl (those outside Islam with whom Muslims might develop treaty obligations). One of the earliest of these treaties was the Baqt, a peace of 651 between a Christian kingdom of Nubia and the Islamic conquerors of Egypt. It perhaps resembles more a characteristic Byzantine accommodation than militant Islamic practice. By the ninth century the Abbasid caliphate at Baghdad, where Thucydides' text was known and studied as was ancient Persian history, was conducting war, diplomacy, and commerce from central Asia to much of the southern Mediterranean basin, on a scale vaster than that of Byzantium. The fifth Abbasid caliph, Harun-al-Rashid (r. 786–809), received a delegation from Charlemagne and sent emissaries to China (there were in fact many such Abbasid embassies to the Tang court at Chang'an).

The Crusades

The papal call for a Crusade to retake the Holy Land in 1095 (Byzantium had lost Jerusalem to Arab conquest in 637) drew Western Europe—the papacy, the Empire, territorial kingdoms, and free-booting noblemen—into the large theater of eastern Mediterranean war and diplomacy. The organization of the Crusades themselves (as "intercontinental operations") required heavy diplomatic effort by the papal chancery and played a role in the assertion of spiritual supremacy by the Pope during the long Investiture crisis. It also opened an era of often conflicted relations with the Byzantine Empire.

At the beginning of the First Crusade, promises were made at Constantinople to return territory conquered from the Arabs to Byzantium, but a Norman nobleman who had seized Antioch proclaimed himself to be the Prince of the city and it took fighting and coercive diplomacy before a treaty (of Devol, 1108) settled the matter. The denouement of the various Crusades and the creation of a series of "Latin Kingdoms" in the Middle East generated significant diplomatic activity—between the Pope, the Eastern Emperor, the Republic of Venice, and these kingdoms, including the Kingdom of Jerusalem, and between the Christian armies and the Islamic forces that opposed them—like the agreements reached between Saladin and Richard of England in 1192. The Fourth Crusade (1204), diverted by the Venetians, seized and sacked Constantinople and imposed a Latin regime there that lasted more than a half century and was formalized in treaties of partition with the rump successor of the Byzantine state.

In the past, IR scholars have not shown much interest in the medieval Crusades, despite their clear significance in the history of the foreign policy of both Byzantium and the Western Church and Empire in establishing long-term relations between the West and the Muslim world, and perhaps in altering the character of states and their relation to the Church in the West. This changed somewhat after Huntington's "clash of civilizations" thesis was popularized in the 1990s, and after 9/11 when "crusading" was rhetorically deployed in descriptions of the American war on terror. Since then there has been a minor flurry of interest in the ways in which the crusading era may be profitably revisited by IR scholars seeking to complicate Realism's picture of a sharp break between medieval and modern mentalities and to establish connections between war and foreign policy and internal changes in the West—between domestic papal peacemaking and crusading rhetoric and diplomacy in the twelfth and thirteenth centuries "as a framework for the conduct of political relations in Europe" (Weiler, 2003, 36), and between the need to find the resources to mount crusading expeditions and the growing centralization of the territorial state. The medieval crusading era has been searched for evidence of the importance of "moral authority" as a "power resource," the importance of belief over interest and structure (Horowitz, 2009; Latham, 2011), the ways "internalized norms, rules, and conventions" give meaning to "conflictual and violent action" (Alkopher, 2005, 719), and, following the lead of the French *Annaliste* historian Alphonse Dupront, the ways in which the Crusades were both a product and a source of potent myth and symbol.

Contextualizing Machiavelli

We have taken a rather circuitous route to Machiavelli's world. One objective has been to "provincialize" Western Europe a little and northern Italy especially, and to suggest that from the world historian's perspective Renaissance Florence was not exactly the *fons et origo* of "modern" political practice. One might argue that the statecraft and diplomacy of Machiavelli's time was not so much a Renaissance invention—the state as a work of art—as the culmination of several centuries of both contact with the wider—and not only European—world, and of local, northern Italian experience. The Italian city-state was of medieval origin and character, and its history long before the late fifteenth century had seen regimes with little claim to either social legitimacy or Christian moral sanction.

As with Thucydides' *History*, it is instructive, from the historian's perspective, to explore various contexts, long and short, within which a canonical work like *The Prince* may be situated and historicized. First, there is the long medieval era in which the city-state system in northern Italy matured. How its character was shaped by social and cultural conditions perhaps unique to that prosperous region, and how its persisting practices of statecraft and diplomacy may reflect not only local but distant influences are issues of some interest. Mid-range, so to speak, contexts would include changes in the nature of the fourteenth- and early fifteenth-century state, the rise of "new" men and their "delegitimated" backgrounds, and whatever continuities and changes may be identified in this period in the character of warfare and diplomatic practices, as well as the significance of early Renaissance humanism, closely associated with the rise of educated laity in northern Italian cities, and how the lessons of antiquity were applied in a more secular understanding of civic virtue. Finally, and most familiarly, there is the near context of Machiavelli's own world, his immediate social and political background and experiences, the sources he plausibly drew upon, and ways in which the political crises of his time informed his most enduring work.

To take the deeper context first, one might begin by noting that we can observe early in the medieval period an emerging "system" marked by conflict and alliance in northern Italy. Whether we are justified in speaking of an "anarchic system of billiard-ball states" in line with IR theory, however, depends on the degree to which appeal to higher authority (emperor or pope) was available and how independent these cities were or could be of these larger (if competing) authorities. By the late medieval period, the decline of the ability of the German emperors to intervene decisively in Italian affairs, demonstrated by the success of the Lombard League, along with the erosion of the higher authority of the pope, much damaged by the move to Avignon in 1309 and the Western Schism of the late fourteenth century, enlarged the independence generally of the Italian states—until dynastic French and Spanish ambitions in Italy a century later threatened to extinguish it.

Figure 5.1 Machiavelli's Italy.

Source: Albert Hyma, *A Short History of Europe, 1500–1815* (New York: F. S. Crofts & Co., 1928).

Of the major cities that comprised the medieval system in northern Italy (Figure 5.1), Venice was the oldest in its identity, prosperity, and (oligarchic) republican ethos. It originated as a refuge among the lagoons of the northwestern Adriatic in late antiquity, closely connected to the Eastern Empire. Charlemagne in the Peace of Nicephorus recognized Venice as Byzantine territory with extensive trading rights in the Adriatic. By 1082, when Venice concluded a trade and mutual defense treaty with Byzantium, the city had become a wealthy maritime republic with lucrative interests in the eastern Mediterranean, Byzantium, and the Islamic Near East. It acquired not only trade but territory, with enclaves and islands in the Adriatic and Aegean region, sought to profit from the early crusading conquests (negotiating, for instance, a treaty of alliance with the Crusader Kingdom of Jerusalem in 1123), and expanded its alliance system and territorial hinterland in northern Italy, while developing transalpine trading connections in northern Europe.

As the Venetian state stepped into much of the trading world the Byzantines had previously dominated, its relations with its former protector became aggressively competitive. When the Fourth Crusade conquered and sacked Constantinople, Venice profited immensely from looted treasure and the assumption of Byzantine trade routes and alliances—negotiating a commercial treaty with the Byzantine successor, the rump Nicaean Empire in Anatolia. Venice's own well-developed system of emissaries and envoys reflects its Byzantine inheritance—one general work on the evolution of western diplomacy has observed that Venice "systematized what it had learnt from the Byzantine world" (Hamilton and Langhorn, 1995, 20)—as well as influences absorbed from the Abbasid and later Ottoman Empires. By the late medieval period, the republic had representatives and informants in every major city in Europe and the Near East, establishing a kind of diplomatic network that made it the "school and touchstone of ambassadors." Its envoys sent voluminous reports (the *Relazioni*) back to the Council of Ten where they were archived for the useful information they gathered.

Venice was the richest and most successful of the maritime city-states, but its competitor on the west coast of northern Italy, the Republic of Genoa, also developed an extensive trade beyond Europe, negotiating a trade treaty with the same Nicaean successor state toward the end of the Latin occupation of Constantinople and subsequently profiting from a close, privileged position in the reestablished Eastern Empire with trading rights to the Black Sea. By the end of the thirteenth century, the city's revenues were larger than those of France and it could mobilize nearly 40,000 troops. Like Venice, Genoa was a mercantile oligarchy that had expanded its Italian hinterland to include most of Liguria in the eleventh and twelfth centuries. It also profited from the Crusades, providing transport, supplies, and bowmen. By 1300 it had a population of ca. 80,000–100,000, less than Venice's 100,000–120,000 but roughly comparable to Florence and Milan and significantly larger than either Paris or London.

As Venice and Florence were both rivals and sometime allies, Genoa and Milan, in the rich Po valley, had a similar ambiguous relationship marked by frequent diplomatic conversation. Milan itself, a leader of the anti-imperial Lombard League, emerged by the late twelfth century as a wealthy center of trade and banking, controlled by a series of strong men and their communal factions until the rise of the Visconti family in the mid-thirteenth century. By the late fourteenth century, Milan had become an imperially appointed dukedom. It also, like Venice earlier, developed a bureaucracy for managing foreign affairs and a system of resident envoys in key states like Genoa that was copied by others. War between Milan and its allies and Venice and often Florence over spreading territorial claims in northern Italy generated both a kind of balancing among these and lesser Italian city-states, and a pattern of alternating conflict and negotiation. Warfare on the peninsula had been common enough through the medieval period, but the growth in prosperity of some cities and their practice of hiring mercenaries (more generally available after the end of large-scale crusading) led by opportunistic *condottieri* or freebooting military "contractors," encouraged its development as a commonplace part of intercity rivalry in the thirteenth and fourteenth centuries.

The second area of contextual interest involves the spread through the prosperous north, with Florence at its center, of secular learning. The salient historical facts behind "the coming of the Renaissance" are those that relate to the rise of individualism (and decline of hierarchical dependency), anticlericalism (and the decline of the church's authority in daily lives—in, for instance, the failing efficacy of excommunication), and materialism (the hope of worldly gain among a growing part of the population). Since Weber, many historians and historical sociologists have looked to the rise of the middling classes—secular lawyers, merchants, bankers, and those generally prospering from their own effort—to help explain these phenomena. Northern Italy, with its profitable woolen textile industry, domestic and foreign trade, and financial institutions, might be expected to lie at the heart of a shift away from a medieval ethos of feudal dependency. Within this enabling social environment and encouraged by the mythologized founding traditions of many Italian city-states, the classics of Greek and Latin antiquity—especially works of history and politics— served in the fourteenth and early fifteenth centuries a new sense of civic pride and virtue. Just how Machiavelli may be related to this "civic humanism" and whether that opens an alternative reading of his most famous work as a text of irony rather than cynicism has become a major bone of contention in the world of Machiavelli scholarship.

Machiavelli can be placed within larger debates about a late medieval intellectual and political crisis, especially in northern Italy, that, fuelled by the spread of a secular education in the literature of ancient Rome and Greece and Petrarch's humanism, eroded the certainties of medieval Christianity among a growing prosperous and secular urban elite. The idea however of a sharp break (in perhaps the early fifteenth century) has always been problematic, both overdependent on the assumption that there had been a "medieval" philosophical and political consensus, and bent on establishing the chronological boundaries of this "Renaissance" (in aesthetics, philosophy, and political discourse). Chronology has in fact been a much contested affair, with some scholars seeing a very early beginning (in the twelfth century), while others have identified elements of medieval thought and attitude extending well into the early modern period.

It is of course beyond the scope of this text to engage the vast scholarly literature on the idea of the Renaissance and its multifaceted character, or whether there was in fact a clearly demarcated shift (and among whom first: The educated clergy? The secular laity? The young?) in aesthetic and philosophical as well as political thought. Suffice to say that some are prepared to accept the idea of a decisive break into the modern, concentrating on key texts like *The Prince*, while others see more continuity and locate changes in political thought and practice in the kind of fluid *social contexts* that underpin the new subjectivities that we think characterize the deracinated individual of the late- and post-medieval world. Apart from those traditional scholars of ideas who, like Leo Strauss, insist on an austere textual analysis and critique, historians generally are likely to sympathize with the latter approach, whether they focus on the short context of the specific social and political environment of Florence during

Machiavelli's lifetime, or the longer context of the European-wide, but especially Italian, late medieval crisis.

The third area of context involves the nature of the fifteenth-century Italian political system, that of the major city-states of Genoa, Milan, Pisa, Venice, Florence (and sometimes Naples in the south), and a number of lesser, often client, cities. It was a region of merchant princes, banking dynasties, and *condottieri*-turned-dukes; of the masters of art and architecture and their rich and princely patrons. These cities, territorial statelets, whether republics or dukedoms, had emerged by the thirteenth and fourteenth centuries with enough resources to empower a politics of competition and expansion, and incessant, if rarely seriously destructive, warfare (though in the mid-thirteenth century Milan had been substantially ruined in a particularly violent decade-long civil war). They expanded into their hinterlands both to buffer themselves from their competitors and to increase their tax yield—important, increasingly, in the hiring of mercenary armies.

Whatever the answers to large questions of interpretation, late medieval Italy provides a fascinating microcosm of anarchic and apparently amoral politics. In Lombardy, the Sforza regime in Milan was founded by Francesco, a brutal *condottiero* employed by the ruling Visconti family into which he married. In Tuscany, the Medici of Florence, from Cosimo, de facto ruler of the city by the early fifteenth century, to the reign of his grandson Lorenzo the Magnificent, established their political power through the profits of their family banking house. The Medici family also would produce four popes. The fortunes of the Gonzagas who ruled Mantua from the 1430s were founded on mercenary service—Francesco I was a *condottiero* who fought for Venice, while Ludovico II was another who fought for Milan, as was Francesco II, who ruled the city in the late fifteenth and early sixteenth centuries. Mantua would shift its alliance according to the favorable winds—sometimes serving on the side of the Papal States, sometimes Venice.

Well before Machiavelli wrote, Italian politics was about wealth and naked force, often deployed by parvenus, rulers with little ability to call upon or need for the traditional mystique of feudal monarchy. The fifteenth century saw the further extension of city-state control over the countryside—in response to Milan's control of Lombardy, the Venetians moved to extend territorial claims in the Veneto, including the cities of Padua and Verona, and along the Dalmatian coast. A series of wars against Milan's Visconti family resulted in a high point of territorial success under the Doge Francesco Foscari in the early fifteenth century, though Venice was ultimately outmaneuvered on the peninsula by the Sforzas.

War itself, though ordinarily limited, was a normal and regular instrument of city-state politics (as Machiavelli would later affirm in *The Art of War*), with little of the medieval chivalric ideal. At least some of these regimes were founded by *condottieri* who were used to shifting their own allegiances according to opportunity and profit. Machiavelli declared that strong armies were the foundation of all states. But the wars of the political system of the Italian city-state, though common, casual, and brutal, were small scale, marked by changing configurations and reconfigurations of alliances, compared to the sustained conflict, international and domestic, that accompanied the rise of the large dynastic territorial states of continental Europe. The military revolution of the sixteenth and seventeenth centuries ensured that these larger units with their deeper resources would prevail over the Italian model.

This patchwork system, including the papacy, reestablished at Rome in the 1420s and often fielding its own military force, was, unlike the emerging territorial states north of the Alps, not dependent on a landed feudal class. The early fifteenth century, it has been argued, saw a critical shift away from an earlier period in which Dante could envision Florence in the context of an imperial system of universal order and authority, toward a more strictly secular and contingent world of the rise and fall of men who were neither patriots nor traditional nobles but self-made opportunists. It was also characterized by a kaleidoscopic pattern of unstable alliances like those of Florence from the 1420s—first with Milan against the papacy and Venice and then with Venice against the expansion of Milan, and then again with Sforza's Milan against Venice. Regarding the alliance of Sforza's Milan and Lorenzo's Florence to oppose the Venetians, a kind of fifteenth-century "diplomatic revolution," Lorenzo himself said that the affairs of Italy ought to be kept in a kind of balance. But it was the revolving wheel of city-state diplomacy, a secret agreement between Florence and Naples against Milan, which ultimately drove Sforza to conclude the fateful alliance with Charles VIII of France that would undo the system by turning Italy into a cockpit for the ambitions of the Valois kings and the Spanish.

Represented as an interstate politics of continual warfare, balancing, and failed attempts at hegemony, and of what a Jesuit writer in a disapproving attack on Machiavelli's presumed amorality later called *ragion di stato* (reason of state), "Renaissance" Italy like Thucydides' Greece has long provided Realist theory with a model of how an anarchic state system tends to work. Historians of the period, however, are less likely these days to accept that there had been an abrupt shift from medieval assumptions (that the goal of diplomacy was the peace of Christendom) to a "modern" understanding of *ragion di stato* and Realpolitik. Recent historical work has explored the ways in which the foreign policy of the fifteenth-century Italian city-state may be set into the longer (medieval) historical context, especially how it continued to be influenced by the politics of imperial and papal conflict, while recognizing that Italy also pointed toward a "developing system of international relations" that reflects the evolution of the concept of sovereignty and the growth of secret diplomacy in bureaucratized, institutional settings, in Milan's *Consiglio Segreto*, the secret procedures of Venice's Council of Ten, or in Florence's *Otto di Pratica* (Mallett, 2001, 61–2, 65).

Do these cities compose what one can regard as a "system" exhibiting Waltzian "third image" constraints? Or, did the varied and fluid nature of their domestic character—some, like the Republic of Florence, having a more democratic tradition, others like the Republic of Venice a confirmed oligarchy, or a Milan dominated by the Visconti and Sforza dukes—significantly determine their behavior as power-seeking or defensive polities? Was republican Florence (at least before or after its domination by the Medici) less likely to engage in expansionist war than, say, ducal Milan? Or do the politics of hard-faced *condottieri*-turned-magistrates and princes confirm, as Morgenthau claimed, "the ubiquity of power drives" that Machiavelli and Hobbes would identify and accept (Morgenthau, 1948, 219–20)?

The Italian city-state *system* represents not only a regionally limited, but a chronologically narrow world. It owed much to the medieval struggle of pope and emperor, and was already in decline when Machiavelli wrote about it, soon forcibly subsumed into the larger system of dynastic European territorial kingdoms competing for hegemony. What was its legacy for this new, more extensive and longer-lived system, if any? Was it an instructive harbinger? Did it exert a more direct influence on those early modern advisors and power-wielders who like most of the educated European elite, knew of, read about, or had, like Henry VIII's chief minister Thomas Cromwell, personal experience of Italian war and politics? Italian fashion—in literature, art, and architecture—spread outward from the peninsula to the gothic north. The rise and fall of Italian power dynasties like the Medicis or the Sforzas provided a contemporary text throughout Europe of secular ambition that, as with the invention of perspective in Italian painting, put the controlling, calculating individual at the center.

Finally, a closer consideration of the Italian, in particular the Florentine, context also directs us to the ways in which the city had changed in the generation before and during Machiavelli's lifetime. Florence had been a communal republic whose prosperity depended on its trade and manufacturing, often dominated by strong men and their families before the rise of the Medici. It has been argued that medieval Florence had been marked by a sense of a "moral universe" of good citizenship, order, and due authority, and that the early fifteenth century saw a secularization of these ideals (Pocock, 1983, 50–3), though also a continuation of tension and contestation between the *popolo* and an increasingly wealthy commercial and noble patriciate. The first Medici period culminated however with stable and prosperous years under Lorenzo (1449–1492), who, once a competing family, the Pazzi, had been brutally destroyed, ruled undisturbed by the resulting papal excommunication and interdict until his death in 1492.

The Florence that Machiavelli knew as a young adult (he was 23 when Lorenzo's reign came to an end), however, was one of violent and repeated domestic rupture, external threat, and political uncertainty. The serially balanced system of northern Italian states was thrown into a fresh crisis by the first of three French invasions in 1494. Charles VIII's Italian ambitions and his demands on Florence led to the humiliation and fall of the Medici, and to a brief experiment in a godly and democratic republic dominated by an articulate and popular preacher, Girolamo Savonarola. Machiavelli's Florence was caught up in the religious enthusiasm inspired by the Apocalyptic preaching of this Dominican friar, whose evangelical popularity was in part a response to the ostentatious wealth of not only the urban patriciate and the Medici, but of the papal court as well. His followers established Florence as a "Christian Republic," and launched a moral attack on drink, corruption, sexual immorality, and luxury that included the destruction of art and literature—the bonfire of the vanities—before the brief puritanical regime was brought down and Savonarola tortured and burned on orders from Pope Alexander VI in 1498.

Machiavelli, who had initially admired the return to the city's republican roots under Savonarola's direction, turned vocal critic, and would famously later inveigh in *The Prince* against the futility of a politics of good intentions, of *profeti disarmati*—unarmed prophets—as being likely to fail without the power to achieve and sustain political goals. When the execution of the friar in 1498 returned the republic to the control of leading families, Machiavelli was offered a job as Second Chancellor (an administrative official), a position confirmed when Piero Soderini was made *gonfaloniere* (or chief magistrate) for life—the post had previously been elective for two months. At the same time, a second French invasion, that of Louis XII in 1498, saw Florence allied with the French in their assault on Milan but also hoping to retake the port of Pisa, controlled by Florence since 1406 but now in French hands. Pisa was important to Florentine trade, the Arno having significantly silted up, and Machiavelli was much involved in the ultimately successful war to retake the city, once the French had left. To the south, Florence was threatened by the expansive and bullying ambitions of the pope's son, Cesare Borgia, while a third French invasion in 1508 threw the Italian system once again into disarray and counter-alliance, and allowed the Medici to plot their return with the aid of the army of Pope Julius II.

In 1512, Soderini was deposed and those who served him, including Machiavelli, were purged. It was in the first year of exile that *The Prince* was written, a work that clearly reflects uncertain times in which anything might be risked and accomplished by calculation and aggressive action. It can be taken, thus, in Pocock's (1975, 154) language, as "the greatest of all theoretical explorations of the politics of innovation." Another scholar has observed that the disorder Machiavelli experienced helps to explain "his preoccupation with the rationality of politics" and with power divorced from Christian morality—as a means of achieving a larger public good (Russell, 2005, 233).

Machiavelli in his time and ours

> Ever since Machiavelli, interest and necessity—and *raison d'état*, the phrase
> that comprehends them—have remained the key concepts of *Realpolitik*.
> (Waltz, 1979, 117)

IR scholars have stressed three reasons that Machiavelli occupies the important place he does in the discipline: (1) his apparent advocacy of amoral expediency in the achievement of strictly secular political ends is evidence of a sharp break in both mentality and practice from the medieval past; (2) he perceptively reveals the true ethic, across time, of the exercise of power by stripping away the normative (i.e., religious or idealist) language in which it is usually wrapped; and (3) he occupies therefore a critical place in the theory and practice of IR as the first "modern" in a discourse that runs from Machiavelli through Hobbes to the present. From the point of view of the historian, the first of these assertions, though commonly made, may be quite difficult to justify. However impressive Machiavelli's oeuvre may be, it is hardly sui generis. His vigorous anticlericalism and his assertion that the ultimate good of the people rests on the firm—indeed brutal—actions of a secular prince resonate with a pro-imperial, antipapal medieval discourse of long-standing, back through Marsilio of Padua's *Defensor Pacis* and Dante's *De Monarchia* to the twelfth-century Ghibellines and beyond. The second as we will see begs the (perhaps unanswerable) question of intention while also raising the problem of the cynic's (partial) vision, and is all the more doubtful if it implies that Machiavelli's infamous text is an accurate description and guide to how politics—including interstate relations—actually operate, in our time as in his (the common viewpoint of Realism). The third is obviously true if one restricts the issue to the construction of an internal discourse in political theory, but again risks reading Machiavelli simply as a (proto-)modernist, or, as Leo Strauss argued, a modern materialist, thus running the danger, as with Thucydides, of creating him in our image rather than as a highly complex figure whose work is located in a special time and place.

Less problematic are investigations of Machiavelli's influence on the subsequent development of political philosophy—either negatively (*The Prince* and its author were commonly quite literally demonized and used as exemplars of what politics was not—or should not be—about) or more positively (drawing often on the *Discourses* rather than *The Prince*) in what J. G. A. Pocock and Quentin Skinner saw as a "classical Republican" Atlantic tradition, or, in a less-humanist-oriented synthesis with Hobbes, what Vickie Sullivan calls a "liberal Republican" tradition reflecting not liberty but Machiavelli's "overarching purpose of war and empire" (Sullivan, 2004, 9–10).

Niccolò Machiavelli and the Florentine Republic

Machiavelli was born into a family of somewhat decayed country nobility (his father had a little rural and urban property, but was dependent on his fees as a Florentine lawyer) and grew to maturity during the height of the Republic's cultural and political prominence under Lorenzo. As an adult, dedicated to the service of the city as administrator and diplomat, he witnessed an era of shifting alliances and intermittent warfare, and the extended crises following the end of Savonarola, the intrusion of France as would-be hegemon, and the extension of papal territorial ambitions. When Machiavelli entered government service, Florence had restored a less utopian republic, but the situation was exposed and delicate, requiring adroit diplomatic maneuvering.

Well-educated within his father's humanist circle, he was familiar with the Roman moralists, especially Cicero (whom he would later parody), with Livy and the history and politics of the ancient Roman Republic, and with some knowledge of ancient Greek philosophy and history—he certainly had read Polybius and Xenophon, and probably Thucydides (either in the original Greek or a Latin translation). In his official service, Machiavelli sought to preserve the Florentine Republic through a citizen militia rather than mercenary *condottieri*, and looked, as a distant hope, to the unification of the city-states into a reborn Italian Republic. His younger and better-connected near-contemporary, Francesco Guicciardini, expressed something likely very close to Machiavelli's own views:

Three things I wish to see before I die, but I doubt if I shall see any of them even if I live a long time: in our city the life of a well-ordered republic, Italy freed from all barbarians, and the whole world set free from the tyranny of these wicked priests. (Quoted by Ridolfi, 1967, 193)

Machiavelli was intimately involved in Florentine diplomatic and military affairs, envoy variously to the French and imperial courts, Rome, and Cesare Borgia, and responsible for organizing and maintaining the Florentine citizen-militia that finally defeated Pisa in 1509. Three years later, however, the deposed Medici conspired with the new pope (Julius II) and the Spanish to defeat Florentine defenses. Soderini fled, the Medici were restored and Machiavelli was stripped of his offices, tortured a little, and sent into exile—which he devoted to study and writing, observing in a letter that "fortune has decreed that knowing nothing of silk manufacture nor the wool business, nor of profit or loss, I must talk politics" (quoted by Hale, 1972, 107).

The Prince[1]

We cannot hope to do justice to the vast literature of analysis and criticism that surrounds Machiavelli's major works generally, and *The Prince* particularly; nor does much of this ongoing industry necessarily directly address issues that are central to the concerns of the discipline of IR. Here we shall take a necessarily brief look at what Machiavelli has to say (without lingering overmuch on the extensive speculation about the ambiguities of *virtù* or *necessità*). Generally speaking, Machiavelli's text, written in the vernacular of Tuscan Italian, is more accessible to a modern reader than Thucydides' often difficult and stylistically complicated Greek. The problem of translation that we observed in the use of Thucydides' *History* by IR scholars is less of an issue here, because the language and, perhaps arguably, the mentality are closer to ours, though even with the modern-seeming Machiavelli the careful historian will be conscious of the dangers of assuming that the author's associations and meanings are transparent and directly translatable to our world.

There has been extended speculation about Machiavelli's sources, whether he knew Greek, how his work may plausibly offer a response to Platonic and Aristotelian philosophy, or to Polybius's presentation of history (and the life of republics) as cyclical, and how it relates to the civic humanism associated with the revival of ancient Roman political and historical texts. Machiavelli, from the nineteenth-century historian Jacob Burckhardt's famous and enduring representation, is commonly seen as the essential Renaissance man—in his invocation of the ancient Roman Republic, his anticlericalism, and especially his pragmatic presentation of governance and the state itself as "a work of art." Machiavelli holds a uniquely central position in the academic canon of political thought—indeed some see *The Prince* as the greatest work of political *theory* ever written, though at least one important scholar argues that, impressive as the work is, it should not be taken as *the* decisive break toward a modern theory of politics—a role one might better assign to Hobbes, who does not in fact acknowledge a debt to the infamous Florentine.

The simple designation of Machiavelli as the embodiment of "the Renaissance" ("Machiavelli lived in the Renaissance, and the Renaissance lived in Machiavelli; the communion between the man and the time seems complete" [Mansfield and Tarcov, 1996, xvii]) and of the origins of modernism may beg the same kinds of definitional, contextual, and boundary questions that, as we saw, arise in the casual use of "medieval" by IR scholars. Moreover, though Machiavelli saw his work as advancing a real rather than ideal "politics," his work is not overtly about political philosophy, or a theory of "the state," or of an abstracted state system. And though his three best-known works, *The Prince*, *The Discourses*, and *The Art of War*, can plausibly be seen as a single "political tryptich," they form a body of work that is full of scattered and sometimes contradictory observations and random reflections based on history and experience rather than a cohering argument and philosophy. The unifying theme is in fact simply the need for the shrewd prince or republican patriot to see things as they really are and how they might be changed. It is this insistence on malleability and innovation that some see as justifying Machiavelli's "modernity" and separating him from the medieval ethos, or indeed from backward-looking Renaissance humanism.

The Prince was ostensibly a practical guide for rulers (a literary genre of the time), based, as Machiavelli claimed, on his own "long experience with modern things." It offered, especially, advice about how to get power and hold on to it for those who were ambitious to rule but who lacked hereditary, traditional legitimacy. Written in the year after his exile and not published until after his death (though widely known among his associates), the book leaves open the question, however, of its intended audience and larger purposes. Clearly he hoped it would advance his claim to employment among the Medici to whom it was twice dedicated. After publication (along with the *Discourses* in 1531, four years after Machiavelli died), it famously caused a storm of outrage, but we do not have Machiavelli's own defense of his intentions. There is therefore inevitably a debate about whether his cynical "advice" should be taken at face value.

Machiavelli tells the reader that he wants to "represent things as they are in a real truth, rather than as they are imagined" (50) and that the prince must study life as it is. The virtue to which a private individual might admirably aspire was not virtuous at all in a prince, who was so to speak outside the bounds of normative morality. Machiavelli's *virtù*, a word that has been the object of great scholarly attention, carries a sense not of Christian virtue but, drawing on ancient Roman usage, of the manly action necessary to master *Fortuna* (goddess of fate, chance, or ill-fortune). In this, Machiavelli rationalizes the world around him—that of mercenaries and violent ambition, of war as simply a common means of achieving or maintaining power, and of treaties as convenient and temporary devices suited to the objectives of the moment removed from any larger ethical considerations or commitments—and thus becomes the philosopher of "reasons of state." To see Machiavelli as advancing a theory that the sovereign state in its relations with other states operates beyond or outside morality, however, requires us to shift Machiavelli from his overt focus on the opportunism of princes to the abstraction of *state* behavior and state "reasons."

Underneath, Machiavelli also seems to assume—and is embraced for this, as was Thucydides, by IR's Classical Realists—that unchanging human nature itself dictates the behavior of princes: "The wish to acquire more is admittedly a very natural and common thing" (14). And this is not unique to *The Prince*, but reflects his earliest writing in his official capacity. A report of 1503 argues that "the world has always been inhabited by men with the same passions as our own" (quoted by Hale, 1972, 47), and the same can be found in the advice he offers in his later *Discourses on Livy*: "men … have and always had the same passions" (III, 43). The argument that Machiavelli's work advances a Realpolitik based on the universality of human desires (ambition to rule, lust for acquisition and power) may overstate his reliance on the classical concept of nature itself, but his assault on the Church and pope (in the *Discourses*) and on the inutility of an effeminate Christian morality (contrary to human nature) cannot be denied. Most shockingly, he approves the cruelest devices of rule as a necessity, praising Cesare Borgia's brutality in the Romagna as conducive ultimately to the public good by ensuring unity, order, and obedience in a violent, anarchic world—an end that justifies the means.

> We can say cruelty is used well … when it is employed once for all, and one's own safety depends on it, and then is not persisted in but as far as possible turned to the good of one's subjects. (31)

Moreover, it was better to be feared than loved—since though, being greedy, men could be bought, being also ungrateful, they did not stay bought unless they also feared you. The trick was to make them fear you without hating you—but Machiavelli also notes in a characteristic aphorism that "one can be hated just as much for good deeds as for evil ones" (63).

The republican in Machiavelli nevertheless may peek out from the advice that "a man who has become prince … should, before anything else, try to win the people over" (34). He argued that princes who depended on mercenaries rather than the citizenry would never achieve stability or security. In neither case, however, is the suggestion of a need for the cooptation of the populace separate from the pragmatic problem of how a clever prince will advance *his* position. He does not, in *The Prince* at least, concern himself with the plausibly different domestic character of nonprincely (that is republican) regimes. This is left to the *Discourses*, though in that work a republic may have as much practical use for employing "tyranny" as a prince.

Finally, to what extent does Machiavelli address interstate relations directly? The prince who has secured or enlarged a state—often by warfare—must of course be concerned with keeping it. He would risk other states balancing against him (if "one power among themselves [the Italian states] should enlarge its dominion … an alliance of all the others was necessary" [38]) and the likelihood of having to defend himself: war was an instrumental and necessary part of winning and holding power, as history generally (and Florentine experience) taught. A prince must not only be a fox; in a society of wolves he must be also a lion:

> A prince … must have no other object or thought, nor acquire skill in anything, except war, its organization, and its discipline … You are bound to meet misfortune if you are unarmed because, among other reasons, people despise you. (47–8)

There was of course nothing here of natural or international law, of Cicero's or Aquinas's idea of a just war, but much suggestive of his own experience in attempting to arm Florence with an effective militia. According to Machiavelli, a war is just if "necessity" (rather broadly construed) compels one to it. In this regard, the book seems as detached and analytical as many of his reports and dispatches. And yet it famously ends with a shift to what, in the context of the times, must be seen as a utopian dream: the prospect that a powerful prince might unite all of the peninsula into a reborn Italian republic, and thus escape the humiliation of its fragmentation and dependency.

So what might be a historian's perspective on *The Prince*, as opposed to the strictly textual analysis of scholars of political thought or his Realist appropriators? Burckhardt's placement of Machiavelli remains influential among many historians, though as we have seen there may be sound historical reasons to challenge familiar clichés defining the boundary between medieval and modern. Apart from this, the historian of international relations might ask, first, whether we can be confident that Machiavelli's book helps us understand the forces shaping and pushing forward the often violent relations between states in his time and place, and, second, whether it more generally reveals universal "truths" about how politics (at both the domestic and interstate levels) operate through, in Realist discourse, stripping away the screening language of idealism and normative morality to reveal the actual motive force of self-interest and *ragion di stato*. This question takes us to a somewhat different historical issue, not whether Machiavelli tells it like it is but how his text operates within a history of ideas and within IR in particular, how it has been used and by whom and for what reasons to create a "scientific" discourse within the discipline.

For those who view IR as largely the child of its "first great debate" between "idealism" and "realism," Machiavelli must take pride of place as the father of Realpolitik in both domestic and external affairs, and *The Prince* is a foundational text in the "science" of politics and the amorality of anarchical international relations. Historicizing critics, however, argue that Realists are too quick to claim Machiavelli as a detached and modern theorizer (his "politics" are those of the fifteenth-century republican or princely Italian city-state, not the nation-state), and focus almost exclusively on *The Prince* while often ignoring the rest of Machiavelli's work—the *Discourses on Livy*, the *Florentine Histories, The Art of War*, his plays and poetry, or the surviving letters and reports he wrote in his official capacities. The major divide in Machiavellian scholarship is that between those, political scientists usually, who see him as the modern founder of Realpolitik, and those, often historians, who, using material from, especially, the

Discourses, emphasize his connections with the civic humanism of the late fourteenth and early fifteenth centuries. Machiavelli, like many of the Italian humanists, idealized the ancient Roman Republic, the greatest city-state-turned-hegemonic-empire in history, a golden age for "Italy" comparing very unfavorably with Machiavelli's own.

One debate centers around the issue of whether Machiavelli meant what he appeared to say, that ethics had little to do with statecraft. Taking his other work into consideration as well as his known sympathy for a citizens' republic, the argument might be made that his most famous work was meant to outrage and thus draw attention to the deplorable immorality of the elite of his time. Was it, in other words, a kind of satire (this was, via Spinoza, Rousseau's reading) ready to be decoded? Whatever the plausibility of this way of approaching Machiavelli's "ironical" guide to princes, most have taken him at his word as a cynical rationalizer of immorality, as, that is, "Machiavellian," a view that the practical and often acerbic advice found in his letters, reports, and dispatches in fact would appear to confirm.

Of course, IR Realists and Neorealists have long seen Machiavelli as one of their own. In an anarchy of sovereign states, necessity prevails; there is an iron logic internal to the system; and there is no alternative to Realpolitik because those who embrace an external or "higher" or absolute morality would simply fail. Consequently, there is a need for what may be called "situational" rather than absolute ethics, or an ethics of "proportionality." Machiavelli after all does not say that all ends in life justify whatever means, just that in affairs of state some ends, beneficial ultimately to the public good, justify immoral-seeming means. And even then a prince should not continue to use such means once the end has been achieved. He even makes an over-subtle argument that a ruler ought to suffer a bad conscience if he uses questionable means so that moral values might survive their necessary violation. Realists have also seized upon Machiavelli's presumed pessimistic view of human nature in order to place him with Thucydides and Hobbes in a linear discursive tradition.

Historians, especially social and cultural historians, tend to be cautious about reading classical texts of political thought without regard to context. J. G. A. Pocock has emphasized the need to see Machiavelli as both the inheritor of the civic humanism of his father's generation and as a student of the "delegitimated" politics of his own time—an era of the rise of new men not supported by tradition, custom, and heredity but self-made and dependent on short-term expedients—and the ways in which this shapes the republicanism he took from his ancient Roman Republican sources. More recently, his younger colleague in the so-called "Cambridge school of interpretation," Quentin Skinner, has emphasized the *pre*-humanist, classical Roman character of Machiavelli's republicanism, while Erica Benner has offered a reading that argues provocatively for the infamous Florentine as actually a *moral* philosopher in the Greek rather than Roman intellectual tradition. Thucydides (referred to in both *The Art of War* and *The Discourses*), Plato, and Xenophon "provide a key to Machiavelli's enigmas" and his most shocking passages "should be read ironically and dialectically" (*Machiavelli's Ethics* [2009], 11, 486). Though Benner's analysis makes a gesture toward historicist contexts, it stresses textual interpretation and depends on what some will consider unsupportable assumptions about Machiavelli's access to and use of Greek sources, as in the parallel she sees between the shocking amorality of *The Prince* and Thucydides' putting extreme arguments in the mouths of suspect speakers. Moreover, though Machiavelli cites Athens as an example of an imperial republic, he does not seem to share Thucydides' compassionate horror of war as tragedy.

Other scholars informed by postmodern literary analysis have moved away from a search for ideological meaning drawn from whatever sources, or indeed for an overarching consistency in hidden or overt messages in order to emphasize the *rhetorical* character of Machiavelli's oeuvre. Feminist scholarship stresses the gendered culture of Machiavelli's time and place and anxiety about masculinity connected to the general late medieval crisis—the waning of dependency and the rise of the ambitious but vulnerable individual. Hannah Pitkin notes that Machiavelli's *Fortuna* is a feminine threat (and "effeminato" a favorite Machiavellian epithet) to be mastered by manly *virtù*, while *Italia* (in the last chapter of *The Prince*) is a woman "beaten, despoiled, lacerated, devastated" who will welcome a rescuing prince as her savior and lover (Pitkin, 1984, 25–6). While such a reading remains grounded in historical-cultural contexts, other explorations of Machiavelli's rhetoric have been more determinedly ahistorical in teasing out the "strategies" of the text, the quite different dissimulations of *The Prince* and *The Discourses*, intended for different audiences. For Mikael Hornqvist, beyond and above "the traditional and pre-modern framework" in which Machiavelli's writing was imbedded, or the "cardboard stage set" of "its Florentine context and its contemporary trappings," Machiavelli's focus on the *cose del mondo* (the things of this world), his pessimistic view of human nature, and his rejection of the status quo reveals the mind of a deracinated modern (Hornqvist, 2004, 6, 284, 289).

In the last analysis, the issue for IR students is how convincingly *The Prince* has been made to support large theorizing within the discipline. No doubt too much has been made (against the grain of the common understanding) of Machiavelli as a civic humanist and republican moralist. But even if one accepts a reading of Machiavelli as indeed the amoralist he seems to be, IR scholars of a critical theory or Constructivist leaning nevertheless have questioned the uses that his most famous work has been made to serve in contemporary IR. Why, they ask, should we take a text that rationalizes the gangster politics of late medieval city-states or Italian Renaissance machismo and generalize it as appropriate to, say, the operation of democratic nation-states of the modern era?

Recommended reading

For work on the growth of the state that engages the medieval era, see Joseph R. Strayer, *On the Medieval Origins of the Modern State* (1970); Charles Tilly (ed.), *The Formation of National States in Western Europe* (1975); and Thomas Ertman, *Birth of the Leviathan: Building States and Regimes in Medieval and Early Modern Europe* (1997). Also, David

Abulafia and Nora Berend (eds.), *Medieval Frontiers: Concepts and Practices* (2002). Bernard Guenée, *States and Rulers in Later Medieval Europe* (1985 [trans. by Juliet Vale]), focuses on the fourteenth and fifteenth centuries. For a controversial critique of the academic use of the concept of "feudalism," see Susan Reynolds, *Fiefs and Vassals: The Medieval Evidence Reinterpreted* (1994). For aspects of the problem of the medieval in IR theory, see Benno Teschke, "Geopolitical Relations in the European Middle Ages: History and Theory," *International Organization* 52 (1998). Markus Fischer's attempt to apply Neorealist theory to (nonstate) medieval actors, "Feudal Europe, 800–1300: Communal Discourse and Conflictual Practices," *International Organization* 46 (1992), 427–66, sparked a sharp Constructivist critique from R. B. Hall and F. V. Kratochwill, "Medieval Tales: Neorealist 'Science' and the Abuse of History," *International Organization* 47 (1993), 479–91.

For Byzantium, begin with Jonathan Shepherd et al. (eds.), *The Cambridge History of the Byzantine Empire* (2008). Also, Jonathan Shepherd and Simon Franklin (eds.), *Byzantine Diplomacy* (1990), including H. Kennedy's paper on "Byzantine-Arab Diplomacy in the Near East from the Islamic Conquests to the Mid Eleventh Century," 133–44. There is a substantial literature on medieval Islam and its "Golden Age" of science, scholarship, and empire. J. J. Saunders' brief survey is still useful for a political overview of Islamic-Western relations before the rise of the Ottomans, *A History of Medieval Islam* (1965). Also see the relevant chapters in W. Montgomery Watt's well-known *Islamic Political Thought* (1998 edn.) and Anthony Black, *The History of Islamic Political Thought* (2nd edn., 2011). The Crusades have generated some interest among IR scholars and international historians recently. See, for instance, Tal Dingott Alkopher, "The Social (and Religious) Meanings that Constitute War: The Crusade as Realpolitik vs. Socialpolitik," *International Studies Quarterly* 49 (2005), 715–37, or Andrew A. Latham, "Theorizing the Crusades: Identity, Institutions, and Religious War in Medieval Latin Christendom," *International Studies Quarterly* 55 (2011), 223–43. The history of diplomacy in the medieval West has been relatively neglected in general texts, but see Guenée, *States and Rulers*, 137–53. D. E. Queller, *The Office of Ambassador in the Middle Ages* (1967) is a useful older source. On medieval diplomacy in one Western kingdom, see Pierre Chaplais' rather technical *English Diplomatic Practice in the Middle Ages* (2003).

There is a vast literature on Machiavelli. Anthony Grafton's "Introduction" to *The Prince* (Penguin, 2003) is a good, concise beginning, as still is J. R. Hale's only somewhat dated *Machiavelli and Renaissance Italy* (1972), supplemented by Quentin Skinner's *Machiavelli* (1981). David Boucher's *Political Theories of International Relations: From Thucydides to the Present* (1998) offers an overview. For a well-known historicist argument locating Machiavelli as a civic humanist, see J. G. A. Pocock, *The Machiavellian Moment: Florentine Political Thought and the Atlantic Republican Tradition* (1975); also, Quentin Skinner's *The Renaissance*, Vol. 1 (1978). For Skinner's more recent views, see "Machiavelli's Discorsi and the Pre-Humanist Origins of Republican Ideas," in G. Bock, Q. Skinner, and M. Viroli (eds.), *Machiavelli and Republicanism* (1990), 121–41. Still useful older works include Herbert Butterfield,

The Statecraft of Machiavelli (1940); Felix Gilbert, *Machiavelli and Guicciardini: Politics and History in Sixteenth Century Florence* (1965); and J. M. Whitfield, *Discourses on Machiavelli* (1969). Roberto Ridolfi, *The Life of Niccolò Machiavelli* (trans., 1963), has long been the standard biography, but also see Corrado Vivanti's *Niccolò Machiavelli: An Intellectual Biography* (2013, in English translation).

CHAPTER 6
THE SOVEREIGN STATE AND THE "WESTPHALIAN SYSTEM" IN EARLY MODERN EUROPE

The Congress of Westphalia (1643–8) and the resulting peace treaties that ended the Thirty Years' War are of great importance in IR historiography. Their significance is in a sense metahistorical, constituting, as this literature often asserts, *the* paradigm break that introduces and structures the unitary, sovereign state system that is arguably with us still. Thus, "Westphalian" is a kind of shorthand for a bundle of concepts central to much IR theory, signifying more than the actual historically specific and chronologically bounded events at the German cities of Münster and Osnabrück.

The European territorial state before Westphalia

The Westphalian settlement of the Thirty Years' War is generally taken in mainstream IR to mark the European-wide acceptance, by treaty, of the concept or ideal of the autonomous, sovereign, territorial state and a state system in which these constitute the basic, irreducible units, answerable to no higher authority, politically supreme within their borders, and pursuing policies legitimately dictated by secular *raison d'état*. This is of course an abstraction of a much messier mid-seventeenth-century political reality. Moreover, the idea that such a new system replaced an earlier one of "feudal" ambiguity is better tailored to the central European (i.e., German) Holy Roman Empire, than to the monarchies and republics beyond—in Italy, the Netherlands, Spain, France, England, or Sweden.

Medieval origins

Just how "sovereign" these states already were involves the complicated history of the origin and development of European (and especially northwestern European) political practice, legal concepts, and popular mentality in the previous 300 or 400 years. Much of the literature on the "medieval origins" of the modern state in Europe revolves around the issue of state sovereignty. While the concept of absolute sovereignty may not be developed in European political theory until the work of Renaissance and Baroque writers like Jean Bodin, Robert Filmer, or Thomas Hobbes, elements of its evolution and practice clearly reach back as far as the twelfth-century emergence of consolidating kingdoms. But beyond the political-legal issue of the growth of royal prerogative within such bounded territories, there is also the wider, contextual issue of changes in popular identity—that is, the growth of a sense of patriotic loyalty that transcends the local, demeans those of other realms, and works against a cosmopolitan sense of the unity of Christendom. The two processes—the emergence of legally sovereign kingdoms and republics and the growth of proto-national consciousness— are closely intertwined. If, as one scholar searching for the origins of the modern state puts it, "a state exists chiefly in the hearts and minds of its people" (Strayer, 1970, 5), such "identity formation" may simply draw upon a settled sense of place and inclusion, as with Machiavelli's Florence, or beg a less spatial, early medieval process of "ethno-genesis"—a much-contested idea, in part because of the way nationalists in the nineteenth century and fascists in the twentieth manipulated the concept of an original people (or *Urvolk*).

Historians, then, are likely to approach the complicated issue of "the origin of the state" (admittedly a somewhat Whiggish project), from a number of angles—social, economic, and cultural, as well as more narrowly legal and political. Modernists tend to pursue social, economic, and bureaucratic lines of argument in tracing the rise of the state; postmodernists have been more interested in a cultural analysis of identity and "imagined communities." In IR, however, with the exception of some Constructivists, the mainstream has construed the Westphalian issue as essentially one of political-legal definition and state practice, and has tightly focused on the innovations, as they are represented, of the European seventeenth century.

The argument for *medieval* origins of the modern state was advanced by a well-regarded historian at Princeton University, Joseph Strayer, whose series of lectures on this theme was published in 1970. Strayer did not contest the "difference" of the medieval political world, but proposed an *evolution* toward the modern concept of sovereignty from as early as the twelfth century in, especially, the kingdoms of England and France: "by 1300 the king of England had not only the attributes of sovereignty, he had, and knew he had, sovereign power. He made laws, formally and deliberately … " (Strayer, 1970, 44). In France, the "essential elements of the modern state" developed from the reign of Philip Augustus (1180–1223), and by the mid-fifteenth century Louis XI was able to consolidate his authority through simple administrative decree. For both kingdoms, these elements included a territorial heartland, permanent institutions of royal justice and finance, the use and development of Roman law, and a degree of stability "essential for state-building." The important test, according to Strayer, for determining the emergence of state sovereignty was whether there had been a significant shift in popular loyalty from family, local community, feudal lord, or church to the crown, as evidenced in the growth of court ceremonial ("the majesty that surrounds a king") long before the Renaissance and Baroque articulation of theories of divine right. While other loyalties do not disappear, there are grounds for arguing that, at least in northwestern Europe, the crown had emerged with a special moral authority and quasi-religious mystique by the fourteenth century. Though these dynastic monarchies were territorially ambiguous and prone to internal feudal conflict (from the English Wars of the Roses of the fifteenth century to the French Fronde of the mid-seventeenth century), the long era witnesses a continuous growth of executive authority—enhanced by the chief business of the state, the conduct of war. Arguably there was also, important to IR, the evolution of a states *system* that saw the growth of regular diplomacy, formal alliances, and treaty-making.

Historical Sociology, indebted as it was to Weberian notions of the importance of bureaucratic institutions and instrumental rationality from the Renaissance and Reformation era on, and to the notion of a sovereignty that is defined by the monopoly of the legitimate means of domestic violence, was slow to embrace the larger time frame for modern state-building, though there was here too from the 1970s a fresh look at premodern eras in the work of Charles Tilly, Perry Anderson, and Michael Mann that dealt with the anticipation of modern state regimes before the Renaissance. Like Strayer, these scholars often associated state-building with the requirements of warfare, a connection that has been widely but not universally accepted.

Within IR, critics of the claims of scientistic structuralism that Westphalia constituted a paradigm shift that it could describe but not adequately explain have attacked both the definitions and the chronology of the Westphalia thesis. The Constructivist John Ruggie proposed in a much-read article of 1993, "Territoriality and Beyond," that sovereignty required not simply the growth of secular, centralized government, but a reconceptualization of "territory," that is, well-defined and exclusionary borders rather than overlapping frontiers and superimposed and tangled jurisdictions. Arguably this shift, in the West at least, had begun by the thirteenth century in the progressive consolidation of two increasingly separate realms—the internal realm of public peace and the external realm of sovereign war. The emerging state system was, therefore, "socially constructed" out of three dimensions of collective European experience: "material environments, strategic behavior, and social epistemology [or 'mental equipment']" (Ruggie, 1993, 152).

Clearly, as Joseph Strayer argued, the germ of the early modern sovereign state is present at least in Western Europe during the High Middle Ages. The wars between France and England demonstrate not only dynastic ambitions, but some idea of nation. These polities were increasingly legally and culturally unified (a slow process) at least at the level of the political and economic elites, though overmighty noble subjects continue through the early modern period to bedevil them with civil war and regional anarchy. There is also evidence of the growth of popular regard for the spiritual and secular authority of the crown. At the same time, there are significant signs that popular reverence for the universal Church—for the pope in Rome or monastic institutions—was waning. From Wycliffe's England to Hus's Bohemia the late medieval Church was on the defensive.

In Italy and in the southern German principalities, the contest between imperial and papal authority had long provoked heated and well-organized factions—the so-called papal Guelphs and imperial Ghibellines of the communes whose emergence as independent city-states had been part of the eleventh- and twelfth-century crisis of imperial authority. The Florentine poet Dante had, in his *De Monarchia*, taken the emperor's side, as the legitimate guarantor of earthly happiness, which required a peace that only the sword could provide. In 1324, an Italian physician and scholar, Marsilio of Padua, produced a work, *Defensor Pacis*, that advocated the authority of the emperor (as defender of the peace) over the universal claims of the pope (then at Avignon). An analogous "imperial" authority had been sometimes asserted on behalf of lesser territorial sovereigns from at least the twelfth century. Marsilio's tract was widely read and debated, and well known in the courts of those looking to justify their own territorial authority, and who were therefore encouraged to see themselves as little emperors within their own sovereign spheres. In fact, according to some scholars, the notion of a continuing jurisdictional contest between universal emperor and territorial princes into the early modern era is something of a scholarly myth: the authority of the emperor, at least since the failure of the Hohenstauffens to reestablish it, had long been more symbolic than real. According to one scholar at least, "at no time in the middle ages did other kings defer to the emperor" (Osiander, 2001, 119).

If late medieval and early Renaissance writers drew on classical antiquity (the Roman Republic) and late antiquity (Justinian's Byzantium) in establishing or rationalizing the sovereign independence of city-states and territorial monarchies, this does not mean that we can ignore the earlier middle ages or see them as some political realists do as chiefly irrelevant to the development of a modern state system. The confused and compromised sovereignty of the medieval period—its mixture of feudal and proto-modern elements, of the universal and the territorial, of conflicting jurisdictions and borderless dynastic ambition—does not of course simply disappear overnight into a Renaissance of secularism, calculating princes, and unitary states. Historians are more likely to see evolution than sudden breaks. In some ways, the late medieval period anticipated the new order, while the new order itself contained elements of past practice and mentality—as a study of a complex and self-contradictory king like Henry VIII of England would reveal. Nor did all of "Europe" move into a political rebirth at the same pace in the same era—the Mediterranean basin, the prosperous northwest, central Europe, and the far north and eastern realms moved if at all at their own pace and in their own way.

In 1994, the political scientist and IR scholar Hendrik Spruyt revisited Strayer's medieval era, informed by the considerable debate in the intervening period over structural change in the European states system and the various approaches of other disciplines like Anthropology and Sociology to the problem of origins. Though accepting much of Strayer's view that the medieval period saw the emergence of "the notion of sovereignty," Spruyt rejects a linear and inevitable evolution of sovereignty, defined as internal hierarchy and external autonomy, in favor of a more historically contingent situation of "fits and starts" where various alternatives ("varieties of institutional forms") to medieval practice emerged out of the decline of the feudal order—the city-state, the league of city-states (like the Hanse), and sovereign monarchies. Rather than the requirements of warfare, which Charles Tilly had argued was the main driver of state formation, the key underlying factor for Spruyt is the spread of trade, the monetarization of the economy and the ascendance of mercantile groups and urban centers, and the "different coalitions and bargains between kings, aristocracy, and towns" that account for institutional variation across Europe (Spruyt, 1994, 4). In France, a "social bargain" between king and burghers allowed for the recentralization of the Capetian monarchy as sovereign over church and nobles; in central Europe the reverse happened—in the emperor's bargain with the nobles against the towns.

Renaissance monarchy: Sovereignty and the dynastic state

The "new monarchies" of late medieval and Renaissance Western Europe were to prove more efficient in the long run than competing types of political organization. On the one hand, the dynastic sovereign state in the Renaissance West was buttressed, as Ernst Kantorowicz famously argued in his influential book, *The King's Two Bodies* (1957), by the medieval concept of the transcendent, undying, spiritual body of the monarch as the symbolic basis for state sovereignty, a kind of "political theology." On the other hand, the humanist reverence for the ancient Roman Republic, so notable among Machiavelli's generation, encouraged ideals of citizenship and service that enhanced the claims of the sovereign state to the public loyalty that lawyer-administrators like Thomas Cromwell devised and encouraged. This coalescence of *internal* authority, it can be argued, also generated a "systemic effect" in interstate relations that saw, through competition and emulation, the spread of the unitary sovereign state, constituted and confirmed through warfare, and the consequent further decline of the feudal principle in interstate affairs.

If the rise of Spain as a European power was symbolized in the mid-sixteenth century by the Peace of Cateau-Cambresis (1559) that confirmed its control of most of Italy, the Spanish inheritance of Charles V's vast empire proved thinly overstretched. Successive decades would see power slip away to the rising regimes of the northwest of Europe: France, especially, but also England, with new players emerging in the United Provinces and Sweden. Historians are likely to search for social and economic factors of importance that underlie whatever political and ideological change may have occurred, and this means engaging domestic (in Waltzian terms, "second image") factors in the creation of any new European-wide "system." These would include the significant resumption of population growth after the series of plagues that had devastated Europe since the fourteenth century. There was, along with a growth in population, a growth in taxable wealth from agriculture and commerce that allowed territorial monarchies to extend their reach by giving them more effective control over the administration of justice.

But the picture is not so simple. The era may have witnessed the "rise of the sovereign state," enshrined in law and a degree of centralization, but securing a secular monopoly of power was a fitful and unfinished business. Rebellion in the sixteenth and seventeenth centuries invariably has at least a feudal undercurrent. Moreover, the patrimonialization of the most remunerative offices, the expenses of a more opulent court, and the ruinous cost of nearly continuous warfare brought inflation and periodic fiscal crisis nearly everywhere by the seventeenth century, undermining these regimes' ability to meet the most significant domestic and external challenges of this period. The phenomenon, however, that most challenged both the old empire and, ultimately, the new monarchies (though it had overtones of class and new-versus-old wealth) was, arguably, less material than ideological. The Protestant Reformation both polarized the international system and, with the rise of Calvinist subversion, threatened the unitary sovereignty of the domestic realm in much of west and central Europe. What began as a humanist critique from within of the abuses and excesses of the universal Church rapidly spread, especially north of the Mediterranean basin, to challenge the basis of the legitimate religious and political authority of pope and emperor.

If the Reformation divided many polities, as in France, it could also serve to enhance the authority of other, often upwardly mobile regimes, as in England, Holland, or Sweden, and of some German princes. The English case demonstrates most clearly how it could be harnessed to reconstruct the ambiguous concept of sovereignty in terms that anticipate the modern unitary state. The parvenu Tudors had famously brought to an end the divisive, exhausting civil wars of the fifteenth century, but the Renaissance state was a fragile thing. It was chronically short of money and doubtful about how far the King's writ (for justice and tax-gathering) ran in a countryside where noble families could still claim a significant degree of loyalty. The Reformation (as an act of state) in England offered practical solutions: not least the assumption of papal revenues and the vast wealth of the monasteries. The legalistic way in which this was accomplished is significant. This involved making explicit, by means of parliamentary statute, the general principle that a king of England was inheritor to both the secular authority of the Emperor *and* the religious authority of the Pope—within the bounds of the territory of the English state: "this realm of England is an empire, and so hath been accepted in the world, governed by one supreme head and king, having the dignity and royal estate of the imperial crown of the same" (Act in Restraint of Appeals, 1533).

Such indivisible sovereignty was not just an extension of the medieval theory of the mystique of monarchy, but in England harnessed and made necessary an institution, parliament, that had been in decline. The Tudors needed as much legitimacy as they could find—at the cost of having also to accept a degree of parliamentary collaboration in the administration of justice, the approval of laws, and the power to tax. And in so doing the authority of the king, that is, the absolute, indivisible sovereignty of the state, was expressed not as the crown alone but as *King-in-Parliament*. The same idea of the indivisible sovereignty of a unitary state could be achieved in other ways—as in an increasingly absolutist France that nevertheless remained an administrative mosaic of traditionally quasi-autonomous regions. If in England and the Netherlands the "rising bourgeoisie" was arguably central to what would be the brokered, constitutional, parliamentary, nonabsolutist state, in France, as Perry Anderson has argued, they were "bought off" by the crown and "feudalized."

The long familiar distinction in much scholarship between limited and absolutist monarchies may, however, be of less importance than it once seemed. Certainly both were dependent on fiscal-military resources and interacted in the states system in much the same way, and in both an emerging rhetoric, a "theory of the state," located the dynastic monarch in a larger idea. The sixteenth-century English formula of king-in-parliament as well as the French (and early seventeenth-century English) absolutist ideology of king-as-patriarch catch the growing sense that the sovereign was less a dynast who "owned" a state, than the protector of the people's security, wealth, and religion.

Renaissance and Baroque diplomacy

Elaborate medieval rituals celebrating, with jousts and feasting, the personal promises that bound princes under Christian oath persisted into the Renaissance but such summitry between monarchs was a rare occurrence, and the fact that treaties were now studiously copied, registered, and archived indicates the emergence of a less personalized, more formal and regular European system of international relations, inspired significantly by fifteenth- and sixteenth-century Italian diplomatic practice. The court of powerful players like King Charles VIII of France, Emperor Maximilian I, or Pope Julius II could be expected to attract a regular host of envoys sent from great and lesser states hoping for influence or information.

Early modern European diplomacy owed much to the Italian model, especially that of Venice. This involved a degree of bureaucracy, if not professionalization, and a regular system of agents sent abroad. Nevertheless, it would be rash, as one scholar has recently observed, to exaggerate the degree to which the Renaissance system anticipates the modern. The "independent" Italian city-states were hardly regarded by larger powers as in any way formally equal (Machiavelli complained of being openly treated as "Mr Nothing" at the imperial court)—something that the elaborate attention devoted to hierarchic precedence reinforced. Moreover, the Italian innovation of the resident ambassador, though increasingly common, was a costly charge on state resources and did not become universal, nor did such envoys yet enjoy the assured legal protection of extra-territoriality (i.e., diplomatic immunity).

There was nevertheless an increase in both what might be called "continuous diplomacy," involving information-gathering and regular reportage, and the reach of regular Western European diplomatic contact—to the Ottoman court in Constantinople and that of the Grand Dukes of Muscovy. It has also been argued, more debatably perhaps, that Italian Renaissance humanism encouraged a rhetorical, representational transformation that focused on the role of the diplomat as mediator, someone who, as Gentili observed, both brings peoples together and keeps them apart. A concern with the *ethics* of mediation could paint the ambassador as either angel or pimp (Hampton, 2009, 3–5 and Chapter 2).

In fact, the ambassadors of the new monarchies played numerous roles—not merely as go-betweens, but as temporizers, negotiators, and bribers of buyable courtiers. The imperatives of "state interest" pursued opportunistically are echoed in the punning observation of Sir Henry Wotton, James I's envoy to Venice, that an ambassador was "an honest man sent to lie abroad for his country." There were, inevitably, Italian overtones of a necessary amorality, of, perhaps, Castiglione's advocacy of *sprezzatura* (the art of appearing artless). It became a commonplace in seventeenth-century manuals for diplomats (as in Juan Antonio de Vera y Figueroa's well-known *Embaxador* of 1620) that though ambassadors should maintain virtuous private lives, dissimulation and deceit were necessary in public life. Abram de Wicquefort, a Dutch double agent employed by Holland, France, Brandenburg, and others and present at the Congress of Westphalia, wrote of the "art" of diplomacy, the need for experience and clear-sighted calculation, and the unimportance of a conventional sense of morality. His observation that a country could afford to be served by bad men, but not by incompetent ones, has a Machiavellian resonance, and indeed he openly admired the scandalous Florentine and recommended his works. By the end of the seventeenth century it had also become a cliché—in a growing literary genre of "advice for ambassadors"—that a diplomat had to have charm and cultivation, the better to be able to discover the weaknesses of those with whom he dealt. But charm, experience, and a flexible conscience were not enough. With the regularization of continuous diplomacy as a function of state, one observer, François de Callières, claimed (in 1716) that the diplomat ought to be *trained* as in other professions—in languages, and in knowledge of the material resources of other countries and "the limits" of their "territorial sovereignty."

Diplomacy was not only about intelligence-gathering, alliance-building, and the prevention, conduct, or resolution of war. It also might involve covertly weakening present or future enemies—especially those who were themselves likely to intervene in the domestic affairs of one's own country. Elizabeth I's chief adviser from 1550 to 1598, William Cecil, Lord Burghley, claimed that in order to counter Catholic subversion in England he intended to "build fires in other men's houses." A generation later the great *eminence grise* of the French monarchy, Cardinal Richelieu (chief minister, 1624–42, of Louis XIII) pursued a similar policy of consolidating royal authority within France while encouraging instability abroad (especially in the Empire) through an extensive system of spies and bribery. With Cecil, there was always ambiguity about whether he was more concerned to preserve Protestantism in the face of a Spanish-enforced counterreformation or the fragile political establishment that he served. These were much the same thing. With Richelieu (though he was nominally a Cardinal of the church), the primary goal was always secular political advantage; that is, a calculating *raison d'état* prevailed. As for ethics, he once observed, "Man is immortal, his salvation is hereafter. The state has no immortality, its salvation is now or never."

For Richelieu, in the era of the so-called Wars of Religion, the enemies of the state might be Protestant or Catholic. He employed a variety of means to counter the Habsburgs: a multilateral network of alliances (as with the Northern German Protestant states), bilateral alliances for coordinated action (as with Sweden), the protection of weak territories to enable the passage of French forces, covert subsidies and the loan of troops short of formal involvement, and of course direct military action. Costly and unpredictable war was, however, the least preferred option. His opportunism dictated that *dialogue between states be continuous*, that diplomacy be ongoing with friend and foe, requiring permanent establishments rather than special envoys. This leads in the next generation to wide acceptance of the idea of the "extra-territoriality" of ambassadors in permanent residence.

In the Realist pantheon, Richelieu takes first place in the era—and yet, his reputation may rest more on his own memoirs than on reality: however shrewd his calculations and intention to further the interests of the state, he can hardly be said to have tamed the nobility (the end of his era saw a dangerous rebellion of disaffected nobles) or, indeed, to have created a system of administrators more dedicated to the interests of the state than to personal profit. His successor Cardinal Mazarin shamelessly amassed a huge fortune and on his deathbed worried, not about the French state but his own family's future.

Westphalia in IR

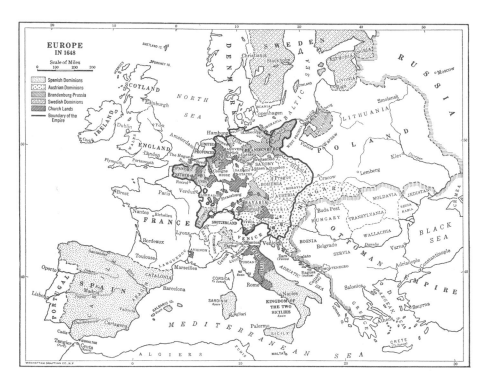

Figure 6.1 Europe at the end of the Thirty Years' War.

Source: Albert Hyma, *A Short History of Europe, 1500–1815* (New York: F. S. Crofts & Co., 1928).

IR scholars of many schools of thought have been until relatively recently remarkably comfortable with reproducing the familiar, but generally unexamined, assumption that the modern system of secular, sovereign, unitary, and formally equal states was born out of, or at least confirmed by, the peace settlement that ended the Thirty Years' War (Figure 6.1). Thanks largely to nineteenth-century nationalist historians, the war (or series of wars from 1618 to 1648) was commonly represented as a struggle of (mostly Protestant) states attempting to defend themselves against the hegemonic designs of the Habsburg Holy Roman Emperor, the Roman Catholic Pope, and the Habsburg Spanish king. Hardly any professional historian would now accept such a view without serious reservations. Nevertheless, in IR's metanarrative the war and its peace continue to be invoked within a number of the discipline's important discourses: first, they represent a definitive move, it is said, from the confused, universal claims of political and religious authority of the medieval world to an anarchic territorial state system that would henceforth operate normatively through the doctrine of balance of power; second, it is claimed that they brought about—through exhaustion and legalistic resolution—the end of the era of religious conflict in Europe both within and among states, and its replacement by an essentially secular *raison d'état*; and third, they confirm that the defeat of the emperor and pope legitimated the central concept of modern interstate relations—that of absolute state sovereignty. There are sound reasons why historians may be uneasy with such conclusions and how the history of this "foundational" event has been misread in the construction of contemporary theories of IR.

The Thirty Years' War and the European state system

Far from expressing or threatening universal hegemony, the Holy Roman Emperor had significantly declined in political clout by the seventeenth century. A lengthy war against Ottoman expansion in the east, heavily subsidized by the imperial Reichstag, left the Austrian Habsburgs bankrupt and politically weakened. Their plight was exacerbated by the decline of feudal loyalties that the Protestantism of many of the German princes encouraged, the personal caliber of those who inherited the imperial crown, and the inherently limiting nature of the imperial constitution. The Empire was a customary system of quasi-autonomous polities roughly countering the theoretical authority of the emperor, whose governing role was limited and who possessed few military resources outside of his own hereditary domains. There was no central government per se and local princes enjoyed a degree of territorial sovereignty, the whole being knit together to some extent by courtly ceremony, the imperial Reichstag that represented electors, princes, and cities, and judicial institutions (imperial courts) to which regional issues and matters relating to the emperor's prerogatives might be appealed. While the Habsburgs enjoyed more authority within their own territories and as elective kings of Bohemia and Hungary, as a whole their *imperial* regime was loosely and ambiguously constructed and their prerogative authority frequently contested. The whole had been threatened by religious upheaval with the rise of Lutheran and Calvinist theology—not only in north German estates and Luther's Saxony, but in Bohemia and Hungary, and even in Vienna itself.

The Treaty or Peace of Augsburg (1555) had been a compromise between the then emperor, Charles V, and the Protestant Smalkaldic League of Lutheran princes that his army had defeated. While it promised that Lutherans would not be punished for heresy and provided that disputes be submitted to the imperial court, it was only subsequently (after 1586) that the doctrine associated with the Peace, *cuius regio, eius religio* (allowing the local prince to decide the religion of his territory) became explicit. Cumulative stresses on this framework of tacit religious pluralism led to the coalescence of polarized Protestant and Catholic armed defensive organization within the Empire and to the determination of Ferdinand II (r. 1619–37), to re-Catholicize the Empire, inspiring among other things a fear that ecclesiastical property transferred to Lutherans would be repossessed. In 1619, a succession crisis in Bohemia set off a more general conflict.

The Thirty Years' War was a long series of campaigns and countercampaigns, pauses and restarts, which can be grouped into significantly different phases. The first was marked by the Bohemian crisis, when Protestant nobles there rejected the new emperor in favor of the election as their king of the Calvinist prince, Frederick, the Elector Palatine. The second (1625–9) saw the ambitious attempt by the Lutheran king of Denmark, sensing the opportunity of a general collapse of Habsburg authority, to extend his power in northern Germany. The third (1630–5) saw the dramatic emergence of Sweden under Gustavus Adolphus, who displaced Denmark in his ambition to extend by military conquest Swedish territorial claims in northern Germany, and perhaps to claim the imperial crown itself. This latter phase also saw the maturing of Richelieu's anti-Habsburg schemes both to weaken Spain by interdicting its connection with the Spanish Netherlands and, as he himself said, "to ruin the House of Austria completely,… to profit from its dismemberment, and to make the [French] king the head of all the catholic princes of Christendom." Finally, the war was savagely prolonged among a devastated people after the 1635 Peace of Prague failed over the divisive issue of amnesty. Fighting continued during the long sitting of the peace congress from 1643 to 1648.

The historical narrative of the Thirty Years' War, long influenced by nineteenth-century Protestant and nationalist historiography, has shifted significantly of late. The 350th anniversary of Westphalia focused revisionist research and publication by specialist historians, often German—though with little apparent impact on the way English-speaking IR scholars conventionally invoke the war and the peace. The most recent history in English, however, Peter H. Wilson's *The Thirty Years' War: Europe's Tragedy* (2009), is an accessible account that makes extensive use of the wide range of current scholarship. In this telling, what emerges is rather less simply or primarily a war of religion (the king of Saxony, a Protestant, supported the emperor, while Catholic France allied with Lutheran Sweden). Nor is it clearly a tale of Catholic Habsburg hubris. The closer and more detailed the examination of the nature of the imperial system, the fighting, and the alliances, the more difficult it is to draw the kinds of general conclusions from them that often appear in textbooks.

The war was, on the ground, brutal and destructive—swathes of central Europe were devastated, the population reduced, and trade and agriculture disrupted, though perhaps not to the extent once assumed in popular memory and by mostly Protestant historians projecting generally from the infamous destruction of the city of Magdeburg. Traditionally the rapaciousness of undisciplined mercenary troops hired by contractor-generals like Wallenstein was blamed for much of the devastation. But some military historians have questioned conventional wisdom about the contract system, and argued that, as a necessity in circumstances where regimes did not have the immediate resources to field large armies, it was rather more effective and disciplined than once thought. Nor does the argument that religious motivation deepened the brutality of troops in the field sit well with the fact that contract armies were not entirely recruited on the basis of faith (indeed defeated troops of whatever confession were often pressed into service by a victorious army). Civilians suffered greatly from pillage and rape in the areas where armies transited, but not necessarily for their faith, and many more died or were driven from their homes by famine and disease. The wars were certainly expensive for the powers concerned. The resources of Sweden were especially overextended and the country's exhaustion (Gustavus Adolphus was killed at the battle of Lützen in 1632) would open the door for the rise of other new players—Russia and Brandenburg-Prussia—in the decades to come.

The Congress of Westphalia and the treaties

Complex negotiations with the object of ending the fighting in the Empire and the eighty years of off and on warfare between Spain and the Dutch Republic began in 1643. The instructions given the main envoys (sovereigns did not attend) were vague about how the "peace of Christendom" was to be achieved, though the French and the Swedes publically invoked the issue of "German liberty" and insisted that the German estates be admitted as full participants. Negotiations ultimately involved the Habsburg emperor (whose representative Maximilian von Trauttmansdorff emerged as the central figure at the conference), the quasi-sovereign princes and free cities of the Empire, the Dutch Republic, and the kingdoms of Spain, France (Richelieu had died in 1642), and Sweden. Negotiations proceeded through intervening years of fighting, though the cities of Osnabrück and Münster were designated neutral zones for the ongoing conference—the one hosting deliberations involving the Empire and its estates, the other the war between Spain and the Dutch. France's dispute with Spain was not addressed. Protestants and Catholics, present at both venues, met separately.

Though medieval church councils were a kind of precedent, the Congress of Westphalia can be seen as the first modern peace conference. There were 194 official participants (178 from the various imperial estates). In all, some 235 ambassadors, plenipotentiaries, and lesser envoys attended, accompanied, often, by numerous staff. The settlement that was ultimately reached in 1648 was in fact more "mixed" and pragmatically limited than some expected—or IR scholars sometimes assume, though interpretation of the congress's consequences and historical importance rests on rather more than the details of the treaties. Beyond the complex arrangements within the Empire (restitution of religious property, representation in imperial institutions, etc.), there were three main international agreements, two signed at Münster involving, first, Spain and the United Provinces and, second, the Empire and France, and a third at Osnabrück involving the

Empire and Sweden. The Peace was widely celebrated at the time, and the published text ran through thirty editions within a year. Its memory was kept alive long after in annual festivals in German cities and towns.

The first article of the treaties at both Münster and Osnabrück referred to a "Christian, general and permanent peace," a nod to the medieval ideal and to papal exhortation (the papacy was nevertheless a largely spent political force and had been excluded from meaningful deliberations). In the current view of researching historians more knowledgeable about the actual events and better versed in the documentary evidence, the IR presentation of the settlement, emphasizing its supposed secularity (the "end of the wars of religion") and the limitation of Habsburg sovereign authority, has tended to oversimplify and exaggerate.

The religious settlement is certainly more complex than often suggested: while the settlement did ensure a degree of toleration, including the right of minorities to practice their religion, this certainly did not "take religion out of politics." Rather than simply confirming the right of local rulers to dictate the theological beliefs of their subjects (as in the years after the Augsburg settlement), Westphalia "fixed" the religious character of states as had prevailed in the normative year of 1624. This was, in fact, a limitation rather than enhancement of the domestic "sovereignty" of these German princes. Nevertheless, most historians would endorse the general sense that the settlement "changed imperial culture" and shifted imperial governance from dreams of recovering a universal (Catholic) character to one of dickering over the relative weight of Protestant and Catholic representation in imperial institutions.

Much has been made of the guarantee that the imperial estates were henceforth free to conduct foreign relations of their own beyond the Empire, to ally with whomever they wished. But this was in fact a limited freedom—they could not wage *offensive* war, and continued to be subject to the jurisdiction of imperial legal institutions. It is hard to justify the common assertion that the settlement directly enabled a system (and doctrine) of sovereign balancing, or that it legitimated the view that these principalities were in fact henceforth fully sovereign. At the most, according to Wilson, it further "eroded" the medieval principle of hierarchy and was "a major step" toward a modern system of formal equality among sovereign states. At the same time, it may be argued that a practical effect of the peace was to save, clarify, and somewhat enhance Austrian Habsburg authority that had waned significantly in the previous century. As Wilson concludes, Westphalia "injected new life into [the Empire's] constitution and strengthened its political culture" (Wilson, 2009, 672, 769, 778).

The "myth" of Westphalia

… the Treaty of Westphalia … made the territorial state the cornerstone of the modern state system. (Hans Morgenthau, 1948)

The actual institution of the balance of power … was an implicit objective of the Peace of Westphalia of 1648, which marked the end of Habsburg pretensions to universal monarchy. (Hedley Bull, 1977)

> ... the shift in Europe from the medieval world to the modern international system ... took full shape at the Peace of Westphalia in 1648. (Daniel Philpott, 2001)

The debate over Westphalia in IR scholarship intensified with the assault on Realism and Neorealism in the 1980s and 1990s, and continues. While scholars would likely agree that the Congress of Westphalia has significance as a diplomatic event and a process—that it encouraged the subsequent development of multilateral diplomacy and, especially, the practice of ending major wars with general conferences—most elements of the standard IR narrative of Westphalia, its presumed suppression of the supposed universalist and hegemonic ambitions of the Habsburg emperors and the establishment of a "Westphalian system" of unitary sovereign states, have been challenged. In very general terms, the commanding idea of a "paradigm break" in the mid-seventeenth century has been vigorously denied by, on the one hand, those scholars who argue, as we have seen, that the sovereign territorial monarchical state was already well developed in western European mentality and practice. Others admit a shift "from medieval to modern" but see this as a long-term phenomenon (especially in mentality), that, in Andreas Osiander's opinion, was "never even completed during the *Ancien Régime*" (i.e., by 1789), and consequently the representation of the settlement found in most IR literature is "a figment of the imagination" (Osiander, 2001a, 121; 2001b, 261). For some, the modern state system was not born until the era of the French Revolution and the normalization of the idea of nation-state.

"Westphalia" constitutes an important "discourse" in IR, and its twentieth-century history throws light on the discipline's own development. An early "idealist" understanding related the Congress and its settlement to ideas of international order and community, seeing in them a forerunner of the League of Nations idea. Though there were alternative, prewar "realist" interpretations of the meaning of Westphalia (the German historian Friedrich Meinecke argued, in his *Machiavellianism* [1924], that it signified the continuing growth of *raison d'état* in European politics), it was not until after the Second World War that the dominant IR representation (among not only Realist, but Liberal Institutionalist, English School, and some Constructivist scholars as well) came to focus on the principle of state sovereignty. The most influential source for the characterization of the Westphalian Settlement as a "pan-European charter" that established a system of sovereign, formally equal states and thus put an end to the hierarchical, universalist aspirations of the Habsburg emperor or the pope was apparently a 1948 article by the international law scholar Leo Gross. To the extent that his views rested on an older historiography (Gross himself was not a historian), they drew substantially from a nineteenth-century nationalist historiography that itself was based in part on anti-imperial propaganda from the early seventeenth century.

Gross's thesis can be challenged, first, in its representation of the consequences of the war and settlement for the Holy Roman Empire. The principalities did not emerge as clearly sovereign; the Empire itself did emerge as an arguably more efficient, consolidated entity; and the Habsburgs, weak and ineffective before the war, became subsequently more rather than less empowered, thanks to their final late seventeenth-century defeat of Ottoman expansionism in the east. Second, the argument that the settlement inaugurated and enshrined secularity and rationality, and a consequent ethos of *raison d'état* that superseded normative morality (religion) in interstate relations, may be hard for historians to justify either as a description of the actual negotiations (the treaties were introduced by an affirmation of Christian peace and sworn to by formal Christian oaths) or the subsequent history of confessional politics in ancien regime relations—especially after Louis XIV's revocation of the Edict of Nantes in 1685 and the intensified late seventeenth-century Austrian Habsburg effort to recatholicize its hereditary domains. Third, the argument that the settlement inaugurated a general system, or "charter for all Europe," grounded in the recognition of absolute sovereignty and characterized by the practice of "balance of power" has been attacked by those who argue that, though one can see already before the Westphalian era a *de facto* system of sovereign states, this was not consciously acknowledged and formalized in international law either before or following the settlement. The Peace was not a multilateral recognition of such a system or of the equality of its signatories. A historian of international law has recently claimed categorically that, contrary to Gross' interpretation, the principles of sovereignty, equality of states in law, religious neutrality, and balance of power "are to be found in none of the three main Westphalian Treaties, at least not as principles of international law" (Lesaffer, 2004, 9).

Finally, critique of the Westphalia thesis has been driven, to a significant degree, by the more general post-Cold War debate over the concept of sovereignty itself (see Chapter 10). It can be argued that the modern state and its ideology of absolute sovereignty may owe more to domestic social and political change (especially the rise of a literate middle-class citizenry) than to Hobbesian political theory, formal treaties, or system logic. In this sense, sovereignty is created on the ground, as it were. For a Marxist like Benno Teschke, the "sovereignty" of the medieval or early modern dynastic regime is not the sovereignty of the mature, industrialized capitalist system, dependent on a shift (which the "myth" of Westphalia cannot address) in the social property relations that "primarily define the constitution and identity" of states (Teschke, 2003, 7). Others, including some Constructivists, would agree that Westphalia is inadequate to explain the character of modern sovereignty, but would argue, less economistically, that the sovereignty of the modern world cannot be fully articulated until the French Revolution sacralized the secular idea of the "nation" as something other than the shifting dynastic patrimony of kings.

Many, perhaps most, historians would now agree with Stephen Krasner that "Westphalia was not a beginning or an end" (Krasner, 1993, 264), though no doubt not everyone would be prepared to argue further, with Sebastian Schmidt, that "it would be best, for the sake of both empirical and theoretical clarity, if the discipline abandoned the use of the Westphalia concept as an analytic construct" (Schmidt, 2011, 603).

War, politics, and seventeenth-century thought

Whether one can accept the centrality of "the Westphalian moment" in defining the future of the European state system, most IR scholars would agree that the long sixteenth- and seventeenth-century era of warfare—both civil and external—saw the consolidation of the dynastic territorial state familiar to subsequent European history, a system of regularized diplomatic relations among such states, including at least the germ of a doctrine of balancing, *and* significant attempts to grapple intellectually with the sovereign nature of states and how their relations in war and peace might be understood and rationalized. In this ferment of political thought, especially in the crucible of the Thirty Years' War, two thinkers emerge of enduring interest for the discipline.

Hugo Grotius (1583–1645), a Dutch lawyer and diplomatist who represented Sweden in negotiations with Richelieu, laid the basis for what would prove to be perhaps the longest "tradition" in IR scholarship—that of international law. His work, located squarely in the context of the long eighty-year struggle between the United Provinces and the Spanish empire and of the conceit that republican Holland was a new Athens, accepted and advanced the concept of the sovereign state freed of imperial hierarchy, and of a system of states in which, though warfare might be a common occurrence, order of a kind might be enforced, not by imperial or papal diktat but through a consensual system in which such wars were legitimated, contained, and to some extent governed by natural law *and* Christian morality. His seminal work of 1621, *De Jura Belli ac Pacis* (Of the Law of War and Peace), was not only an application of the Roman idea of natural law to the developing realm of European international jurisprudence, but in fact the first systematic description of a state *system*.

Though Grotius can be somewhat misleadingly pigeon-holed in IR as a founder of the Idealist or utopian tradition contrasted with that of Realists, his work, as Garrett Mattingly long ago explained, was grounded in the self-interest of security-seeking sovereign states: "he aimed to show that on these terms it is in the interest of the State to accept the rule of law, since to preserve its existence there must be some community of nations" (Mattingly, 1955, 294). There is a very substantial literature on Grotian thought and the international law tradition, but this has for whatever reason been, especially since the emergence of Realism after the Second World War, rather marginal to the central interests of the discipline. As Quincy Wright in his study of the history of war succinctly put it, "the practice of statesmen … followed the precepts of Machiavelli rather than those of Grotius" (Wright, 1942, 334–5).

In its canon of historical texts, one mid-seventeenth-century writer occupies central place in IR discourse, the English clergyman Thomas Hobbes (1588–1679). Famously, the *Leviathan* of 1651 (in the parts of interest to political theory scholars who generally ignore the rest of this monumental work) sets out an argument for the "Absolute Sovereignty" of the ruler—both within the state and in his relations with other states—and grounds this idea, not in Christian morality (the divinity of kings), but in rationalist and materialist conclusions drawn from the atavism of human nature. Again, as with

Thucydides or Machiavelli, there is inevitably some tension between the approach of those scholars of political thought who examine texts in terms of their internal argument, timeless meaning, or the dialectic they advance within a linear discourse, and many historians who would wish to place Hobbes contextually, to historicize his master work as the product of one who was himself caught up in the displacement, chaos, and fearful uncertainty of civil war and for whom any secular authority, however arbitrary, which worked to bring social and political order was justifiable. With the rise of a more aggressive Calvinism, the demands of individual conscience threatened royal (including imperial) authority as well as that of the church, and civil wars and fragile compromises followed in France, the Empire, and finally England. It was these historically specific times that undergird Hobbes's vision and gave it its special motive in the need to reestablish order and hierarchy. The fact that he wrote in English, rather than scholarly Latin, suggests his interest in reaching a wide audience, to persuade Royalist *or* Commonwealth citizen-subjects fearful of their lives and property that "the end of Obedience is Protection."

For Realists, a direct line runs from Thucydides (whom Hobbes translated), through Machiavelli (whom Hobbes likely read, but did not acknowledge) to the *Leviathan*. Hobbes is, in this tradition, not only a philosopher of human nature and the protective sovereign state, but a pessimistic observer of the nature of states themselves, expressed in the anarchy of their ever-warring opportunism. He portrays mankind, though naturally violent, as driven by fear of death consensually to yield primitive autonomy (war by everyone against everyone) to a prince or commonwealth in an irrevocable agreement to ensure a less fearful existence. One might note that some feminists like Anne Tickner have argued that Hobbes text reflects a "stereotypically masculine" *partial* view of human nature and by extension of the international system. "Human nature" contains both masculine and feminine, conflictual and cooperative "elements of social reproduction and interdependence as well as domination and separation" (Tickner, 1994, 37–38). When Realists like Morgenthau, as well as Neorealists like Waltz, adopt a "Hobbesian" view of the system of states—as an anarchy in which the contest for power is unrestrained by either higher authority or a sense of social cooperation—they are transposing Hobbes's dubious and gendered psychology of humans as individual actors to the interstate realm of sovereign relations.

By his setting aside ideas that justified obedience to a sovereign as divinely appointed arbiter of morality, Hobbes is also made to anticipate and confirm Realism's rejection of the higher ideals of international law and liberal human rights as effective forces in international relations. One should note in passing that what Hobbes actually says or means may not correspond to the common IR usage of "Hobbesian." Some have argued that too much has been made of Hobbes's convenient device of grounding the origins of the sovereign bargain in an entirely hypothetical theory of the (original) human condition in order to remove the state itself from the realm of moral conduct. Hobbes in fact himself suggests that anarchic brutality was an aspect of only the primitive first phase of human life, and he elsewhere expresses a concern for an ethics beyond expediency.

If Hobbes is going to be central to the discipline of IR, there is a need to back away from Hobbes's own inherently ahistorical arguments about the mythic *origin* of political society and ask what does he actually say about *interstate* relations. On the one hand, he seems to assume that the freedom of action which a commonwealth has is directly analogous to that which all humans have in the absence of a sovereign power to keep them in awe. While individuals in society are constrained to act in an orderly and peaceful manner by the sovereign's monopoly of coercive power, conflict occurs between states because they are unconstrained by higher authority. Sounding quite Machiavellian, he observes that "Force and Fraud, are in warre the two Cardinall virtues." It is less clear however whether such a condition is inevitable and perpetual: why would relations among states not be guided by the same principle that, according to Hobbes, transformed the anarchy of human individuals into sovereign communities— whereby a bargain is struck exchanging dangerous chaos for the peaceful enjoyment of life and property? Finally, in the advice he offers the Sovereign, Hobbes suggests that the defense of the state does not lie only in preparation for battle, but in the avoidance of "unnecessary wars." Expediency, in the form of Prudence, may thus dictate a civilized moderation.

Ultima Ratio Regum: War, balance of power, and international law in ancien regime Europe

The long period following Westphalia—down to the French Revolution—can be seen as a unity, dominated by a European system based on the sovereign state (often a dynastic state). Though these states might be "confessional" regimes where, as in Louis XIV's France or in late Stuart and Hanoverian Britain, full citizenship was restricted to those of a single faith, the system as a whole was at least partially secularized: a theoretically universal "Christendom" was replaced in common usage by the word "European," and religious oaths in treaties disappear. Certainly diplomacy and warfare often seem to suggest the pursuit of naked state (or dynastic) advantage rather than religious fraternity: England fought three wars against the Protestant Dutch, and both Protestant and Catholic states allied to resist Bourbon hegemony. Nevertheless, at the level of *domestic* mobilization it must be admitted that religious identities remain, perhaps even grow in importance—to reemerge, like the Protestant patriotism of the English, as powerful factors in the establishment of nations out of dynasties.

Many would argue that the absolutist territorial state that matures on the continent after Westphalia, in France especially or in Brandenburg-Prussia or the westernized Russian empire, is evidence of the arrival of the modern system of unitary sovereign regimes, Great Power politics, and antihegemonial balancing. While the Holy Roman Emperor's theoretical authority over the German princes may not have been as diminished or constrained by Westphalia as was once thought, the real basis for the power of the ancien regime Austrian Habsburgs now lay not in the Empire but in their resecured control over their Austrian and Bohemian domains. The decisive defeat of the

Ottoman Army before the gates of Vienna in 1683, the subsequent freeing of Hungary from Turkish rule, and the suppression of a revolt by the Hungarians, freed them to participate as a Great Power equal in the eighteenth century.

Of course, the *kind* of sovereignty implied in the rule of dynastic monarchs differs from that of the modern nation-state. Dynastic realms were not necessarily fixed territorially, and might expand or shrink according to the politics of marriage or the accident of inheritance. Interstate relations in the ancien regime as a whole nevertheless often seem to approximate a Realist model characterized by shifting alliances and frequent warfare. The use of sovereign force and the threat of force were casual, frequent, and conducted apparently with little regard for justification in international law or the ancient concept of a "just war," however much the European system might also have been, in English School terms, culturally a "society of states." The motto stamped on Louis XIV's canon, *Ultima Ratio Regum* (the Last Argument of Kings), had, one might argue, a Realist as well as ironic meaning.

And yet, though Louis was often at war, he carefully regulated the use of force, never insisted upon total victory, and generally combined war with diplomacy. In the century that followed, familiarly modern diplomacy was more or less formalized throughout Europe, accompanied by literary genres of handbooks of practice, ambassadors' memoirs, and philosophic investigations of what "international law" might mean and how it might be applied. War itself was also theorized in handbooks. Armies were better organized and state-controlled, and wars were by and large limited to the pursuit of specific national and dynastic interests, rarely threatening an existential crisis. The one state to go to the wall, Poland, did so not as the result of the rage of unlimited, unconditional warfare, but through the peculiarity of its domestic constitution, the cynical operation of dynastic ambition, and Great Power balancing.

After the Peace of Utrecht and the death of Louis XIV, the European state system assumed a character that would in essentials endure until Napoleon destroyed it, though, with a turn of the kaleidoscope of historical contingency, Sweden (after the Battle of Poltava in 1709) ceased to be a major player, as did the United Provinces, checked globally by the phenomenal growth of British naval might. Britain emerged as a critical "balancer" in Europe by virtue of the maritime commercial wealth it was able to employ. Along with France and Austria, two other "powers" came to the table: the Russian empire after Peter the Great and Brandenburg-Prussia.

War and the state

Military historians and IR scholars, often Realists who are committed to calculating comparative state capabilities, have encouraged a subgenre in the discipline that searches out significant eras of "military revolution"—that is, the moments of critical shift due to new weaponry, tactics, and organization. Some have argued that such a compartmentalized focus can exaggerate the importance of material factors and ignore the social, cultural, and economic realms from which they spring. Or that a true "history of warfare" must include not only material factors and specific practices but what might be called the changing "culture of war"—how, for instance, warfare might be affected by ideals of aristocratic honor and service and an elite tradition of *la gloire de guerre* (the Palace of Versailles contained a *salon de guerre* featuring a statue of Louis as Mars, the god of war). To speak of the culture of war, of course, is to speak of much more than the practice of war. As Jeremy Black has recently observed, "What can be termed the culture of *gloire* linked the military to both politics and the social elite, and also provided a vital organizational tool as *gloire* provided a lubricant of obedience" (Black, 2012, 63).

In the Europe treated by this chapter, the idea of critical "military revolutions," inaugurated by Michael Roberts (1956) and elaborated by Geoffrey Parker (1988), has drawn special attention to the sixteenth and seventeenth centuries. From the late medieval period, success in war, it is argued, came to depend on post-feudal military recruitment and organization, training in firearms and artillery (though the use of massed pikemen remained common until after the Thirty Years' War), and the growth of a more efficient state able to extract the resources to pay for weaponry and mercenaries. Sixteenth-century Spain was able to deploy a seasoned, highly professional army for use wherever required—though with imperial interests extending from Italy and the eastern Mediterranean to the Netherlands, Spanish finances were overstretched: the sack of Rome was caused by lack of pay.

Much has been made of the supposed rational innovations introduced in the Swedish Army by the early seventeenth century—mobile cannon and firing by salvo as well as a system of national conscription—and proven on the battlefield during the Thirty Years' War. Liddell-Hart called Gustavus Adolphus the "founder of modern war." Though there remains some skepticism about theories of military revolution for the earlier period, certainly armies by the late seventeenth century were more controlled affairs than in the wars of religion when marauding masses sporadically despoiled the countryside. Strategic and tactical calculations were helped along by the development of a disciplined infantry fighting "in line" and trained in concentrated musket-fire, lighter cavalry as an auxiliary force, more mobile light artillery, a more professional officer class, and improved systems of supply (by the eighteenth century armies generally paid for requisitioned food and fodder for the well-provisioned bivouacking of troops in winter).

In the late seventeenth century, Louis XIV conceived of all Europe as a potential "theater of war." His success in achieving a unitary state where nobility were subordinated and royal authority prevailed over local resistance also enabled the raising of a standing army answerable to the crown rather than entrepreneur commanders. Frequent war as an instrument of *raison d'état*, however, both required and encouraged a fiscal-bureaucratic and centralized state. There is a chicken-and-egg debate about whether the resources of the new state enabled and encouraged war, or whether more frequent recourse to war itself was the major factor in the emergence of the centralized state.

While Classical Realists may see war as an inevitable corollary to the lust for power embedded in human nature, Neorealists see war in the post-Westphalian world as arising chiefly out of the logic of the competitive, anarchic state system, a logic that prioritized the prime objective of state security through the operation of (a military) balance of power. Many historians of course would want to look beyond human nature and underneath system constraints for the myriad fiscal, social, technological, and perhaps constitutional factors that enabled and also perhaps encouraged states to go to war for a variety of purposes.

The centralized, bureaucratic fiscal-military state

The states of late seventeenth-century and early eighteenth-century Europe have traditionally been distinguished by their domestic organization and underlying philosophy: divine-right absolutism prevailed in Spain and France, justified by a professor of law at Toulouse, Jean Bodin (1530–96), whose *Six Books of the Commonweal* (1576), composed during the civil war period, argued that sovereignty *ought* to mean "*la puissance absolue et perpetuelle*" (absolute and perpetual power). The prince was answerable only to God. A hundred years later these ideas were developed and promoted at the court of Louis XIV in the eloquent sermons of Bishop Jacques-Bénigne Bossuet (1627–1704): God, he wrote, was to be found in a trinity of "*le roi, Jesus-Christ et l'Eglise*" (the king, Jesus Christ, and the Church). Forms of constitutionalism, on the other hand, typified the Dutch Republic and Sweden, but most obviously England after the Glorious Revolution of 1688.

It used to be a commonplace that the French absolutist model was uniquely characterized in the Baroque period by a great *dirigiste* minister like Louis XIV's Jean-Baptiste Colbert who grappled with fiscal and bureaucratic reform more efficiently to extract resources and direct an economy that could, with difficulty, undergird the hegemonic wars of the French state. Constitutional states, in theory, were characterized by fitful governance and awkward parliaments. Nevertheless, *both* absolutist and constitutionalist states developed in this era a more effective bureaucratized fiscal-military system of administration. What gave the United Provinces and England an advantage was their more disciplined approach to state expenditure, their ability to collect taxes that were viewed as legitimate by much of the population, and, critically, their ability to tap into the private financial sector on better terms through an institution like the Bank of England and a national debt guaranteed by the state (a Dutch invention). Where France and Spain failed was not in an excess of centralization but in the inability of even a ruthless modernizer like Colbert and those who followed to root out the older device of "patrimonialization," that is, sale of offices of state as hereditable property for ready money. In Spain by 1650, there were some 30,000 proprietary office holders in Castile alone; in France the right to collect taxes was, disastrously, farmed out to aristocratic families in exchange for the promise of fees paid back to the center. In Britain, centralized fiscal and administrative reforms, and especially the effective land tax, as well as the credit facilities guaranteed by parliament created the means to fight land wars in Europe, subsidize allies, and develop a global navy—by far the most capital-intensive form of military expense of the era.

Louis XIV and the threat of French hegemony

The "Sun King," who came to the throne of France as a minor as the negotiations at Westphalia commenced, reigned in sole control of the state from 1661 until his death in 1715. His chief geopolitical interest lay in dominating the Spanish Netherlands and extending French influence in the Holy Roman Empire, a continuing French objective that embraced the ambition of making the Rhine the natural border of the kingdom *and* becoming, as Richelieu had proposed, the dominant power in Europe. Certainly by the conclusion of the French-Dutch war in the peace of Nijmegen (1678–9), there could be little doubt that France was the most powerful nation in Europe, a prominence that rested on the largest tax-paying population in Europe. The series of wars—and the regime was almost continually at war—were fought for the most part in the Netherlands and the Germanies though there was now a global dimension as French interests extended to the New World and Asia.

The regime tended to use diplomacy as a means of untying or preventing coalitional opposition and settling matters after military campaigns. French became the language of diplomacy, which had been Latin, and French "style" dictated the public face of diplomatic ritual, indicating not only the dominance or threatened dominance of French state power but the spread of French cultural influence and language throughout the courts of German princes and kings and as far east as St. Petersburg. Louis XIV received envoys from much of Europe and beyond—the Ottoman alliance was revived (1669) and there were reciprocal relations with Morocco, Persia, and the Far East (Siam). French Jesuit missionaries were sent to China (1685), while earlier missions to India and New France in America were extended.

The development of regular, continual diplomatic relations in late seventeenth-century Europe also owes much to the opposition that French ambition generated among other states—as in the League of Augsburg (1686), known as the Grand Alliance after England joined in 1689. France's political ambition was challenged in a series of major wars fought by such shifting alliances; the last, the War of the Spanish Succession, ended with a peace that, many scholars have argued, established a "doctrine" of balance of power as an explicit principle of the European system. Nevertheless, the era from Westphalia to Utrecht can as easily be characterized as one of political, military, and cultural hegemony—a continuity, under France, of the long tradition of imperial universalism—as of a new systemic balance among equals.

Louis XIV's last war (the War of the Spanish Succession, 1701–14, a continuation of the War of the Grand Alliance, 1689–1694) was forced upon him by a coalition of other European states led by the Habsburg Emperor—the Dutch Republic, Britain, Prussia (as an electorate of the Empire), and Savoy among others—in response to his hopes of claiming the Spanish inheritance for his grandson and heir apparent, thus uniting the two kingdoms (the Austrian emperor asserted his claim to the throne for his own son). The peace negotiations that followed—concluded in the treaties of Utrecht (between France and Spain, and between Britain and the Dutch, 1713), Rastatt (between France and Austria, 1714), and Baden (between France and the Holy Roman

Empire, 1714)—figure significantly in IR discourse as confirming the doctrine of the balance of power, a practice that IR system theory sees as functionally integral to an anarchic system of sovereign states motivated by the prime objective of defensive security. As many historians of diplomacy and IR scholars, of both the English School and Waltzian structuralist variety, continue to emphasize, the Treaty of Utrecht was the first European treaty that *mentioned* the doctrine of balance (in the preamble to Article VI): "obtaining a general Peace and securing the Tranquillity of *Europe* by a Balance of power." Whether this amounts to a new norm, the simple recognition of a structural constraint, or, in the words of one skeptical scholar, merely "obliging references" to the ideal of balance, may be debated. Clearly the chief balancer was, and would be in the years to come, Britain, and it was arguably Britain that profited most from the settlement—not only because it served to *balance* Europe but because it advanced British *hegemony* at sea. The peace was widely referred to as "*la paix anglaise.*"

We should bear in mind the ambiguity of much IR discourse about "balance of power," perhaps the most pervasive concept (some would say cliché) in the discipline. It can be either (or both) a *doctrine*, that is, a proscriptive creed (a principle, a historically constructed belief), or simply a somewhat ahistorical behavioral *response* to threat, a systemic practice. As the era of the European ancien regimes is often cited as especially prone to the clockwork operation of the balance of power, it is well to consider some complicating issues. First, it would appear that the balancing mechanism is clearly situational rather than universal, a calculation of where one's interests may lie—in balancing or bandwagoning, or, as in the case of the British, in balancing in Europe while seeking its own clear hegemony at sea and within its larger (formal and informal) imperium. Second, the discourse of balance tends to assume its defensive character—against a threatening hegemon like France—but not all coalitions can be thus explained. Those assembled by the Great Powers against Frederick II's Prussia can be better explained as attempts to keep down a *rising* Power seeking to join the club than as defensive responses to a hegemonical threat.

On closer inspection platitudes about the clockwork mechanism of balance become, then, a little less convincing. Certainly French dynastic designs on Spain were thwarted. But the war reveals other motives than the neatly adjusted balance of Europe—Austria, though losing its own claim to the Spanish throne, got most of Spain's territories in Italy and the Netherlands; Britain, which had begun secret negotiations with France (Callières advised that "secrecy is the very soul of diplomacy"), feathered its own nest, achieving the profitable Asiento (the right to trade slaves in Spanish dominions) and a perpetual occupancy of the strategically important territories of Gibraltar and Minorca. And at the end of the day there was little in the treaties that much altered France's dominating position on the Netherlands' border or in the Rhineland. In retrospect, French hegemony on the European continent was never as real a prospect as the narrative may suggest. Had France been genuinely capable of dominating Europe by force of arms, then balancing might have been less effective in the face of the temptation to bandwagon that many smaller states, seeking to preserve what they could, would have faced. Moreover, hegemonic threat is a matter of place and perspective. To many German and Italian noblemen and peoples, the Austrian Habsburgs remained the chief hegemonic concern.

In short, the *practice* of European war and diplomacy may display an element of timely balancing, and the British would come to see themselves as the chief continental balancer—pursuing their own hegemony elsewhere—but "balance of power" was not seen yet as a doctrine of, in Watson's words, "continuous mobile equilibrium." As Michael Cox, Tim Dunne, and Ken Booth have argued, "the notion of a 'balance of power' was less a norm than a rationalization," not of a defensive need for security, but of the aggressive pursuit of power, territory, and commerce (2001, 10).

War, eighteenth-century Realpolitik, and "the Shape of Prussia"

In the era between Utrecht and the French Revolution, one can speak of a degree of institutionalization and rationalization of the conduct of European foreign relations, increasingly associated with a continuous interstate conversation through an era of intermittent warfare and peace negotiation. Spain and Savoy-Piedmont created secretariats of state for foreign affairs in emulation of French practice and Peter the Great established a College (ministry) of Foreign Affairs toward the end of the Great Northern War (1700–21) with Sweden. A decade later the Prussians organized a Department of External Affairs. There were reforms in the Austrian State Chancellery following the loss of Silesia to Prussia (in the War of the Austrian Succession, 1740–8), and in 1782 the British (following the loss of the American colonies) finally replaced the confused domestic and foreign jurisdictions of their two secretaries of state (for the northern and southern departments) with a single Foreign Secretary.

After Utrecht, Austria, which continued to push the Ottoman Empire back in the Balkans, came to be viewed as the principal opponent of French ambition on the ground. Hanoverian Britain, though it maintained a direct dynastic interest in the security of Hanover, relied more on financial subsidies than, as in the War of the Spanish Succession, large-scale military intervention. With French ambitions held in check, and the Austrian power base within its hereditary lands and Hungary confirmed, the most significant challenge to the conservation of the European system or society of states in the eighteenth century was the rise of the Russian empire in the east, and, more immediately, the emergence of Brandenburg-Prussia, a north German state whose growing power was founded on the basis of bureaucratic (rather than divine) absolutism.

The scattered territories that comprised the north-German Electorate of Brandenburg, dynastically combined with the duchy of Prussia after 1618, historically had provided a poor basis for princely ambition—or indeed for survival in the violent world of the wars of religion. In 1640, Frederick William of Brandenburg, the "Great Elector," began a calculated effort to consolidate and expand this territory through marriage and diplomacy (the Treaty of Westphalia gave him part of Pomerania, and a war with the Poles a decade later provided more land in the East), the rapid construction

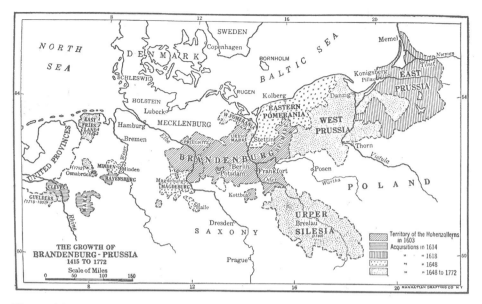

Figure 6.2 The rise of Prussia.

Source: Albert Hyma, *A Short History of Europe, 1500–1815* (New York: F. S. Crofts & Co., 1928).

of a centralized efficient bureaucracy, and the creation of an army larger than his population would normally have provided (Figure 6.2). Brandenburg-Prussia (a kingdom after 1701) was a variant of the absolutist state, based as it was on administrative absolutism rather than divine right. Its rulers managed to avoid aristocratic patrimonialism and reduced spending at court in order to accumulate a special treasury for use during wartime. Reforms accelerated after 1715 under the Elector's grandson Frederick William I (of Prussia) with a modernized administrative law code, a nationalized officer corps (the king himself wrote the army's first handbook of field regulations), and a further significant increase in the size of the army. By 1732, a new method of recruiting and maintaining the army, the *Kantonsystem*, created a kind of local reserve.

The Prussian bureaucracy, militarized in its organization, and in part recruited from veterans and from service-oriented landowners (Junkers), was built around a cadre of university-trained officials. This official class collected taxes levied directly by the crown without approval from the estates (aristocratic opposition was bought off by giving them tax exemption). What was missing was a public credit system that could absorb the costs of a sustained war—a problem for Prussia throughout the century. The army grew very substantially from 40,000 in 1713 to nearly 200,000 by the end of the war-filled reign of Frederick the Great. Though armies, including that of Prussia, were still recruited heavily from mercenaries, they were more professionally disciplined. In Clausewitz's words, warfare "became more regular, better organized, and more attuned to the purpose of war—that is, to its political objective" (1831, 395). Within western and central Europe, cautious commanders jockeyed tactically for chessboard position.

In some sense, Frederick II (the Great) of Prussia (r. 1740–86) is the perfect embodiment of the theory and practice of the doctrine of reason of state that regarded warfare as a flexible instrument of politics. He once asserted that the civilian population should not even be aware that wars were taking place. Frederick employed cold logic in identifying what was necessary to make Prussia a Power, and pursed that objective with a singularly focused vision. His was also a concept of the state that was more than the dynastic ambition of a ruling family (the Hohenzollern) or the common view that stressed the patrimonial nature of royal authority: as Frederick famously said, rulers should be "first servants of the state."

In eighteenth-century Europe, *maps* became more significant—in defining the state as a matter of "logical" borders rather than ill-defined frontiers and jurisdictions, and in the conduct of war and diplomacy. The French foreign office set up its own geological section and map-making was subsidized for use on the continent, for expanding territories abroad, and for navigation at sea. The problem for Frederick was Prussia's patchwork lack of territorial coherence, its modest size, and its relatively small population for taxation and recruitment into the army. He would need to rectify Prussia's "shape": as the young Frederick had written in 1731, it was necessary to "*corriger la figure de la Prusse*" (correct the shape of Prussia). This could only be done by force, a spirited offence; the Prussian army, he said, was particularly suited to the offensive.

Frederick went to war with great audacity and against solemn treaty promises for the sole object of state advantage. His successes were due to his swiftness of action and his persistence in the face of apparently overwhelming odds—assuming that in the end alliances against him would conclude that the sustained effort to defeat him was not worth the candle. This conviction amounted to what Clausewitz later would call a kind of "moral superiority" (i.e., *intensity*; Frederick had little interest in the Lutheran pietism that had moved his father and grandfather). This certainty and focus was necessary to compensate for the material weakness of Prussia's exposed position. The opportunity arose when Maria Theresa succeeded to the Austrian throne. Frederick, who had promised like the other powers to respect her succession, fell on the prosperous German-Austrian province of Silesia in 1740 with the intention of quickly occupying it—and then negotiating.

The War of the Austrian Succession brought Prussia Silesia and with it a population of 1,300,000 (a 60 percent increase for Prussia) and an increase of 42 percent in state revenues. This allowed Frederick very substantially to expand his army before the start of the next war (the Seven Years' War) where he planned to do the same in Saxony. Nearly crushed by a vast alliance of Austria, Saxony, France, and Russia, Frederick fought first on one front and then on another, managed to destroy France's military reputation at the battle of Rossbach (1757), and in the end survived—without Saxony but retaining Silesia. Moreover, success and survival in the two wars with Austria had the added benefit of further weakening the Austrian Habsburg position within the Holy Roman Empire—a shift in perception that enhanced Prussia's image not only as a Great Power but as Austria's chief rival as "protector" of the German principalities. Having achieved much of what he wished for, Frederick then became a cautious and defensive ruler, making clever use of diplomacy to keep his kingdom out of large conflicts.

A society of sovereigns: International law, war, and the balance of power

In this era, the major figures in the philosophy of international relations, rather than extending the Bodin and Hobbesian tradition of absolute sovereignty, chose to develop the lawyerly ideas of Hugo Grotius. The university of Jena, founded in Lutheran Saxony, became a major center for speculation about international law (international law was of special interest, one can imagine, for central Europeans of lesser states likely to be arbitrarily handled by Great Powers). The most important thinker in the immediate post-Westphalian era is, in fact, not much discussed by IR theorists, though the English School scholar, Martin Wight, acknowledged that he coined the term "systems of states." Samuel von Pufendorf (1632–94) was born the son of a Lutheran minister in a Saxony that had been devastated in the religious wars. At the University of Jena, he read Grotius and Hobbes, whom he would attempt to synthesize, and wrote a book, published in 1661, on what he called "Universal Jurisprudence." In 1667, he published a widely read tract attacking the Austrian emperor, arguing that the Holy Roman Empire had after Westphalia become a "monstrosity"—neither a "regular kingdom" nor a republic. Moving to the University of Lund in Sweden, he wrote his major work, *De Jure Naturae et Gentium* (The Law of Nature and Nations, 1672, also titled "On the Duty of Man and Citizen"). Here he returned to the problem of the just and unjust wars, concluding that, as opposed to Hobbes, the state of nature was one of a fragile peace rather than constant warfare, and that it was human nature to seek to preserve peace. States, which were after all but the sum of the innately sociable individuals who were their citizens, had, like individuals, a moral persona.

For Pufendorf, then, states were sovereign individuals (moral or immoral persons) to whom the concept of natural rights and obligations should apply: that is, he attempted to reconcile justice and utility, the self-interest of states and their obligation under natural law. After Pufendorf, this tradition of speculation about the law of nations in an era of frequent warfare dictated by *raison d'état* was carried on by the Silesian-born early Enlightenment philosopher, Christian Wolff (1679–1754), who also studied at Jena, and his protégé, the Swiss-born Emer de Vattel (1714–67), the characteristic philosopher of the eighteenth-century sovereign state system. In a sense Vattel's work absorbs the Utrecht settlement into the mainstream of thought on international law. Enjoying the patronage of the king of Saxony, Vatel wrote a book in 1758 on the law of nations (*Droit des Gens*), which, building on Grotius and Pufendorf, made explicit the idea of a formal equality of all sovereign states—at least in legal-diplomatic terms—and the principle of *noninterference* inside the borders of the state. For Vattel, "balance of power" had an ethical aspect: no power *ought* to be in such a preponderant position that it could "lay down the law to others."

Nevertheless, in these years the metaphoric concept of "balance" is increasingly presented not as the normative value to which it is clearly related (the golden mean, the moderation of power) but as a universal rule, a mechanistic fact: "I do not think," Herbert Butterfield once observed, "that it can have been an accident that the doctrine of a European equilibrium became so fashionable … just at the time when the world had become familiar with parallelograms of forces, and men were beginning to see the heavenly bodies beautifully equipoised" (1966, 141). By the mid- and late eighteenth-century tracts and pamphlets expanded on the discovery of this principle of the politics of nations. The philosopher David Hume (1711–76), in a well-known brief essay "On the balance of power" (1747), traced the concept back to Xenophon and Thucydides and saw it as simply "founded … on common sense and obvious reasoning." Hume, however, more Grotian than Hobbesian, stops short of calling balancing through warfare a law of international politics, admitting that "above half of our wars with *France*" owed "more to our own imprudent vehemence" than to attempts to balance against "the ambition of our neighbours."

Adam Watson entitles the eighteenth-century chapter of his English School text, *The Evolution of International Society* (1992), "The Age of Reason and of Balance." Though as Richard Little has emphasized, "balance of power" was a powerful *metaphor*, it can nevertheless be exaggerated as either a law of the modern state system or exactly descriptive of international politics in the century when it was most acknowledged. One scholar, David Kaiser, has scoffed that "balance" was an ideal that was invoked only when it suited powers to do so. What *is* characteristic of the times is a remarkably fluid diplomacy that saw states turn from balancing to bandwagoning and back to balancing as it suited them. As Kaiser has said, "with the exception of the United Provinces, every European state fought both with and against the French during the reign of Louis XIV" (1990, 198).

Recommended readings

For the practice of foreign relations in the pre-Westphalian era, one should begin with Garrett Mattingly's long-standard account, *Renaissance Diplomacy* (1955), supplemented with more recent scholarship, for example, Michael Mallett's "Italian Renaissance Diplomacy," *Diplomacy & Statecraft* 12 (2001), 61–70. For a recent general narrative text on early modern war and diplomacy, see Jeremy Black, *A History of Diplomacy* (2010) and *European International Relations, 1648–1815* (2002). The standard biography of Cardinal Richelieu, available in English translation, is Carl Burckhardt's three-volume *Richelieu and His Age* (1967). For the extensive debate in IR over Westphalia, see, in addition to those cited in the text, Derek Croxton, "The Peace of Westphalia of 1648 and the Origins of Sovereignty," *International History Review* 21 (1999), 569–91. Leo Gross's article, "The Peace of Westphalia, 1648–1948," was published in the *American Journal of International Law* 42 (1948), 20–41. For an example of push-back by those defending the significance of 1648 and the origins of the "Westphalian order," see Sasson Sofer, "The Prominence of Historical Demarcations: Westphalia and the New World Order," *Diplomacy & Statecraft* 20 (2009), 1–19.

The Peace of Utrecht and the scholarly debate over the balance of power it supposedly enshrined can be followed in, for instance, Evan Luard, *The Balance of Power: The System of International Relations, 1648–1815* (1992), but also see Richard Little, *The Balance of Power in International Relations: Metaphors, Myths and Models* (2007).

Both Grotius and, especially, Hobbes have generated a large scholarly literature in political theory generally and among IR scholars. For Grotius, see the collection of essays edited by Hedley Bull, Benedict Kingsbury, and Adam Roberts, *Hugo Grotius and International Relations* (1990). Edward Keene, *Beyond the Anarchical Society: Grotius, Colonialism, and Order in World Politics* (2002), contests Bull's analysis and puts Grotius into the context of expanding European colonialism. Hobbes can be approached through David Armitage's recent general text, *Foundations of Modern International Thought* (2013), Part II, the succinct introduction provided by Ian Shapiro to the 2010 Yale edition of the *Leviathan*, "Reading Hobbes Today," ix–xxiii, and the third volume of Quentin Skinner's, *Visions of Politics*: *Hobbes and Civil Science* (2002). Also see L. M. J. Bagby, *Thucydides, Hobbes and the Interpretation of Realism* (1993). A. P. Martinich, *Hobbes: A Biography* (1999), provides a fairly recent, well-contextualized life. For some thoughts on Hobbes's use of anarchy as metaphor, see Michael C. Williams, *The Realist Tradition and the Limits of International Relations* (2005), ch. 1.

For the development of the fiscal-military state in Britain, see John Brewer, *The Sinews of Power: War, Money and the English State, 1688–1783* (1989). Giles McDonogh's relatively recent *Frederick the Great: A Life in Deeds and Letters* (1999) offers a full, somewhat debunking treatment. On Pufendorf, see David Boucher, "Resurrecting Pufendorf and Capturing the Westphalian Moment," *Review of International Studies* 27 (2001), 557–577. Edwin van de Haar's article, "David Hume and International Political Theory: A Reappraisal," *Review of International Studies* 34 (2008), 225–42, takes an English School approach. Also see Frederick G. Whelan, *Hume and Machiavelli: Political Realism and Liberal Thought* (2004).

CHAPTER 7
NATION, STATE, AND EMPIRE IN THE LONG NINETEENTH CENTURY

This chapter treats the era from the revolutionary and Napoleonic wars to the Great War of 1914–18, the historiography of which has long been central to our general understanding of how a multipolar system or society of states operates. That the European era and its politics of statecraft, from the Congress of Vienna in 1815 to the Paris Peace Conference in 1919, should occupy such a prominent position in a discipline that purports to universal truth draws from more than an unexamined Eurocentrism in its practitioners. Before the rise of a global America, that most tangible-seeming factor in the social science of war and peace, *power*, could be regarded almost as a European monopoly, asserted through its technologies of war, industry, communication, and commerce and confirmed in formal and informal global empires.

The Europe of the pre-First World War Great Powers bulks large in the discipline because its practice of balancing and Realpolitik can be made to model the workings generally of any system of unitary sovereign states in a condition of international anarchy. For the historian, however, the narrative of Great Power war and diplomacy and the uses to which it has been put in IR raise a number of important issues. The most prominent of these is the powerful impact in the nineteenth century of an understanding of the state as a "nation," that is as a people, and of a sovereignty that was implicit not in the state per se but in the collective popular will that the state represented and served. This idea, revolutionary at the end of the eighteenth century, became normative across much of Europe and the New World in the long era that followed and promised to transform the dealings of states with each other and with "suppressed" or incomplete nationalities in ways that traditional historians of the art of diplomacy or IR structural Realists have been reluctant to appreciate. In the most autocratic of powers—Prussia or Austria from the end of the Napoleonic wars, and even Russia by the end of the nineteenth century—the need for the dynastic ancien regime to put on the clothing and speak the language of nationalism, indicates, to many historians at any rate, that factors other than system constraints and defensive security were increasingly in play. "Public opinion"—whether the press-informed views of the expanding professional, commercial, industrial, and financial elites or the passions of the crowd in the street—came to complicate as never before the calculations of the makers of foreign policy.

The challenge is precisely that of identifying the degree to which interstate relations in Europe may have been shaped by domestic and global factors—public opinion and the development in some powers of representative institutions, the invention of "national" ethnicities, the maturing of a liberal-capitalist industrial economy and its global markets, the enhanced state resources generated by commerce, finance, and industry, or imperial projections of sovereignty far beyond Europe. In other words, it is much more obvious than in the previous century that both domestic and extra-European contexts—political, economic, and social/cultural—demand attention by scholars attempting to understand the "system" and whatever constraints it may or may not have imposed on decision-makers. It may also suggest a wider sphere for IR analysis in the relations of *peoples*, and their self-understanding as more than, or other than, states. By the end of the nineteenth century, few statesmen could have claimed, as had Emperor Joseph II of Austria at the end of the previous century, that "I know no 'peoples,' only subjects."

This is not to argue that foreign policy was not still in the hands often of those least sensitive to these changes. There is yet some considerable plausibility in accounts of nineteenth-century statecraft—from Castlereagh and Metternich to Bismarck and Salisbury—that emphasize the calculations of statesmen who operated, or sought to operate, above the domestic fray. But most historians, certainly, and many Neoclassical Realists as well, appreciate that no Great Power in this era can be adequately understood as an international actor without considering, in addition to the personality and psychology of their decision-makers or the constraints of the international system, large historical forces of, say, nationalism, ethnic identity, aggressive, penetrative free-trade liberalism, or the revolutionary class-consciousness of at least important fractions of the lower orders. At the very least, these forces contributed to a new complex reality not well understood by those traditional statesmen who attempted to ignore or sought to manipulate them.

This chapter will address the character of the nineteenth-century state system in Europe, its domestic and imperial/global contexts, and its common understanding and use by IR scholars. We shall follow the periodization adopted by diplomatic and international historians of Great Power politics, while keeping in mind that those who would see international relations as a profound expression of social and cultural, as well as political, forces might prefer a somewhat different schema.

The European system restored and maintained

The relations of the victorious European powers in the aftermath of the titanic struggles of the twenty-five-year revolutionary and Napoleonic era—the nearly constant warfare, the destruction and rearrangement of sovereign states, and the failure of coalition after coalition to balance against the French—has long been a major focus of international political and diplomatic history. Inevitably the central figure for much of this scholarship is the German-Austrian statesman, Clemens von Metternich, as central to the understanding of the "restored" European system in this era as Bismarck is to that of the latter part of the century.

For IR scholars convinced of the essential continuity of the Westphalian paradigm, the lesson to be learned is that Napoleonic France *had* ultimately been defeated and the system restored, and one finds little interest among structural Realists in viewing the struggle against revolutionary and imperial France as other than confirmation: for them, what matters most is that system logic and constraints ultimately prevailed over a would-be hegemon in 1815, just as it would in 1918 and 1945. For many others, the story of the restoration of European order through the "concert" of the Great Powers that served to preserve a general peace for forty years afterward holds considerable interest as more than a simple return to a balanced Westphalian order. Notably, the historian Paul Schroeder challenged the presumption of a continuity of crude, mechanical balancing. In a major study that engages at the level of the political-diplomatic system (rather than, say, pursuing the complex interplay of revolutionary forces and concepts), he argues that there was a significant "transformation" around 1800, a shift away from the war-prone version of eighteenth-century anarchy to one that involved a collective determination to preserve peace and stability (Schroeder, 1994).

Popular sovereignty, nationalism, and IR

A still larger argument can certainly be made for a significant "paradigm break" at the end of the eighteenth century. The American and French Revolutions enshrined the powerful concept of popular sovereignty, while Napoleon's battlefield diplomacy broke up and remade the European system with a vengeance. There was, arguably, a change in the conduct and purpose of war itself. Larger armies and grand revolutionary or imperial ambitions threatened the absolute destruction of states, not border rectification.

At the end of a generation of nearly constant warfare and the making and remaking of "nations," the ancien regimes—much altered, except for the Russian autocracy, by the need to mobilize their peoples—set about the impossible task of "restoring" a Europe of traditional, dynastic states roughly balanced through diplomacy and limited war. But the congress of powers assembled in Vienna, like those that followed, operated in a radically new context: the old Europe in which a dynast could claim to be the state had been swept away and when peace was restored the old bottles of the past had to accommodate the new wine of citizen armies, popular politics, and nationalism. Does this matter for IR analysis? Some would argue that balance of power is balance of power and sovereignty is sovereignty whether exercised by an ancien regime monarch, a constitutional and perhaps representative government, or a self-made emperor. In order to begin to answer that question, we need to consider how the world changed between the fall of the Bastille in 1789 and the reconstruction of Europe in 1815.

The French Revolution and its challenge to the state system and to the idea of sovereignty

The European eighteenth century witnessed a developing sense of the autonomous self, especially among the prosperous, respectable, often urban, professional and commercial middle classes who were increasingly uncomfortable with hierarchical systems of personal subservience and dependency. In Western Europe and British America, such feelings, rife with political meaning, extended into the very modest middling sort and among self-educated artisans. The nascent concept of the "nation" as more than the patrimony of a dynast became contested ground: what was it, who spoke for it, who "owned" it? The American revolution advanced constitutionalism and the ideal of the citizen-state, while Rousseau's much-discussed concept of the "general will" held that authority rested on a mystical popular sanction even in autocracies. At the same time, many middle-class Germans of the scattered central European principalities looked to free themselves from French cultural imperialism in a growing sense of commonality—a "Reich of the spirit."

The central issue of the Age of Revolutions (as Thomas Paine called it) is the relationship between state and people, and rejection of either patriarchy or a supposed contract between monarch and subjects. Where exactly would sovereignty lie if divorced from the sovereign? Is it divisible? For whom does government speak? The French Revolution would resolve the paradox of sovereignty by replacing the majesty of the King with that of the nation. This radical act demanded the *construction* of a more truly unitary state in place of the mixed quasi-feudal character of the monarchy, its estates of the realm, and the ancient regions of France. The Jacobin radicals intended the Oath to the Nation to supplant loyalty not only to the anointed and paternal monarch, but to *les pays* (the traditional localities) as well. To these questions were joined Enlightenment theories of philology and culture, of the nation as a people or *Volk* with its own language and historically developed character, and a concept of "rights"—universal human rights, perhaps, as well as the rights of the citizen.

What kind of meaning should IR find in the revolution in Paris in 1789 that inaugurates the long era of this chapter or that in Moscow and St. Petersburg in 1917 that in some sense concludes it? The central issue for the discipline raised by the concept of the nation and of popular sovereignty, and by revolution and the prospect of revolution (what Marx called the sixth Great Power), is not only whether they become factors in the Realpolitik calculations of statesmen but whether they interact in some significant way with the operation of the international system itself. After all, the concert of European powers as envisioned by "the doctor of revolutions," Clemens von Metternich, or the "Holy Alliance" as dreamed by Alexander I, were not so much instruments of the balance of power as, in their essence, counterrevolutionary combinations.

The relation of revolution (a mass aspiration to establish a radically different society) and the revolutionary state to the international system has been raised, as we have seen, by the sociologist Theda Skocpol and latterly by the IR scholar Stephen Walt, for whom revolutions are "unit-level" (i.e., domestic) events that, influenced it may be by international ideologies, must operate nonetheless within the state system. Others have noted that revolutionary success in mobilizing and organizing the resources of the nation, as in republican France, can have a certain systemic effect in leading other states, as in Prussia, defensively to adopt similar reforms. Fred Halliday has argued (1999) that revolutions, exemplified by the French Revolution, not only aspire to change the international system through, say, the ideal of fraternal states replacing that of competitive states, but also inspire counterrevolutionary interventionism. The very definition of state security, awarded primacy in Realist theory, may be contested by revolutionaries and counterrevolutionaries alike and boundaries, the distinction of inside and outside, may become irrelevant.

In mainstream IR or indeed much diplomatic history, revolutions are usually regarded as breakdowns, temporary ruptures, from which a state recovers to rejoin the society or system of other states. Hedley Bull excluded revolutions as an ordinary mechanism of international society. In the short run, revolutions may produce new states that pursue a foreign policy distinct from that of status quo powers, but the system exerts its constraints and the revolution succumbs to the need for diplomacy. This is the message of David Armstrong's *Revolution and World Order* (1993). Yet, it is hard to deny the *sustained* importance of the American and French revolutions, and the ideologies that promoted them, to the international system. They played a significant role in universalizing the national idea by undermining the legitimacy of ancien regimes and by experimenting with ways to define, ritualize, and legitimize new nations.

The era also encouraged conceptions of a state system that might involve more than the violence of constant balancing warfare—something radicals tended to identify with the atavistic ancien regime. At the University of Göttingen, Arnold Hermann Ludwig Heeren (1760–1842) retreated, as it were (he was no radical), to the history of the ancient world. In 1800, however, he published a *History of the European State System* that (anticipating a central tenet of the English School) argued that, though independent, states could be regarded as moral persons who had long shared, in Europe at least, a common culture; they constituted historically a kind of society or family of nations. At Königsberg in East Prussia, the idealist philosopher, Immanuel Kant (1724–1804), had gone further and posed, in a tract, *Perpetual Peace* (1795), written in the midst of the turmoil of the first years of the French Republic, the idea that it might be possible to construct a more peaceful society of (republican) states through some form of international organization. He was as dismissive as any Realist of the international law tradition: "Hugo Grotius, Pufendorf, Vattel and many others (all tiresome comforters) are still faithfully cited to *justify* an offensive war, even though their codex ... does not have the least amount of *legal* force." Since republics were not *patrimonia* but societies of individuals with a rational and moral predisposition, they were less likely to go to war, and be more aware of mutual self-interest (in, for instance, the "spirit of Trade, which cannot coexist with war") and mutual, that is, universal, "rights." The "general will (within a people, or in the relation of various nations among each other) … makes the concept of right effective." Though informed by a kind of Enlightenment cosmopolitanism, Kant, it should be noted, did not propose a universal world government, but rather a federal structure of independent states. He admitted that war was "a regrettable expedient in the state of nature," but suggested that a *society* of independent republics would regard war among themselves as irrational—though they might need to defend themselves from war-prone nonrepublics (Kant, 1795, 79, 92, 101–2).

Warfare and international politics: A military revolution?

In the era of Kant's essay, warfare was transformed by the French Republic's struggle (at first defensive, then offensive) against the counterrevolution and by its employment of the *levée en masse*, a conscripted citizen army. Subsequently, the large, renewable resource of "the nation in arms," combined with the superiority of French staff work and the corps and divisional structure of French armies, enabled Napoleon's reconceptualization of how armies might be used. This may not only have been a matter of new resources, however. The era of the Revolution, it has been argued, saw a *cultural shift* from a military ethos of "forbearance" to one of attack. Together, these changed, it may be argued, the ways in which force and the threat of force would play out in international politics. In contrast to the cautious chess-playing of many eighteenth-century generals with carefully scripted, limited objectives, Napoleon, the supreme opportunist, once observed that one might fight simply to see what happens.

The failure of Europe, that is, of the several successive coalitions, to balance effectively against Napoleon was due not only to Napoleon's destruction of opposing powers—individually and together—in battle, but to the attractions of bandwagoning with the French, something that was dependent, as Napoleon knew, on his sustaining the appearance as well as the reality of hegemonic power: "My power depends on my glory and … [it] will fail if I do not feed it on new glories and new victories." Traditional warfare of territorial adjustment was transmuted under Napoleon into a hybrid of revolutionary, nationalist, and dynastic ambition; his armies humbled empires and reconstructed Europe both in the field and through his coercive diplomacy. War was frequent ("I regard any conclusion of peace as a short truce") and necessary—not least to fund the French army and to reward his officers with land and cash from indemnities. But Napoleon's wars, though involving masses of men and, often, heavy casualties, were intended to be quick rather than drawn out. There was diplomacy during the conflicts, which were followed by settlements that advanced his current objectives. A bully in negotiations, Napoleon saw treaties as short-term fixes, and had, unlike Frederick the Great before him or Bismarck afterward, little interest in creating lasting solutions once some immediate territorial or political ambition had been gratified.

The art of war

War lies at the heart of international relations and of the discipline of IR. Its best-known systematic study is that of Carl von Clausewitz (1780–1831), *On War* (published posthumously and unfinished in 1831). Clausewitz, famous for his dictum that "war is nothing but the continuation of politics by other means," was a Prussian general and director of the Prussian Military Academy who had fought in the Napoleonic wars. In the work for which he is renowned, he sought to present warfare not as moral or immoral but as a *phenomenon present throughout history* that could be studied, not as a science exactly because of the role of chance and of what he called unanticipated "friction" in combat, but as a field of human activity. As he says, war is *a social activity* like commerce, litigation, or politics. His study thus fits into the Enlightenment project of trying to comprehend all human activities more systematically.

Nevertheless, Clausewitz argued that analysis of the present that is grounded in general patterns and rules drawn from history was likely to err. He observed that war was often like a game of cards, and that chance, and how to exploit it, might be better understood as a factor (there is a line that runs from Clausewitz to modern "game theory"). Though his study references history—especially the wars of Frederick the Great and the then-recent campaigns of Napoleon—it does not offer a general theory drawn from past experience: history moved, and tactics and strategies that were appropriate to the world of fifty or a hundred years past were poor guides to the present (Frederick the Great's tactics had been made obsolete by Napoleon)—just as the experiences of his own world would be inadequate guides in the future.

For Clausewitz, what had most importantly changed in his lifetime was that war in Europe had become general rather than limited, involving the mobilization of the whole state and people with a strategic field encompassing all of Europe (Clausewitz, it might be claimed, invented the concept of "escalation"). Frederick and Napoleon were geniuses, he argued, in the way they grasped the unique situations in which they lived. Such genius involved not only tactical savvy, but larger intellectual and emotional (i.e., psychological) qualities, strength of character, and also a kind of intuition that he called the successful general's *coup d'oeil* or inward eye that could instantly recognize an opportunity. The genius also, he thought, possessed the insight that if war were to be taken up in the pursuit of whatever objective, it had to be engaged in *without reservation*, whether the objective was limited and defensive or the total domination of an enemy. As he said, war is by definition an act of force: "If one side uses force without compunction, undeterred by the bloodshed it involves, while the other side refrains, the first will gain the upper hand" (Clausewitz, 1831, 84). Statements like this have served to place Clausewitz in the pantheon of Realist writers, though nowhere does he justify the decision to go to war for whatever purpose. If he is clearly outside the Grotian "international law" tradition that has sought to understand what a just war might be or to create rules of conduct, neither can he be regarded as a glorifier of war for its own sake.

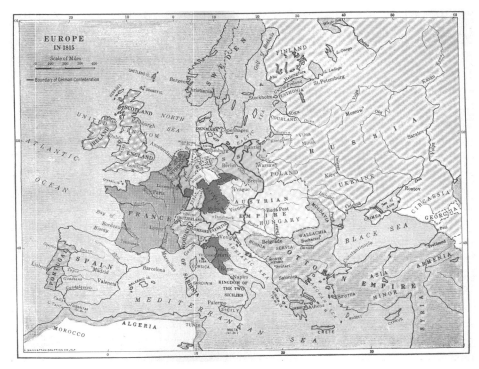

Figure 7.1 Europe and the Congress of Vienna.

Source: Albert Hyma, *A Short History of Europe, 1500–1815* (New York: F. S. Crofts & Co., 1928).

Vienna and the Congress System

In this era, states seem less the billiard balls of IR theory than malleable and divisible polities, and domestic sovereignty a dubious and challenged thing: the Jacobin revolutionaries threatened subversion of other states, while the powers they faced fought not only for territory and to restrain threatened French hegemony—traditional motives—but to change the revolutionary regime in France. In some countries, as in the Netherlands or northern Italy, local people rose up against their own "sovereign" governments in anticipation of French "liberation." The Prussian and Austrian monarchies were only able to retrieve their position by putting themselves at the head of a new kind of patriotism.

This was what the Congress of Vienna faced in recreating the "system" of the eighteenth century (Figure 7.1). The wars of the Republic and the Napoleonic Empire forced surviving regimes to reform their own bureaucracies, finances, and military organization, as well as pay lip service to a new nationalism. The large powers generally grew larger and more powerful at the expense of smaller states, but also more confused (Michael Mann says "polymorphous")—as old regime monarchs, and their militaries, confronted new classes and new forms of state-as-national identity, encouraged by expanding popular institutions of association (clubs and societies of all kinds proliferated). National newspapers and journals became fora for the widespread discussion of domestic and foreign policy (at least among the bourgeoisie).

Like Westphalia in 1643–8 and Paris in 1919, the Congress of Vienna is an iconic event in the history of European politics and diplomacy, one of the great moments for the working of the multipolar European Great Power system. It was attended in person by the sovereign majesties of some of the powers (Austria, Russia, Prussia, Denmark; sovereigns had not attended the Westphalia Congress) and by foreign ministers, significant advisors, and numerous staff. The four Great Power Allies (Britain, Austria, Prussia, and Russia) and Bourbon France were joined by lesser powers like Denmark and Spain (but, at Russia's insistence, not by representatives of the Ottoman Empire), while driven by ambition or fear a host of the concerned rushed to Vienna to put their cases for the large and minor German states (the king of Saxony was, however, not invited). They met in Metternich's rooms on the Ballhausplatz in the Austrian capital (twice occupied by Napoleon) after the French Emperor had been sent into his first exile in 1814. Though it had been expected that the business of settling a peace would take at most a few weeks, the conference in fact lasted from September through the winter and following spring, and through the "hundred days" of Napoleon's return to Paris, into June of 1815.

The Congress of Vienna has long attracted a popular narrative of the personalities involved, their machinations, and the consequences of their handiwork for the era that followed. For diplomatic historians, the conference has been the subject of intense study based on the surviving archives of personal correspondence, memoirs, and official papers. Among the key players, the commanding figures were the Autocrat of All the Russias, Tsar Alexander I (1777–1825), who like Wilson in 1919 would act quite independently of his foreign ministry advisers; Charles Maurice de Talleyrand (1754–1838), long-surviving representative of the restored Louis XVIII of France; Robert Stewart, Lord Castlereagh (1769–1822), the foreign secretary and plenipotentiary of a British government that was content to let him exercise a nearly complete independence of judgment; and Clemens von Metternich (1773–1859), the Austrian minister who would take center stage in European affairs not only at the conference but for subsequent decades.

Metternich, later chancellor of the Austrian Empire, was born in the Rhineland to a father who was an aristocrat and diplomat (for Austria). A youth at the University of Strasbourg at the outbreak of the French Revolution, his career in the Austrian service, facilitated by family and marriage connections, saw his rapid rise—ambassador to Berlin and then, in 1806, to Paris. From his appointment as foreign minister in 1809 (after Austria had been defeated and Vienna occupied a second time by Napoleon), Metternich's chief objective was to return Austria to influence—first through a dynastic marriage (of Emperor Francis I's oldest child Marie-Louise to Napoleon) and latterly, after Napoleon's fall, as the "arbiter of Europe" in whatever arrangements might be made for the restoration of European "order." France, under whatever regime, was to be restrained by positioning Austria as protector of a reformed German Confederation and as the dominant Power in post-Napoleonic Italy. At the same time, Metternich was also concerned that neither Prussia, a competitor for leadership of the smaller

German states, nor, more importantly, Russia, with its vast potential for interference in Western Europe, emerged in a commanding position in the postwar world.

As Metternich said, "No great political insight is needed to see that this Congress could not be modelled on any which had taken place." Its scope was to be wide-ranging and its organization reflected this: there were special committees established to consider the German, Swiss, and Italian questions, the abolition of the slave trade, and the regulation of international waterways. An important innovation, on Castlereagh's suggestion, was a "statistical committee" to research, especially, the facts of population in contested regions.

Beyond the divisive territorial issues that required in any event attention as the French imperial regime collapsed, the conference faced two overarching objectives: that of guarding against a future, resurgent France, and that of securing not only a "balance" among the other Great Powers, but their active, enduring collaboration in preserving future order. France itself, unlike the defeated powers of Germany and Austria in 1919, secured a place at the table of "Allied" powers at Vienna—not as an enemy but, through Talleyrand's adroit pleading, as a "legitimate" restored state. The idea or project of a *Concert* of the Great Powers, to be sustained after the settlement, was the notable consequence of the Congress; it would require and ensure Austria's continuing status for years to come.

A few months prior to the fall of Napoleon, Castlereagh had negotiated an alliance (of Britain, Austria, Russia, and Prussia, the last of the successive coalitions against France that had been inaugurated by the British Prime Minister William Pitt, the Younger, in 1793) not only to secure the French Emperor's final defeat but to "fix the means of maintaining against every attempt the order of things which shall have been the happy consequence of their efforts"—that is, to pursue together and enforce a stable peace. The agreement at Chaumont included an explicit declaration that it had for its object "the maintenance of the balance of Europe, to secure the repose and independence of the Powers." Subsequently, upon the restoration of the Bourbon monarchy, the two treaties of Paris (before and after Napoleon's Hundred Days) dealt separately with French territorial boundaries and reparations. The powers at Vienna dealt with wider issues involving the states system itself: myriad territorial "adjustments," the restoration of "legitimate" sovereigns, and the claims and counterclaims of the dispossessed or ambitious, but also, ultimately, the erection of a system of collective security (the Concert or, subsequently, Congress System) whereby the Great Powers would meet periodically or in time of crisis. That is, the Great Powers at Vienna were to prevent future conflict, not through a mechanical reliance on the laws of balancing, but through the active policing of stability by the most powerful European states.

Vienna did not attempt to restore, in facsimile form, the Europe that Napoleon had destroyed. The key issues involved the fate of Saxony (whose king had allied with Napoleon and whose territory was coveted by Prussia), the future of other German states once part of the defunct Holy Roman Empire and the character of the association of those that survived in a new *Bund* or federation, the claims, including those of the pope and of Spanish Bourbon legitimists, to this or that part of Italy, and, most divisive of all, the disposition of the large central European territories once part of the partitioned Kingdom of Poland. In the event, Russian gains in Poland were balanced by Austrian gains in Italy (Lombardy and the Venetia, including Venice) and Prussian acquisitions in the Rhineland (rather than all of Saxony). The Low Country became a buffer between France and Prussia by joining Belgium and Holland into one state; the German states of Saxony and Bavaria were to serve the same function between Austria and Prussia: Germany, one delegate said later, had to be a kind of shock absorber and hence had to remain disunited in the interests of peace, preserving the "balance through an inherent force of gravity." Rather than a contentious restoration of the Habsburg-dominated Holy Roman Empire, a new "German Confederation" (of fewer and larger German states) was established under the presidency of Austria—strong enough to discourage French aggression, but too weak itself to threaten the European balance.

Like Westphalia more than a century and a half earlier, Vienna was an unusual example of multi- rather than bilateral negotiation, a conference deliberating European-wide issues. Vienna's multipolarity was of course largely restricted to that of the Great Powers, hardly influenced by the many lesser states whose fates were decided around the Congress tables. Nevertheless, in the aftermath of the defeat of Napoleon, one finds, overlaying the logic of interests of state, an articulation of a concept of an *international system* as a "community of states," a "general concert," a "cultural family," a "society of nations." One might also note, with Jeremy Black, that religion, which some claim progressively receded as a factor after Westphalia, returned in this era as a powerful force: it was, in England and elsewhere, a source of opposition to revolution and to Napoleon, it of course informed Alexander's reactionary project of a Holy Alliance, and—most importantly—would in the nineteenth century contribute significantly to ethno-national identities (Black, 2002, 18, 20).

The system policed, 1815–22

In the years following Vienna, conservative statesmen looked back on the turmoil brought to the European state system by the French Revolution and Napoleon's ambition, and hoped to devise alliances and a process that would operate to conserve the status quo. There were, in their eyes, two great threats of instability: war between the Great Powers, which could open the door to popular revolt, and nationalistic liberalism that threatened the integrity, especially, of autocratic multicultural empires. These concerns highlighted the fact that the balance-of-power regime of the eighteenth century, marked by frequent limited wars followed by negotiated, balancing peace settlements, might no longer be adequate. Famously, Tsar Alexander I, regarded by many as an enlightened "liberator" who had earlier expressed liberal sentiments and was no special friend of Bourbon legitimacy, became obsessed with a kind of evangelical messianism, determined to resist ungodly revolution and to preserve the role of religion in public affairs through a Holy Alliance of Russia, Austria, and Prussia (the Austrian emperor is supposed to have remarked that he did not know whether these proposals should be discussed in the Council of Ministers or the confessional). The Holy Alliance aimed to secure the conservative character of lesser regimes throughout the European system. It was accommodated by Metternich, if not Britain, but had ceased to have much force by the time of Alexander's death in 1825.

More tangibly, Metternich's concern after Vienna was to institute a *process* through periodic congresses of the Great Powers that would head off war among the powers while (unintended in Castlereagh's original project) suppressing radical liberalism in Spain, the Germanies, Greece, or Italy. The Quadruple Alliance was continued through a series of subsequent congresses. There were five by 1822, when the system of regular meetings was abandoned, largely due to British reluctance to intervene in the domestic affairs of states. Thereafter, ambassadorial (rather than ministerial or head of state) congresses served to sustain the idea of Great Power regulation, as a "concert of Europe," at times of impending crisis or war—as at the London conference of 1830 that followed the Belgian revolt against the Netherlands, or (less successfully) that in 1864 on the Schleswig-Holstein issue.

The system challenged and remade

Though some version of the concert of the Great Powers is manifest throughout the long nineteenth century, the conservative restoration envisioned in the post-Vienna structure promoted and defended by Metternich came under increasing stress from the rise of domestic liberalism in the West (itself symptomatic of deep shifts in social and economic forces there) and the emergence of a powerful current of ethno-nationalism in Poland, Spain, Greece, Hungary, Italy, and the Germanies. A French revolution against the Bourbon Restoration in 1830 opened fissures throughout Europe that promised to bring the whole structure down. Another in 1848 did so, if only briefly. Violent regime change throughout western and central Europe seemed likely as radical and liberal opposition commanded the streets of first Paris, then Berlin and Vienna. Of the powers, only autocratic Russia, "gendarme of Europe," was a secure-seeming bastion of counterrevolution, intervening to save the Austrian Empire (though not Metternich, who was forced to retire), Prussia, and Hungary. That revolution was again mastered—due to Russian and Prussian military intervention but also to the domestic anxieties of a protection-seeking liberal bourgeoisie—should not conceal the fact that the restored concert, and the stability and power of key members (Britain, France, perhaps Prussia), now depended to some degree at least on the uncertain foundations of bourgeois liberalism.

The French problem, Austrian weakness, and new nations

The French political instability and the danger that a more populist government there would encourage instability elsewhere through emulation or direct French promotion of liberal and nationalist forces emerged as a central threat to the working of a system dedicated to maintaining the status quo. These fears seemed confirmed when the revolutionary disorder in Paris in 1848–9 led inexorably to the emergence of a plebiscitary neo-imperial Bonapartist regime under a nephew of Napoleon I, Louis-Napoleon. The Second Empire (1852–70) raised traditional fears of the return of French expansionism—of Napoleonic *gloire* and ambition. France remained the largest, most populous state in western and central Europe, and by mid-century was undergoing both a rapid industrialization and a booming financial sector. Moreover, Napoleon III sought not only to advance traditional French objectives (in, say, the Middle East), but rhetorically to advance France's hegemonic role in Europe as that of a chief promoter, protector, and exploiter of the emerging politics of ethno-nationalism. His embrace of the Polish and Italian causes directly threatened the integrity of those conservative powers that had sought to balance against France in the decades since Vienna.

The long nineteenth century is sometimes presented as a hundred years of peace, evidence of the successful working of a concert system that, while not preventing war among Great Powers, at least ensured that these did not spread to engulf the continent as a whole as had happened in the era of Napoleon I—or would, announcing the breakdown of the system, in 1914. Though the concert failed to prevent a major conflict among three of the Great Powers (and the Porte) in 1854, the Crimean War did not become a European-wide conflict and the negotiated settlement at the Congress of Paris in 1856 can be seen to have endorsed the guiding concept of balance generally (against supposed Russian expansionism) and the need for the system to shore up the disintegration of the Ottoman regime lest its territories, as spoils of war, serve to threaten that balance. The key had been the refusal of Austria to join with Russia against France and Britain as Russia expected it to do.

During Metternich's time Austrian weakness, as a confused if absolutist multicultural (increasingly multinational) state, may have worked to its advantage. It was socially conservative and its politics cosmopolitan (at least in Vienna). It was a threat to no other power. It was territorially satiated. Austria was also protected by the sense that it was necessary to the system. Its territory could not be allowed to fall to any of the other continental powers. In the decades that followed 1856, however, exposure of the Austrian Empire's weakness would make it another "sick man" of Europe, raising concern that its status as a Great Power—or indeed as a continuing state at all—was in doubt. Metternich's principle of defending the status quo and avoiding war had encouraged respect for treaties and consultation among the powers. The revolutions of 1848, the fall of Metternich, and the rise of Napoleon III in France and Bismarck in Prussia saw the coming of an era of cynical Realpolitik in which war was again a calculated means of revising the system. If the Great Power wars after Crimea were bilateral conflicts that did not involve the rest of the powers, cumulatively, the wars of 1859, 1864, 1866, and 1870 effected as significant a transformation of the European system as an all-power war might have done.

In 1859, Napoleon III moved quickly to head off a European congress and defeated Austria in Italy (neither liberal Britain nor absolutist Russia was willing to "balance" against France). Defeat in Italy weakened Austria and prepared the way for the emergence of a united Italy—and for a Prussian bid to replace Austria as the dominant power over the lesser German states that Otto von Bismarck (1815–98) regarded with contempt as "little sovereignties." In 1864, Prussia, under the masterful guidance of Bismarck, appointed minister-president of Prussia from 1862, allied with a hesitant Austria to defeat Denmark before an all-power conference in London could act—this secured Schleswig-Holstein and made Prussia dominant in the Bund. In 1866, Bismarck's Prussia defeated Austria (French support was withheld, and Russia—still smarting perhaps from the "betrayal" of 1854—did not intervene), removing Austria from the German Federation and positioning Prussia for the last of the three wars of German unification.

In 1870, Bismarck maneuvered Napoleon III into declaring war on Prussia, adroitly ensuring that there would be no Great Power interference or attempt at congress arbitration. The defeat of France was swiftly followed by the declaration of a Prussian-dominated German Empire that excluded Austria—a Germany that had been created by acts of violence ("blood and iron," in Bismarck's language) rather than the liberal constitutionalism that the failed National Assembly of 1849 had envisioned.

Why, some IR scholars have worried, did balancing, as a system law, not operate to block the rise of Prussia/Germany? The failure of the powers to balance against a Prussia that was clearly acting in a "normatively disruptive" way has produced some debate. Mearsheimer argues that, in 1864 at least, the stakes seemed too small to generate aggressive Great Power balancing. Others emphasize miscalculation and "buck-passing," domestic factors, or the fact that Prussia's "legitimation strategy"—the use of rhetoric that variously appealed to both dynastic concerns and nationalist sentiment—served to defuse any concerted Great Power response. In the last analysis, however, credit seems most due to Bismarck's special genius for creating uncertainty among other states about Prussia's intentions, and isolating and encouraging differences among potential opponents.

New nations

The romantic nationalism that proliferated in the nineteenth century constituted both an immediate and potential intrusion of the domestic into the operation of the Great Power concert by unsettling the regimes of the conservative powers, adding a powerful irredentist motive to those of system stability and state security, and complicating the math by which the system balanced. Europe saw the disappearance of many small principalities that had acted as buffers between Great Powers, the engorgement of a former power as a likely new hegemon (Prussia), the addition of one (*soi disant*) Great Power (Italy), and a proliferation of small sovereign and quasi-sovereign states in eastern Europe and the Balkans that were deeply committed to their own ethnic identities in the imposing context of a "Macedonian salad" of cultural diversity.

Greece had led the way and its success announced the progressive dissolution of the Ottoman regime in Europe, creating, as had long been feared, a cockpit in the Balkans for at least a potential competition among the powers. The "Eastern Question" would bedevil late nineteenth-century European politics. Greece was followed by the long struggle for an Italian republic (successfully hijacked by the monarchy of Piedmont-Sardinia and its ally imperial France), to the significant cost of the Austrians. The most dramatic game-changer, however, was the emergence of a new German Empire built on Bismarck's wars and diplomacy and threatening, with its great population, industrial progress, and military prowess, whatever balance the system had maintained since the defeat of Napoleon I.

With the destruction of a role for Austria in the Germanies or in Italy, the Austro-Hungarian Empire, as it was reconstituted after the war with Prussia, found itself repositioned as a lesser power clinging to its historic status, torn by its own nationalist minorities, and looking toward the Slavic east as a (hoped for) solution to both its domestic and international condition. It would emerge from its *Ausgleich* with the kingdom of Hungary as a declining and nervous power less likely to balance with Russia. Austria's diplomatic role increasingly served to partner Bismarck's Germany: she remained neutral in the Franco-Prussian War in 1870 and, though joining the Three Emperors' League (Russia, Germany, Austria) in 1873, portentously negotiated a Dual Alliance with Germany in 1879.

War and the nation-state

Do nationalism and the idea of the nation-state change the ways in which the sovereign state system operates? Do they change the reasons states go to war, the way they go to war, and the way they conduct their wars? In the face of Kantian optimism about the inclination of democratic regimes to stay at peace, it has long been accepted that nationalism and ethnic identity—closely associated with nineteenth-century democratization—served to promote conflict, a perspective encouraged by the post-Communist fate of the Balkans at the end of the twentieth century and recently endorsed by Andreas Wimmer in *Waves of War: Nationalism, State Formation, and Ethnic Exclusion in the Modern World* (2013). Although many Realists hold that states have to operate within the external constraints of the system, regardless of whether they are dynastic, liberal/democratic, multicultural empires, or ethnically constructed, some military historians have argued that there are "cultures of warfare" and that the culture of the democratic nation-state may affect both military performance and strategy; some Constructivists would argue that "identity politics" may subvert rational calculation. Though many historians would sympathize with the Constructivist view, the massive prominence of Bismarck in maintaining the recreated state system would seem to argue for the powerful importance of rational Realpolitik and an awareness of the security dilemma. Bismarck, essentially a loyal monarchist, both disparaged and sought to manipulate democracy and nationalism.

Ethnic nationalism was the second "big idea" in the politics of the long nineteenth century (revolution was the other), powerfully instrumental in the creation of Greece, Italy, and a Prussian-dominated German Empire (though with German Austria outside its borders, Bismarck's Germany was not the *Grossdeutschland* envisioned by liberal nationalists). It also seeped into the ethos of dynastic empires like Russia and Austria, which were multicultural but within which there was a dominant ethnicity. Nationalism as populist patriotism, however, whether ethnically constructed or not, became a huge force everywhere—and traditional elites had to accommodate this (very awkwardly in the Austrian case).

How, then, might nationalism impact the idea of *reason of state*, that is, the determination of state interests? Clausewitz well understood the difference to the conduct of warfare that the national idea—that is, the idea of the general will rather than mere dynastic ambition—made to warfare in his lifetime. It clearly affected the means by which the state could defend itself or seek to impose its will on others. Though the expansive and revolutionary concept of the entire nation in arms was made more prosaically and normatively operational in the latter half of the century through (limited) conscription, more narrowly defined terms of shorter service, and the creation of large reserves of those men who had performed their national service, the national idea implied an *absolute character* to warfare, in part to justify the general sacrifices of the people. The object of such war carried out by the nation in arms was a matter no longer of check and countercheck but the annihilation (*Vernichtung*) of the enemy. It was this reading of Clausewitz that Helmuth von Moltke, the Chief of the Prussian General Staff in the 1850s and 1860s, pressed upon his officers. War should never be half-hearted; its object was the total defeat of an enemy, and he recommended his officers read Homer, the Bible, and Clausewitz.

The new German Empire was hammered out by Bismarck and von Moltke on the anvil of war, and though Bismarck then worked to stabilize the new European power constellation he had created, the idea that the nation's destiny had been born out of war and the supposed warlike ardor of its people constituted a central element of the "Prussianism" that seemed often to lie at the heart of the German ethos. Clausewitz, ironically not himself a pan-German nationalist, had emphasized what he called the "moral" aspects of war—by which he meant the force that came from courage, conviction, and audacity. The "spirit of boldness" that characterized the greatest commanders and armies of the people would spill over as it were into the character of the state itself: "A people and nation can hope for a strong position in the world only if national character and familiarity with war fortify each other by continual interaction" (226). He admitted that a people "fortified" by experience of warfare would also be likely to develop a hatred of other nations and especially the desire for revenge, passions that governments would be compelled to control—and perhaps make use of. In 1883, Colmar von der Goltz published a much-read work, *Das Volk im Waffen* (*The People Armed*). In it he says that Clausewitz as much as Goethe was the father of his nation.

Realist theory asserts that the most important state interest is survival (self-defense) and assumes the rational pursuit of this primary goal. But the nationalist ethos is inherently built on emotion—patriotism, brotherhood, and blood—rather than calculation. Clausewitz assumed that the natural state of the European system was one of balance, of status quo, and this balance itself was maintained in part by a state being able to threaten the annihilation of an opponent to enhance its negotiations. But what if the nation is seen to be not a fixed, territorial entity or a dynasty, but something in the process of becoming, a destiny, a people—many of whom may regrettably live outside the formal boundaries of the present state?

The politics of irredentism (from the Italian *irridento*—the unredeemed) follow naturally from Greek, Italian, and German independence and unification and added a significant motive for the resort to war in order to "finish" the national destiny; it also threatened to pull apart multiethnic states like the Austrian, Russian, or Ottoman empires. Governments everywhere, autocracies as well as democracies, became more dependent upon (and anxious about) public opinion and were tempted or driven to a politics of ethnicity in order to shore up their domestic position even when Realpolitik and state security may have counseled otherwise.

International Relations in Europe and abroad after 1870

The narrative of European diplomacy in the era from 1870 to the outbreak of the First World War commonly revolves around (1) the increasingly strained efforts of the master of the reconstituted concert system, Bismarck, to preserve Germany's gains and security within a balanced European system; (2) the extension of European concerns to include the "diplomacy of imperialism" as powers competed for territory and spheres of influence in Africa and Asia; and (3) the failure of Bismarck's successors, an epigone generation, to match the judgment and guile necessary to keep the system in trim. The classic scholarly study of the era is A. J. P. Taylor's *The Struggle for Europe, 1848–1918* (1954).

Taylor and many scholars who followed treated the narrative as one, largely, of politics and diplomacy, though some like Arno J. Mayer in his 1981 text, *The Persistence of the Old Regime*, have emphasized the social and cultural conditioning of the traditional elite who dominated the making of foreign policy and of the bourgeoisie who deferred to them. Others, including historical sociologists like Michael Mann and Anthony Giddens, have more recently reengaged the older Marxist perspective and drawn attention to ways in which the economic changes impelled by industrial capitalism affected the nature of the modern nation-state, the role of its military, and its means of waging war. Mann has advanced the notion of "polymorphous factionalism" as characteristic of a nation-state like Germany where competing old elites, capitalist elites, the military, and the bureaucracy produced confusion and contradiction rather than Weberian rationalism, culminating in the aggression that led to war in 1914—"German aggression was not considered or 'realist'" (Mann, 1993, 798).

At the heart of Taylor's influential work, however, was the political-diplomatic Balance of Power (capitalized by Taylor) and his assertion that it "determined everything for Bismarck," a "calculation almost as pure as in the days before the French Revolution" (Taylor, 1954, xx and 240). Though Taylor himself was no theorist, his work has been regarded by many IR scholars as endorsing a Realist perspective. More recently, Paul Schroeder has taken exception to this view, arguing that balance of power may take different forms and serve different purposes. Taylor, who uses the concept as largely a figure of speech, hardly advances a systems theorist's mechanistic view of balancing. Beneath the surface of Taylor's text, there is another balance of power "struggling to get out," a "sort of ideal" that in fact did not much determine policy. According to Schroeder's reading of Taylor, the critical issue is not "balancing" as such, but the ways in which alliances were operated—more for the restraint and management of *allies* than for the projection of power (Schroeder, 2001, 16–20). It was the abandonment of this purposeful use of alliances after Bismarck that put Europe on the slippery slope to general war.

The late nineteenth-century European system—and its failure—has been of enduring interest to diplomatic historians, for whom the period continues to offer a (perhaps no-longer-so-rich) mine for dissertations and scholarly debate. Within Political Science IR, the variety of Realists find here a never-failing source of confirmation of system logic, Realpolitik, the security dilemma, or (for Offensive Realists) the drive for power maximization.

While Offensive Realism seeks confirmation in the pre-First World War breakdown of the concert system, its theory appears to have less traction when applied to the long-peaceful post-Vienna or Bismarckian eras. It has, for instance, been argued that a compulsive drive to maximize power does not well explain the apparent restraint of both Alexander I and Nicholas I in pursuing Russian advantage in the West or in the declining Ottoman Empire. As Matthew Rendall puts it, "The concert of Europe's members were good defensive realists … If great powers are as aggressive as Mearsheimer claims, Russia should have taken all it could get away with" (Rendall, 2006, 524, 530). And in the era dominated by Bismarck, the Iron Chancellor's elaborate structure was designed, not, it would seem, further to advance German hegemony, but to conserve its position in a classic example of a Great Power decision-maker concerned with the security dilemma. The later risk-taking and drive for *Weltmacht* reflects, from the Neoclassical or Defensive Realist perspective, disastrous incompetence rather than the dictates of a natural drive for power maximization. Others, including many historians and some Realists, would turn to domestic factors in explaining both moderation and aggression.

Great Power diplomacy in late nineteenth-century Europe

Gordon Craig observed that the diplomatic balance of power system in Europe worked best in the first half of the nineteenth century when, for the most part, foreign ministers did not have to worry much about public opinion (Craig and George, 1990, 32–3). By the 1870s, most European powers, Russia excepted, were if not democracies, parliamentary regimes, and public opinion became an important consideration in the making of foreign policy—and even in autocratic Russia there was increasing concern to co-opt Slavic nationalism in shoring up its illiberal foundations. As the middle class took a more active interest in the politics of the state, its own interests and ethos became instrumental, and romantic nationalism was especially powerful among the prosperous, newspaper-reading middle classes.

By the late nineteenth-century, war and empire also became the stock in trade of a cheap, illustrated, mass-market popular press that could jingoistically work up public passions among the lower middle and working classes made literate by state education and given the vote in Britain, Germany, and France.

Finally, the mature development of an industrialized, exporting economy in Western Europe had a far-reaching influence on the practice of international relations by (1) adding well-developed commercial and financial interests to those state interests of security and prestige that traditionally inform the politics of international relations; (2) pitting free traders like Britain against protectionist powers like Germany; and (3) making success in war ever more dependent on industrial weapons technology and an ability to pay for it. Arms races came to threaten to destabilize the European balance by the early twentieth century. And finally (4) an advanced industrial economy also meant a numerous industrial proletariat, the loyalty of which was an increasing concern. A patriotic war might have domestic advantages for the ruling elites by distracting the underclass from socialist internationalism.

The nineteenth-century diplomatic establishment

In spite of the popular force of demotic nationalism, the nineteenth-century diplomatic system and its practitioners remained to a significant degree cosmopolitan and elitist—French was the accepted language of diplomacy and *top* diplomats continued to be, throughout Europe, recruited from the traditional social elite—but with a growing meritocratic element among the professional civil servants who served them.

Prussia led the way toward meritocracy among its diplomatic officialdom—though a German ambassador to the end of the era would be expected to have a "von" or "zu" in his name. Already by the early nineteenth century admission to a diplomatic career in Prussia was normally by examination; candidates had to have completed three years at university, passed the two first examinations required by the state civil service, and served for eighteen months in provincial government. If then selected by the minister, they had to work for a year as unpaid attachés before sitting further examinations in modern political history, commerce and law, and oral and written French.

Foreign office and diplomatic personnel changed most in the French Third Republic after the fall of Napoleon III in 1870. The dominant Radicals sought to democratize government service: competitive examination was required of all candidates after 1877, and by the early years of the twentieth century a diploma from the *Ecole Libre des Sciences Politiques* ("Sciences Po," founded in 1872 to train a foreign policy elite) counted for more than aristocratic background. In liberal Britain, on the other hand, the traditional landed classes managed to cling to positions of considerable influence. The British civil service reforms that mandated competitive examination after the Crimean War were not fully implemented in the Foreign Office, where nomination (i.e., "connections") remained a common means of entry and family wealth an important prerequisite. As one would expect, in autocratic Russia the foreign service—a large cumbersome affair—remained significantly aristocratic, yet even here there were gestures toward meritocracy: after 1859, Russian diplomats had to pass an examination in modern languages, "diplomatic science" (i.e., international law, economics, and statistics), and writing—but nobles were admitted "in personal right" and an ambassadorship required both wealth and connections.

In most of the Great Powers, foreign service bureaucracies at home grew significantly, as did the diplomatic corps abroad. In Prussia, the foreign office moved into new quarters in Berlin's Wilhelmstrasse in 1819; the French Foreign Office was moved by Napoleon III to the Quai d'Orsay in the late 1850s; Britain saw, from the 1860s on, an extensive rebuilding of Whitehall in a grand Italianate style, including a new Foreign Office between Parliament and Downing Street. Of the eastern empires, Austria's foreign affairs bureaucracy had long shared, on the edge of the Hoffburg in Vienna, the eighteenth-century building in the Ballhausplatz where the Congress of Vienna met in 1815; in Russia, however, a massive new building in the center of the capital St. Petersburg was opened in 1827 for both the general staff and the Foreign Ministry.

In the last analysis, throughout Europe the character of those who were recruited to work in often elegant and substantial edifices did not change as much as the introduction of examination and the promotion of middle-class men by merit might suggest. Pre-First World War foreign offices and the diplomatic corps were strongly marked by an ethos of aristocratic superiority and wealth.

Bismarck's system

Bismarck, it is said, violated the concert of Europe in order to build up Prussia, and then worked hard to recreate it in order to protect Germany. Unlike Metternich, his loyalties were not to Europe in the abstract but to the Hohenzollern dynasty. Its power and self-interest were to be advanced by any means necessary, in an elaborate game of chance divorced from morality. "Politics," he said, "is the art of the possible." Having broken the Austrians and the French, Bismarck's new German Empire (proclaimed at the Palace of Versailles in 1871) was in danger of being regarded as the kind of hegemon against which other nations had in the past sought to balance, while the annexation of Alsace and Lorraine ensured enduring French enmity. Bismarck's objective for the next twenty years was to prevent balancing against Germany by (1) encouraging a concert of conservative powers (the so-called Three Emperors' League of Germany, Russia, and Austria [1873 and 1881]) and (2) keeping potential enemies from combining against the Reich (France and Britain; France and Russia). This is the last classic period of a system of "cabinet diplomacy" operating at the level of Great Power negotiation (public and secret) to adjust a balance that would preserve general peace. For Bismarck to operate effectively at its center, Germany had to be seen to be a *satisfied* power without threatening ambitions.

The Congress of Berlin (June–July 1878) is the great set piece of late nineteenth-century multilateral European diplomacy. It successfully prevented a war among Great Powers and enhanced Bismarck's role as "honest broker" of the European system. A war between Russia and the Ottoman Empire had resulted in the humiliating Treaty of San Stefano that stripped the Porte of much of its European territory in the Balkans, creating a large Bulgaria with access to the Aegean—through which Russian designs might proliferate. This concerned the British because the spread of the Russian sphere of influence at Constantinople, in the eastern Mediterranean, and in central Asia threatened their interests, and because the collapse of Ottoman power threatened the balance in Europe generally (something that also concerned Bismarck). The Austrians were concerned about the threat the newly independent Balkan states might pose to their own influence in the region. Britain and Austria demanded a congress to adjudicate these issues.

Held at Bismarck's chancellery, the congress was attended by chief ministers and foreign secretaries—Bismarck as chancellor of the German Reich, Benjamin Disraeli as prime minister of Great Britain, Prince Gorchakov as foreign minister of Russia, and Count Andrassy as foreign minister for Austria-Hungary. The Porte, France, and Italy were also represented and there were delegates from the Balkans. Russia yielded: Bulgaria was sharply reduced, independent states of Montenegro, Serbia, and Romania recognized, Austria-Hungary allowed to occupy Bosnia-Herzegovina, Turkey to reoccupy Macedonia. The result was a defeat for Russian ambitions and a great victory for Disraeli, though Bismarck's role may have damaged his own ability to keep Russia on side in future diplomatic maneuvering. The elaborate structure Bismarck erected, of course, was likely to fail eventually. It was undermined in the end by his own failing powers, the impatience of a new Kaiser, and the rise of a more aggressive generation of German leaders with more overt designs to advance German hegemony.

Imperialism and the international relations of (European) empires

The imperial pretentions and multicultural character of the premodern autocracies of Russia, Austria, and the Porte remained, with difficulty, outside the Western European ideology of the sovereign nation-state. After defeat by the Prussians and the *Ausgleich* (union with Hungary) of 1867, the Austrian ruler of what was now known as the Dual Monarchy remained emperor of Austria, with territory reaching from the Adriatic in the south to Polish Galicia in the north, king of Bohemia (the Czechs), Hungary, and Croatia, and (potential) suzerain of the contiguous Balkan territories. Meanwhile, Russian expansion meant the imperial regime had come to dominate a vast number of peoples in the west, the east through central Asia to the Pacific, and the south beyond the Caucasus. Though the tsar ruled over Roman Catholic, Orthodox Catholic, Protestant, Muslim, and Jewish peoples, in fact the unreformed autocracy increasingly emphasized its role as protector of the orthodox Slavs. Finally, in theory the Ottoman Empire stretched from Baghdad in the East to Morocco in the West, and the Sultan claimed both sovereign political power and religious authority as caliph, but beyond Anatolia his reign was increasingly a loose matter of formal suzerainty that, as in Egypt, involved the de facto independence of local rulers. Austrian and then Russian pressures ate away at Ottoman control in the Balkans and the Black Sea, as did independence movements in the early nineteenth century, and the regime survived as a "power" only through the protection of the British and French.

Though composed of very different, largely contiguous territories and peoples, these empires interacted in the European system as theoretically unitary sovereign states while in fact being awkward conglomerations held together principally by the personal authority of the Emperor, Tsar, or Sultan. They were, in the era of the nation-state, anomalies.

Nation-state imperialism and the first globalization

The European global empires of the early modern and modern period were very different. They were extensions of unitary nation-states (the British monarch was not an "emperor" until Disraeli had Victoria rather belatedly proclaimed empress in 1876; France, after 1870, was again a republic); that is, they were essentially European sovereign states that had managed to export colonists to some areas and acquire direct or indirect rule over non-European peoples. By the late nineteenth century, their "imperialism" was a competitive, expansionist ideology composed of elements of traditional power politics involving geopolitical gamesmanship, but also undergirded by social Darwinism, racism, a liberal imperialism that emphasized the civilizing mission of the West, and, perhaps, economic necessity as their metropolitan base grew in industrial capacity and financial wealth in an era of competition for European and world markets and increasingly marginal returns. For IR all this poses a number of questions: how and to what degree might this more energetic European competition abroad affect the practice of Great Power politics in Europe; how might these empires "fit" the Westphalian concept of absolute sovereignty; and, finally, how did the new imperialism, its advocates as well as its critics, shape a new understanding of international law?

Colonies both added to the resources these powers could employ within the European theater and created another dimension of conflict and negotiation—as trade, finance, and warfare became global and the conference system devised to balance and settle European affairs was, less effectively perhaps, extended to the consideration of areas where European states had projected their presence abroad—or wished to. That is, the calculus of threat, security, and balance became more complicated and inevitably the diplomacy of imperialism had sometimes unintended consequences— as when the British and French in 1904 settled their differences in Africa through an Entente Cordiale that seemed to confirm German fears of encirclement in Europe.

Certainly strategic geopolitical thinking took on global dimensions. The threat that Russia would develop hegemonic capabilities through her imperial expansion in Asia had been a concern among British statesmen for some time. A Regius Professor of Modern History at Cambridge University, John Robert Seeley (1834–95)—following perhaps Alexis de Tocqueville's 1835 prediction of a coming global bipolarity of "two great nations ... the Russian and the Anglo-American"—argued as early as 1881 that future power lay with states that could control a great continental land mass. The

British could only survive as a power if they compensated for their nation's small size by achieving the continental equivalent in her colonial empire. Otherwise, the future, he said, would belong to Russia and the United States. In the early twentieth century, Japanese imperialists would follow much the same logic.

The end of the century saw the rise of an additional power from outside the European land mass. The American naval officer and teacher, Alfred Thayer Mahan (1840–1914), had written in 1890 an influential study of sea power in history, and his geopolitical speculations were regarded by many as a blueprint (following the British example) for achieving or confirming through a global naval presence the world status now expected of a Great Power. The United States' war with Spain in the Caribbean and the Pacific at the end of the century and Theodore Roosevelt's sending of the Great White Fleet (sixteen battleships) around the world in 1907–9 announced America's application to membership in the Great Power club. At the end of Britain's hard-fought (second) Boer War in southern Africa (1899–1902), Halford John Mackinder (1861–1947), an Oxford-educated geographer and a founder of the LSE, observed that "the world has rapidly seen an expansion of the theatre of international politics. The European phase of history is rapidly passing away. A new balance of power is being evolved" (Mackinder, 1902, 350).

In terms of IR theory, there is a problem that, though these empires in their relations with each other may be seen in Europe as the unitary states of Realist theory, in the world beyond their character is much more ambiguous. In their relations with lesser states abroad a system of balance did not obtain; the imperial powers were hegemons that exerted a coercive influence over nominally sovereign states (as with China). At the same time, however, within their spheres of direct control their own "sovereignty" was hardly grounded in a "domestic monopoly of violence." In India, Britain only gradually came to exert an effective suzerainty, and then often nominally through local elites and princes. Their claim to sovereign "rule" over millions was a very fragile assertion and their coercive power rested not so much on the physical force of their military as on their maintaining the *perception* of effective control.

In IR there has been a lively debate in the last decade or so over just how empire and imperialism relate to the theory of the state and its sovereignty. The discipline was largely framed around the Westphalian ideal; European empires were either seen as somewhat anomalous or simply as projections of European sovereignty abroad—as in Bull and Watson's *The Expansion of International Society* (1984), which assumes that sovereignty, its concept and practice, was diffused by Europe throughout the world. Recently, this view has been challenged and complicated by those who argue that coming to grips with the ambiguities of imperial sovereignty may help us understand the weaknesses of the Westphalian model itself and the ways it may have obscured "the relations of mutual constitution through which states, societies, and other international phenomena are produced" (Barkawi and Laffey, 2002, 112). The idea of "zones of mutual constitution," they argue, may help redress the prevailing idea of the unitary, sovereign state in Europe, just as a better understanding of the complicated European encounter with non-European subaltern peoples may redress the idea of an uncomplicated "exportation" of the concept of sovereignty to the rest of the world (for more on sovereignty in IR, see Chapter 10).

The theory of sovereignty, and by extension, the security interests of the sovereign state, then, are complicated by late nineteenth-century imperialism, a kind of globalization that not only intensified the interplay of European and other societies abroad but was characterized by the growth of vested corporate interests within and beyond the European state—manufacturers (including armament manufacturers), commercial exporters, and financial investors. Is economic advantage simply part of the political calculus of state power, or do these interests "drive" policy forward in ways that challenge the notion of political sovereignty and may actually weaken and damage state security? Do they have agendas that have little to do with state interests at all?

There has been a long debate over the influence of financial interests behind especially British imperial expansion. Lenin (following the British radical liberal John Hobson) argued during the First World War that finance capital's need for high returns on investment lay behind imperial expansion, resulting in a global Armageddon among competing capitalist imperial powers. Most economic historians now doubt that the balance sheets of imperialism confirm that financial objectives of well-placed bankers were paramount (either in South Africa, as Hobson thought, or in igniting the First World War). Nevertheless, global economic interests, and the fiscal and commercial institutions associated with them, increasingly became factors that system theory, concerned as it is principally with political balancing and state security, cannot easily accommodate.

Sovereignty presumes, in IR theory, an absolute authority within the boundaries of the modern state. But is empire unitary or plural? Before the First World War the British had devolved, with privy council oversight, most responsibility for domestic (if not foreign) affairs to several of its settlement colonies. The whole thing was British, but the dominions were not part of a British state in the sense that Algeria was regarded as part of metropolitan France. Then there is the issue of sovereignty for the states that fell within this or that sphere of influence. What are we to do with China, which was forced to yield to Western demands for treaty ports and extraterritorial rights and which suffered the humiliation of Western intervention during the Boxer Rebellion? Even more ambiguously, there is the theoretical sovereignty of the independent states of Latin America, which had been shielded from the European powers they broke away from (not by the Monroe Doctrine but by the British Navy), only to become subject to the dictates of their European creditors—not least the British. What late nineteenth-century Latin American country could be said to be really sovereign? Rather, they were part of what has been called an informal (or free-trade) imperialism exercised by European governments and investors. Their own sense of being sovereign was sustained perhaps by the internecine wars that broke out from time to time in the Americas, but they were hardly autonomous agents in the way suggested by Westphalian theory.

And finally, it may be argued that the spread and institutionalization (through trade treaties and the gold standard) of global capitalism involved for the powers themselves, enmeshed in its international system, a vulnerability to speculation and global economic processes and cycles that diminished their own autonomy.

The diplomacy of imperialism

The late nineteenth century saw intense competition in Africa and Asia among the imperial powers for sovereign territory and *spheres of influence* (apparently the first use of this phrase in formal diplomatic exchange was in 1869 when Russia claimed that it did not consider Afghanistan within its "sphere of influence"). Imperial ambitions had, of course, played an important, if often subsidiary, part in European negotiation and settlement since Utrecht, involving in most cases the rising British challenge to the global empires of Spain and France, but, it can be argued, they did not often impinge on the balancing strategies in Europe of the concert of powers—though Bismarck attempted to deflect the French toward its overseas empire and away from *revanche* (revenge) and the recovery of Alsace and Lorraine. Toward the end of the century this changed. *Weltmacht* (world power) came to be seen as definitional of Great Power status, not only in a post-Bismarckian Germany searching for "a place in the sun." Powerful political lobbies advocating a "forward" policy confronted decision-makers in France and Britain, as well as the German Reich, and even Austria-Hungary can be seen to embrace expansion in the Balkans as a form of ersatz imperialism.

Great Power competition beyond Europe came then, in a fin de siècle of heightened anxiety over economic and geopolitical security, to seem less marginal to multipower politics *in Europe*, and the "Diplomacy of Imperialism" (the title of a prominent 1960 study by the Harvard historian William L. Langer) takes center stage in the pre-First World War era. The progressive weakening of the Ottoman Empire had drawn European powers into Near Eastern affairs; the Great Power concert quickly moved on from dealing with the "Eastern Question" in 1878 to attempting to sort out the "scramble for Africa" in 1884–5—in another Berlin Conference, again presided over by Bismarck. The following decades witnessed crises abroad that threatened a system that, centered in Europe, was global—from the Anglo-Russian competition for influence in central Asia and Afghanistan to the Fashoda incident (1898) where Britain and France came close to war in the southern Sudan, the second Boer War (1899–1902) when Germany provided materiel and moral support to the Afrikaner Republics, or the diplomatic sabre-rattling of the Moroccan crises. Anticipation that a general war in Europe might well result from such imperial conflict was widespread, though of course when war did come the *casus belli* had little immediately to do with Great Power imperialism in the wider world.

Realism posits that the *system* of competing sovereign states dictates the terms of engagement, however much the scope of competitive ambition may be raised to include the whole globe or whether the nations in competition may be motivated by contrasting ideologies. William Gladstone, the great Liberal British statesman of the second half of the nineteenth century and four times prime minister, preferred arbitration to war and denounced Disraeli's imperialism as tawdry and theatrical, while many in his own party were "little Englanders" who were vehemently opposed to expanding an empire they saw as expensive to run and dangerous to democracy at home. And yet, in 1881 Gladstone sent the British fleet to bombard Alexandria and began an occupation of Egypt that would last for more than half a century. This seems to fit the Realist model—though the extent to which the further expansion and entrenchment of the Egyptian–Sudan commitment was driven by a highly volatile public opinion may not. Or, to take Disraeli's own imperialism, though there was much romantic oratory about the Jewel in the Crown and how the British must become an imperial people, in the end Britain's movements on the global chessboard were, it can be argued, dictated more by the traditional requirements of (an extended version of) geopolitical security—to counter the threat from other states (Russia or France)—than a new imperial mandate dictated by an imperial ideology. In fact, British (defensive) imperial expansion carried on regardless of whichever party was in power.

On the other hand, the emergence in Western Europe of what might be called a popular culture of imperialism raises serious problems for any Realist analysis based on simple *raison d'état*. Imperialism came to be entrenched in the popular mind by state schools, adventure novels, and a chauvinistic press at the same time that European countries were expanding the franchise and education to the lower classes. Consequently, statesmen were increasingly vulnerable domestically to jingoistic pressures (these could also of course be manipulated) that complicated calculations of state advantage and security in foreign relations. Nationalism and imperialism came to affect the mentality of "cosmopolitan" European elites as well, adding an intangible factor in the power-maximizing geopolitical strategies of Realpolitik. Bismarck had had no special use for empire abroad and did not see German interests as best served by imperial adventure, but for many of the coming generation, not least for the young Kaiser William II, *prestige* came to play as large a role as security; the perception of Germany's interests changed and required an expansive (and bullying) posture, a battle fleet, and colonies. It is hard not to see this as a psychological and ideological turn—rather than something dictated by the interests of state or even by German industrialists and investors.

Similarly, in the mid-century it had been still possible for British intellectuals and politicians to debate whether Britain's interests were best served in sustaining an expensive formal empire or whether an industrial and commercial nation was better served by global free trade. But by the turn of the century for many the Empire had become its own reward, conferring a kind of national manhood. In that sense, an imperial sensibility and subjectivity may have changed the terms of the game; empire became part of cultural identity and its preservation was an existential matter for many Britons as late as the 1950s.

Imperialism and international law

The traditional understanding of international law was significantly impacted by imperialism—especially by what might be called "liberal imperialism," the idea that the global spread of European "civilization," while often coercive, would lead to the diffusion of social, economic, and cultural progress (as in the worldwide assault on the slave trade). Africa during and after the imperial "scramble" was the preferred locus for the rhetoric of the civilizational benefits of empire, and at the Berlin Conference the abolition of the interior slave trade was offered as the central rationale for the extension of European sovereignty and influence.

It has often been argued that the early era of European contact with Asian, South Asian, and Near Eastern states and local rulers had involved a degree of respect for their sovereignty—expressed in the treaties made with them (though this can be exaggerated for Asia, and clearly did not obtain in the Americas). To some extent, the legal scholar Charles Henry Alexandrowicz argued, this had rested on a tradition (from ancient Rome through de Vitoria and Grotius) of natural law universalism that was steadily undermined in the nineteenth century by the spread of European empires and the concept of legal positivism—that law derives not from ancient or religious ideals of justice, but more prosaically and narrowly from what is ordered and practiced by state institutions. Peoples lacking such institutions (and a codified legal regime) may then be considered to be without law or legal rights as properly understood unless they came under the protection of the imperial sovereignty of a European state.

While the force of legal positivism may not adequately explain the destruction of the sovereign identities of colonized peoples, it seems clear that by the late nineteenth century liberal imperialists effectively limited the (previously universal, in theory) field of international law to those who were "civilized"—that is, to Europeans, former Europeans, and those who had been or were being tutored by them and were, so to speak, their wards. The new international law, one scholar has recently observed, was "forged out of the attempt to create a legal system that could account for relations between the European and non-European worlds in the colonial confrontation" (Sylvest, 2008, 406). In this, the old doctrine of *terra nullius* (territory not claimed by a recognized sovereign state and thus "belonging" to no one) was revived—with a special reference (as at the Berlin Conference) to Africa and its peoples. In 1888, the Institute of International Law (founded in Lausanne, Switzerland, in 1873) devoted its annual meeting to discussion of the meaning, scope, and application of *terra nullius*—whether "savages" have sovereign rights, whether they have property rights, whether they can sign treaties yielding up these rights, and so forth.

The coming of the Great War

However much imperial contest abroad may have been symptomatic of Great Power rivalry in Europe, the European system did not ultimately fail because of it. War, when it came, was not, as had been sometimes predicted, a direct result of *global* competition. Nor did war become inevitable because of—or not *only* because of—secret treaty commitments and timetables of mobilization; national publics expected it and many wanted it. Just what *it* was, and would tragically become, was less apparent—though some now argue that the German General staff at least not only sought a general war, but expected it to be a long and bloody affair that would result, not in a secure status quo, but the establishment of a clear political, military, and economic German hegemony.

Though all of the powers saw an eruption of populist war frenzy, the July 1914 crisis and the build up to it can be described in orthodox terms drawn from Classical Realist, Neorealist (a.k.a. Defensive Realist), or Offensive Realist models. Fear of the growing population, industrial productivity, and military power of Germany, amplified no doubt by the arrogance of its new leadership, inspired the kind of "nightmare of coalitions" that had been Bismarck's bête-noir: anti-German balancing by France, Russia, and, ultimately, Britain, while Austria-Hungary depended upon German protection and ceased to be an independent balancer. The multilateral European system became one of armed bipolarity, though Italy, preoccupied by its own imperial adventure in Africa, stood apart. One might note in passing that Neorealist claims (drawing of course on the Cold War) that a bipolar system is more stable and less likely to lead to general war than a multipolar system attempting balance seem here to be less convincing. This drawing apart of the powers into opposed camps had been prevented for a generation by Bismarck's adroit and devious maneuvering. But his system collapsed in the face of heightened German diplomatic bullying and risk-taking, the Franco-Russian alliance, and a British need for support in sustaining its (overstretched) worldwide commitments.

Some scholars would now argue that war became inevitable, not when the series of early twentieth-century Balkan wars finally escalated into a wider confrontation, or when the assassinations in Sarajevo served as an unanticipated trip-wire, or when Germany provided Austria-Hungary with a "blank check," but in 1905, when Russia's severe and unexpected humiliation at the hands of the Japanese and the domestic revolution that followed fatally damaged perceptions of Russian effectiveness in the balanced alliance system in Europe (as well as providing an incentive for a panicked Russian establishment to seek to distract its restive population with bellicose gestures in defense of Slavic nationalism). In some sense when a general war came, it was the weakest of the allies (Austria-Hungary and Russia) who precipitated Armageddon in an area that few sober statesmen in the nineteenth century would have thought vital to their national interests. After all, Bismarck once said that all of the Balkans was not worth the bones of one Pomeranian Grenadier.

IR and the origins of the Great War: Diplomacy and beyond

Though the consequences of the Great War—revolutions, regime changes, and the dismemberment of key players—were of a magnitude not witnessed since Napoleonic times, political narratives of the drift into war have often focused on somewhat narrow issues. It has long been popularly thought that the war came almost by accident as the creaking mechanisms of secret treaty obligations, mobilization timetables, and ossified contingency planning made it somehow inevitable once a relatively minor incident—the assassinations at Sarajevo—triggered unintended and unwanted results. Though secret commitments—most notably that of Germany to support Austria-Hungary in an offensive war—may have been instrumentally critical, and the German "blank check," perhaps foolish, was *the system* heading toward resolution by force anyhow? That there was not only a sense of inevitability, but a logic demanding war now rather than later was suggested by the view of the German and Austrian military that they would soon face not a demoralized and recuperating Russia but in a few years a modernized, industrialized, and thus unbeatable foe.

Much of the ongoing scholarship has revolved around the subject of war aims—especially German war aims. The postwar (highly politicized) academic investigation into war aims was inspired and heightened by the debate over the "War Guilt" clause of the Treaty of Versailles (Art. 231). But there are war aims and war aims: diplomats and their instructions are generally concerned with well-defined, relatively immediate and narrow goals, and instrumental strategies. Larger issues are more speculative. What factors beyond those of diplomacy, balance of power, competitive military capabilities, and the dictates of an anarchic states system come into play? The most commonly invoked realm is that of economic interests. These can be precise and political, as in, say, Britain's concern over German protectionism and the anticipated German economic domination of *Mitteleuropa*, access to newly strategic resources like oil, the defense of the French holders of Russian bonds, and so forth. A corollary is the presumption that important economic interests, well-placed financiers and manufacturers, may have exerted pressure on national policymakers. Fritz Fischer created a storm in the 1960s (especially in his 1961 book, *Germany's Aims in the First World War*) with his thesis that the war was eagerly supported in Germany, not merely by a declining Junker aristocracy and the army's General Staff, but by liberal politicians and commercial interests—and that getting a place in the sun meant not only freeing Germany from encirclement but seizing a commanding share of world trade.

On a more general, global level, while Marxist-Leninist arguments of the inevitability of war among capitalist-imperialist states competing for market share has failed to achieve much traction among historians of international relations, the revelation of the secret wartime negotiations between the allied powers and Italy (in the 1915 Treaty of London) and Russia (promising Constantinople), and between Britain and France over postwar disposal of the Ottoman Empire (in Mesopotamia, Syria, and the Lebanon)—the Sykes-Picot agreement of 1916—certainly highlighted issues of the hidden aims of imperial aggrandizement. If few scholars are willing to argue that the Great War can be clearly blamed on the ambitions of finance capitalists and imperialists, nevertheless the argument can be made that the global expansion of the pre-World War economy and the tight integration of world markets made it more difficult for powers to mobilize resources (capital and labor) for an extended conflict, intensified the "security dilemma," and made the outbreak of war more likely (Rowe, 1999).

Finally, some historians of European culture and collective psychology have moved from issues of economic interest, imperial advantage, or offensive-defensive military strategy to the eruption of the *irrational*—which swept aside both fine calculations of national interest and the progressive liberal internationalism of the annual Universal Peace Congresses (from 1889) or the Hague Conferences of 1899 and 1907. This can undermine political theory that depends on rational expectations and, alternatively, that which rests on assumptions of the universality of the "urge to power." Psychologically, the war can be seen, not in terms of power maximization, but as an *escape*—according to a once-popular Freudian analysis—from the psycho-sexual repression of the straight-laced bourgeois societies of Western Europe. In late August, each of the capitals of the combatant nations saw crowds cheering the news of war. Workers ignored the warnings of their socialist leaders while middle-class boys finishing school volunteered in their thousands. Psychological factors may of course also play in the minds of policymakers and diplomats, neither themselves immune to nationalist enthusiasm nor able to gauge the passionate motives and actions of their opposing counterparts. If, as much Realist theory maintains, the system depends on the rational calculation of state interest, then irrationality and misunderstanding are issues of some importance. Some IR scholars would see in 1914 evidence of problems of "perception"—of threat or of inevitability—as psychological factors of great analytical importance. "Perception," according to Jervis, builds on itself and may encourage escalation.

What, then, has IR taken from the long preoccupation with the causes of the Great War? How has the debate over the failure of the European system to prevent a general war among the Great Powers in 1914 been made to reflect or address a more general debate over its methods, theory, and practice? Most obviously, the search for origins begs questions about the operation of the Westphalian system and what most Realists regard as its chief mechanism for either preserving general peace or countering the threat of a single power's hegemony—the balance of power. For the historian A. J. P. Taylor, the war was not caused by the system of balancing, but by its "breakdown"—due to the weakening of Russia, a German habit of bullying, or the way that mobilization schedules, the Schlieffen plan, or the unsustainable costs of the arms race encouraged generals and statesmen to abandon balance for preventive aggression. Much the same message is to be found in Barbara Tuchman's popular history of the crisis, *The Guns of August* (1962).

Many Realists (especially Neoclassical and Defensive Realists) follow some version of this analysis, that the coming of a general, long-sustained, and extraordinarily bloody and exhaustive conflict was *unintended*, if not exactly accidental. To blame was, variously, the security dilemma, a spiral of escalation, misperceptions of one's opponent's intentions, and a contemporary (German) belief that vigorous offense was the best defense, what Stephen Van Evera and Jack Snyder have called the "cult of the offensive." Attention has also been drawn to the way alliances actually work. The structuralist Kenneth Waltz and others have suggested that efficient balancing might be prevented by "buck-passing" (where one power might pass to another the responsibility for initiating action) or "chain-ganging" (where a stronger power may be committed to action by a weaker ally). Added to the debate has been a further perspective that system breakdowns may often reflect a crisis of "power transition," where rising players contribute to the loss of system stability and increase the likelihood of aggressive (perhaps unilateral and irrational) action on the part of transition losers.

The historical record has been made to support any variety of analyses, though evidence now suggests that the German military was aware of—and presumably prepared to accept—the likelihood that the war would be long and difficult, and that there was, so to speak, a window of opportunity for seizing hegemony in central Europe before Russia modernized. For some this has been enough to confirm that Germany was not dragged into the war (chain-ganged) by its weaker ally, Austria-Hungary, or locked into war by the Schlieffen plan or mobilization schedules, but entered with its "eyes wide open." Mearsheimer and the Offensive Realists have gone further and suggested that the war resulted not from the failure to balance in a timely fashion, but from a general tendency for states poised to achieve hegemony to run considerable risks to maximize their power—German mobilization simply reflected a determination to seize what it could, though just why Germany did so in August 1914 rather than earlier is not perhaps very well explained.

In the last analysis, many historians would bring the origins debate back to the decision-makers—the disaster of Wilhelm II's style and the inadequacy of his advisors to understand what they were doing, the factor, that is, of pure incompetence. Just before the guns of August, German Chancellor Theobald Bethmann-Hollweg despairingly complained of the cumulative effect of the foreign policy initiatives he had had to endure: "A Turkish policy against Russia, Morocco against France, fleet against England, all at the same time—challenge everybody, get in everyone's way, and actually, in the course of all this, weaken nobody" (quoted by Byman and Pollack, 2001, 125).

Recommended readings

For one example of scholarship questioning the standard nineteenth-century chronological divisions that stress war and peace, see Hudson Meadwell, "The Long Nineteenth Century in Europe," *Review of International Studies* 27 (2001), 165–89. For IR and the revolutionary concept of popular sovereignty, see Fred Halliday, who offers a Marxist perspective in *Revolution and World Politics* (1999), and Stephen Walt's *Revolution and War* (1996), a comparative, Realist approach that nevertheless acknowledges the importance of domestic contexts and ideology. Beyond IR scholarship, per se, there is a vast literature on nineteenth-century nationalism and citizenship. See, for instance, Rogers Brubaker, *Citizenship and Nationhood in France and Germany* (1992). Friedrich Kratochwil's "Citizenship: On the Border of Order," in Lapid and Kratochwil (eds.), *The Return of Culture and Identity Theory* (1996), 181–97, offers a Constructivist perspective. For some general implications of the emergent nation-state, see Anthony Giddens, *The Nation-State and Violence* (1985).

The period as a whole has been addressed briefly by Paul W. Schroeder, "International Politics, Peace, and War, 1815–1914," in T. C. W. Blanning (ed.), *The Nineteenth Century: Europe, 1763–1848* (2000), 158–209, while his *Transformation of European Politics 1763–1848* (1994) offers an in-depth interpretation of the era, and of balance-of-power thinking, before and after the Congress. On the Congress of Vienna itself, the old standards by Harold Nicolson (1946 and 1961) and Charles K. Webster (1965) are still worth reading. For more recent interpretations, see Henry Kissinger, *A World Restored* (1973), and Mark Jarrett, *The Congress of Vienna and Its Legacy: War and Great Power Diplomacy after Napoleon* (2013). Also, G. John Ikenberry, *After Victory: Institutions, Strategic Restraint, and the Rebuilding of Order after Major Wars* (2001), chapter 4: "The Settlement of 1815," 80–116.

On Clausewitz, the introductory essays by Peter Paret and Michael Howard in the Princeton edition of *On War* (1984) are still useful. For European warfare in the post-Napoleonic era, see Deborah Avant, "From Mercenary to Citizen Armies: Explaining Change in the Practice of War," *International Organization* 54 (2000), 41–72, and D. S. Showalter, "Europe's Way of War, 1815–64," in Jeremy Black (ed.), *European Warfare 1815–2000* (2002), 27–50. For the debate over the idea of military cultures, see Victor Davis Hanson, *Carnage and Culture: Landmark Battles in the Rise of Western Power* (2001).

Taylor's *The Struggle for Europe* can be supplemented with George Kennan's *The Decline of Bismarck's European Order: Franco-Russian Relations, 1875–1890* (1979) and Richard Langhorne's *Collapse of the Concert of Europe: International Politics, 1890–1914* (1981). A recent and full biography of Bismarck is available in English: Jonathan Steinberg's *Bismarck: A Life* (2011). Richard Ned Lebow also offers a critique of Taylor, and of the general historiography of the origins of the First World War, in "Agency versus Structure in A. J. P. Taylor's Origins of the First World War," *International History Review* 23, 1 (March 2001), 51–72. For recent work on imperialism and international law, see Calvin Sylvest, "'Our Passion for Legality': International Law and Imperialism in Late Nineteenth-Century Britain," *Review of International Studies* 34 (2008), 403–23, and Andrew Fitzmaurice, "Liberalism and Empire in Nineteenth-Century International Law," *American Historical Review* 117 (2012), 122–40.

The literature on the origins of the First World War is extensive. Of the post-Second World War scholarship, Luigi Albertini's three-volume analysis, *The Origins of the War of 1914* (trans. from the Italian, 1952–1957), has been influential among historians of diplomacy. For relatively recent commentary, see John W. Langdon, *July 1914: The Long Debate, 1918–1990* (1991); Anita Mombauer, *The Origins of the First World War: Controversies and Consensus* (2002); Richard F. Hamilton and Holger H. Herwig (eds.), *The Origins of World War I* (2003); and Mark Hewitson, *Germany and the Causes of the First World War* (2004). For debate among IR scholars since the 1980s, see, for instance, Steven Van Evera, *Causes of War: Power and the Roots of Conflict* (1999), and Keir A. Lieber, "The New History of World War I and What It Means for International Relations Theory," *International Security* 32 (2007), 155–91. For a critique of "power transition" theory, see Benjamin Valentino and Richard Ned Lebow, "Lost in Transition: Critical

Analysis of Power Transition Theory," *International Relations* 23 (2009), 389–410. On "chain-ganging" in IR theory, see Thomas J. Christensen and Jack L. Snyder, "Chain Gangs and Passed Bucks: Predicting Alliance Patterns in Multipolarity," *International Organization* 44 (1990), 137–68, and Dominic Tierney, "Does Chain-Ganging Cause the Outbreak of War?" *International Studies Quarterly* 55 (2011), 285–304. For the "cult of the offensive," see Jack Snyder, *The Ideology of the Offensive: Military Decision Making and the Disasters of 1914* (1984), and Steven Van Evera, "The Cult of the Offensive and the Origins of the First World War," *International Security*, 9 (1984), 58–107.

CHAPTER 8
THE FAILURE OF DIPLOMACY, NEW AND OLD, AND THE END OF EUROPEAN HEGEMONY

And it is worth remembering that it was not the new but the old diplomacy, with the return to alliances and bi-lateral diplomacy, that failed so disastrously in 1939. (Steiner, 2001, 30)

Conventional explanations of the origins of IR as a discipline attach great significance to the era of the First World War, the peace settlement that followed, and the failure of that peace by the end of the 1930s. On the one hand, the so-called Idealist tradition regarded the war as the climactic failure of the old European system with its autocratic empires, *raison d'état*, Realpolitik, power-balancing, and secret treaties, opening the possibility of a new era where the Grotian tradition of international law and international institutions—with an admixture of Kantian "democratic peace"— would make possible a more orderly global society of interdependent nations. From this perspective, the very scale of the horror of the First World War made grotesquely obsolete the old diplomacy. Liberal idealism considered itself progressive and rationalist (liberals thought they could construct a better—more logical and humane—system of international relations). It also offered an alternative to the other radical restructuring of the world system on offer, that of the Bolshevik revolutionaries in post-1917 Russia.

On the other hand, what came to call itself, after the collapse of the hopes of the League of Nations, the Realist tradition would argue that the New (Wilsonian) Diplomacy, by naively disregarding the timeless character of power politics grounded in human nature and the Hobbesian anarchic international system, was, like Machiavelli's unarmed prophet, doomed to failure. Another great war was the consequence and a power-balancing approach to international politics was sensibly, in this tradition, reestablished thereafter. Their perspective was one that enshrined a cyclical, repetitive historical narrative and denied the improvability of mankind generally. As in Thucydides' day, so in ours, the powerful do as they wish, the weak what they must.

In fact, this dichotomy conceals, as we have seen, significant variation. On the left there was a sharp distinction between liberal or progressive internationalism, which stressed the cooperative interdependence of peoples or nations, and socialist or revolutionary internationalism, which stressed class conflict and, as had Lenin, viewed with great suspicion a League of (capitalist) Nations. While Liberal Internationalists may have dominated the emerging field of IR, there was little consensus among them either in the interwar period or later over "collective security" and the legitimate use of force.

Varieties of Realism, on the other hand, also came to endorse among themselves different readings of the (at least limited) rationality of security-seeking or power-maximizing states. There is at least one kind of consensus. The interwar era is heavy with meaning, if rightly read.

War and peace

The negotiations at Paris in 1919 and the Treaty of Versailles have never ceased to attract general and specialist interest—from the attempt to blame the harsh peace of reparations and national humiliation for the emergence of the dictators and another world war to the view that, in light of subsequent German resurgence, the treaty and reparations system were not severe enough. What should the discipline of IR take from this this war and this peace?

First, the rapid spread of a general war in 1914 seems to have announced a significant break with the way the European system had worked since Napoleon's fall to ensure that wars, when they came, remained relatively limited. One can of course debate whether the system ultimately failed or worked—after all, Germany's hegemonic ambition was in the end thwarted by a combination of powers. But the struggle was of a magnitude never before witnessed, and resulted in revolutions, regime changes, and the dismemberment of empires. Second, does the character of something that approaches total war and a demand at the peace conference for total surrender look toward a future where *diplomacy* loses its ability either to prevent wars or to restore a collaborative peace? Does force become, as in the Second World War, absolute and constitutive of a super-realism that encompasses the death of the European system as a *society* of states and of the norms that had served to impose limits to violence and encourage the resort to negotiation? Finally, do the League and afterward the United Nations (UN), as world organizations, constitute a radical break with the European past, or, through liberal (and liberal imperial) concepts of international law and arbitration, the globalization of a particular Western tradition?

The issue of the war aims of the Great Powers, and of Germany in particular, figured centrally in the long scholarly debate over the origins of the Great War—a debate that was fuelled by the selective publication during and after the war of documents from the archives of combatant nations. The so-called "war guilt" clause may have been inserted specifically to justify reparations, but came to carry a much larger importance in the resistance to the "Diktat" of Versailles in Germany and the selling of the peace settlement in the Allied states. Because the war forced combatant states to make unprecedented claims on their peoples, governments were constrained to evolve ever larger aims to justify sacrifice on an unprecedented scale. It is this populist context that most distinguishes the negotiations in Paris from those a century earlier in Vienna. Selective "leaks" to an eager press during the conference played a calculated role in deliberations, and the "Big Four," as political leaders of democratic regimes, were especially sensitive (or, in Wilson's case, should have been) to domestic electoral considerations. In place of the cool detachment of a Metternich or a Castlereagh, we have the "tiger" Clemenceau, *Père la Victoire* (father victory), beloved by the press for his outspoken commitment to total war, a non-negotiated peace, and severe reparations; Orlando, *Premiere della Vittoria* (premier of victory), desperate to take back to the Italian people the territorial gains promised them in 1915; and David Lloyd George, a "goat-footed" radical-liberal who had fought an election in December of 1918 amid calls to hang the Kaiser and squeeze the Germans (for reparations) until the pips squeaked. Woodrow Wilson, a stiff-necked Presbyterian academic idealist who was determined to bring his understanding of America as a "beacon of liberty" to bear on the reconstruction of a more moral and democratic world, had announced his intention to replace the "balance of power" with a "community of power," and had been encouraged in this messianic mission by the heady outpouring of popular adulation he received in the streets of Paris, London, and Rome.

Importantly, the great conference that assembled in Paris in 1919 saw professional foreign office and treasury civil servants, special researchers and aides (recruited often from the universities), and generally those who had been co-opted into the preparation of elaborate peace planning, firmly subordinated to the political leaders who attended in person. Paris became a kind of summitry, a personal diplomacy of the Big Four who tended to relegate their own foreign secretaries (with the exception of Italy's Sonnino) to the sidelines. As an experienced historian-diplomat has observed, "it is almost always a mistake for heads of state to undertake the details of a negotiation" (Kissinger, 1994, 230).

The Paris Peace Conference and its consequences

It is to be regretted that public opinion appears to countenance the view that the doctrine of the Balance of Power can be neglected. It is, and will remain, a fundamental point just as much after the establishment of a League of Nations as it has been before. (James Headlam-Morley, classicist, historian, and member of the British delegation in Paris)

In the spring and summer of 1919, the victorious allies looked out on a Europe that, even more than in 1815, could not simply be put back to status quo ante (Figure 8.1). First, revolutions in Berlin and Vienna had turned those empires into democratic republics, while red revolutionaries ruled in Moscow and, briefly, Budapest. The Ottoman regime likewise had been destroyed and its much-reduced successor would soon become the secular Anatolian state of Turkey. Second, as had not been the case in 1815, there were millions of displaced refugees, while throughout central and eastern Europe new states rushed to create their own borders before the conference could define them—anticipating Wilson's call for self-determination of peoples by creating de facto nations on the ground. Ethnic cleansing was rampant from

Figure 8.1 Postwar settlements 1919–23.

Source: Erik Goldstein, *Wars and Peace Treaties 1816–1991* (London: Routledge, 1992), by permission of Taylor & Francis Books UK.

Armenia to the Baltic. Third, Germany and Austria, though new republics, were not represented at the table, but were expected to sign whatever the Allied powers demanded. Nor were the new rulers in Russia, who had signed a separate peace with Germany, represented.

According to mainstream IR, the guiding principles of the old system since Westphalia had been the concepts of sovereignty and the balance of power. The first held that states should not meddle in the internal affairs of other states. This principle was of course disregarded during the war, but afterward Allied intervention in Russia and Soviet subversion and propaganda in the West suggest a significant shift in practice harkening back to the era of the French Revolution. Nor was the 1919 settlement especially designed to establish a lasting balance of power—a goal in 1815—though some British negotiators appear to have been concerned to preserve enough German power to offset that of a victorious France. In fact, the likeliest state to dominate in the future through its population and probable economic hegemony (Germany) was neither substantially diminished nor conciliated by a treaty that one of the victorious powers (the United States) refused to ratify, two others (Britain and France) viewed—for different reasons—with skeptical misgiving, and the fifth (Italy) resented as the mutilation of its hard-won victory.

The postwar configuration was less a Great Power consortium or concert than a confusion of motive and intention—bedevilled by continuing French security concerns and the bitter revisionism of the Germans, and by the emergence of new, often aggressive, smaller regional states, ambitious beyond their resources and defined by a narrow ethnic identity at odds, often, with their own multifarious populations: Poland, Czechoslovakia, Hungary, Yugoslavia (the kingdom of the Serbs, Croats, and Slovenes), as well as fragments of the Ottoman Near East. With the economic exhaustion and imperial overextension of Britain—historically Europe's chief balancer—the system, such as it was, became inherently less manageable and, to the degree that America and Russia remained largely outside, less inclusive. Any reordering through international or supranational institutions that drew on an international law tradition that had been a relatively minor motif in Western international relations since the seventeenth century was likely to be fraught with enormous difficulty. Nevertheless, might one claim, as some Liberal Internationalists aver, that the League of Nations and the Court of International Justice at the Hague at least planted the seeds—institutionally and in the collective consciousness—of a cosmopolitan regime that would constitute a significant break with sovereign state anarchy and the mechanisms by which it worked?

The war and the Treaty of Versailles did establish a new environment—if not an effective new structure or commanding ideology—for the practice of international relations. The result of the war and the peace was neither a rebalanced Europe nor a community of nations, but a radically changed Europe in which two of the former powers simply ceased to exist (Austria-Hungary and the Porte) and two others (Germany and Russia, the two most populous nations in Europe) became, for a while, pariah states, while the wartime "Associated" power, the United States, withdrew from any regular participation in European affairs (staying outside the League but returning in 1924 to take a role in the London Reparations Conference). Though the Weimar Republic joined the League (as a permanent member of its Council) after the Locarno Conference of 1925 settled the issue of its Western boundary with France and Belgium, the Soviet

Union, deeply distrusted in the West, would remain substantially outside the European community even after Stalin moved to join the League and negotiate an anti-German treaty of "Mutual Assistance" with France in the mid-1930s.

The Twenty Years' Crisis

If the *European* system had in some sense become a *global* system in the nineteenth and early twentieth century thanks to Europe's imperialism and its worldwide commerce and finance, the period after the exhausting Great War saw an increasing erosion of overstretched European control. The British Empire may have reached its territorial zenith in the 1920s as a result of its absorption of German colonies in Africa and the extension of its sphere of influence in the Near and Middle East via the system of "mandates," but American commercial and financial interests had taken advantage of British wartime withdrawal to expand in Latin America and elsewhere.

Though the United States continued to press for the repayment of war loans, took a major role (via the Dawes and Young plans) in the restructuring of European reparations, and came to be deeply involved in funding those reparations payments, it largely withdrew from European political affairs while continuing to nurture large designs in the Pacific and Far East. These ambitions, like those of the expanding Japanese Empire, were constrained but hardly diminished by the naval disarmament conferences of 1921–2, 1927, 1930, and 1932. Moreover, European global influence was, to read the signs of disorder from Egypt to the Raj, not only vulnerable to competing extra-European Great Powers. There were nascent independence movements in the Dutch East Indies, India, French Indochina, and North Africa. European resources, exhausted by the war, were further strained by a slow recovery thereafter, well before the Great Depression diverted attention to domestic social and economic crisis, exacerbated the revisionist assault on the Versailles settlement, undermined liberal democracy, and encouraged autarchy rather than globalism.

Hope for a new European—indeed new global—international order rested for many on the League of Nations. Wilson had compromised his vision in Paris in order to achieve his primary goal, the League (it is the first part, articles 1–30, of the Treaty of Versailles), which he hoped would rectify mistakes and unresolved impasses of the settlement. These hopes involved, in the face of the awkward structure of the organization defined in its covenant, the prospect that the League idea would evolve and its underlying principles become normative, at least among the democracies of the postwar world. That is, the League was, in the minds of its liberal proponents, not only an institutional arrangement but a *learning process*. IR scholars, chiefly Realists, have naturally enough focused on the failure of the League and collective security to deter or punish aggression and the body's increasing irrelevance in the darkening 1930s descent toward another great war. On the other hand, there has been increasing interest in aspects of the League's work not directly associated with its failed disarmament and international security agendas.

Since the end of the Cold War, there has been a (continuing) surge of scholarly interest in the interwar growth of multiple visions of cosmopolitan internationalism. The distinguished diplomatic historian Akira Iriye has written of the rise of a "cultural internationalism" characterized by an "internationalist imagination" that transcended states and considerations of state power. Internationalism was promoted not only within the League but beyond, by the movements and organizations that mushroomed in the 1920s (like the International Institute for Intellectual Cooperation, established in 1926) advocating cosmopolitan cultural exchange. For these and their advocates, the importance of the League lay not so much in the details of its structure or even the effectiveness of its international security arrangements, as in "the group consciousness rising from the national to the international unit" (Mary Follet, *The New State*, 1918, quoted by Iriye, 1997, 58).

As one scholar has recently argued, the interwar years consequently saw a "widening global community" that presaged a shift "from international relations to international society" (Gorman, 2012, 319). This was expressed in the emergence of nongovernmental institutions like the Carnegie Endowment for International Peace and the creation of the League's own international civil service. Liberal Institutionalists have returned to the League and the ways its various agencies and commissions—like the International Labour Organization, the Health Committee, and the Economic and Financial Organization (an umbrella for various agencies) or those set up to oversee the administration of mandates, the European refugee problem, and the rights of minorities—may have fomented *lasting* transregional and global perspectives and cooperation, and served as a legacy for the later work of the UN. That is, as Susan Pedersen has argued with reference to the mandates system, they served to generate, if not new practices, then a new "language of international norms" (Pedersen, 2006, 581).

The widely perceived failure of the League was closely associated with its promise to bring about a fundamental change in the anarchic, war-prone international system. But at the heart of the League lay an ambiguity—whether it offered an alternative to Great Power balancing as Wilson had envisioned or by drawing the powers into its processes recreated something like the old concert system in new clothes. As Martin Wight once observed, the League both enshrined the Grotian doctrine of the legitimate use of force against a delinquent state violating the law of nations and institutionalized the idea of a balance of power. The League was not, as some had envisioned, a supra-state authority, but an agreement among sovereign states who promised to submit their differences to arbitration. Carr's representation of the League as an institution dominated by "utopian" idealists does not adequately convey the complexity of motive and practice that the League idea in fact involved.

Some version of collective security under the League through sanctions and if necessary force via Article 16 was attractive to different groups and different states for different reasons: some Idealists (but not confirmed pacifists) hoped it would encourage alternative methods of conflict resolution, or, were these to fail, an institutionalized coercion of rogue states; small countries hoped to find in it some protection without subordinating themselves to a Great Power; and the overextended, exhausted status quo powers (Britain and France) were willing to work within the League (in parallel with traditional diplomacy) in hopes of finding there some relief from the burden of European and global security. It was an institution, however, that seemed to many to offer more to small nations fearful to protect their new boundaries than to Great Powers.

The League was a world organization which came to include much of Latin America, the dominions of the British Empire and India, Abyssinia, Liberia, Turkey, Iraq, Iran, Afghanistan, China, and Japan, and though the United States remained outside, it had a consul-general in Geneva to liaise with the League. It was, however, most concerned in its early days with reestablishing order *in Europe* and with issues that overlapped state sovereignty, like those involving stateless refugees and minority rights. Though small states (and France) wanted coercive action to be automatic where League rules were violated, Article 11 of the Covenant required that before a call for collective action could be binding on members, there would have to be a unanimous vote in the League Council. Attempts to make arbitration compulsory and action against aggressors automatic were successfully resisted by, especially, Britain, which was concerned that its overstretched resources might be committed to European issues of little significance to its own imperial security.

Traditional Great Power diplomacy continued to operate in parallel with, as well as within, the League. Further negotiation was needed to complete the peace of 1919, make adjustments in eastern Europe and Anatolia, and later to redress the reparations system and advance naval disarmament. The most important Great Power conference of the period was that at Locarno (1925). Locarno was meant to reassure France (which had made defensive treaties with Poland and the Czechs and occupied the Ruhr) that Germany would not militarize the Rhineland. Confirming western borders, it left open final resolution of eastern European issues, though these might be submitted to the Court of International Justice. As a modus vivendi or *détente* achieved by direct negotiation outside the auspices of the League, Locarno has usually encouraged a Realist reading of, especially, Britain's interest in European "balancing," though at least one IR scholar has suggested it may have some relevance in understanding the dynamics, and limitations, of the Kantian "democratic peace"—Weimar, Britain, and France being of course nontotalitarian regimes.

The much-touted "spirit of Locarno" (the statesmen representing Britain, France, and Germany each received the Nobel Peace Prize) marked the highpoint of interwar optimism about the pacific resolution of differences among democratic peoples, and was followed by the Kellogg-Briand Pact (1928), a largely symbolic renunciation of war (it was not a ratified "treaty") by its signatories which included the United States, France, Germany, Italy, Britain, Poland, Czechoslovakia, and Japan—many others were added the next year, including the Soviet Union. Viewed with hindsight of course, Locarno can be better portrayed as an end than a beginning, or even as the first installment of appeasement.

The system challenged

A Draft Treaty of Mutual Assistance of 1923 and the Geneva Protocol of 1924 were attempts to enhance the League's coercive power. They were consistently opposed by the British Conservatives (in government for most of the 1920s), who saw the League as essentially a conciliatory rather than a policing body and were fearful they would be dragged into war in support of indefensible boundaries negotiated too quickly in 1919. Consequently, the French renewed their efforts to create and sustain a traditional alliance system (in eastern Europe) to balance a resurgent Germany.

Japan's challenge to the system began with the occupation of Manchuria (1931) and its attack on Shanghai (1932). The League had been apparently successful in defusing through threatened coercion a Greco-Bulgarian dispute, but to arbitrate disputes involving a major power was another matter. The Japanese military occupation of much of Manchuria led to a League Resolution in October 1931 but any call for Japanese withdrawal was deprived of binding force because of Article 11 (the Japanese voted against and refused arbitration). Another League Resolution in December called for withdrawal and set up a commission to study the issue. When this commission reported critically in 1933, Japan, which had formally established a protectorate in Manchuria, voted against acceptance and withdrew from the League (the same year Hitler withdrew from the League's disarmament conference and then from the League itself).

A vigorous League response to aggression depended on Britain and France (from outside the League, the United States was alternatively tough- and conciliatory-sounding toward Japan), but many among the British and French political class regarded Japan as a useful bulwark in the East against Bolshevism. Moreover, the international financial crisis of 1931 and subsequent economic difficulties greatly distracted policymakers from the crisis in the East. Failure to discipline Japan, however, led directly to Mussolini's aggression in Abyssinia in 1935, and the League's failure to endorse serious sanctions against Italy, largely due to the resistance of the British who had hoped via the so-called Stresa Front (of Britain, France, and Italy) to keep Mussolini either aligned with the West or neutral in the mounting crisis over German demands for revision. This was followed by Hitler's remilitarization of the Rhineland, German and Italian intervention in the Spanish Civil War, and, in 1937, Mussolini's withdrawal of Italy from the League.

In addition to the bilateral security treaties between France and eastern European states, there were secret understandings between Soviet Russia and Weimar Germany (following discussions at Rapallo in 1922)—ostensibly on trade but accompanied by secret agreements that allowed the Germans to begin to rearm and retrain. This persistence of the old diplomacy was dictated by the security concerns of, especially, France, and the determination of some states, especially Germany, to revise the Versailles Treaty, and can be represented, by Realists, as merely the expected resurfacing of the primacy of *raison d'état* in what remained in spite of the League an essentially anarchic sovereign state system. A new element, however, was provided by the rise of an ideology—fascism, and in the Nazi case fascist racism—

which embraced war, not as "politics by other means," but as a cleansing and positive expression of a virile state and people.

In IR scholarship, this ideologically driven attitude poses a significant problem for structural theory: if war is regarded by some players as not a *means* for achieving security, balance, or power maximization, but as desirable in and of itself, the rational calculus upon which much of Realism rests is brought into question. This in turn raises a larger, more general question: to what extent does ideology—in Walzian terms, a second image variable—enter into the analysis of a state system? On the one hand, traditional balance-of-power historical analysis, from Carr's *The Twenty Years' Crisis* (1939, 1946) to A. J. P. Taylor's *The Origins of the Second World War* (1961), has tended to set aside or minimize the importance of ideas in preference for the realities of power and the pragmatism or opportunism of even fascist key players. On the other hand, popular post-Second World War historiography emphasized totalitarian ideologies and the perverted motives and ambitions of seriously neurotic dictators. Recently, some Neoclassical Realists have attempted to accommodate the ideological element by emphasizing at least the *use* of ideology to generate the public opinion that empowered dictators to pursue schemes that other types of regimes hesitated to embrace.

Fascist foreign policy and its institutions

Do interwar totalitarian foreign relations differ significantly from the style and substance generally of those of the Westphalian sovereign state system? Certainly the public rhetoric of *fascist* foreign policymakers, a Hitler or a Mussolini, was often marked by a bullying and gratuitous belligerence that apparently scorned traditions of diplomatic nicety (though some of Wilhelm II's clumsy pronouncements before the First World War suggest that the fascists had no monopoly on bombast). Speeches at a party rally were of course as much for domestic as foreign consumption, and could belie a continuing, altogether more traditional intercourse among foreign service professionals.

In Italy, there was little change in the foreign ministry until the late 1930s, and while Galeazzo Ciano's public pronouncements could reflect the penchant for the overblown of his father-in-law, *Il Duce*, Dino Grandi, Fascist minister of foreign affairs 1929–1932, later proved an adept and amiably ingratiating ambassador in London—unlike his German counterpart, Joachim von Ribbentrop, whose crude bluster and personal vanity managed to offend most of those with whom he dealt. But as in Italy, there was considerable continuity in the German foreign office. Much of the bureaucracy remained traditional in outlook and practice, and was presided over until 1938 by the aristocratic Konstantin von Neurath. Nevertheless, fascist regimes in both Italy and Germany often simply sidelined the professionals in making and implementing foreign policy. Well before von Neurath was moved out of the Wilhelmstrasse, Ribbentrop had organized a parallel Nazi foreign policy apparatus, and when he himself became foreign minister in 1938 he immediately set about a belated "Nazification" of the remaining personnel.

For IR scholars, then, a question arises over the way bureaucracies, guided (in Weberian terms) by an at least instrumental rationality, must relate in totalitarian systems to political leaders motivated and empowered by the mystique of the charismatic leadership principle and by goals of racial superiority or global revolution that reach far beyond *raison d'état* as traditionally conceived. German National Socialists fused the concepts of leader, race, and nation in a way that would seem to make much state-centric IR theory inadequate or inappropriate, just as the suicidal *Götterdämmerung* of the German nation would in 1945 appear to negate any rational concept of state security.

Of course, ideology may often be restrained by political reality. Lenin and Trotsky anticipated a European-wide socialist revolution that would, inspired by that in Russia, make the traditional diplomacy of the bourgeois state obsolete. The history of Soviet foreign policy in the interwar period is, however, to a large degree, that of a reluctant and defensive accommodation with the reality—that is, persistence—of a nonrevolutionary European state system. But the Realist view that Stalin (according to Kissinger, a "supreme realist … the Richelieu of his period") *simply* returned to the traditional forms of international relations once the revolutionary ardor of the Bolshevik era had burned itself out or was extirpated, and that this was a result of the constraints of the international system, is a serious oversimplification. In fact, Russian foreign policy followed, as is well known, a dual course in the interwar years. On the one hand, there was that of the *Narkomindel*, the foreign office bureaucracy concerned with the promotion of Russian state objectives through seeking formal recognition and the establishment of the institutional apparatus of diplomacy, embassies and emissaries, public treaties, and secret understandings with other nations. On the other hand, there was the conviction of the inevitability of success—that history was on the side of the communist system—and, institutionally, the more subterranean, international efforts of the *Comintern* (the Third International), a parallel bureaucracy devoted to coordinating Communist movements abroad and spreading revolutionary (and pro-Russian) sentiment among nations whose internal "sovereignty," presumably, posed no greater theoretical barrier than it did to Britain's Secret Intelligence Service or, latterly, the CIA.

Appeasement, Munich, and Great Power diplomacy

The narrative of international relations in the interwar era—most recently and exhaustively treated in Zara Steiner's monumental volumes *The Lights That Failed* (2005) and *The Triumph of the Dark* (2011)—has commonly been broken into two stories or discourses, that of the hopes and failure of the League and that of the hopes and failure of "appeasement." These are of course intertwined tales, and each, as a Constructivist IR scholar has recently argued, has drawn on and promoted complementary "lessons of history" in its narration: the "lesson of Versailles" and the "lesson of Munich." The former involves the way widespread assumptions about the "unfair" treatment of the defeated peoples in the severe peace settlement of 1919 undermined the structure of that peace, including the commitment of powerful members of the League's Council to defend it against the aggression of aggrieved revisionist states. It encouraged Western leaders to embrace or at least cease to resist the appeasement of those states; the lesson of Versailles led to Munich. The lesson of Munich, often intoned in the later twentieth century, involves the contrasting understanding that revisionist and opportunistic aggressors— especially those of the totalitarian variety—must be dealt with from a position of strength and determination. Hans Morgenthau came to argue that "in combining Munich and Versailles, the lesson dictated how these environments were defined: compromise, or appeasement, could take place among liberal states, but faced with non-liberal states, like the Soviet Union, American foreign policy would have to focus on security rather than inclusion" (quoted by Rasmusen, 2003, 513). Cold War Realism was far more likely to invoke the lesson of Munich than that of Versailles.

As we have seen, IR political theory has commonly made use of historical precedent and analogy, while historians have often been justifiably critical of drawing lessons from one era and simply applying them to another. Whether Realist analysis may accurately explain the failures of appeasement in 1938 may be argued, but the invocation of the "lessons" of Munich in very different eras and under very different circumstances—from Britain's confrontation with Nasser during the Suez crisis to America's involvement in Vietnam or the first and second Iraq Wars—perhaps says more about the way the narrative of international relations can shape a lasting "security culture" or worldview than it does about the actual veracity and utility of such lessons.

"Appeasement" of course, as a pejorative term, largely derives from the lesson of Munich and the dramatic failure of revisionist policies to prevent the coming of a second Great War. Earlier usage had often been more positive than negative. Dealing with dictators in the 1930s did not necessarily change the logic; indeed, a "just" revision of Versailles would, it was hoped, undermine the fascist rhetoric of grievance—Mussolini's "mutilated victory" and Hitler's "Diktat." For IR, the key issue is less the concept of appeasement per se, as compromise itself, central to the operation of a sovereign state system grounded in negotiation and balance, is either wise or foolish according to historical context, but rather the shift from the international institutions and processes of the League or the Court of International Justice back to a traditional form of bilateral and multilateral Great Power negotiation.

The appeasement of the late 1930s—from Chamberlain's trips to Berchtesgaden and Bad Godesberg to the four-power conference at Munich—was a return to a tradition of Great Power settlement, with lesser nations relegated to positions as impotent (and absent) observers, but in the context of the glare of publicity and public opinion and in conditions where the Western powers were too disunited to be able to impose significant balancing on Germany. Neither this return to traditional negotiation among the powers, nor the decision to go to war in 1939 over Poland, can however, according to the distinguished Cambridge historian of international relations Zara Steiner, confirm a Realist reading of interwar international relations. Contrary to either Defensive or Offensive Realist theory, Western policymakers, and especially appeasers like Neville Chamberlain, were not influenced by issues of strategic deterrence, military rearmament timetables, or political-economic considerations so much as by largely domestic politics and morality. Moreover, *perceptions* of fascist intentions, the consequences of granting their demands, and even the (exaggerated) assessment of their military strength were largely based, she argues, on nonmaterial factors such as a deep (and unjustified) sense of Western military inferiority and the persistence of a guilty conviction that revisionist demands contained some moral justification: "states are not, in reality, rational, unitary actors ... decision-makers or states often act out of ignorance and misperceive or misjudge the power equation ... Mearsheimer is wrong when he claims that it does not matter who heads the government" (Steiner, 2010, 130, 137). A Defensive *or* Offensive Realist response would of course observe that Realism does not in fact assume that fallible policymakers are uninfluenced by their ignorance, misperception, and concern with domestic and moral factors, but that the consequences of their irrational behavior is the likely failure of their policies and perhaps catastrophic damage to the security of the states they represent. Both appeasement and war are "pathological consequences," according to Waltz, of a multipolar system.

What has not been sufficiently explored, according to some, is the political-economic context of 1930s appeasement. Though Steiner's dense treatment of the pre-appeasement era in *The Lights that Failed* extensively explored the economic diplomacy of European reconstruction, as did Charles Maier's *Recasting Bourgeois Europe* (1975), she is dismissive of economic determinism in policymaking. There was of course a crude economism to be found in the contemporary 1930s socialist critique of appeasement. However, no current international historian has yet set out as well and thickly argued a case for a political-economic interpretation of the appeasement era as Arno Mayer did for the Paris Peace conference (in his comprehensive study of the *Politics and Diplomacy of Peacemaking* [1967]), though a number of IR scholars, including Gilpin and Wendt, have explored aspects of "economic appeasement" in the 1930s, and new work in this area is informed by left-IPE and revisionist Marxist analysis.

That being said, the late 1930s turn away from collective security and disarmament within the auspices of the League toward direct face-to-face negotiation has generally been seen by Realists in largely political terms, as the regrettably delayed return to crisis management by the powers. But the Munich conference itself can hardly be compared with the great conferences of the nineteenth century (or even with Locarno). It was a rushed affair, held in a major city of the most belligerent power (which set the agenda) rather than on neutral turf, not instructed or much informed by professional foreign service staffs (who were not even allowed to make official notes of the proceedings), and begun and finished in a single day and evening. This was hardly, in fact, serious summitry. Moreover, two Great Powers—Russia and the United States—were not parties at all.

Munich, intended to defuse the confrontation between Germany and Czechoslovakia over the Sudetenland, was shortly followed by the absorption of the Czech rump into the Reich, and the subsequent abandonment by Britain and France of any attempt to settle matters through a concert of powers. Crude balancing returned with a vengeance, as the West scrambled to guarantee Polish security and, belatedly, to seek a defensive arrangement with the Soviet Union—a half-hearted affair countered by Germany's swift and secretly negotiated masterstroke of the Ribbentrop-Molotov Pact. As German troops poured across the Polish border on September 1, 1939, one might say that *both* the new and the old diplomacy had failed—the open covenants of the internationalist dream of self-determined democratic peoples, enshrined in international law and the League, *and* the resort to old world concert and balance. Whether either might have been able to operate successfully if more vigorously pursued may beg the question whether any system of international relations could have functioned to prevent war among all the Great Powers in the poisonous autarchic environment of the Great Depression and the rise of fascist belligerence.

Carr's thesis in his *The Twenty Years' Crisis*, written during the Munich crisis, advanced the argument that idealism had been inadequate when dealing with rising and revisionist powers and with the historical-material realities of the time. If the League idea was inherently unrealistic in the face of large historical forces, Carr, as we have seen, was nevertheless more ambiguous than many Realists who followed him on how—or whether—power and morality might be reconciled in foreign affairs. Moreover, any analysis of the failure of the League must go further than its presumed "utopianism." It was, as an institution dedicated to peace and security, hobbled from the beginning by its governing constitution and by the Great Powers who both distrusted it and dominated it. Though it accomplished much in lesser areas of international organization and cooperation, it was never the radical "idealist" instrument envisioned by those true utopians who had wanted, not an international or federative body, but a world polity with elected delegates rather than an assembly of representatives of national foreign ministries.

Beyond the problems posed by its awkward institutional character, the League was inhibited as an effective "society" of nations due to the steady growth in the number of active members of the international community and the simultaneous breakdown of the homogeneity of that community—divided as it became by ideology and the diverse constitutive natures of those democracies, quasi-democracies, nondemocracies, and totalitarian regimes both inside and outside the League. While among IR scholars, some Liberal Institutionalists might object that, given time, such a transnational structure would itself have influenced the character of global culture and encouraged the growth of cooperation through a process of learning, others have argued that in the 1930s at least the lack of shared normative values and perspectives fatally inhibited any such growth. As Craig and George observe, with a degree of nostalgia,

An important reason for the relative effectiveness of the nineteenth-century system was that its members were bound together by a common historical tradition, by cultural and religious ties, and [in the case of the monarchies of Europe] by familial relationships … This kind of homogeneity did not survive the [first world] war. (Craig and George, 1990, 58)

Nor did Europe as law-giver to the global community survive the *Second* World War.

The Second World War and "the provincializing of Europe"

By the end of 1940, Germany had established a European hegemony under Hitler that was more complete than Napoleon's—destroying any chance for the traditional system's balancing through European coalition. American armed neutrality, Russian weakness, and Japan's alliance made effective *global* balancing against the Axis powers also seem unlikely. This changed with the entry of the United States, the "arsenal of democracy," into both the European and Pacific theaters of war, and with the surprising resistance of the Russians to the German eastward advance in 1941–2.

German success rested on its military professionalism and a strategy of swift conquest (Blitzkrieg) before the limits of its war economy—its fiscal and material resources—were exposed. The thrust into Russia on an unprecedentedly broad front was a gamble. It failed due in large part to the simple vastness of the Russian state, the endurance of its large population, the industrial resources fortuitously provided by the brutal state planning of the 1920s and 1930s, and, importantly, Stalin's ability to tap into deep reservoirs of Russian nationalism. Doomed perhaps in any event, the German assault also failed because of Hitler's personal, inflexible domination of both strategy and tactics. Aggressive Nazi foreign policy had been one of high risks, often in the face of far more conservative senior diplomatic and military officials. Its successes, and the initial success in the West of Hitler's war leadership, secured the Führer's position and made inevitable the pursuit of *Lebensraum* (living space) for the German race in the east that had been, it appears, his ultimate objective. This raises issues of interest for IR.

Though after Munich Hitler continued to use the language of treaty revision and the self-determination of ethnic Germans (in Danzig) to justify his further aggression, this was merely a screen. The fragmentation of Czechoslovakia and the incorporation of Bohemia into the Reich allowed free play for his dreams of an eastern policy of territorial expansion—through and beyond the Polish state. This drive eastward is most easily accommodated in Realist theory as a bid to secure strategic raw materials (and keep them from a likely geopolitical as well as ideological enemy—the Soviet Union), the oil and minerals increasingly necessary to maintain (as in defensive Realism) or expand (according to offensive Realism) the military power of the state. This is more or less congenial with a view that there was an important Realpolitik logic in German expansion—though a logic that seemingly ignored the fact that German *economic* hegemony in eastern Europe was already, with little risk or cost, significantly binding those states to its political will.

The historian Niall Ferguson has asked whether Hitler was therefore a "quintessential offensive realist?" To answer this question, one has to consider the logic of Nazi risk-taking in 1938 (when Britain, France, and Czechoslovakia might well have defeated a German offensive). Ferguson believes not: "Hitler was anything but a realist, offensive or otherwise, in September 1938. He was a very reckless gambler" (Ferguson, 2010, 182). Admitting that the move east in 1941 *can* be explained in Realist terms by the imperative to secure resources, and that there was a logical (if perverse) case to be made for Lebensraum as a necessity for a densely populated Germany, nevertheless the pursuit of a brutal policy of extermination to "clear" rather than "liberate" the conquered territory was instrumentally *irrational* in the immediate context of the wartime need to foment anti-Soviet support in the Ukraine and elsewhere. This policy can best be understood as an ideological commitment to racial purity and the cleansing nature of warfare—in the face of the immediate interests of state security, that is, of winning the war. The same of course can be said for the drive to divert resources from the war effort to the destruction of European Jewry.

Global alliance

Though one can of course present the wartime motives of the *Allies* in ideological terms as well, of the defense of liberal capitalism in Europe and abroad or the survival of Marxist-Leninist socialism, these come to the fore more blatantly after the final defeat of the Axis powers opened the question of what was to follow. The wartime alliances, across ideological boundaries, strongly suggest the Realist notion of the primacy of *state* survival through coalition balancing against a would-be hegemon—as in the eras of Louis XIV, Napoleon, and the Kaiser—but with, ultimately, a significant difference. Though those conflicts had had a global dimension, as did their negotiated settlement, they had seen the restoration of a Great Power state system, and did little to challenge European (especially British) preponderance in world affairs. While it is true that Napoleon, like Hitler, had threatened the destruction of sovereign states in a new order, and the First World War had been an existential catastrophe for autocratic European empires, the European system itself had retained its self-referential character postbellum. While Euro-Asian Russia briefly dominated the heart of Europe at the end of the Napoleonic wars, it had not attempted to sustain a postwar hegemony in the West. America after the Paris Peace conference in 1919 even more thoroughly renounced its interest in or responsibility for European security arrangements—though its banks and commercial interests were significantly engaged even before the war ended in eroding European (especially British) global hegemony.

The wartime conferences

As at Chaumont and Vienna in 1814–15, the Allied powers toward the end of the Second World War saw themselves as the sole arbiters of the complex issues that would arise with the cessation of hostilities, and as at Paris in 1919 the political leaders of those powers, Churchill, Stalin, and Roosevelt, were uninclined significantly to delegate their authority to ministers and foreign service professionals. On Roosevelt's insistence, both the British Foreign Secretary, Anthony Eden, and the American Secretary of State, Cordell Hull, were excluded from the discussions between Churchill and Roosevelt at Casablanca (January 1943) that led to a policy of "unconditional surrender" of the Axis powers. Harry Hopkins was Roosevelt's personal envoy (as Col. House had been Wilson's) in London, and the main intermediary in working out the details of Lend-Lease had been not a state department functionary but W. Averell Harriman, a businessman who was later appointed US ambassador to the USSR.

The Tehran conference (in December 1943) was, however, preceded by a conference of ministers in Moscow to air their agendas and priorities—for Russia the pressing need for an Anglo-American second front, for the United States the establishment of a successor to the League, and for all three the need to begin discussing plans for postwar Germany. At Tehran, Roosevelt, hoping to establish a close relationship that would ensure Russian cooperation in policing the postwar world, was prepared to deal with Stalin in the face of Churchill's deep reluctance to commit to a cross-channel rather than Mediterranean offensive, and with scant regard for the details of a balancing territorial settlement that his more traditionalist British ally held important. The growth of the American presence in Western Europe and the Soviet victory at Kursk presaged an inevitable shift in the Big Three dynamic away from Great Britain. In fact, the conference had originally been intended as a bilateral, personal, summit between Stalin and Roosevelt, and the two leaders both stayed in the Soviet embassy; Churchill, at the British legation.

The first meeting of the three saw Stalin and Roosevelt prevail against Churchill on the central issue of Operation Overlord, an absolute commitment to an Anglo-American invasion of the coast of France in May (or thereabouts) of 1944. Stalin, for his part, committed to join the war against Japan in the Far East after German capitulation, an important Anglo-American objective. Churchill, who in the next year would fly to Moscow to engage in his own bilateral diplomacy (with the American ambassador, Harriman, as observer only), raised the issue of postwar Polish borders—the so-called Curzon line in the east and the probable inclusion of some German territory in the west—which Stalin used as an opportunity for a little geopolitical horse-trading: a "chunk" of East Prussia, including Memel and Königsberg, would give Russia an ice-free Baltic base (he also raised the issue of Turkey's control of the Black Sea straits and warm-water outlets in the Far East). The final topic of discussion was the likely "dismemberment" of Germany and the inevitable issue of borders and reparations. When Churchill reminded Stalin of the First World War Bolshevik slogan, "no annexations, no indemnities," the Marshal replied "I already told you, I have become a conservative" (quoted in Roberts, 2007, 17).

In February of 1945, with the collapse of Germany imminent, the three met again in the Russian Crimea at Yalta. This proved a more elaborate event than Tehran; the Allied leaders were accompanied by larger and more varied delegations of ministers, and the foreign secretaries Eden, Molotov, and Stettinius met separately on especially conflicted issues. In plenary session, the three leaders discussed the postwar settlement, including the Polish borders (accepting the Curzon line in the east but reserving final consideration of the western, German, border pending a formal peace settlement). The Polish border issue was, however, less divisive than the emerging issue of the character of the provisional Polish government (already established by the USSR), and Churchill's concern that it be broadly based to include the Polish government-in-exile in London.

The division of Germany into zones of occupation was less contentious, though Stalin was contemptuous of the proposal that the French be granted a zone of German occupation (they "have only eight divisions"). The demand for unconditional surrender and occupation by the Allies of the defeated Axis countries reflected Allied conviction that the Armistice of 1918 had been a mistake.

Roosevelt wanted further confirmation of the Soviet promise of support for the conquest of Japan and was prepared to exchange this for Japanese territory (the Kurile Islands and southern Sakhalin) and more or less a Soviet sphere of influence in much of eastern Europe (in any event a de facto reality), where the United States, though concerned to see the establishment of democratic regimes, had no clear strategic or economic interests. As a concession to Anglo-American concerns, Stalin agreed to a Declaration on Liberated Europe: to assist the liberated peoples "to solve by democratic means their pressing political and economic problems" and, alluding to the Anglo-American Atlantic Charter of 1941, "the right of all people to choose the form of government under which they will live."

Of the other issues addressed in plenary session, the establishment of a successor to the League at the end of the war mattered most to Roosevelt. The Soviets were promised full participation, with a Great Power veto right. Finally, the Soviet insistence that significant reparations ("in kind"—i.e., goods and industrial plant) be extracted from the Germans, and that, as the ally that had suffered the most, the USSR should receive the lion's share saw both Churchill and Roosevelt raise the specter of "the lesson of Versailles." They agreed to establish a reparations commission.

The final Big Three conference, that near Berlin at Potsdam in July of 1945, was marked by the attendance of a new, inexperienced (and somewhat Anglophobic) American president, Harry Truman, who was dependent on his advisors—generally, like his secretary of state James Byrnes, more suspicious of Russian motives, especially over the provisional Polish government, than Roosevelt had been. Stalin's first meeting was with Truman, confirming, perhaps, a degree of British subordination. In any event, midway through the conference British representation changed, Churchill having lost a general election to the surprise of everyone. The new socialist prime minister, Clement Attlee, already in attendance, and his foreign secretary Ernest Bevin nevertheless continued to voice British geopolitical concerns—about the USSR's domination of the reconstituted eastern European states, its threat to Turkey and Iran, and its insistence on a role in the Mediterranean.

Though Stalin's strong suit in dealing with the Americans was his confirmation of Soviet support in the invasion of the Japanese homeland (a delighted Truman claimed "I've gotten what I came for"), the atomic bomb, dropped on Japan just four days after the conference ended, would bring the war to an unexpectedly swift conclusion, confirm American domination of the postwar Japanese settlement, deprive the Russians of their trump card in continuing negotiations, and seriously unbalance British plans, predicated as they were on having another year or two before the end of the war to put their eastern empire back on its feet and their finances (before Lend-Lease was terminated) in better order.

General principles were established and details left to foreign ministers. The 1936 Montreux convention on access to the straits between the Black Sea and the Mediterranean was, at Russian insistence, to be revised (though the proposed changes were subsequently rejected by Turkey), and territorial trusteeships for the Italian colonies were assigned. New, western-moved, Polish borders were confirmed, as were the German occupation zones. Reparations proved not to be such a thorny issue since neither Byrnes nor Stalin wished to treat divided Germany as a single economic unit. Germany was to be disarmed and denazified, and there would be "war crime" trials for German and Japanese leaders and those officers and officials associated with wartime atrocities.

Together, these three Conferences may suggest the grand style of the Great Powers of the past, whereby the fate of lesser states had been settled almost casually without consultation. They certainly seemed a repudiation of the kind of process envisioned by Wilson's League—though like Wilson, Roosevelt had been hopeful of a postwar world of interdependent, democratic nations and was willing to let much with which he might disagree go ahead in the hope that a successor to the League, the UN, would this time, and with active participation by both the United States and the Soviet Union, later rectify things. In any event, the Soviet Union had sacrificed more of its population than the Western Allies, and importantly, like Russia in 1815, had a vast army on the ground. Though the American right would complain loudly that the Roosevelt administration was "soft" on Communism, it can be argued that Soviet postwar preponderance in central and eastern Europe simply reflected this fact.

After the Second World War, the centrality of Europe in world affairs was much changed. Its Cold War importance was that of the dangerous boundary zone between antagonistic superpowers, rather than the cockpit of autonomous Great Powers. Hitler had smashed the continental state system, but in the end Germany itself, ruined, depleted, and divided like much of central Europe, ceased to exist as a unitary sovereign state. The British clung to the semblance of a formal empire, and the French to rather less than this. There was to be the mirage of influence in their seats on the UN Security Council and in Britain's expensive commitment to nuclear weapons, but Churchill's hope of sustaining and projecting global influence into the future as one of the "Big Three" came to be regarded by the Americans as nonsense well before the Suez debacle revealed the hollowness of British pretensions.

By the conference of Tehran in 1943, there was already an emerging bipolar global system—not only that represented by the non-negotiable confrontation of Axis and Allied powers, but within Allied summitry, as Britain came to count for rather less than its American and Soviet interlocutors. Well before the end, it was appreciated everywhere that "Europe," at the heart of the world's diplomatic system of international relations for 300 years, would count for much less than the peripheral powers of America and Russia. This fact was clear in (1) the relative weight of the United States and Russia vis-à-vis Britain in the wartime conferences, and the failure of the British to reassert their traditional role of European balancer, (2) the rapid loss of empire by France and Britain during the war and after, (3) the construction of the new (American dominated) world financial system at Bretton Woods in 1944, and (4) the creation of a UN located in New York City with a large non-European majority in its Assembly.

The devastation of much of Europe was much worse than during and after the First World War. By 1945, European war dead numbered perhaps as many as twenty-seven million Russians and seven million Germans, amounting to some 10 percent of the German population, 13 percent or more of the Soviet population, and as much as 16 percent of the Poles. European Jewry—those who had not been able to emigrate—suffered of course proportionately much more than this: the six or seven million who were killed represented the large majority of that population. There were, again, masses of refugees, persons displaced by war, but this time as many as twenty million. About twelve million people had been expelled or fled westwards after 1944.

Europe was occupied. During the war, over a million Americans had been stationed in Britain; in 1945, the Americans, British, and Russians occupied Germany (with a zone of occupation carved out of the American sector for the French); the Americans engineered the successor state in Italy, and became, to the annoyance of the excluded British, the sole ruler and law-giver to the Japanese people. The Bomb, the Marshall plan, and the Cold War in general point in the same direction—that the political reality of global international relations reduced Western and central Europe to a subordinate status, and would continue to do so militarily, financially, and culturally for a generation.

Can we nevertheless say that the *European system* was globalized? Only in the sense that, as the number of independent states mushroomed with decolonization, the apparatus of sovereign state relations followed the *form* of European diplomatic convention: the system of ambassadors with immunity and the formal myth than states were autonomous and that other states would not seek to subvert their domestic sovereignty. In fact, the new "system" rested less on the idealization of sovereign state equality in a condition of international anarchy than on the reality of the *dual hegemony*, within their own spheres of influence, of the Soviet Union and the United States.

The end of empire

The exhausting struggle in Europe fatally undermined the ability of those combatant and occupied European powers with imperial regimes abroad—Britain, France, the Netherlands, and Belgium—to maintain their global pretentions during the war or to restore them afterward (Portugal, as a neutral, was able to maintain a longer lease on its own African empire). European imperialism was in any event already deeply challenged by the nationalist movements on the ground that had flourished since the Peace Conference of 1919 had denied them the "self-determination" it extended to eastern Europe. After 1945, the rapidity and scope of decolonization radically transformed global international relations.

The Netherlands were never able to resecure authority in the Dutch East Indies after the Japanese surrender, and an independence struggle was swiftly followed by the proclamation of an Indonesian Republic in 1949. For the British Empire, the wartime loss of its naval supremacy in the Pacific, of Hong Kong and its Singapore base, also undermined its prestige in the East generally and in the south Asian subcontinent where the postwar Labour Government quickly negotiated an end to the Raj and independence for India, Ceylon, Pakistan, and Burma. Sudan's independence had been promised during the war, Palestine was evacuated in 1948, and nominal Egyptian independence (largely ignored during the war) was made tangible by the officers' coup of 1951. British presence and interests remained of course entrenched in many newly independent countries like Malaya (where Britain was committed to fighting a long counterinsurgency) and in ex-mandates like Iraq, Iran, or Transjordan, but were tenuous.

The collapse of France in 1940 signaled a more complete end of imperial effectiveness abroad. The Free French had committed postwar France to the granting of responsible government in Africa. In Asia, the Japanese conquest of French Indochina made resumption of imperial control all but impossible and a war of liberation followed. Two years after the definitive French defeat at Dien Bien Phu in 1954, Morocco and Tunisia were granted independence but a long struggle ensued to retain Algeria, as a department of France with a white settler community of over a million. By 1962, when the Algerian civil war, having torn apart the French Fourth Republic, was concluded with Algerian independence, the "winds of change" were blowing through both French and British Africa, while in the vast central African Congo, Belgian plans for an extended, phased decolonization process ended abruptly in 1959 with riots and independence the next year—to be followed by an extended civil war.

Roosevelt had told Churchill that he did not intend to fight in order to preserve the British Empire, and Anglo-American relations in wartime India were often strained. American administrations from Truman to Eisenhower accepted, by and large, that decolonization was inevitable and that the United States ought not to be seen to prop up formal imperialism. This stance, made brutally clear to Britain and France during the Suez crisis of 1956, was informed by the growing need to keep the non-Western world within the orbit of the West, for strategic security interests but also to ensure the economic orientation of new postcolonial states toward the United States. Meanwhile, America increasingly assumed the global security obligations of the former British and French empires—in Greece, Turkey, the Middle East, and Indochina.

IR scholarship's characteristic Eurocentrism, its overwhelming preoccupation with the pre-Cold War history of the state system of the European subcontinent and its larger meaning for the discipline's theory and practice, has meant that *imperialism* has been significantly understudied and undertheorized—being treated, if at all, both as largely irrelevant to processes and constraints inherent in the Westphalian order in Europe and as an extension of that competitive, sovereign state anarchy to the larger world. This line of reasoning encourages the common view that the postimperial, decolonized world simply reproduced the European system either, as English School and some Constructivist scholars might imply, through the tutelage of its erstwhile imperial masters or, for structuralists, because the sovereign anarchic system imposed its constraints on new nations wherever and whenever they might emerge. While some scholars have probed the connections between early-twentieth-century imperialism and internationalism, and others (Liberal Institutionalist, Constructivist, and IPE scholars) have been concerned with the ways in which European empires anticipated, and perhaps configured, the interconnected, globalized world of the modern era, there has been very little in mainstream IR theory that encourages the study of the actual process of decolonization on the ground locally and its meaning for the culture(s) of international relations.

Top-down IR scholarship that assumes for purposes of system analysis the "globalization" of European sovereignty (even as Europe itself lost its hegemonic role abroad and indeed much of its own sovereignty) was surprisingly resistant to the important historiographic shifts in the 1980s and 1990s in the understanding of imperialism and postimperialism that followed from the local perspective of postcolonial and subaltern studies. Feminist IR scholarship has attempted to redress this bias, but remains largely a minority voice in the discipline. This recalcitrance has impoverished IR's ability to understand contemporary regional—or indeed global—conflict that might not be state-centric, and what it comprehends as the "failed-state syndrome" of many postcolonial societies.

While this is not the place for a close analysis of the locally complex and varied experience of decolonization (for which there is a large and growing literature beyond the discipline of IR), one might note that postcolonial states were in a sense often set up to fail through hastily drawn boundaries that ignored important ethnic divisions, the imposing of secular constitutions enshrining principles of governance somewhat alien to local cultures, the legacy of European-educated elites that divided rather than unified the postcolonial "nation," or, importantly, the subordination of new states, on the one hand, to the economic constraints of a Western-dominated global capitalist order or, on the other, to extravagant and unsustainable Soviet model projects of socialist modernization.

To the extent that IR was interested in decolonized peoples following the Second World War, it was chiefly in how such new nations (as states) might relate politically to the bipolar world of the superpowers—as, that is, pawns in the global chess-match of strategic Realpolitik and the politics of economic aid and development. Had the discipline been prepared to take more seriously the understanding of non-Western peoples as more than or other than states, and as agents rather than objects, it might have been better prepared to respond not only to the Vietnam war as more than a problem of "containment," but also and importantly to the nonstate conflict ("terrorism") that has emerged with a vengeance since the end of the Cold War. A more serious engagement, informed perhaps by cultural history and historical sociology, with the manifold implications of the end of empire and the decolonization that followed might have enabled a better (and more predictive) understanding of our contemporary world.

The postwar settlement

The First World War was to have been, as H. G. Wells famously said, the war to end war. But for complicated reasons the structures erected to ensure arbitration in place of armed conflict—the League and the world court—were barely adequate to contain the traditional politics of force and intimidation when attempted by small states and notably unable to channel Great Power relations into a new pattern. The "new diplomacy," based on ill-defined Wilsonian principles of openness and conciliation, meant to ensure that democracy rather than elites and vested interests would prevail, failed—partly because the various foreign service establishments never really believed in it. By the late 1930s, the traditional system of state balancing and power politics was back with British and French rearmament and, concurrently, a personal diplomacy of "appeasement" ending in a traditional-seeming Great Power conference at Munich. But these also failed, and the world was engulfed in another war much more devastating to its civilian populations than the first. How did its resolution differ from that of previous all-power wars?

Economic issues generally were much more to the fore in 1945 than in 1919, when the probable effect of reparations on the world economy had received little sustained attention, though thereafter the economic side of restoring European order was much debated and came to touch "on almost every aspect of [post-First World War] diplomacy in a manner that had no real equivalent in the pre-war period" (Steiner, 2001, 20). The collapse of the global economy in the early 1930s, the turn toward policies of economic autarchy by democracies as well as totalitarian states, and the failure of the World Economic Conference in 1933 ensured a heightened sense of the centrality of economic factors in formal and informal international relations. In the administration of the British and French empires, economic development received much attention in the interwar period, while it has recently been argued (David Ekbladh, *The Great American Mission* [2011]) that, though he had helped destroy the 1933 economic conference, Roosevelt's domestic schemes for depression-era recovery, like the Tennessee Valley Authority, formed a basis for subsequent American designs for global "modernization" in Asia and elsewhere. In the words of the internationalist Harry Dexter White at the US Treasury, the goal was to create a "New Deal for a new world" (Steil, 2013, 1). During the Second World War, the US administration of Lend-Lease set a precedent for the employment of trained economists on the staffs of American diplomatic missions, broadening their agendas and anticipating postwar "dollar diplomacy." Roosevelt and his advisors assumed that America would be well set to dominate the postwar global financial and commercial system without, it was hoped, the continuation of a large military presence abroad. There was emphasis on postwar planning that centered a *dollar-dominated* financial system and a *global free-trade* regime that would redirect trade from semiclosed former colonial empires to US markets (a *pax Americana* rather than a *pax Britannica*).

Bretton Woods and the global financial system

The Bretton Woods conference of over 700 delegates from 44 countries, held in New Hampshire a month after the Anglo-American D-Day invasion of Nazi Europe, concretely positioned the United States as the fiscal arbiter of what would be the restored global postwar economic system. This gathering, perhaps even more than the

Allied Great Power wartime conferences of Tehran, Yalta, and Potsdam, symbolized the reality of American military, political, and economic hegemony—at least in the non-Communist world. The United States (as Churchill said, "You have all the gold") sought to arrange for the future stability of a postdepression, postwar world a monetary system that was based explicitly on the dollar and free from the kind of exchange controls with which the British hoped to shore up sterling's international (or at least Empire-Commonwealth) role.

American economic clout had been expressed from the 1920s in interwar negotiations over the system of reparations payments and the repayment of war loans, but Bretton Woods was a far more extensive affair. The objective was to reestablish a stable international system without simply reverting to the gold standard—by substituting the dollar as the global reserve currency, linked to a fixed rate for gold and with intervention by a US-dominated World Bank and an IMF to prevent destabilizing monetary fluctuations. Britain's most prominent economist, John Maynard Keynes, who made six official trips to the United States in the 1940s, wanted an autonomous global currency and bank, and a global stabilization fund with unlimited ability to call on members (i.e., the United States). The United States, however, was unwilling to give *carte blanche* to the new international financial institutions and demanded strict quotas on the amount nations in trouble could draw; voting rights in the IMF and the World Bank (the International Bank for Reconstruction and Development) were weighted to favor the largest creditor nation. Everyone else, including Britain, was a debtor and the United States unsurprisingly got its way.

After war ended, the enormous need for reconstruction in Britain and elsewhere in Europe led to a dollar shortage; the United States ran huge trade surpluses, which meant reserves in the United States continued to expand while the rest of the world endured continued trade deficits. The intended consequence of the reconstruction of the global financial system was that America was able to confirm and institutionalize its global victory in the sterling-dollar rivalry, to replace the British Empire as the financial as well as military hegemon of the new world order. During the sterling crisis of 1947, the *Economist* would observe that though not many believed that it was the conscious aim of American policy to bankrupt Britain, "the evidence can certainly be read that way" (Steil, 2013, 330).

Peace, again

The war ended with the invasion and collapse of the Axis powers. Unconditional, non-negotiated total victory was accompanied by the occupation of Germany, its European allies, and Japan, which, though the Japanese homeland was not invaded, also surrendered unconditionally. The Italian fascist regime had collapsed a year earlier and its successor allied with the victors. There was a more definitive destruction of the aggressor states than when the November Armistice ended the First World War. Both Germany and Japan suffered a total loss of sovereignty and new constitutions were to be largely dictated to them. But what was the immediate and long-term legacy of the manner of the war's closure for the system of international relations?

The global settlement involved, not a single great conference as in 1919, but a series of agreements across what was already an emerging divide between the West and the Soviet Union. These discussions and treaties were prefigured by the wartime conferences of the Big Three at Yalta and Potsdam. After the Japanese surrender, a Council of Foreign Ministers (representing Britain, the United States, and Russia) met, first, in London in September and October, and subsequently in Moscow in December to establish the groundwork for a settlement. This was followed by a European peace conference held in Paris from July to October 1946. Paris, 1946, was however no grand congress of all the powers as at Westphalia, Utrecht, or Vienna. As at the conference of victorious allies at Paris in 1919, however, it dealt with the restoration of boundaries and, at Russia's insistence, determined the reparations which Germany's allies were to be assessed (the Western powers abjured reparations for themselves and were disturbed by the onerous amount the Soviets demanded). Prewar Czechoslovakia was recreated (with the Sudetenland now denuded of its German-speaking inhabitants), and in eastern Europe boundaries were more or less reset according to the borders of January 1, 1941, except for those of Poland. Italy lost its colonies. Reparations and boundaries largely reflected the interests of the Soviet state—as the ally which had suffered the most, and which had substantial control on the ground in eastern and central Europe. Stalin had already begun to strip assets out of Romania and Germany for transport back to the Soviet Union. The reality on the ground suggested of course the Soviet Union's likely domination of the newly restored states, and though a gesture toward the ghost of the League and the newborn UN was made by affirming that the liberated states were to secure "the enjoyment of human rights and of the fundamental freedoms, including freedom of expression, of press and publication, of religious worship, of political opinion and of public meeting," no enforcement mechanism was seriously proposed. A separate four power treaty envisioned for occupied Germany fell victim to the nascent Cold War and was not concluded until 1990.

Broadly considered, the Second World War settlement also included the parallel establishment of the UN (a conference of fifty allied nations signed its charter in June of 1945) and the war crimes trials. Like the direct governance of Germany and Japan by military authority, the tribunals in Nuremberg (both the International Military Tribunal and the American-conducted Nuremberg Military Tribunal) and Tokyo signal the suspension of sovereignty and of the idea that the leaders of sovereign states are shielded in international law from personal liability. The trials however offer something of a contradictory perspective. On the one hand, the formal process was that of a court—that is, it claimed to apply and expand traditions of international law and subsequently affected the development of international jurisprudence. On the other hand, it was justice meted out by the victors in devastated and supine countries and simply reflected the realities of power. Some in the West, like the pioneering IR scholar Quincy Wright at the University of Chicago or the chief justice of the US Supreme

Court, Harlan Fiske Stone, attacked what they saw as the hypocritical misuse of nineteenth-century international law traditions (a "high-grade lynching party" as Stone said), while George Kennan recommended summary execution of Nazi leaders rather than "show trials" suggestive of Stalin's purges in the 1930s. Though Stalin himself is reported to have said, perhaps jokingly, that the Allies should simply have shot 50,000 Nazi officers and party members, the Soviets, though they had not been members of the wartime United Nations War Crimes Commission, played a "substantive role" at Nuremberg (Hirsch, 2008, 701–2).

Clearly "Europe" as the center of global international relations was finished (though it took Britain and France some time to realize this); the Americans (with the bomb) and the Russians (with the largest army in Europe) were the arbiters of whatever peace would follow, though the Russians were somewhat discounted as a *global* force until 1949. The Americans after Bretton Woods would dominate global economic as well as political relations. In terms of system change, there were, or seemed to be, two factors of significance: *the United Nations* and *the American monopoly of the atomic bomb*. The UN was a gesture toward the aspirations of the League, though with a Great Power "concert" at its heart in the Security Council; the bomb asserted such hegemony as no state had ever possessed before. Both implied a break *and* a continuity with the traditional anarchic, balancing system of sovereign powers that, IR argues, had prevailed since Westphalia. Both also are closely involved in the origins of the so-called Cold War that followed closely on the heels of optimistic hopes and institutional designs for a new, pacific world order.

Finally, one might observe that IR scholarship that is significantly invested in a close reading of the political and military ambitions and strategies, wartime alliances, and armed and confrontational peace that followed the Second World War has been less interested (characteristically) in what one might call the cultural, rather than Realpolitik, basis for the Cold War. First, it might be argued that the enduring reading of the history of the unhappy 1930s as "the lessons of Munich," entrenched in the popular as well as administrative mentality, greatly heightened misperception and narrowed negotiable space across the Cold War divide as well as between a democratic West and much of the Third World. Second, cultural historians might observe that the totality and brutality of the Second World War, the disappearance of any line between civilian and combatant, the whole-scale inhumanity of the Holocaust or the pattern bombing of thickly populated cities, the total mobilization of resources and the pervasiveness of propaganda, like the commitment to a complete victory of annihilation and the determination to punish the defeated by hanging their leaders, "denazifying" their peoples, and converting their governmental systems to resemble those of their occupying powers, had a lasting effect thereafter on Cold War mentalities and practices.

George Orwell's postwar novel of a future dystopia, *1984*, often misread in Cold War America as simply an attack on Soviet totalitarianism, is as much about the enduring rhetoric, bureaucratic authoritarianism, and mentality of the wartime experience as about ideology. If, for mainstream political IR, the Cold War begins with Stalin's 1946 Bolshoi address and George Kennan's "long telegram," some historians would look to the construction of a wartime psychology of fear and paranoia, and see, not a sudden break from wartime alliance to peacetime confrontation, but on the domestic level at least a kind of continuity.

Recommended readings

Among the voluminous scholarship dealing with the Paris peace conference, see Erik Goldstein's brief but useful survey, *The First World War Peace Settlements 1919–1925* (2002). For fuller treatments, see Margaret Macmillan, *Paris 1919: Six Months that Changed the World* (2001), and Norman A. Graebner and Edward M. Bennett, *The Versailles Treaty and Its Legacy: The Failure of the Wilsonian Vision* (2011). For the highly politicized and selective opening of state archives in response to the demands of the New Diplomacy and the debate over war guilt and the Versailles Treaty generally, see Keith Wilson (ed.), *Forging the Collective Memory: Government and International Historians through Two World Wars* (1996). In comparing Paris, 1919, with other major postwar settlements, G. John Ikenberry has offered a utilitarian analysis in *After Victory: Institutions, Strategic Restraint, and the Rebuilding of Order after Major Wars* (2001).

The flurry of interest in international society in the interwar years can be explored in Timothy Dunne, *Inventing International Society* (1998); Daniel Laqua (ed.), *Internationalism Reconfigured: Transnational Ideas and Movements between the World Wars* (2011); Daniel Gorman, *The Emergence of International Society in the 1920s* (2012); Mark Mazower, *Governing the World* (2012); and Glenda Sluga, *Internationalism in the Age of Nationalism* (2013). Also see D. Long and B. Schmidt (eds.), *Imperialism and Internationalism in the Discipline of International Relations* (2005). For recent work on the League beyond the issue of collective security, see Susan Pederson, "Back to the League of Nations," *American Historical Review* 112 (2007), 1091–117; Keith David Watenpugh, "The League of Nations' Rescue of Armenian Genocide Survivors and the Making of Modern Humanitarianism, 1920–1927," *American Historical Review* 115 (2010), 1315–39; and Patricia Clavin, *Securing the World Economy: The Reinvention of the League of Nations, 1920–1946* (2013).

On Carr, in addition to the scholarship cited in Chapter 1, see Graham Evans, "E. H. Carr and International Relations," *British Journal of International Studies* 1 (1975), 77–97, and William T. R. Fox, "E. H. Carr and Political Realism: Vision and Revision," *Review of International Studies* 11 (1985), 1–16. A reconsideration of the utopians Carr attacked can be found in David Long and Peter Wilson (eds.), *Thinkers of the Twenty Years' Crisis: Inter-War Idealism Reassessed* (1995). Also see Jeanne Morefield, *Covenants without Swords: Idealist Liberalism and the Spirit of Empire* (2005). For a critique of Realist analysis of the coming of the Second World War, see Zara Steiner, "British Decisions for Peace and War 1938–1939," and Niall Ferguson, "Realism and Risk in 1938: German Foreign Policy and the Munich Crisis," in May, Rosecrance, and Steiner (eds.), *History and Neorealism* (2010), 129–54 and 154–84. The heated debate over A. J. P. Taylor's controversial 1961 text can be traced in Gordon Martel (ed.), *The Origins of the Second World War Reconsidered* (1986). The large literature on appeasement can be approached through Steiner's *The Triumph of the Dark*. Also see Peter Neville, *Hitler and Appeasement: The British Attempt to Prevent the Second World War* (2009). For an approach informed by a Marxist reading of the political economy of appeasement, see Alexander Anievas, "The International Political Economy of Appeasement: The Social Sources of British Foreign Policy During the 1930s," *Review of International Studies* 37 (2011), 601–29.

On Bretton Woods, see Benn Steil, *The Battle of Bretton Woods: John Maynard Keynes, Harry Dexter White, and the Making of a New World Order* (2013). For scholarship on the other wartime conferences, see Paul D. Mayle, *Eureka Summit: Agreement in Principle & the Big Three at Tehran, 1943* (1987); S. M. Plokhy, *Yalta: The Price of Peace* (2010); Fraser J. Harbutt, *Yalta 1945: Europe and America at the Crossroads* (2010); and Wilson D. Miscamble, *From Roosevelt to Truman: Potsdam, Hiroshima, and the Cold War* (2007).

There is a large literature on the International Military Tribunal (IMT) at Nuremberg. For the "legality" of the Nuremberg trials and international law, begin with Robert K. Woetzel, *The Nuremberg Trials in International Law* (1960); also George Ginsburgs and V. N. Kudriavtsev (eds.), *The Nuremberg Trial and International Law* (1990). For the less-well covered, but jurisprudentially important American-organized NMT, see Kim C. Priemel and Alexa Stiller (eds.), *Reassessing the Nuremberg Military Tribunals: Transitional Justice, Trial Narratives, and Historiography* (2012), and Kevin Jon Heller, *The Nuremberg Military Tribunals and the Origins of International Criminal Law* (2011). For the trials in Japan, see Yuma Totani, *The Tokyo War Crimes Trial: The Pursuit of Justice in the Wake of World War II* (2009).

CHAPTER 9
COLD WAR AND POST-COLD WAR

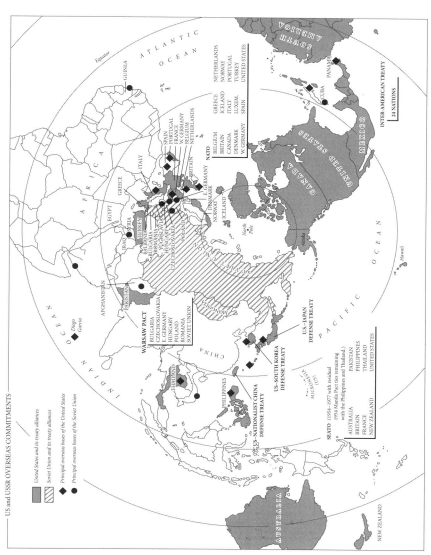

Figure 9.1 A bipolar world.

The *American* discipline of IR, reinvented, as it were, by Realists after the Second World War, can almost be said to be itself an artifact of the Cold War. It was handmaiden to the United States' sustained postwar global posture, and certainly experienced a serious crisis of identity—and perhaps risk of obsolescence—with the *fin de siècle* collapse of the Soviet Union. Moreover, to a very great degree other schools of IR thought evolved over this half century in critical dialogue with the tenets of Cold War Realism and Neorealism as expressed in the work of Hans Morgenthau or Kenneth Waltz. While it may be that the intellectual roots of American IR can be said to lie in the late nineteenth-century academy, as has been argued by Brian Schmidt, it has most flourished as a coherent discipline in the era when political scientists were much courted for what contribution they might make toward an understanding of Soviet decision-making and the formulation and rationalization of anti-Soviet policy. As a result, while the international history and world history/world systems fields take a longer and wider view, IR as practiced in the United States became to a great extent contemporary politics as viewed from Washington. The Cold War is important not only because it raised critical issues for the discipline—how a multipolar system became and operated as a bipolar one (Figure 9.1), what impact nuclear weapons had on decision-making, or how global superpower hegemons related to the rest of the world's states and peoples— but also because IR as a contemporary political discourse has been to a significant degree formed around the Cold War and these issues. It subsequently had to adjust quickly to the emergence of a *post*-Cold War paradigm in which the existential fears of hair-trigger nuclear holocaust ceased to haunt a world defined by dangerous confrontation, tense balance, and precarious détente.

Western representations of a defensive Cold War were certainly challenged in the 1970s by the revisionism of some radical scholars, though neoconservative post-revisionism in the decade that followed secured more influence in the halls of power. Since the end of the era, the partial opening of archives has led to further revisionism and debate by historians and political scientists—as has inevitably the widening distance (now more than a quarter-century) between ourselves and the discipline as it was practiced and understood in the midst of a phenomenon that to many scholars of that time seemed timeless (or at least likely long to endure). In the first place, one can question the very concept of *the* Cold War. The term itself apparently originated with George Orwell in 1945 and came into common usage by the early 1950s as a metaphor to describe superpower stalemate, best evidenced perhaps in Churchill's iron curtain speech, the continued division of Germany (and Berlin) in the absence of a peace treaty, the emergence of two opposed alliance systems (NATO and the Warsaw Pact), and a wary condition of constant, nuclear-armed vigilance between ideological foes. But was there a single half-century Cold War or many cold wars, depending on period and perspective (the common perspective of much IR scholarship is that of the Anglo-American West)? The general understanding of Cold War is as a military and political/diplomatic phenomenon, but there was also a cultural Cold War and an economic Cold War.

One might begin with questions of definition and perspective. Western Cold War scholarship—and this would include both historical narration and political analysis—has been accused of "myth-making," of viewing selected key events (like the Berlin airlift or the Cuban missile crisis) as "heroic history" confirming American leadership of the Free World. The narrative perspective—whether Soviet or Western—is that of the superpower. Its focus on global strategy, crisis management, and decision-making renders largely invisible, or so subaltern and postcolonial scholars argue, much of the world in which the Cold War was played out; or, at least relegates these peoples to the condition of objects of protection or pawns in a larger game rather than active subjects. Much recent scholarship, more "historiographically self-aware" than that generated during the era, has dwelt upon the *experience* of the Cold War within its various arenas, European, Asian, African, or Latin American—resulting in some splintering of *the* global Cold War of the superpowers and a contesting of rhetorical representations.

The Cold War, for instance, was cold from the standpoint of those powers that refrained from using their weapons of mass destruction on each other. It is altogether another matter from the perspective of the millions of non-Western peoples who died in the numerous very hot proxy wars and insurgencies of this half century—in Greece, Malaysia, Korea, Indochina, Africa, Latin America, and Afghanistan. One scholar skeptical of the dominant East-West framing of the Cold War has observed that both superpowers pursued an (informal) imperialism vis-à-vis the rest of the world, more suggestive perhaps of a continuity of Great Power *Weltpolitik* than a break with the pre-Cold War past. European imperialism established global networks; the Cold War superpowers and their threat of world-destructive nuclear warfare might be said to have furthered and perhaps completed this globalization.

The rhetoric of narration, then, is important not only in defining areas of research and analysis but in shaping the popular culture's understanding of these times. For instance, what we call the Cold *War* might equally be termed, as in the title of a study by one of the era's prominent scholars, the Long *Peace*. There has been no general conflict between or among Great Powers since the end of the Second World War, though regional conflicts, so-called "proxy wars," proliferated. If the era was one of peace, however, it was a strained and dangerous peace of armed tension. What gives the Cold War its special character is not merely the sustained tension between mutually suspicious powers but the admixture of ideology, global reach, and nuclear weapons—whose world-destroying power of course has established the special narrative character of this era. And yet, a historian might observe that ideological conflict and existential struggle can be found elsewhere in history. The eminent historian of international relations, Ernest May, started *his* survey course on the Cold War in 1789.

Much IR theory has viewed the Cold War era as essentially a matter of *state security*, through a lens that emphasizes the more or less rational interplay of powers within a bipolar system of balanced deterrence. But cultural and sociological analyses provide other lenses. Something might be gained by viewing the Cold War as a conflict between two contiguous ecumenes, like those of Byzantium and Islam. This would center issues of identity and identity construction as well as those of ideology and security. A "societal constructivist" scholar has recently argued that much might be gained by viewing the various stages of the Cold War as shifting discourses about difference. How, for instance, did the Soviet and American political elite understand the "other," and how do these understandings relate to the domestic self? A political-economic approach may also help reveal ways in which the *idea* of a threatening Cold War was generated and reinforced domestically by power elites (economic as well as bureaucratic and political). Following the lead of an earlier radical revisionism that centered American economic imperialism rather than "security"—as in William Appleman Williams' *The Tragedy of American Diplomacy* (revised and enlarged in 1972)—one recent provocative study by a scholar of the left shifts the representation of the early, foundational, Cold War period from the themes of *Communist* expansionism, military power, geopolitics, and national defense to that of the *United States*' "primary goal" of creating and preserving a self-serving liberal economic order—observing, for instance, that the dollars pumped into Europe by the Marshall Plan served to sustain the flood of American exports (Cardwell, 2011).

A cultural, social, and political-economic reading of the Cold War has been, however, more attractive to historians, Constructivists, and some IPE scholars than to political Realists. Much mainstream IR scholarship continues to emphasize bipolarity and nuclear deterrence, though decision-making analysis has also proliferated, drawing attention to assumptions about rational calculation. There was a real danger that Soviet or Western miscalculation might have led to the "mutually assured destruction" (MAD) by which the system purportedly stayed in balance—a balance of terror rather than a balance of power. Many, if not all, scholars would now accept that the scenario long advanced by Washington-oriented Realists of the need to counter, in the interests of global and national security, an aggressively expansionist Communist empire substantially misread the essentially defensive character of Stalin's regime and those that followed. Whether this was more the result of psychological misperception or willful misrepresentation may be debated.

More than metaphor, but what kind of reality?

In the last analysis, as one scholar has recently observed, the Cold War will probably continue to "defy any single master narrative" (Nehring, 2012, 949). Certainly the view from Belgrade or New Delhi, Prague, Warsaw or Budapest, or "frontline" Berlin, was different from that from Washington or Moscow, and different still from the perspective of London or Paris—one-time Great Powers reduced as it were to a sometime reluctant bandwagoning with the Americans. Not since the ancient empires of the Middle East and China had formal alliances, and the balancing that they may represent, meant so little in the actual expression of power. The dominant narrative of the Cold War by the early 1960s is that of the nuclear-armed superpowers and their "eyeball-to-eyeball" stand-off—though the perceived impossibility of actually *using* these arsenals at least left the door open to a much more conventional contest of arms.

The term "Super Power" was first used in 1944, and applied to the United States, the British Empire, and the Soviet Union—the "Big Three" of Tehran, Yalta, and Potsdam. Financial exhaustion, perhaps the domestic agenda of the socialist Labour Government, and the end of the Raj effectively removed even a nuclear-armed Britain from the superpower category. The apparent return of a *concert* of Great Powers in the creation of a UN Security Council made up of the United States, Russia, Britain, France, and China proved largely a mirage. This was not only due to the power inequalities among these states (though after 1949 the Soviet Union's development of nuclear capability ensured a perceived if not actual condition of bipolarity). The policing concert Roosevelt had envisioned, a concept suggesting that born out of the Congress of Vienna in 1815, was undermined by the apparent subordination of Britain, France, and [Nationalist] China to America's determination to use the institution to isolate and contain the Soviet Union, and, consequently, by the USSR's frequent recourse to its veto.

In spite of the formal worldwide extension of the system of diplomatic relations in the Vienna Convention of 1961—a consequence of the proliferation of independent states following decolonization—the realm of professional diplomacy can be said to have shrunk even further in the postwar world with (1) the disappearance of the more fluid balancing that had characterized a multipolar system, (2) the growing prominence of direct ministerial activity (the American Secretary of State from 1953 to 1959, John Foster Dulles, travelled some 56,000 miles and attended 50 conferences) and of summitry between superpower leaders (from Geneva in 1955 to Reykjavik in 1986), (3) reliance on the deterrent formula of MAD rather than on dialogue, and (4) the increased importance of intelligence services as quasi-autonomous players rather than adjuncts of foreign affairs and defense ministries. The well-funded Central Intelligence Agency (CIA) and its "covert operations" were a submerged part of a vast American "intelligence community" that included the National Security Agency, the Defense Intelligence Agency, and the State Department's Bureau of Intelligence and Research. Meanwhile, the Soviet diplomatic missions abroad were subordinated to the interests of the KGB (state security) and GRU (military intelligence), who constituted a high proportion of resident staff in any Soviet mission. Given also the way embassies and legations were increasingly expected to function as sites for "public relations" (i.e., propaganda) events—film series, music and art exhibitions, and guest speakers— one might legitimately wonder whether their chief purpose, East or West, was any longer "diplomacy" at all. As Zbigniew Brzezinski, later National Security Advisor in the Carter administration, said in 1970, if foreign ministries and embassies "did not already exist, they surely would not have to be invented" (quoted in Hamilton and Langhorn, 1995, 232).

Early Cold War

Historians tend to impose chronological breaks upon their data for purposes of analysis and narrative. Certainly there is considerable reason to consider the metaphoric Cold War not as a single confrontational, bipolar phenomenon of global international relations that endured from 1946 to the collapse of the Soviet Union in 1989–1991, but as a shifting phenomenon marked by important unifying themes like the omnipresent threat of nuclear war but also by distinct phases, characterized by the emergence of new players (the People's Republic of China or a rearmed West Germany), the cathartic shock of dangerous confrontation (the Cuban missile crisis), an altered subjective co-awareness (from "they are the Other" to "they are somewhat like us"), calculation-upsetting technologies (of, say, nuclear yield, delivery systems, and targeting), or sharply shifting domestic political and social contexts. In Chapter 2, we observed that important schools of post-Second World War IR may be historicized, that is, closely related to chronological changes in the character of the Cold War—from confrontation and containment to stasis and détente, confrontation redux, and finally "the triumph of the West." A reasonable schema of these overlapping periods would begin with an early, and dangerously unstable, confrontation marked by the rapid militarization of counterpoised geopolitical, ideological, and economic systems divided by an "iron curtain," shock (in the West) of discovering that the American nuclear monopoly could not be sustained and that thermonuclear devices were capable of destroying all life, and a series of crises that threatened to turn Cold War into a real war that would be a relatively brief but catastrophic, history-ending Armageddon.

The hopeful view that Stalin's Russia might be pursuing limited rather than expansionist security interests in eastern Europe (as a defensive zone) seemed to conflict with Stalin's speech of February 1946, affirming a belief in the impossibility of a peaceful accommodation with global capitalism, and the opportunistic pressure the Soviets appeared to be bringing to bear outside Europe. In this immediate postwar period of apprehension and some uncertainty at the State Department and in the Truman administration generally, what has come to be known as the "long telegram" played, it is often argued, a catalyzing role. This was an extended memorandum written, two weeks after Stalin's Bolshoi address, by George Kennan, then deputy chief of the US mission in Moscow. Kennan sought to locate Soviet interests in a historical as well as ideological and regime context, and wrote of the "neurotic insecurity" reflected in Russian temperament and national character. The Soviet regime, fearing capitalist encirclement, *was* expansionist, and expected conflicts within capitalism to provide opportunities, but was not likely to be recklessly adventuristic; they would, however, probe any "timely and promising" soft spot. Though the Soviet problem should be approached like "a major strategic problem in war," it could be solved without recourse to "any general military conflict." The next year, Kennan expanded on the consequences for American policy in an article in *Foreign Affairs*, which he published anonymously as "X": what was needed was a "long-term, patient but firm and vigilant containment of Russian expansive tendencies."

Kennan's message has often been represented as an influential *Realist* response to the USSR's emergence from the war as a rising challenger to the United States' global position, one which helped to shift the Roosevelt-era State Department's culture of alliance and accommodation to one of wariness and vigilance. In this sense, it may be compared with Morgenthau's *Politics Among Nations* (1948), which similarly stressed

Russia's historical "national character" in an attempt to counter the threat of America's relapse into isolationism. Kennan's emphasis on history, culture, and ideology, as well as the internal dynamics of the Soviet regime and his relatively moderate recommendation of a policy of patience and containment, locates him within Classical but not structural or Offensive Realism. At the end of the day, however, it may well be that political IR as well as historians of diplomacy and foreign policy have exaggerated Kennan's influence in an administration that, arguably, was already searching to rationalize, for domestic as well as international reasons, a foreign policy of confrontation. Truman and his Secretary of State, James Byrnes, took the continuing occupation of northern Iran by the Soviets to the UN early in 1946; the mid-term elections did not go well for the administration, and in March of 1947 Truman brought his own, less nuanced reading of Kennan's message of containment to Congress in what was called the "Truman Doctrine"—a successful attempt to get funding for Greece and Turkey. It can be argued that, in order to secure support from a Republican Congress that wanted to reduce expensive global commitments, the Truman government knowingly exaggerated the Soviet threat (Republican senator Vandenberg encouraged Truman "to scare the hell out of the American people" [quoted by LaFeber, 1996, 477]).

The years immediately following the Truman doctrine saw the rapid American construction (the foundations had been laid in the war) of what some scholars have called the "national security state." The National Security Act in 1947 aimed to coordinate intelligence operations (it established the CIA) with unified military planning through a National Security Council that, like the National Security Advisor (from 1953), effectively moved the coordination of defense policy into the president's executive office. In 1950, responding to both the Soviet Union's atomic bomb test (and anticipating that both the United States and the USSR would achieve a thermonuclear capability in the near future) and the Chinese communist conquest of the mainland, the council produced a secret policy paper (NSC-68) that recommended a "rapid build-up of political, economic, and military strength" to support a global, and more confrontational than Kenan had envisioned, policy of confrontation with the Soviet Union.

Though some IR scholars remain chiefly concerned with the ways in which such early Cold War developments in the United States simply express the system logic of a necessary power balancing, others, especially since the end of the Cold War, have been interested in how an obsession with national security itself transformed public culture, national identity, and the definition of national interests. One can speak of the emergence of a "new ideology of national security" that effectively altered the nature of the state itself not only by massively shifting resources to perpetual defense and enhancing the "imperial presidency" vis-à-vis the other branches of government, but by cultivating a powerful sense of mission and global responsibility.

The first phase, marked by a real danger that false perceptions of intentions and the psychological dynamics of escalation would lead to general nuclear war, is book-ended by the Czech coup and Berlin crisis of 1948, on the one hand, and the Berlin crisis of 1958–1963 and the Cuban missile crisis of 1962, on the other. It encompasses the nuclear arms race, a rhetoric of mutually incompatible values, and the creation of the enduring architecture of a bipolar Cold War international system—the division of Europe and, especially following the Korean War (1950–3), the creation of alliance systems in the Middle East and Asia. In Europe, the Marshall Plan, the US-dominated NATO (in 1949), and the inclusion of a rearmed West Germany in Western defense strategy was countered by the founding of a German Democratic Republic (East Germany) and, in 1955, the organization of Soviet satellite states into a parallel "mutual assistance" security organization, the Warsaw Pact.

The Soviet Union under Stalin had encouraged the North Korean regime to gamble on a war of unification, and after Stalin's death in 1953 continued to foment "national liberation" movements but also to court influence among newly independent and so-called "nonaligned" states. The United States moved to prop up the French in Indochina with financial assistance, and, in parts of the world where the British had some influence and historical presence, it looked, with rapidly diminishing expectations however, to their support in containing Communism—in Greece, the Middle East, and (more successfully) Malaya. Though there was British and Australian support (under an American commander) for the war in Korea, increasingly American administrations encouraged formal regional defense agreements like the 1954 South-East Asia Treaty Organization (SEATO) and the 1955 Baghdad Pact—later the Central Treaty Organization (CENTO)—which they expected to dominate directly or indirectly. America's status as superpower protector was confirmed in the 1950s by the deterrent thermonuclear "umbrella" it offered its allies. When Britain opted to pursue its own nuclear deterrent, the US Congress moved to prevent the sharing of American nuclear weapons technologies; the British decision to proceed without American help was, like France's later *force de frappe*, perhaps as much aimed at sending a message to Washington as countering the Soviet threat.

The nuclear Cold War

The perception of a balanced superpower nuclear capability may *ultimately* have made for a more stable system, but this outcome was by no means obvious in the 1950s and early 1960s. From the Western perspective, it was unclear (1) how rational an ideologically driven Soviet leadership might be (in the absence of meaningful diplomatic dialogue much was invested in the arcane business of Kremlinology); (2) how vulnerable the West might be to domestic communist parties, as in Italy or France; (3) how stable the nuclear stalemate might be in light of the rapid development of missile technologies in the Soviet Union; and (4) even if the nuclear standoff was effective, whether the presumed superiority of the conventional Soviet force in Europe could so easily be "balanced" by the threat of a nuclear response. On the one hand, the theater use of low yield nuclear weapons, which would compensate the West for its disadvantage on the ground, might lead to catastrophic escalation; on the other, the position that Washington would take (under Eisenhower) that the United States would retaliate against any assault with a full nuclear strike against the Soviet Union depended upon the believability that the West would in fact commit itself to thermonuclear annihilation of millions of people to, say, preserve the independence of West Berlin.

In IR terms, the early Cold War was a "conflict-laden" type of international system, even though bipolar. The Soviet Union seemed, as a "rising" challenger to American hegemony, to continue after the death of Stalin to exert opportunistic pressure, in Berlin especially, while courting third world leaders with military and economic aid ("rouble diplomacy") and, as in East Germany in 1953 or in Hungary in 1956, maintaining robust domination of its satellite states. It clearly made significant technological and economic progress in the two decades from the end of the Second World War, while Americans—in the era of late 1950s recession, Sputnik, and the "missile gap"—seemed fixated with the threat of their relative decline, concerns that of course were belied by the reality of American global military and economic supremacy but heightened the psychological tensions that might have led to war. Though the missile gap panic engineered by Kennedy in 1960 was electioneering fiction, and by 1962 the United States had intermediate-range nuclear missiles operational in Britain, Italy, and Turkey, the American nuclear *advantage* was in fact rapidly diminishing.

The era of dangerous confrontation was characterized by the continuing tension over the divided city of Berlin. The extended Berlin crisis of 1958–63, according to one scholar "the central episode of the Cold War" (Trachtenberg, 2001, 13), was arguably provoked not by Soviet expansionist ideology but by defensive fears that the Federal Republic would be allowed by the United States to develop a nuclear capacity of its own, as well as by its need to stabilize the East German regime. Khrushchev, however, did not respond favorably to Kennedy's status quo overtures at the Vienna summit meeting in 1961—a meeting held only weeks after the failure of a US-supported invasion of Cuba to dislodge its Marxist regime and followed within less than a year by the secret Soviet deployment of medium-range nuclear missiles on the island. The era came to an end, as it were, with the cathartic trauma of the Cuban missile crisis.

The Cuban Missile Crisis and IR

The Cuban crisis of 1962, the "thirteen days in October," has achieved a kind of popular cultural status as the representative event in a dangerous, pre-détente Cold War, where nuclear confrontation was closest to a trigger point. It was high-stakes, televised drama (from discovery of the missiles, the US quarantine, and the Soviet withdrawal), the "most dangerous moment in human history," and has been the object of much scrutiny by historians and political scientists in the half-century since, including a flurry of scholarship following the post-Cold War release of Soviet and American documents, memoirs, and interviews. The fiftieth anniversary was marked by the declassification of documents and a series of events, discussions, and scholarly papers organized by the Wilson Center's Cold War International History Project and another "retrospective" by the John F. Kennedy Presidential Library, while an oral history project (1989–92) aimed to develop Cuban perspectives often submerged in the drama of US-Soviet confrontation.

In IR, most Realists have tended to view the crisis as confirming the primacy of geopolitics and state security over ideology, the importance of rational calculation, and—though the crisis threatened nuclear catastrophe—the operation of bipolar nuclear deterrence and the quid-pro-quo balancing, secretly negotiated, of Soviet withdrawal from Cuba in exchange for American withdrawal of medium-range nuclear missiles from Turkey. The crisis also generated interest in the issue of perception and misperception (a team of scholars at Stanford looked back to Europe in 1914 for a comparative perspective on the dangers of unintended escalation), the use of cognitive psychology to anticipate crises and defuse them, the application of game theory in modeling high-risk decision-making, and how the crisis might serve to test "expected-utility" and "prospect" theories borrowed from behavioral economics. The most influential work of IR scholarship derived from the crisis, however, is that of the political scientist Graham Allison in his important study of the domestic, bureaucratic context, *Essence of Decision: Explaining the Cuban Missile Crisis* (1971).

Allison argued that *organizational cultures* have a significant impact when decisions have to be made quickly with less than full information. Of the three models he explores, the first, that of the rational actor, central to Realism, was the least adequate. The other two, those of organizational process (standard operating procedures) and bureaucratic politics (how organizations defend their own role and perspective), suggest, especially in time of crisis, the limits of rational choice decision-making. Alison's work inspired substantial discussion in the 1970s and 1980s, though it had perhaps more attraction for political and social scientists than for historians, many of whom find a deep knowledge of the key decision-makers more useful than an understanding of the organizational culture of bureaucrats whose advice is often ignored.

Finally, there has been concern among some historians about the way the dominant crisis narrative has both stressed the American or Western perspective and contains the event in a Cold War rather than wider historical frame. While the partial opening of Soviet archives after 1991 and the publication of Soviet memoirs have made available a Soviet reading of the October crisis (and of the Cold War generally), the addition of a Russian perspective has for the most part entrenched an understanding of the crisis as a matter of superpower confrontation and the bipolar Cold War. As Fidel Castro complained when he viewed the film *Thirteen Days*, "where are the Cubans?"

An oral history project organized from 1989 to 1992 encouraged a reconsideration of the dominant narrative of the crisis that had sidelined the Cubans as having "vacated their sovereignty." How in fact might the inclusion of a (subaltern) Cuban perspective add something important in the analysis of IR? In the first place, it restores a voice that opens the crisis discourse to more than psychological and process-focused issues of decision-making and management in Washington and Moscow. It locates events, not only in the special superpower dynamics of the Cold War, but in a much deeper continuity of the pursuit, say, of American interests in Latin America. The *Cuban* concern to preserve its fragile revolutionary regime from the threat of US intervention was a product not only of the Bay of Pigs invasion but of a history running back to the late nineteenth century. From this perspective, the Cold War narrative actually serves to obscure deeper causal factors like the historic, long-sustained defense of American capitalism, that is, Yankee imperialism, in Latin America and beyond.

Within the Cold War narrative, the Cuban missile crisis is important not only in the business of policy and decision-making analysis and IR theory-testing, but also in the way it can be seen to have led to a transition out of an era of acute and dangerous confrontation to a search for a more stable system. Within nine months, the first limited test ban treaty was signed, and in the next few years at least some in the US foreign policy establishment began to view Soviets less as a utopian/ideological (i.e., nonrational) enemy, and more as an increasingly conservative adversary looking for security and global stability.

There is another narrative, not often addressed in IR scholarship but which some Constructivists and historians might argue has importance for transnational relations: that of the "idealist" voice represented by the antinuclear movements that had been galvanized by the threat of thermonuclear weapons in the late 1950s. This antinuclear/antiwar discourse (and the "horror and antipathy" with which public opinion came to regard the radioactive consequences of nuclear war graphically revealed and memorialized in Japan) contributed to what has been called the *nuclear taboo*—a deep, visceral repugnance at the possibility of actually using nuclear weapons that can be said to have become part of the normative morality of many in both East and West. A Constructivist might argue that this sense lends support to the argument that there was more behind the long, balanced peace of the Cold War than simple deterrence.

The nuclear factor came to play differently within the different schools of IR and historical thought. That grounded in moral idealism argues that the appalling prospect of any nuclear use (not a careful balance of nuclear threat) served to prevent war between superpowers simply because it was too horrible to contemplate. A psychological break with the past over the unacceptable consequences of the use of force had occurred. Early in the nuclear Cold War, Classical Realists assumed that prudent self-interest would restrain nuclear powers from actually using their arsenals. Subsequently, however, the enhanced destructiveness of *thermo*nuclear weapons, their rapid proliferation, and the swiftness of their missile-born delivery suggested that the dangerous system of antagonistic balance required skilled, careful diplomacy and an expanded role for international regulation. It has been argued that the threat of a thermonuclear "omnicide" led early founders of Realist thought like Morgenthau, Niebuhr, and Kennan, to "revisit" their understanding of deterrence in an anarchical system and "correspondingly, to let go their earlier belief that a world state was neither desirable nor possible" (Campbell Craig, 2003, xvii).

Neorealists, however, viewed the bipolar system as inherently stable; there was no need to refer either to morality or clever diplomacy since the system operated automatically given the rational choice of the major actors in an environment of MAD—so long as one side did not have a significant survivability advantage.

There is a consistency in Waltz's controversial insistence that the proliferation of nuclear weapons among lesser states might bring with it greater rather than less stability. Of course, the calculus of MAD on which the Neorealists built their vision of system stability only operates effectively if nuclear powers are determined to conserve their positions. One might wonder whether Hitler would have regarded nuclear weapons as a means to preserve system balance and to enhance security. In its last stages the Third Reich embraced the self-immolation of the German Volk, and today might there be those who could perceive the state itself as suicide bomber?

Mid and late Cold War

The end of the dangerous early Cold War was marked by the resolution of the Cuban crisis and the sobering awareness of a nuclear catastrophe averted, the dampening down or defusing of the threat of war in Europe that divided Berlin had posed, and the high symbolism of the "hotline" link between Washington and Moscow that was established in 1963. Though the 1960s and early 1970s saw the superpowers' determination to keep allies on side—in Vietnam, Czechoslovakia, or Chile—the era also saw the reestablishment of diplomacy. The test ban treaty of 1963 was followed in 1968 by a nuclear nonproliferation treaty and, in 1972, a strategic arms limitation agreement and an antiballistic missile treaty between the United Sates and the Soviet Union—the first fruits of the coming era of détente— while "cultural exchange" programs suggested a certain gesture toward the goal of mutual understanding.

The Cold War is generally treated as, in its essence, a superpower confrontation. The IR structural concept of bipolarity is grounded in this perspective. But, as suggested above, a different Cold War might be viewed from a different, broader perspective. This involves more than acknowledging the tendency of the two hegemons to globalize their security concerns and draw into their orbits lesser states—or the tendency of lesser states to bandwagon with them, concepts that are familiar to mainstream IR. Rather, one might observe that as the era developed, each power found it increasingly difficult to *manage* lesser allies beyond (and sometimes including) those within their expected spheres of influence in Eastern Europe, Latin America, and Asia. This may be expected as a decolonized "third world" sensed that their attractiveness as allies or neutrals gave them some leverage—Tito, Nasser, and Nehru explored the possibilities. Mao quickly sought to become more than a Marxist protégé of Stalin, and both Adenauer and Ulbricht proved awkward and demanding for their respective patrons. As Gaddis (2005, 128–9) has put it, "Tails were beginning to wag dogs … 'dominos' found it useful, from time to time, to *advertise* a propensity to topple."

It can also be argued, in opposition to a crude version of structural Realism, that there was an element of "learning" over time involved in the working of an international system of bipolar confrontation. As the Cold War continued, a mutual fear of escalation to thermonuclear war encouraged "rules of prudence" in the management of rivalry. Moreover, the fact that nuclear weapons had not been used in the early Cold War—in a preventive strike by America on the Soviet Union or in Korea—and that Eisenhower had appeared to rule out limited nuclear conflict, encouraged a cumulative and habitual reluctance to contemplate the use or threat of use of such weapons, a taboo which became deeply entrenched, however much subsequent US administrations and military planners might have flirted with (and developed contingency plans for) the "flexible use" of theater-deployed nuclear weaponry. The flip side of this phenomenon, as one Constructivist scholar has observed, is however that the sense of the impossibility of actually using nuclear weapons may carry with it an unintended "permissive effect" of shielding a non-nuclear resort to violence from "normative opprobrium" (Tannenwald, 2007, 46–7). In other words, the self-denial of a nuclear option in some sense made more acceptable the Cold War and post-Cold War resort to conventional violence in pursuit of national goals.

Vietnam and American IR

Like the Korean war, that in Vietnam remained non-nuclear, though as a conventionally fought conflict it cost the United States over 58,000 dead and 150,000 wounded, and of course many times this in Vietnamese civilian and military casualties. To the extent that it is considered primarily a Cold War "containment" conflict, from the perspective of an American foreign policy establishment, rather than, from the perspective of the Viet Cong, as a colonial insurgency and postcolonial war of national liberation, it carries a number of meanings and issues for IR schools of thought as the decade-long central global event of the middle Cold War period between the Cuban missile crisis and 1970s détente. The American IR community was fractured by the conflict, but not altogether along the lines of a pro-containment Realism versus an antiwar Idealism. Some among the older generation of American Realists like, most notably, Hans Morgenthau but also Reinhold Niebuhr and George Kennan, were opposed on both ethical and practical grounds, while many "Cold War Liberals" were ready to embrace war in Indochina as a battle against communist totalitarianism and endorse the export by force of arms of American democratic values and institutions.

Among the post-Morgenthau generation of "security studies" Realists who remained committed to a policy of global containment, the debated issues were how to carry on the war, whether through continued self-imposed limits (on the bombing of the north, the interdiction of its shipping, etc.) or through a more robust offensive that risked regional expansion. Latterly, the central issue became whether and how negotiations might be begun, with whom, and with what agenda. As the struggle persisted without a clear resolution, however, a further discourse emerged about the probable impact of a perceived loss in southeast Asia on American public opinion and the constraints that might impose on future American foreign policy. A feared loss of American reputation became a factor in continuing a war, whether wisely or otherwise begun, to a face-saving conclusion. The issue of prestige, and the rhetorical use of this intangible by political leaders then and since, has provided some ground for those scholars who have sought to emphasize the social and discursive construction of "interests."

During the early Cold War of confrontation, most Realists had assumed that security interests were relatively clear-cut, as were the strategic costs and benefits of containment. These calculations, strained in Korea, became more tenuous still as the Vietnam morass consumed men and resources for little appreciable gain against a foe that was difficult to characterize as simply a manifestation of global communist expansionism. The Vietnam experience, then, brought into question the definition and calculation of security interests. It also brought into focus intimate connections between the domestic and the international. Historians of the Vietnam era quickly came to center their narratives on the critical problem posed by the dramatic loss of public support for the United States' commitment to containment in southeast Asia. The foreign policy establishment, however, had been slow to appreciate the importance of the ways in which a domestic consensus was necessary in enabling foreign policy. The democratic public was, ordinarily, assumed tacitly to legitimize the actions of its representatives. Vietnam became a vivid illustration of the consequences if such an assumed consensus disintegrates. Woodrow Wilson's failure to sell the League at home or George W. Bush's to sustain support for his war in Iraq may be others.

Though the discipline of IR, much concerned with the theory and practice of bipolarity and the Cold War search for security, has not devoted much of its literature to the Vietnam imbroglio, the long war in fact encouraged alternatives to the mainstream Realism that had dominated the American field since the beginnings of the Cold War. Scholars from the left, where anticolonialist and Marxist theory provides an integrative approach, early on offered a critique, though this tradition remains marginal to the main thrust of IR as it is taught in the Anglo-American world. But many Realists themselves were forced to engage the difficulty of calculating security interests and the complex problem of how power is defined, how the ability to project state power may be limited by a state's domestic condition, and the inappropriateness of much Cold War scholarship on deterrence and nuclear capabilities in understanding a war of counterinsurgency. At the same time the deeply divisive debate over the morality of the war encouraged a return in some quarters of IR scholarship to issues of a just war, the limits of the use of force, normative values, and human rights—topics that had been more or less shelved during the early Cold War. By the early and mid-1970s, the "defeat" of American intervention in Vietnam, the abandonment of the Breton Woods system, and a global recession challenged the idea of, especially American, superpower autonomy, emphasized the limits of power, and encouraged, as in the work of Keohane and Nye, a turn to the transnational and ideas of (Neo)Liberal Internationalism and Institutionalism. On the other hand, some like Waltz were encouraged to leave this tangled melange of issues for the refuge provided by a more austere form of systemic analysis in structural Neorealism.

Détente

The lesson of Vietnam for many in the IR community was that of *limits* on the exercise of power, in parts of the world where the ability of the United States to use force was little enhanced by its nuclear throw-weight and in situations where there was little of the domestic cohesion needed to pursue a sustained and costly policy that involved significant casualties. Another lesson seemed to be that even a superpower had need of traditional diplomacy in a world that threatened the erosion of its power and influence. The United States came to see itself as a declining, or at least overextended, power. It committed reluctantly to negotiation with the North Vietnamese by the late 1960s, something the "world community" applauded but that did not lead to a lasting or face-saving resolution. On the other hand, the Johnson administration's move to open negotiations with the Soviet Union on nuclear reductions, tabled in response to the Soviet suppression of the Czechs in 1968, anticipates the Nixon administration's active pursuit of détente in the 1970s.

The pursuit of direct diplomacy (not encouraged by Dulles's state department in the 1950s) had much to do with the emergence of China, as the domestic chaos of the Cultural Revolution subsided, as a rising—and from 1967 thermonuclear—power. The widening split within what had been perceived as a global communist bloc (there were Sino-Soviet border clashes in 1969) presented the United States, and its National Security Advisor schooled in the history of Realpolitik, Henry Kissinger, with an opportunity of effectively pursuing traditional diplomacy. As he told President Nixon, "We have to play the balance of power game totally unemotionally … we need the Chinese to correct the Russians" (quoted in Black, 2012, 115).

Kissinger, who relegated the UN to the background in the administration's search for an end to the Vietnam War, also opened direct bilateral talks with the Soviets on strategic arms limitation 1969–70. In 1971, however, the National Security Advisor himself made a secret trip to Beijing, followed by Nixon's historic visit and American recognition of the communist regime—a foreign policy coup that was intended to bring pressure to bear on the Soviet Union to negotiate on a variety of issues including Vietnam. A few months later, the Nixon–Brezhnev Moscow summit saw the signing of both the SALT-I treaty and an antiballistic missile treaty, as well as largely symbolic agreements on cooperation in environmental protection and space exploration— to be followed the next year by Brezhnev's visit to the United States and in 1975 by the nonbinding Helsinki Accords (which endorsed existing borders; renunciation of violence; nonintervention in the internal affairs of states; human rights; and cooperation in a range of cultural, educational, economic, scientific, and humanitarian areas), events that signaled at least some investment in the stabilization of Cold War relations.

Though Kissinger's position as White House advisor further subordinated the state department professionals and Nixon's own secretary of state, his playing the China card in his negotiations with the Soviet regime, like his "shuttle diplomacy" in search for a Middle East settlement, signaled a return to a tradition of Great Power negotiation. The Achilles' heel of détente proved, however, to be the problem inherent in selling a foreign policy of compromise to the public and Congress after a quarter century in which successive administrations had assiduously cultivated the rhetoric of Cold War animosity and confrontation. The pursuit of détente in fact was itself often submerged in a sea of Wilsonian rhetoric to avoid, presumably, the charge that it was merely appeasement disguised. Nevertheless, Kissinger's policy, however much it was intended to exploit Soviet weaknesses and was accompanied by a sustained anticommunist presentation, faced serious criticism and congressional obstruction at home—often in the name of the human rights not only of the suppressed "satellite" nations of Eastern Europe but of (especially Jewish) Soviet citizens. Efforts to defuse the arms race through international agreements and constructive dialogue meant legitimizing the Soviet state—or at least accepting its position as a co-equal Great Power—and the division of Europe.

Détente was not only driven forward by America's defeat in Vietnam, the opportunities opened up by the Sino-Soviet split, or the fact that West Germany itself was moving toward its own accommodation with communist East Germany and the Soviet Union. At its heart it was grounded in (mutual) assumptions that the postwar system of European and global division had stabilized and would remain so for the foreseeable future. Such a view of an enduring status quo world was shared by most IR Realists, and many Liberal Internationalists hoped that such system stability would serve to defuse apprehensive concerns about security and encourage an *evolution* toward a more peaceful, interdependent world. Neither adequately anticipated the possibility that significant technological advance in weapons systems—multiple nuclear warheads, more accurate targeting, or more sophisticated antiballistic systems of defense—would threaten the assumptions of continued security balance or that domestic factors in each superpower could quickly undermine the progress (perhaps in any event less real than it appeared) toward a sustained modus vivendi.

Behind détente was the assumption that the major players constituted relatively stable, predictable societies—the Soviet government under Brezhnev seemed an essentially conservative regime. History however teaches that in the long run change happens: Carter's SALT-II negotiations failed to get congressional approval in the face of the Soviet invasion of Afghanistan; the development of the cruise missile, the (threatened) development and deployment of the neutron bomb, and Reagan's star-wars initiative served to upset the stability which détente required. Moreover, the last years of the Soviet Union would suggest that the whole edifice of state stability upon which much IR theory is predicated can erode from within largely unseen, producing a crisis not of the military and economic apparatus of power, but of will and legitimacy.

The end of the Cold War

The growing difficulty of selling détente to the American Congress, destabilizing advances in weapons technology, the Soviet intervention in Afghanistan, and the election of the conservative Republican Ronald Reagan to the US presidency in 1980 heralded a drift back into a Cold War of heightened rhetoric and a (defensive and offensive) arms race. Though the 1970s had seen significant recession in the West, the Soviets experienced a relatively much worse and apparently intractable economic stagnation that undermined the ability of their geriatric leadership to respond to the security challenges posed by an American administration that seemed to embrace, not the idea of coexistence, but that of a winnable Cold War.

The rapid pace of the computer and information revolution in the West enabled and encouraged a more aggressive American pursuit of military superiority—leading some to call for rejection of the carefully negotiated limitations (a key element of détente) on the development of effective antiballistic missile defenses. From the perspective of Moscow, an impenetrable American defensive shield (via Reagan's futuristic Strategic Defense Initiative) had more to do with offense than defense, enabling as it would a winnable nuclear war. It would render ineffectual the ruling Cold War balancing concept of MAD, and some Soviet military planners contemplated the, admittedly desperate, argument for a preemptive strike.

The dangers inherent in a heated-up Cold War driven by new technologies the USSR could hardly match, the heavy burden of defense spending in an economy that was in decline, and the belated passing of a generation of leaders who lacked the interest or ability creatively to rethink Soviet foreign and domestic policies led to a surprising change in the character of the Soviet state in the mid-1980s under the direction of a new, younger General Secretary, Mikhail Gorbachev, and his reformist "new thinking" about restructuring and openness (*perestroika* and *glasnost*). In foreign policy, this meant arms control accommodation rather than confrontation, culminating in the Reykjavik summit in 1986, the beginning of an exit strategy in Afghanistan (1987–9), and portentously a tacit rejection of the Brezhnev doctrine whereby the USSR was committed to the use of force to preserve Soviet-style socialism in the Warsaw Pact countries.

Though the objective of the new thinking may have been the preservation of the (reformed) communist system, the process spun out of control and the ability of the Soviet state to hold its regime together dramatically eroded due to the rapid destabilizing of the satellite regimes, the accelerating economic difficulties surrounding the attempt to shift from a less militarized budget to one that advanced the production of consumer goods, and, perhaps most importantly, the uncontrollable dynamic of an accelerating domestic loss of faith in the governing system and its apparatus. Unprecedentedly in the history of Great Powers, the USSR simply collapsed, in peacetime, like a house of cards.

Gorbachev's optimism that top-down new thinking would shore up the USSR internally, that Moscow-supported social democratic leaders in the Warsaw Pact would encourage those peoples to stay within the Soviet sphere without crude coercion, and, failing this, that closed borders and satellite buffer states were no longer necessary for the defense of the Soviet state and its socialist system, proved inaccurate or insufficient. The argument of the American political right that the collapse of the Soviet Union was the result of the United States ratcheting up the costs of defense to the point of unsustainability in the Soviet Union has some traction, but is overly simplistic in its understanding of the relations between domestic and external factors.

The sudden end to the Cold War through, not evolutionary processes of accommodation and diplomatic détente, but the inability of one of the powers to sustain its role, was unanticipated by any school of thought within the discipline of IR. It was most damaging, however, to the theories of then-dominant (at least in America) structural Neorealism, which had been deeply invested in assumptions about the inherent stability of a bipolar system. It begged the question of Realism's centering of military power in its analysis of state security as the primary factor in "politics among nations." Significantly, as Gaddis has observed, "the Soviet Union collapsed, after all, with all its military forces, even its nuclear capabilities, fully intact" (Gaddis, 2005, 263). Another scholar has called the embarrassment among Security Studies academics like "the effects the sinking of the *Titanic* had on the profession of naval engineers" (Katzenstein, 1996b, xi). How, in the following decade or so did the discipline attempt to come to grips with a sea-change it had failed to anticipate?

Cold War history and IR scholarship

A big question for the discipline of IR—one which brings in its train many collateral issues—is, broadly put, to what extent can (or should) the course of the Cold War be ascribed to ideology, that is, to ideas and values, to what extent to the systemic dynamics of Great Power politics? And ought IR, as a science of politics, to privilege the latter over the former?

The confrontation has commonly been represented as that between two opposed systems of economic order and governance, that of a capitalist West based on the concept of private property, individual rights, and a more or less "free" economy and that of a Marxist socialist and totalitarian regime based on collectivist values, public ownership, and the ideal at least of social equality. In addition, the role of religion has been prominent in narratives of the Cold War from the beginning: many Christians (especially American Protestants) viewed the struggle as one against godless communism, while at the same time it was common for Western analysts to portray Soviet communism as itself a kind of ersatz religion. The role of ideas is also central to the *end* of the Cold War. The "new thinking" of perestroika and glasnost was not simply a response to external security and economic pressures, but also addressed a crisis within Marxist ideology. Finally, as we have seen, post-Cold War Constructivism has sought to examine the long conflict less in terms of political power and strategic maneuvering, choosing to explore the subjective side of the creation of opposed identities and values and how these may be mutually constructed and reproduced during the long evolution of the Cold War era.

Alternatively, on the other side of this interpretive divide some are prone to ask whether the Cold War and its end might be better or more scientifically understood as the play of factors familiar to IR Realism: the rise and fall of challengers and hegemons, the pursuit of security, the balance of power, and the constraints of an anarchic system. Those, both international historians and political scientists, who see the Cold War principally in terms of Great Power politics would probably agree with the historian (and moderate Realist) Marc Trachtenberg who has argued, "instead of a great rupture separating us from the past, there is a deep continuity" and, consequently, a need to "historicize, to normalize, the Cold War." While such a perspective may bring into doubt a structural emphasis on the uniqueness of mid- and late twentieth-century bipolarity, it would at the same time resist overstating the role of ideology and values: the Cold War should be seen essentially "as a political process, with its own dynamic, unfolding over time, and about which moral judgments are often quite problematic" (Trachtenberg, 2001, 10, 16). Others have observed that the issue is not whether the Cold War can better be explained by ideas or by the exercise of power, but how exactly power and ideas relate to one another.

Postmortem analysis of the Cold War was energized by the suddenness of its unanticipated demise. The 1990s saw a general assault on the theories of Realism and Neorealism that had failed to predict its end, or, more exactly, the *nonviolent* nature of its end. IR scholars like Waltz, Stephen Rock, and other Realists argued as late as 1988 and 1989 that there was no prospect in sight of an end to bipolarity and an armed balance, and moreover that there was little evidence in history of declining powers peacefully yielding up their hegemony. Much of the post-1989 critique was directed by historians and historically informed moderate (Classical) Realists against the rigidities of structuralist Neorealism in particular and more generally against scientific attempts to predict how systems operate. A number of IR scholars, and not only Constructivists like Friedrich Kratochwil but prominent mainstream practitioners like John Gaddis and Richard Ned Lebow, were quick to draw attention to the failure of forecasting, the inadequacy of so-called "power transition" theories (which failed to anticipate peaceful change), and the insufficiency of bipolarity as either a descriptive concept or an overriding determining factor. "The Soviet response to decline," Lebow baldly stated, "is not one captured by any realist theory" (Lebow, 1994, 263), while a prominent historian of the Soviet Union, Robert Conquest, simply and provocatively advised: "If you are a student, switch from political science to history."

Though initially some scientific Realists were caught off guard and driven to argue unpersuasively that the demise of the Soviet Union was too singular an event ("one data point") upon which to challenge scientific political theory, a more vigorous debate developed through the decade that followed. It was argued, for instance, that power transition theory had been concerned with the probable war-like responses of hegemons defending themselves from rising powers, not with what might happen when a rising challenger like the Soviet Union fell into decline without ever effectively achieving parity with the only really global superpower, America. A political scientist at Princeton, William C. Wohlforth, offered perhaps the most articulate defense of a moderate (i.e., what would come to be called Neoclassical) Realism, admitting that scientific theory was "weak" though useful, that structuralism had difficulty explaining change, and that the apparent stability of the long Cold War had less to do with bipolarity than with the ideological belief by both powers in their ultimate victory. When this persistent belief was finally undermined in the Soviet Union by the increasing difficulty of providing both security and a domestic standard of living comparable to that of the West, the response, like that of declining challengers generally, was to attempt reform rather than war (Wohlforth, 1994/1995).

Central to the Neoclassical Realist response was a willingness to incorporate domestic, especially economic, factors in explaining the sudden end of the Cold War. An emphasis on comparable economic capabilities had of course long been a part of the West's attempt to predict the course of the Cold War. From the 1940s and 1950s, the American intelligence community employed macroeconomic methods for calculating the gross national product (GNP) of the Soviet Union and its ability to meet rising costs of defense or offense, though gauging the performance of a nonmarket economy proved a difficult business. By the 1970s changes in economic modeling led the CIA to recalculate significantly upward its estimates of actual military spending by the Soviet Union. This helped undermine détente and drive forward the more aggressive arms race of the late Carter and Reagan era.

Though moderate Realism acknowledged the importance of ideas (new thinking), it tended to see these largely as expressions of a domestic crisis (the crumbling of the Soviet ability to satisfy the consumer demands of its citizenry) that had been fatally exacerbated by competitive security demands. This analysis was a close fit with both the journalistic reading of the sudden Soviet collapse and the self-justificatory boasting of the American neoconservative right. A substantially different view was endorsed by a Neoliberal reading of the events of the late 1980s, not just in the Soviet Union, but in the satellite states of Eastern Europe. This likewise drew attention to the failure of structural Neorealism to anticipate the end of the Cold War, but broadly attacked the "myths" of Realpolitik generally for underplaying the role of ideas and values in explaining system change. One prominent critic, in his 1993 presidential address to the International Studies Association, went so far as to speak of the confirmation of "Wilson's vision" and the rediscovery that "the motives that animate the goals of states are not immutable" and called for "a principled realism emphasizing liberal ideals" (Kegley, 1993, 135–43). Other critics argued that the entire Cold War could best be seen, not as a bipolar version of the traditional state system and its balancing dynamic, but as evidence of a radical reconceptualization of international relations by two powers both of whom had universalized their global vision in ways that challenged traditional notions of sovereign equality and thus "changed the rules of the game."

For the Soviet Union, the end of the Cold War can be seen as a Communist Party "legitimation crisis," a crisis that cannot simply be represented as an economic crisis. That is, crude economic determinism—the argument that the West had simply pushed the Soviet empire beyond its ability to adapt—is inadequate to explain a much deeper, domestic, and essentially intellectual crisis within both the party elite and a growing civil society. The critical conundrum—why the Soviet leadership withheld the use of military force to preserve the party, the state, and the Warsaw Pact bloc—cannot be answered by Realist assumptions of rational calculation alone, without also appreciating that decision-makers were presented with "a fundamental option of an ideological character" (Lévesque, 1997, 20). For their part, historians have tended to see in the end of the Cold War and the ensuing crisis of structuralist

IR some confirmation of their suspicion of "the quest for grand patterns" and the complicated business of reading an era and its events through theory rather than on their own, perhaps unique, terms. Musing on the need to rewrite the history of the Cold War era now that we are outside it, the historian John Gaddis wrote a defense of "particular generalization" in place of the social scientist's "general particularization," of a reality of complexity and contingency, and of the historical search for the way processes and structures change over time: "Historians know that every concept is buried in a context, and the only permanent thing about contexts is that they shift" (Gaddis, 2001, 321).

Post-Cold War

The quarter century since the end of the Cold War has been one of ferment for the discipline of IR. There was, first, a period of reassessment driven by the apparent replacement of a system of balance for one dominated by hegemonic America—symbolized by the successful coalition the United States assembled to defeat Iraq in the Gulf War of 1990–1991. How stable such a "unipolar" system might be sparked a flurry of speculation and prediction across the IR spectrum. Second, the early and mid-1990s saw an optimistic revival of Liberal Internationalism, Liberal Institutionalism, and democratic peace theory—abetted by positive readings of the expanding European Union project and of "globalization." A seminal, much-debated text of this era was Francis Fukuyama's "The End of History" (1989 and 1993). For some IR scholars, the "new world order" that was emerging from Cold War stasis indicated the need for an "historical turn" in IR theory to understand such dramatic changes—the end not just of the Cold War but perhaps of the 350-year-old Westphalian era. Some, especially those committed to critical theory, "discourse ethics," and the concept of "cosmopolitan democracy," wrote of the dawning of a "post-Westphalian state" in which absolute sovereignty, already challenged by international capital markets and production and mass migration, was being transformed by a new normative vision of the state and of citizenship, one that would be more inclusive of multicultural subnational and transnational identities and loyalties.

By the end of the decade, however, the prospect of maintaining a liberal world order seemed much less sure in light of the violent conflict in the Balkans (a *continuation* of history, many observed), the prospect of the resurgence of right-wing chauvinism in both a reunited Germany—somewhat exaggerated as it turned out— and a much-reduced Russia, and the difficulties the United States and the UN encountered in furthering a global human rights regime (in the Balkans, Somalia, or Rwanda). IR Realism, chastened and fragmented by the unexpected end of the Cold War and the difficulty of forecasting the course of interstate relations or the nature of the unfolding new state system, and challenged by the rise of varieties of Constructivism, revived in the troubled late 1990s.

Nevertheless, whatever the difficulties of policing the new order, the prospect of a state system that was not in immediate danger of nuclear war—or indeed of conventional war among the powers—left the discipline without one of its founding concepts, that security, security threat, security dilemma, the politics of war, and the politics of the prevention of war, lay at the heart of IR as a scholarly field. Overall, Realism was for a while on the defensive and there was a precipitous decline in national security studies in the 1990s. At the same time, there was some pressure, especially from the left of the discipline, to expand the definitions of state security so important in IR theory to embrace ecologism, the concept of "environmental security," as well as to include standard-of-living issues (food and famine) as security factors, leading as they might to the instability or "failure" of a state. This required the redefining of state interests in ways that centered a growing need for interstate cooperation and international institutions rather than the inevitability of geopolitical conflict.

There was a surge of interest in the discipline in IPE as the former Soviet states rushed to adopt the institutions and practices of the liberal, capitalist world order, while corporate and financial globalization continued apace, and in the coming of a single globalized *civil society*, a community of communities, in which, it seemed, states themselves would become less important and local authority more constrained by a regime of universal norms. One scholar wrote of the cumulative force of "the internationalization of human rights norms" since the 1960s and 1970s (Donnelly, 1999, 75). In this post-Cold War, interdependent world, Liberal Institutionalists reaffirmed a commitment to international law and institutions—that is, like their opponents the Neorealists, to *rational choice* in the pursuit of interests rather than how those interests and norms may themselves evolve. The chief issue was how to achieve security (often defined more broadly than in terms of power) that involved constructing, through multinational institutions, a positive rather than negative identification of state interests—of seeing the international system not as anarchy but as a cooperative society.

While some sociologists, like Martin Shaw, found that the abrupt end of the Cold War challenged them to pay more attention to theorizing the international and the new globality, social Constructivists and "new normative" theorists (including some feminist scholars intent upon deconstructing patriarchal culture) found in these events justification for their emphasis on domestic processes that created identities, interests, and moral values. Echoing what the English School had long maintained, an increasing number of American IR scholars were prepared to argue that "norms are not static; they are contested and [historically] contingent" (Katzenstein, 1996a, 3). As Peter Katzenstein argued, state interests could no longer be taken for granted as they were in the Cold War. There had been from 1988 to 1991 what John Mueller has called a "quiet cataclysm" in the perception of world politics, "the functional equivalent of World War III," but demonstrating that radical change can occur quickly without a violent resolution (Mueller, 1995, 1–3). There was a need to consider many kinds of power and to recognize that the power state actors seek may be defined by cultural as well as military factors.

The end of history?

For many European scholars, postwar French and German amity symbolized and systematized by the European Union constitutes a significant break from the competitive state system of the past. It is now inconceivable, they argue, that European Union members would resort to war and balance as they have done for centuries. Moreover, the progressive evolution of the European Economic Community to the European Union and its transnational network of financial, trade, and legal institutions, political and social norms, and a common immigration policy, seemed to point, especially in the 1990s, to the coming of what John Ruggie called "the first truly postmodern international political form"—one that problematizes the very concept of state territoriality (Ruggie, 1993, 140). This would constitute a dramatic shift in normative expectations unpredicted by Realist theory, though anticipated perhaps in the Liberal concept of the "democratic peace."

The most forceful expression of the idea of a break with the past at the end of the Cold War was expressed, however, by Francis Fukuyama in an essay of 1989—later expanded into a book—on what he called the coming "end of history" in the fulfillment of globalized liberal, free-trade democracy, a world free of ideological conflict and marked by increasing interdependence, diaspora, and transnational (postnational) culture, presided over by the United States as global policeman. Though with a philosophic grounding in German idealism (Kant and, especially, Hegel), Fukuyama's argument also owes something to the utopian strain in classical nineteenth-century political economy. This optimism about the dawning of a new era was contested from rather different positions. Adam Watson, in pondering what kind of new global society of states might emerge, wrote more ambiguously of operative values or codes of conduct derived from what he calls the "hybrid culture of western and non-western norms" (Watson, 1992, 307). A yet more guarded view was expressed by Henry Kissinger: the new order, unlike that after the Congress of Vienna, "will have to be built by statesmen who represent vastly different cultures" without much indication that transnational norms would emerge. Moreover, it would be, he predicted, an order that the United States could neither dominate nor, as in the past, withdraw from (Kissinger, 1994, 27).

Though the idea of a democratic peace (that democratic nations would be far less likely to war against each other) did achieve a greater respectability through the work of scholars examining the historical evidence, others remained skeptical of that evidence (too few cases), or suspected a hidden assumption that war itself was either an abnormal pathology or a problem of misperception (see Chapter 10). And some Realists, while accepting the fact that democracies have been since the Second World War less likely to war with each other, see this as simply a side effect of Cold War bipolarity. John Weltman in his own wide-ranging review of the history of war from the Greeks to the present drew attention to the increasing lack of utility (of benefits over costs), at present, of warfare rather than some emerging democratic ideological homogeneity. Writing after the first Gulf War, he argued that general war would be replaced in the future by more localized conflicts that were less costly and more manageable (Weltman, 1995, xi–xii).

The return of history

After the Gulf War, the first major international crisis of the post-Cold War period was the disintegration of Yugoslavia and the eruption of what many represented as a genocidal war in the Balkans. The "national problem," suppressed by Tito's communist regime, reemerged with a vengeance—the return of history. On the other hand, history does not repeat itself exactly. The Balkan conflict did not endanger the larger European peace. At the same time, there were apprehensions that, though the Soviet Union had disappeared, postcommunist Russia would reemerge from its economic meltdown with the same national security interests and perhaps regional ambitions that had marked the Russian Empire of the eighteenth and nineteenth centuries. Moreover, academic Realists had a large investment to protect, and some sprang to defend (in favored journals like *Security Studies* and *International Security*) an analysis based on power relations rather than normative change. In 2000, Waltz poured scorn on the idea of a "withering away of the power of the state" as a "wish and an illusion," the mirage of peace-promoting economic interdependence (asymmetrical and thus more likely to lead to conflict), and democratic peace theory generally (Waltz, 2000, 10–18). The most aggressive response, however, came from John Mearsheimer.

Most Realists assume that unipolarity is the least stable of all structures. Arguing from a stubbornly Realist position, Mearsheimer (an ex-US Air Force officer at the University of Chicago) asserted in 1990 that not only Russia but the Western European states were likely to return to a more aggressive pursuit of their interests. The disappearance of the balanced equilibrium of the Cold War would ultimately plunge the world once again into multipolar aggression; far from ushering in peaceful interdependency, the global economic system would inspire national competition and resentment of dependency, and would likely be marked by economic blackmail and brinkmanship. The democratic peace of postwar western Europe was but a phenomenon of its time, and could prosper because security responsibilities had been assumed by the superpower hegemon. In his analysis, he drew on historical evidence that he claimed showed that liberal institutions "have mattered rather little in the past" (Mearsheimer, 1990, 49).

Mearsheimer called this view "offensive realism" as opposed to the "defensive" Realism of Kenneth Waltz. To the Neorealist idea of a system seeking equilibrium, he opposed the idea of states perpetually and aggressively not seeking to balance but to maximize their power: a post-Cold War policed by a single super power would be a short-lived phenomenon—not because others would balance against the United States, but because rising would-be hegemons would seek to displace it. States were inevitably power-hungry expanding units. Far from leading to global peace, the disintegration of the Soviet Union would see the rise of new interstate rivalries—like the Balkans writ large—and the fading into irrelevance of international institutions like the UN.

But his predictive analysis, restated and expanded in a book in 2001, has yet, with regard to Europe at least, to find much confirmation in the twenty-five years since the end of Cold War bipolarity. To many historians, Mearsheimer's historical proofs seem tendentious and have trouble explaining why Britain in the nineteenth century and America in the twentieth did not seem to act as aggressively expanding, power maximizing Great Powers should. His detractors probably outnumber his supporters, though the impressive rise of China and its more assertive posture in the last decade, the current difficulties experienced by a European Union divided by immigration and fiscal issues, and, most recently, Russia's seizure of the Crimea and promotion of civil war in the Ukraine, have made his predictions seem somewhat less far-fetched than they appeared in the 1990s.

Post-9/11

Much of IR theory, and especially Realist theory, has been concerned with the definition and advancement of "national interests." During periods of security crisis, as in the early Cold War, the most tangible interest was that of survival. With the end of the Cold War, the defining of national interests became much more complicated. For historians this is not surprising. Interests and the normative context of interests can be expected to change over time—something Martha Finnemore explored in the late 1990s in her study of *National Interests in International Society* (1996). With the disappearance of a stable-seeming bipolar world, attention was refocused on factors beyond those of balance, stability, and security, on concepts and values drawn from religion or nationalism or cultural revolution (all of which are visible in, say, Iran after the fall of the Shah's secular regime in 1979).

After the end of the Soviet system, some scholars—Samuel Huntington being the most prominent—speculated about the ideological-cultural global divisions of a persistent "civilizational" character likely to reemerge after the fall of communism (see Chapter 10). The terrorist attacks of 9/11 seemed to confirm these fears. They also inaugurated a second postwar era that challenged the optimism of the Liberal vision of global interdependency but that raised difficult issues for a Realism that had placed the state and the state system at the heart of its understanding of IR. Though America's invasion of Afghanistan, where the regime had harbored the planners of the Al-Qaeda terror attacks, suggested a bridge between nonstate actors and states, G. W. Bush's advisors were less successful in their attempt to harness the threat posed to the West by Al-Qaeda to their desire to "finish the job" in Iraq in 2003—deploying a melange of Realist and Liberal rationales (antiterrorism, humanitarian regime-change, and "weapons of mass destruction") to justify the promotion of American interests in this geopolitically important, oil-rich region.

In the first decade of the twenty-first century, antiwestern transregional, transnational violence certainly suggested a less benign form of globalization, one that was unanticipated in either classical or structural Realist or Liberal thought, while the rising power of fundamentalist religion in much of the Muslim world (though not only there) has revived an interest in civilizational thinking long considered passé by many modern historians. Some Realists would of course argue that however intractable-seeming, destructive, and pervasive "terrorism" has become in the early twenty-first century, it does not constitute a tangible security threat to the survival of the state in the way that Great Power warfare does. But quite apart from the fact that nuclear-armed nonstate actors may threaten devastation quite comparable to that of interstate warfare, others would reply that IR theory that cannot or refuses to accommodate the most prominent feature of the international politics of our time has little to offer as a *useful* social science.

At the same time, some familiar areas of IR scholarship have in fact been nurtured by the "global war on terror." The problem of the expanded surveillance and use of force against nonstate actors has drawn the attention of scholars of human rights law to a range of issues. Military scholars have turned from the Cold War to, on the one hand, the challenge of "postconflict" stabilization (as in Iraq and Afghanistan) and, on the other, how to organize defense or offense against an enemy that is neither a state nor a centrally organized and directed force. Scholarship that had focused on the Cold War security state and its intelligence-gathering has now a wider field in the current era of vast informational and computing resources. 9/11 has engendered an antiterrorist security regime with greatly enhanced capabilities and little public oversight.

Recommended readings

Begin with Melvyn P. Leffler and Odd Arne Westad (eds.), *The Cambridge History of the Cold War*, Vols. I–III (2010), a massive compendium of themes that can also be followed in the specialist publications, *Journal of Cold War Studies* and *Cold War History*. Also John Lewis Gaddis, *We Now Know: Rethinking Cold War History* (1997), S. Autio-Sarasmo, "A New Historiography of the Cold War?" *European History Quarterly* 41 (2011), 657–64, and John Lamberton, *The Cold War* (2011). For recent studies questioning the superpower paradigm, see the anthropologist Heonik Kwon's *The Other Cold War* (2010) and the essays in Joel Isaac and Duncan Bell (eds.), *Uncertain Empire: American History and the Idea of the Cold War* (2012), especially Odd Arne Westad's "Exploring Histories of the Cold War: A Pluralist Approach," 51–60. William C. Wohlforth has written from a Realist perspective on the historiography of the Cold War, "Historical Science and Cold War Scholarship," in Elman and Elman (eds.), *Bridges and Boundaries*, 351–8. For a Constructivist approach, see Ted Hopf, *Reconstructing the Cold War: The Early Years, 1945–1958* (2012). For Soviet foreign policy, one may still consult Adam Ulam's three substantial volumes, though the partial opening of Soviet archives after 1991 has added detail and raised some issues of interpretation. See, for instance, Vojtech Mastny, *The Cold War and Soviet Insecurity: The Stalin Years* (1996), and Vladislav Zubok and Constantine Pleshakov, *Inside the Kremlin's Cold War: From Stalin to Khrushchev* (1996).

For the idea of the national security state, see Michael J. Hogan, *A Cross of Iron: Harry S. Truman and the Origins of the National Security State 1945–1954* (1998). A recent overview of the nuclear Cold War can be found in Richard Dean Burns and Joseph M. Siracusa, *A Global History of the Nuclear Arms Race: Weapons, Strategy and Politics* (2 vols., 2013). On Berlin, see Richard D. Williamson, *First Steps toward Détente:*

American Diplomacy in the Berlin Crisis, 1958–1963 (2012). Among the extensive literature on the Cuban missile crisis, see, most recently, Sheldon M. Stern, *The Cuban Missile Crisis in American Memory: Myths versus Reality* (2012), and David R. Gibson, *Talk at the Brink: Deliberation and Decision during the Cuban Missile Crisis* (2012). For the Russian perspective, Aleksandr Fursenko and Timothy Natali, *One Hell of a Gamble* (1997) and *Khrushchev's Cold War* (2006), as well as Svetlana Savranskaya, *The Soviet Cuban Missile Crisis* (2012). For the often neglected Cuban perspective, see James G. Blight, Bruce J. Allyn, and David A. Welch (eds.), *Cuba on the Brink: Castro, the Missile Crisis and the Soviet Collapse* (1993), and Mark Laffey and Jutta Weldes, "Decolonizing the Cuban Missile Crisis," *International Studies Quarterly* 52 (2008), 555–77. Also Odd Arne Westad, *The Global Cold War: Third World Interventions and the Making of Our Times* (2007).

For a recent treatment of Morgenthau's opposition to the Vietnam war, see Lorenzo Zambernardi, "The Impotence of Power: Morgenthau's Critique of American Intervention in Vietnam," *Review of International Studies* 37 (2011), 1335–56. On the Vietnam- and post-Vietnam-era issue of prestige in the calculation of national security interests see Jennifer L. Millikin, "Metaphors of Prestige and Reputation in American Foreign Policy and American Realism," in Francis A. Beer and Robert Hariman (eds.), *Post-Realism* (1996), 217–38.

For the debate over the sudden end of the Cold War and its meaning for Realism, see, for instance, Jeffrey W. Legro and Andrew Moravcsik, "Is Anybody Still a Realist?" *International Security* 24 (1999), 5–55. For Waltz's defense, see "Structural Realism after the Cold War," *International Security* 25 (2000), 5–41. More general discussion of the meaning of the end of the Cold War can be found in Lebow and Risse-Kappen (eds.), *International Relations Theory and the End of the Cold War* (1995). Also, Sasson Sofer, "The Prominence of Historical Demarcations: Westphalia and the New World Order," *Diplomacy & Statecraft* 20 (2009), 1–19. For a critical theory perspective see Andrew Linklater, "Citizenship and Sovereignty in the Post-Westphalian State," *European Journal of International Relations* 2 (1996), 77–103. For some critical responses to Fukuyama, see Gordon Marsden (ed.), *After the End of History* (1992). Post-Cold War triumphalism and its oversimplified view of the Cold War era is treated in Ellen Schrecker (ed.), *Cold War Triumphalism: The Misuse of History after the Fall of Communism* (2004).

Martin Shaw's view of the need to globalize IR can be found in his "The Global Revolution and the Twenty-First Century: From International Relations to Global Politics," in Chan and Wiener (eds.), *Twentieth Century History* (1999), 191–210, and "Globality and Historical Sociology: State, Revolution and War Revisited," in Stephen Hobden and John M. Hobson (eds.), *Historical Sociology of International Relations* (2002), 82–98. For an historian's skeptical response to Mearsheimer, see Jonathan Haslam, "John Mearsheimer's 'Elementary Geometry of Power': Euclidean Movement or an Intellectual Blind Alley?" in May, Rosecrance, and Steiner (eds.), *History and Realism* (2010), 322–40.

PART III
CONTEMPORARY INTERNATIONAL
RELATIONS AND THE USES OF HISTORY

The unanticipated end of the Cold War and the problematic of global "terrorism" at the beginning of the twenty-first century resonated powerfully through the discipline of IR, unsettling long-held assumptions about the nature of the field, the building blocks of its theory, and the applications and outcomes it might offer for the practice of international relations in the contemporary world. The reverberations continue into the second decade of the new century, amplified by the manifest failures of American designs in Iraq and Afghanistan, the perplexing complications of an Arab Spring gone awry, and the apparent flimsiness of a supposedly "normative" international commitment to human rights.

The confusion of analysis, the policy failures, and the shock of unintended consequences have undoubtedly damaged the claim of IR to be a predictive social and political *science* while at the same time enhancing the role of history—viewed either as *contingency* (unexpected things happen) or as *process* (the inevitability of change, including structural change)—and of historical narrative. Fin de siècle uncertainty about boundaries—between outside and inside, ourselves and dangerous others, regional and global, ideological and social, state and civilizational—has bedeviled the analysis of the post-Westphalian (or neo-Westphalian) New World Order, brought History back in as a discipline equipped to explain eras of transformation, and led to what some call a "fourth debate" in IR regarding the use of historical facts, methods, and concepts.

The school of thought thrown most on the defensive has been that of structural or Neorealism, though neither have Liberal Institutionalism and its overly optimistic reading of the effects of globalization fared very well. The reemergence of China and, possibly, Russia as plausible Great Powers has served to revive an older geo-political tradition in the discipline, and its use of history as a reservoir of lessons drawn from a familiar long—if largely European—narrative. At the same time, the rise of "fundamentalism" in the Middle East and elsewhere has focused attention on the motivational beliefs of nonstate actors and on the familiar issue of "agency," while also encouraging a revival of the concept of "civilizations" as enduring, supranational historical phenomena. History—providing not only chronology and "evidence," but an interpretive narrative of ideas, passions, and cultures—has returned to the center stage.

CHAPTER 10
CIVILIZATIONS, THE MYTH OF SOVEREIGNTY, AND THE DEMOCRATIC PEACE: THE END OF INTERNATIONAL RELATIONS (AS WE KNOW IT)?

In this concluding chapter, we shall consider the contemporary use of history and historical narrative in thinking about civilizations, in interrogating the core concepts of "sovereignty" and "state," and in assessing cosmopolitanism and the impact of a globalized realm of international and transnational institutions on the future of international relations and of IR.

The West versus the rest?

Arnold Toynbee's grand narrative of all known civilizations, *A Study of History* (12 volumes, 1934–61), sought for regularities in their generation, growth, and disintegration. Though in some sense his work suggests that of other post-First World War philosophers of Western Decline (José Ortega y Gasset and Oswald Spengler), Toynbee was not motivated by fatalism so much as a hope that moral regeneration (like Butterfield, Toynbee was a practicing Christian) might enable an escape from cyclical decline and the creation of a more stable and just world order. Impelled, apparently, by his reading of Thucydides, he sought "spiritual" rather than material factors in civilizational progress. This sharply separated his work from that of the interwar Marxists or the *Annales* school—though Fernand Braudel would offer his own single-volume text, *A History of Civilizations* (1963 and posthumously in 1987 as *A Grammar of Civilizations*), grounded in material but also "moral" culture and drawing on "all the social sciences."

The overambitious reach of Toynbee's opus and his lack of interest in original, empirical research led to the rapid waning of his reputation among professional historians well before his death in 1975. But his global reach and his insistence that history not be trapped by the nineteenth-century tradition of national narrative offered some inspiration to a new generation of "world" historians like his biographer, William McNeill. McNeill's own world history project has pushed some in IR to embrace a much longer chronology and a less Eurocentric frame for its analyses and encouraged a search for multiple discontinuities and greater global cultural diversity than scholarship of the

Westphalian order allows. At the same time, elements of cyclical declinism (national, cultural, civilizational) reappeared in the late twentieth century in the revival of historical Sociology, in the Culture Wars debates, and in the historian Paul Kennedy's hugely popular book *The Rise and Fall of Great Powers* (1987)—whose implied warning seemed to be buried by end-of-the-Cold-War American triumphalism. The threat if not the certainty of civilizational decline, however, soon resurfaced the 1990s in the work of the political scientist Samuel Huntington.

Samuel Huntington and The Clash of Civilizations

Toynbee's civilizations rose and fell serially and were not essentialized as immutable expressions of uniquely unchanging, incompatible, and competitive world views; they did not of necessity "clash." Similarly, the world history project has advanced global diversity, hybridity, and change rather than stasis and conflict. However, the most striking and influential post-Cold War expression of civilizational thinking in IR, that of Samuel P. Huntington (1927–2008), offered a reading of civilizations at odds with much, if not all, late twentieth-century scholarship. His vision was of a world in which conflicting cultural norms would reemerge after the Cold War. The central question would no longer be "Which side are you on?" but "Who are you?," a provocative riposte to the much-talked about end-of-history liberalism of one of his Harvard students, Francis Fukuyama. Huntington's 1996 work, *The Clash of Civilizations*, predicted neither globalized homogeneity and transnational hybridity nor even some version of the reemergence of traditional multipolar state-system balancing but the aggressive opposition of historically and culturally constructed world views and value systems that would reassert themselves as diametric political alternatives—East versus West, Greco-Roman versus Muslim or Chinese.

It may be argued whether the Gulf War (1990–1) or the new Balkan Wars (1991–9) confirmed Fukuyama's or Huntington's view (as crises dealt with by an American-led police action, or as evidence of cultural fault lines), though the subsequent rise of Al-Qaeda terrorism seemed superficially at least to endorse Huntington's view of the reemerging, divisive force of culture and ethnicity—driven forward by the increased interaction of peoples of different civilizations (globalization as a source of conflict rather than fusion), the "de-Westernization" of postcolonial elites, and the resurgence of global religious identities. Huntington invokes history (as Realists often do), but his critics were quick to seize on the difficulties raised by his selection and use of historical evidence, his centering of intercivilizational difference in explaining "fault-line wars," his invocation of the "bloody borders" of Islam as evidence of its inherently violent character, his neglect of forces like nationalism that can cut across civilizational boundaries and fragment the realms of religion and ethnicity, and his general subordination of the socioeconomic factors behind intercivilizational conflicts. In 1997, the debate entered the global public political realm with the call of Mohammed Khatami, Iranian minister of culture and newly installed president, for a "dialogue of civilizations" that would work to correct misconceptions and defuse hostility, a call that seized attention both generally (the United Nations General Assembly declared 2001 to be a "Year of Dialogue Among Civilisations") and among some IR scholars already sharply critical of Huntington's much-discussed thesis.

Though criticisms of Huntington and civilizational analysis generally were drawn from across the spectrum of IR schools of thought, those most critical tended to come from the anti-Realist end, arguing, for instance, that Huntington's schema essentially reproduced Realist assumptions by replacing "states" with "civilizations." The idea of dialogue rather than inevitable conflict also was attractive to those scholars influenced by critical theory and the concept of a (past, present, and, especially, future) globalized "international public sphere," a realm of cross-cultural conversation and of "reflexive and empathetic subjects" (Lynch, 2000, 314).

The civilizations debate, as a historical discourse about either clash or dialogue, prompted a general reconsideration among at least some sections of the discipline about definitions and demarcations: how should IR "read" civilizations, what are their (highly debatable) boundaries, and how can the discipline avoid embedded "orientalist" assumptions and prejudices? Publications have proliferated with titles like *Civilizational Identity … in International Relations*, *Civilizations in Dispute*, *Civilizations in World Politics*, or *Civilizational Dialogue in World Order*. Inevitably, much of this discourse has drawn on the language and concepts of historical Sociology and Anthropology in defining just what a politics of civilization might involve. Robert Cox, among others, has observed that any contemporary attempt to draw geographical boundaries (fault lines) around civilizations is "an exercise in futility," given the globalized world of communication and migration in which we live. Beyond geography, one might, he argues, center notions of time and space, the tension between individual and community, and spiritual cosmology, while accepting that none of these are fixed. Civilizations should be thought of as "processes or tendencies," and as shifting substrata beneath civil societies, states, and international relations generally (Cox, 2000).

Within and beyond the historical and future state: The limits of sovereignty

It may be argued, from a civilizational perspective, that sovereignty as we know it is a largely Western construction that, when globalized, conflicted with non-Western traditions, understandings, and practices—especially in the Arab world and the Far East, as observed in the tension between the state and "God's rule" in the Muslim *ummah* or in China's historical relationship with tributary peoples. The conflicted search for synthesis with Western notions of territoriality and autonomy continues, perhaps intensifies, with the reemergence of these worlds from global marginality.

We have seen that the concept of the absolute sovereignty of the state has been central to much IR scholarship from the beginning of the discipline—in both its aspects, as domestic authority (the state's "monopoly of violence") and as the external, unitary authority that defines the relationship of one state to others. One finds it most forcefully endorsed in varieties of Realism, but also regarded as a fundamental foundation in the Grotian tradition of international law. It is largely accepted in American IPE and as a starting point in Liberal approaches to international institutions and processes. The school of IR most critical of the "reification" of the idea of sovereignty, Constructivism, itself has been divided over whether the state and state sovereignty, however much they beg to be deconstructed, should continue to be central to the discipline.

Historians have questioned the absolute nature of Westphalian sovereignty in the European past, while recognizing that we are dealing with an intellectual and legal construction, in a sense a convenient fiction, rather than political reality. Critiques of the use of the concept of sovereignty must therefore be careful of what is called the "descriptive fallacy," that is, assuming the concept can be empirically disproven by comparing the ideal with actual practice. At the same time, those IR scholars who casually accept Westphalian sovereignty as a basic concept in understanding state behavior past and present may also be guilty of turning a convenient fiction (a Weberian ideal) into a hard analytical fact. Moreover, some who do not question the importance of the idea of state sovereignty in the (European) past may nevertheless challenge its current descriptive power and its future. Globalizations of one kind or another (transnational capitalism or the liberal universalism of the human rights regime) may cast doubt on the substance and continued use of the concept of absolute state sovereignty.

There has in fact been what one might call an explosion of scholarship on sovereignty—as an intellectual tradition, as the basis for international law, and as a central concept in IR theory—in the late twentieth and early twenty-first century, much of it inspired by the ongoing project of the European Union, the gathering movement to create a global human rights regime, and the contemporary problematic of nonstate actors. Much of this debate has turned in one way or another to history to confirm or confront arguments that center a supposed decline of the state in contemporary or future world affairs.

Diplomacy and treaty-making, and much international law, presume that states are unitary actors—in effect, individuals. The state that may have been literally an individual in the era of dynastic absolutism became a collective individual in the modern era. This fiction lies behind, for instance, the "billiard ball" concept in Neorealist IR theory whereby the unitary state is the basic unit of analysis—whatever the messy, fragile, and conflicted reality might be of the domestic character of a state or the external constraints that might hinder the exercise of its "sovereignty" in the real world. For most states, the absolute sovereignty of the Westphalian state system does not, and never did, correspond to an actual, historical monopoly of violence internally or an independence of action externally. If IR is going to employ the concept of sovereignty, it is important to understand its practical and theoretical limitations, and to understand the nature of sovereignty as actually practiced in any historical era: sovereignty is not a constant, but may shift over time, due to political changes and to large social and economic factors. Are we living in a world where the distance between the legal fiction of sovereignty and the actual ability of states to act in a sovereign manner has widened or narrowed?

Decolonization after the Second World War created a world of politically sovereign peoples freed from Western empires. The end of the Cold War similarly saw the emergence of states that had been only nominally sovereign within superpower hegemonic security alliances but now were more or less independent actors in the world system. The new elites that came to run postcolonial states naturally insisted on the familiar form of sovereignty that had characterized their European metropoles—despite the fact that many of these new "nations" had highly arbitrary geopolitical and ethnic boundaries, and may have lacked much of the legitimacy that Weber assumed characterized the state, or the force to make authority real within their borders. There is much talk of "failed states" and illegitimate regimes. Severe economic constraints may be imposed by either the action of international organizations or the iron discipline of a punishing and constraining global capitalism. Popular identities—globally constituted—may not align with national identities and so may work against the coherence of the state. At the turn of the century, a "State Failure Task Force" reported 136 occurrences from 1955 to 1998 of failure most common in decolonized, impoverished countries (Krasner, 2004, 91). All of this should be of importance to a discipline that has been tenaciously state-centric in its theory and practice.

Reassessing the concept of sovereignty

Summing up, rather provocatively, what they regarded as the trap of, especially American, state-centric IR theory, Yale H. Ferguson and Richard W. Mansbach claimed a few years ago that the Realist worldview now "seems reactionary and naive, the foreign policy equivalent of creationism in natural science." From the historian's point of view, such a state-centric world "never fully existed, certainly does not exist now, and will never exist" (Ferguson and Mansbach, 2007, 530–1). The last couple of decades have seen, in fact, an outpouring of scholarly work on the concept of sovereignty—some by political and social historians but most by political scientists like Stephen Krasner, who titled a collection of essays *Problematic Sovereignty* in 2001. Realism tended to see Westphalian sovereignty as an unproblematic given of the modern international system, a usage attacked by postmodernists like R. K. Ashley in the 1980s who regarded the concept as simply a "metaphysical conceit." For Krasner, it was more than this, but always an "organized hypocrisy"—that is, its defining characteristics, "territory, autonomy, recognition, and control," have never provided an accurate description of its actual practice (Krasner, 1999, 237). In the 2000s some came to see it as not only a legal or political fiction (whether a useful or an obscuring fiction) but also as something that is socially constructed and therefore historically fluid.

The "formal-legal" definition of sovereignty has been subjected to the sharp critique of scholars like Daniel Philpott, who emphasized "tortuous evolution" and revolutionary shifts—especially those caused by, he claims, the impact of decolonization (Philpott, 2001, 16 and Part III). Raia Prokhovnik has stressed more generally the malleability of the concept, its "dynamic and mutable" nature, over different historical eras, and its shifting political vocabulary—from that of the absolutist Bodin to the popular (domestic, performative, and active) sovereignty derived from Locke and Rousseau (Prokhovnik, 2008). Political historians like Paul Schroeder and James Sheehan have focused on the sovereignty of the eighteenth- and nineteenth-century European state system as "both a [unified] doctrine and a [plural] set of activities" (Sheehan, 2006, 2). Others have emphasized the "dark side" of sovereignty, which frequently, from the standpoint of small states, meant destruction, mutilation, or being relegated to buffering or junior balancing in the interests of greater powers. *The concept of sovereignty best suited states that had enough power to express it.*

Much of the long debate over the meaning of sovereignty has revolved around the degree to which it expresses "a natural state of affairs" in a balancing system or whether it is better seen as an *ideology* and a specific form of *legitimization*. Long ago Quincy Wright argued (in *A Study of War*, 1942) for seeing sovereignty as not simply a descriptive aspect of the state system, but a concept that was made to serve different purposes as its function shifted over the centuries: for absolutist thinkers like Bodin it was a solution to the problem of overmighty subjects (aristocrats who might challenge the king); for mercantilists it justified the view that commerce was but an extension of the power of monarchs; for Grotius it was the means of devising an international law that, by identifying the state as an individual with the sole competence to make war, would hold rulers responsible for the actions of their states in times of war. Some like the feminist scholar Jean Elshtain, employing a psychological approach, have argued that the legal convention that the state is an individual is related in the West to the development of *the sovereign* [and masculine] *self* since the Reformation. Machiavelli's state is an individualist prone to conflict, competition, and, especially, self-justification. In this sense, sovereignty is more of an aspiration (for legitimacy) than description. Most states are in fact internally plural and externally dependent in a hierarchical system.

David Lake, among others, has drawn attention (2003) to the inadequacy of any hard, legalistic definition (that sovereignty is absolute and indivisible), and calls for a definition, a "new sovereignty," that does not have such difficulty accommodating the reality of hierarchy in international relations. A more subtle approach might be to step outside the legal notion of absolute sovereignty in order to take account of the ways in which "sovereign" states may nonetheless acknowledge the special *authority* of another state, not merely because of its coercive power but through a kind of trust that confers legitimacy to hierarchy—a kind of contractual relationship that is historically created. This condition arguably prevailed in the Western alliance during the Cold War, or in the carefully constructed, US-led first Gulf War coalition. But by acting unilaterally a decade later in the second war in Iraq, the United States endangered this legitimacy and risked losing its "authority" as global hegemon (Lake, 2007, 79). Lake posits that global hegemony often rests more on the legitimacy of authority than on mere material power.

Some Constructivists would go further and argue that sovereignty, as a social institution, is a matter of identities, and identity is always *relational*. In a much commented upon and reprinted essay of 1992, "Anarchy Is What States Make of It: The Social Construction of Power Politics," Alexander Wendt made the claim that there can be no sovereignty without an "other." It has, that is, an intersubjective character—the sovereignty of a state is not constituted by material capabilities so much as by the existence of difference, of other "sovereign" peoples. The sovereign identity of a state is constructed through social interaction and perception (of, say, trust or challenge). Many scholars are now prepared to see sovereignty as "historically open, contingent and unstable" (Bartleson, 1995, 2), as socially constructed and fluid over time (Biersteker and Weber, 1996), and as a social norm justifying the "ascendant moral purpose" of the modern state by "an appeal to higher-order values" (Reus-Smit, 2001, 528). At the same time, many would argue that, however problematized and contested, "the sovereign state remains the only game in town" (Bickerton et al., 2007, xiii), while for legal scholars like Martin Loughlin sovereignty must remain "a foundational concept" (Loughlin, 2003, 55–6).

Contested sovereignty?

For some historians and historical sociologists, it is useful to consider sovereignty not from the top-down perspective of the prince (and the convenient fiction of the state as an individual) but from the ground up (the state as plurally constituted). Feudal states were clearly plural, but even absolutist regimes of the early modern period—like totalitarian states in the modern era—relied on at least a tacitly consensual relationship with the ruled. A prince may claim absolute authority over his people, but reality suggests a negotiated process of give and take, even in the greatest tyrannies. Modern concepts of citizenship of course imply collective will, democratic legitimation, and national identity as part of the theory and *practice* of sovereignty. But democratic legitimation also implies that the sovereign state is a perpetually contested realm. Sovereignty is not simply a legal given, but is dynamically constructed through shared understandings and agreements about authority. This is not a matter of Hobbes' irrevocable contract between people and Leviathan, but a fluid process of constant reproduction and reconstruction. As two scholars of modern transnational human rights advocacy networks have observed, "changes in these practices and understandings should in turn transform sovereignty" (Keck and Sikkink, 1998, 37).

Broadly, history reveals periods of significant redefinition of the "sovereign self" as a collective response to ideas and to new economic and social contexts. These resulted in the conversion of masses of people to new normative concepts of the individual's relationship to the state—as happened in the Protestant Reformation, the French Revolution, or the dissolution of colonial empires. Sovereignty as an aspect of (a usually dynastic) state shifted to the modern sense of the sovereignty of a self-determining people—a sense that was extended to the many new states created after the First World War and after decolonization. In many of these, newly empowered elites claimed a domestic and external sovereign right for their peoples but found themselves to be only nominal rulers of polities yet to be constructed as unitary in any modern understanding.

Sovereignty-as-people rather than as territory or dynasty became especially an issue in decolonized parts of the world: in Africa and south Asia territorial boundaries, lines drawn on a map, often represent the arbitrary whim of colonial powers. Consequently, decolonization led to bitter civil wars, as in the Congo and Nigeria, and a legacy of continuing interstate conflict, as with India and Pakistan.

Finally, changes in social networking and technologies of communication may enhance or undermine sovereignty. Benedict Anderson famously argued (in *Imagined Communities*, 1983) that the proliferation of printed media—newspapers and pamphlets—propelled a sense of simultaneity and national identity in the early modern Western state through growing literacy, self-awareness, and a sense of community that would later be replicated in a non-Western colonized world resisting dependency. But communication and networking can also work against the legitimacy of the sovereign state. The recent history of a more mobile global population, of diasporas and internet-inspired virtual communities, and of the terrorism of nonstate actors suggests that the degree to which states could claim either a primacy of identity and loyalty or a monopoly of violence has diminished significantly. As one scholar, Daniel Deudney (1995, 216), has said, "States today have a monopoly on the ability to *legitimize* violence, but," contrary to Weber, "they do not have the ability to *monopolize* violence." The coherence of Anderson's imagined community of the nation is more fragile as identities that may command a higher loyalty for many proliferate within and outside the formal state.

Some may suggest that none of this matters, that in analyzing international relations as a system we are concerned only with the legal expression of sovereignty among nations—a unitary authority that allows a state to "act" as a unit. Whether a government is actually weak or strong, the state cohesive or chaotic within its borders, it is still "sovereign" in the eyes of other states and possesses thereby the right to sit at the table and the capacity to negotiate and make treaties. But if we want to explore the nature of post-Westphalian international relations as a system and attempt to use such explorations to predict or hypothesize state behavior, then it is not enough that sovereignty be simply a useful fiction. It must represent some tangible part of reality. Certainly the degree to which sovereignty expresses an objective reality both within a state's borders and among other sovereign nations is a legitimate concern in IR theory and, especially, practice.

The ability of a government to express its will internally or externally is, of course, significantly affected by the resources it might command; these in turn reflect at some level the degree to which its population identifies with the state. Hitler's expression of German sovereignty—*ein Volk, ein Reich, ein Führer*—was even under the Nazi police state a myth and aspiration, propaganda that aspired to create a racialized norm. In reality, most state elites have great difficulty "speaking" for the diverse kinds of people they represent. Nor is the art of international relations blind to this—hence the resources since the sixteenth century that have been put into shaping public opinion at home and weakening other states by encouraging civil unrest and "fifth column" sympathizers—as when Goebbels (wrongly as it turned out) assumed that millions of German Americans could be a powerful asset in Roosevelt's America.

Minorities within and outside the state have nevertheless historically constrained and channeled the practice of sovereign relations. Internal conflict—the divisiveness of ethnicity or the antagonism of social class (often these are related), insofar as they may reduce loyalty to the state and the legitimacy of its elite—may weaken the sovereign player in international relations; at the same time, the romantic understanding of the state as a sovereign people, an ethnicity or race, powerfully encouraged a politics of *irredentism*—the need to complete the destiny of the nation by uniting the people within arbitrary and unnatural borders with "unredeemed" co-nationals beyond—in nineteenth- and early twentieth-century Europe. Once powerful sources of international conflict, such romantic aspirations of national completion were embarrassed by fascism and seemingly shared its fate. Suppressed during the Cold War, and, it can be argued, substantially weakened by the global mobility of peoples and the multiculturalism of the postmodern state, the politics of national completion (or restoration) nevertheless made a return, not only in Milosevic's Greater Serbia, but in the potentially much more destabilizing ambitions of Putin's Russia, and bedevil the international relations of non-Western peoples in the Middle East, South Asia, and Africa.

Partial sovereignty?

After the Second World War, the great increase in the number of polities that claimed sovereign status, and were so recognized by the UN, and which from 1961 ratified in growing numbers the Vienna Convention on Diplomatic Relations, has been commonly regarded in IR texts as evidence that the Western concept of unitary, absolute sovereignty spread throughout a postimperial world of newly sovereign peoples. But claiming internal and external sovereignty and being able fully to practice such sovereign independence were of course quite different things—a fact that legal and diplomatic representations tend to obscure.

For one thing, during the Cold War the hegemonic superpowers imposed informal and formal constraints, both on alliance "partners" and well beyond in the "third world," that significantly reduced these countries' de facto independence. Soft and hard coercion ranged from the economic suasion of rouble and dollar diplomacy to regime change through covert subversion and direct military intervention. The central "front-line" state in the Western alliance, the West German Federal Republic was, from the foundational Basic Law of 1949 to reunification after 1989, by any standard only a partially sovereign entity due to the lack of a formal peace settlement, the continued presence on German soil of American and British military units (no longer "occupiers" but NATO "allies"), and its subordinate status within the American-dominated NATO command. It was also dependent at least in the early years of the Marshall Plan and the "economic miracle" on its commercial and financial connections with the United States. Much the same of course can be said of Japan, with its US-mandated constitution, its reduced defense force, the retention by the United States of military bases long after occupation ended, and its integration into the global structures of American-policed neoliberal capitalism. In Eastern Europe, the constraints were no doubt more direct and arbitrary, and limits on what was at best only a very nominal sovereignty of the Warsaw Pact states were made starkly clear in the German Democratic Republic in 1953, Hungary in 1956, Czechoslovakia in 1968, and Poland in 1980–1.

Associated states and the pooling of sovereignties

West Germany's own somewhat anomalous postwar condition made its transition into the quasi-federated European Economic Community and later Union relatively easy and attractive. Central Europe was no stranger of course to the historical ambiguities of partial sovereignty, as we have seen in the constitutional complexity of the Holy Roman Empire both before and after Westphalia. After the Empire's end in the Napoleonic era, the small states of the German Bund or Confederation remained ambiguously sovereign at best, within the competing spheres of influence of Austria or Prussia—until bought or coerced into Bismarck's Second Reich (where some, like the kingdoms of Bavaria or Saxony, retained a special, privileged identity). If some have seen in the old Holy Roman Empire a parallel with the "neo-medievalism" of the European Union, one might also argue that the Austro-Hungarian Empire/Monarchy after 1867, with its confused administration of peoples claiming various forms of their own sovereign identity, anticipates the (intentional) ambiguity of sovereignty in the modern "European idea." As the historian (and anti-European Union partisan) Alan Sked has observed, "The European idea, in short, recalls the Austrian one, the so-called *Österreiches Staatsidee*" (Sked, 1989, 3). Whether this historical legacy advanced or hindered the development of the European Union as either "superstate" or "normative power," to use the terms of current debate, is nevertheless obscure.

Historians are perhaps more likely than political scientists invested in a theory of the state or those international legal scholars whose starting point is the binding nature of agreements among sovereign states to interrogate the distance between the idea of sovereignty and political and economic reality. They are also more likely to identify significant shifts over time in both the practice and mentality of "sovereign" relationships—often the result of historical contingency and altered material and social circumstances rather than an autonomous evolution of political thought. One scholar has suggested, for instance, that a diminishing of "hard" sovereignty in the modern world can be traced in part to the fearsome consequences of nuclear technology that has, as he puts it, "turned billiard balls into 'eggs'," and sent states searching for protection—beyond sovereign balancing and power projection—by creating cushioning "egg cartons," protective international institutions and norms, as emerging nonstatist strategies of security (Deudney, 1995, 228–9).

Sovereignty in a transnational world

Of late, the discipline of history has increasingly turned to the idea of "transnational history" as an "umbrella perspective" in tracing the creation over the long past of our increasingly interconnected world. This turn highlights the descriptive and interpretive promise of "perspectives such as historical comparison, (cultural) transfers, connections, circulations, entangled or shared history" and threatens to displace the privileged position of the nation-state in historical analysis (Struck, 2011, 573–4). Similarly, and from at least the early 1970s, a significant minority of IR theorists, following Robert Keohane, have been concerned with the problem transnational communication, transnational actors, and international organizations pose to the state-centric study of IR. An ongoing process of "enmeshment" in networks of formal and informal "regimes," the overlapping of polities—their "nesting" in one another, it is argued, means that we can no longer conceptualize the states' system as one of autonomous, hard billiard balls: "the system, like the process of historical change, might be viewed as 'sticky'" (Zacher, 1992, 60; Ferguson and Mansbach, 2008, 373).

At the same time, there has been an increasing interest in the role of *identities*, especially those of religion and ethnicity, which can provide a degree of state coherence and defensive unity when substantially majoritarian (as in postwar Poland), but divisiveness when not or when they overlap state boundaries. The problem of multiple, layered identities (is "nationality" a primary or secondary layer?) and the intersubjective formation of identity complicates any idea of a "civic culture"—as the issue of the veil worn by some Muslim women in France, a state with a historically well-entrenched tradition of the civic sphere, seemed to suggest.

Diasporas in an increasingly migratory, interconnected world and the way modern media and the internet serve to create virtual global communities both within and beyond the borders of the state—where national minorities can achieve a sense of presence and identity through contact with those beyond—have clearly altered the context in which states operate and undermined their assumptions of sovereign primacy. At the same time, such media-enhanced transnational identities may also serve to fragment the "global civil society" which some post-Cold War scholars optimistically anticipated. The considerable attention devoted to diasporas by sociologists and anthropologists as well as scholars of multiculturalism generally has only slowly led to any significant attempt to incorporate these issues into IR theory. Issues of transnational identity have been most attractive to Constructivists, though recently there has been a more general interest in "diaspora mobilization" by state elites as well as nonstate actors.

Sovereignty and political economy

Much was said at the end of the last century about the ways in which a post-Cold War globalization—of international capital markets and relations of production—would encourage both the "obsolescence of force" between major powers and a vision of a "post-Westphalian" era, with the European Union as the model for "new concepts for universal political organization" (Linklater, 1996, 78–83). Twenty years on, such wishful obituaries for the competitive sovereign state system seem less prescient. For one thing, the form that global capitalism assumed in Russia and many of the other successor states of the Soviet empire and elsewhere has, as "crony capitalism" or "oligopolistic neoliberalism," assumed a character that owes much to the statist, autocratic historical traditions of those cultures. For another, the early twenty-first century has seen a growing propensity for Western powers to employ coercive economic sanctions that illustrate, not the autonomy of the global marketplace but its manipulation by powerful states.

Nevertheless, taking a long historical perspective, it can hardly be denied that the contemporary neoliberal political economy exerts, even in the absence of overt manipulation by powerful states for political objectives, a significant influence on the sovereignty of many states. The claim that globalization has significantly "eroded the borders" of *powerful* states may be debatable, but many would assert that the globalized economic system (IMF, World Bank, GATT, and WTO capitalism) sharply hedges the independence of the more *vulnerable* states of (not only, but most obviously) the "underdeveloped," decolonized world. Here a contradiction quickly arose whereby the sovereignty that postindependence elites intended to use to create a modern state proved illusory in the face of the external constraints imposed by a global political economy. There has been in the early twenty-first century some revival of the concepts of dependency and neocolonialism popular in the radical discourse of the 1960s and 1970s.

The apparent autonomy of multinational corporations from state control in a borderless free-trade world, once a favorite subject of IPE and globalization studies, is now questioned by many scholars who seek to reaffirm the centrality of the twenty-first-century state (at least in the developed world). The coercive nature of corporate power beyond their home base, however, remains a chief focus for those who challenge the reality of the sovereign independence of many postcolonial peoples. In the last analysis, and in the real world, the "sovereignty" of a state thrown into severe crisis by a global recession and then coerced into an austerity that may unravel whatever social fabric the nation possesses, can hardly be compared to that of those states that dominate or at least more comfortably negotiate the disciplines imposed by neoliberal capitalism. Some IR scholars have become increasingly aware that the analysis of so-called failed states calls for more than a search for ways to address domestic sources of political instability. Stephen Krasner has called for institutions of "shared sovereignty" and de facto trusteeships—while admitting that this would "smell ... too much like neo-colonialism" (Krasner, 2004, 107). Such a perspective of course begs for a long historical view of ways in which the modern constitution of a global economic regime was anticipated by and perhaps still rests upon the original globalizations that followed the eras of "discovery," slave–sugar mercantilism, and free-trade imperialism.

Finally, there is the perspective explored by, among others, Saskia Sassen, who has taken as her subject the *local* as locus for a globalization that may impact state sovereignty—the ways in which, for instance, cities operate in the cross-border world of the globalized economy, and localized political and social struggles link laterally with like movements elsewhere, leading to what she has called the "partial denationalization of specific components of national states" (Sassen, 2003, 4). A complicated interaction of local culture and global political economy has served further to amplify the crisis of sovereignty in weak states both East and West, North and South.

Human rights

There has been, especially since the end of the Cold War, a significant expansion of what one can call a global human rights regime—in international law and through international institutions and humanitarian interventions. What might a historical understanding of the evolution of human rights discourse and practice hold for IR? How have human rights rhetoric and agendas since the Universal Declaration of Human Rights in 1948 and the Geneva Convention of 1949 down to the current trials of Balkan or African war criminals constrained and limited absolute sovereignty both as a normative concept and in practice?

Human rights, per se, were not emphasized in the charter of the League of Nations beyond reference to humane conditions of labor, the just treatment of peoples in non-sovereign dependencies (mandates), and the protection of "minorities" in the new nations of eastern Europe. The proposal for a High Court of International Justice was dropped in 1920 due to conflict over the extent of its reach and just what crimes (of persons or states) against "the universal law of nations" might involve. Subsequently, the League's Permanent Court of International Justice (1922–46) exercised only a narrow jurisdiction restricted to the settlement of international disputes among states.

Fascist abuses in the 1930s, however, prompted many, like the British novelist, Fabian socialist, popular historian, and futurologist H. G. Wells, to move from the concept of "minority rights" to the more extensive, generalized realm of (human) rights protection. Wells initiated a "Rights of Man" campaign in 1939 that gained some influence in the United States. Wartime experience, Roosevelt's "four freedoms" (of speech and worship, from want and fear), the revelation of Nazi "genocide" (a term coined in 1944), and the war crimes trials led to the adoption by the UN General Assembly of a Universal Declaration of Human Rights in December of 1948. The limited concept of the rights of "minorities" within states, which had been used to advance the irredentist claims of expansionist fascist powers in the 1930s, was set aside in favor of a more generalized concept of individual welfare that embraced both a concern for "positive rights" (like education and health care) as well as freedom from abuse by the state. The Declaration was followed by a UN Commission on Human Rights, an advisory body reporting to the General Assembly—though it refused to take up cases brought by individuals or groups (like the NAACP in America). Any enforcement of a human rights global regime was of course bound to be problematic, especially as postcolonial states jealously regarded their newly established sovereign independence.

The successor to the League's Permanent Court of International Justice, the International Court of Justice (or World Court) established in 1945 inherited its limited jurisdiction. In the years that followed, the human rights agenda, though usually associated with the left, as are the leading human rights watchdog nongovernmental organizations (NGOs), came to have a complicated pedigree. From the beginning of the Cold War, human rights abuses in the Soviet Union were amplified by the anticommunist West as convenient weapons in diplomacy and domestic politics. Nevertheless, from the

1960s one can speak of a shift toward the expansion and internationalization of (at least the rhetoric of) human rights norms and the entrenching of human rights in the foreign policies of many states (albeit as a "secondary interest" rather than a prime national interest like security). This was marked at the UN by the creation of an International Convention on Racial Discrimination (1965) and International Covenants on Economic, Social and Cultural Rights and on Civil and Political Rights in 1966.

Though the political right again appropriated the language of human rights in its resistance, in the United States, to the policy of détente with the Soviet Union, this was in conjunction with a broadening of the concept beyond Cold War antagonism—as in the European Union's endorsement of global human rights, or in NGOs like Amnesty International. There was an expanding range of persons (women and children) recognized to hold rights and of the somewhat elastic concept of genocide. The large-scale massacres of civilians by the Pol Pot regime in Cambodia (1975–9) was widely condemned. By the 1990s, actual genocide seemed to be the objective of some Serbian nationalists during the Balkan Wars. This was followed by the Rwandan tragedy of mass killings of Tutsis by Hutus in 1994. These human disasters led to world condemnation and pressure at the UN for intervention and the use of international legal process and courts to prosecute perpetrators (though this would often require the cooperation and organization of force by Western powers). In 1993, following a Security Council resolution, an International Criminal Tribunal to investigate and prosecute war crimes in the former Yugoslavia was established; the following year a similar court was set up to prosecute crimes in Rwanda.

After the end of the Cold War, then, there has been both an institutional and what may be called an incremental "normative" deepening of the human rights regime (Donnelly, 1999, 88), seen in 1993 in the Vienna World Conference on Human Rights, the Yugoslavia and Rwanda tribunals, a continuing proliferation of nongovernmental human rights organizations, and a significant expansion of international intervention. But expanding the realm of *domestic* human rights abuse (unless defined as genocide) that might call for Great Power, European Union, or UN intervention posed considerable difficulty, not only in the contradictions and lack of consistency one finds in liberal human rights doctrine, but in the practical business of negotiating around the global concept of state sovereignty. When the International Criminal Court (ICC) was established in 2002 with a remit to prosecute individuals for crimes against humanity (war crimes, genocide)— upon referral by either individuals or states—its jurisdiction was rejected by a significant number of UN member states, including the United States and Israel.

Concurrently, there has been growing tension over the Western origins and Eurocentrism of the global understanding of just what constitutes a human right (especially prominent in issues of religious freedom or of sexuality and gender). The rights discourse is historically closely related both to Christian churches and the secular Enlightenment, while the ICC has been more concerned with abuses of human rights in Africa than in the West.

Though there is a long (and continuing) tradition of viewing the expansion of institutions of "global governance" as an outgrowth of an ethical "cosmopolitanism," scholars like Mark Mazower and Samuel Moyne have emphasized the way the history of internationalism generally and the "politics of humanity" especially provide ample evidence of how powerful (Western) states have shaped and selectively embraced institutions and doctrines (like the "Responsibility to Protect," or "R2P," of 2005) to serve their own interests. In line with the Eurocentrism critique often expressed by non-Western observers, this can suggest that humanitarian intervention uncomfortably parallels the earlier "civilizing mission" of late nineteenth-century imperialism, and inherits something of its orientalist bias. Nevertheless, Western human rights discourse may, it has been argued, be able to find and explore common ground in non-Western traditions of, say, Islam or Chinese Confucianism. And in the last analysis, as one defender of expanding international norms says, "Culture is *not* destiny" (Donnelly, 2003, 88).

Less controversially, as the will to intervene militarily to stem human rights abuses has waned, the role of the UN and of myriad NGOs in practical matters of human well-being—in disaster relief, child welfare, disease eradication, protection of wildlife, and ecological issues—has grown. There has been a significant increase in the number, resources, and reach of human rights NGOs in the post-Cold War era of the 1990s and subsequently, involving often an active cooperation among groups acting within states and across state boundaries, sometimes in collaboration with state authorities, but often in opposition to the conventional understanding of state sovereignty. Though NGOs are arguably of growing importance in IR, the ambiguity of their role (as both lobbies for a host of policy issues and as activists on the ground) has made them something of a blind spot in a discipline much more familiar with the business of state power and state security. Nevertheless, some scholars would insist that many of the soft issues of human rights, global ecology, and human welfare are inherently—sooner or later— likely to impact upon state security. The need for more attention to local and global social conditions as a focus for IR has been emphasized by some scholars like Jan Aart Scholte (a coordinator of the "Building Global Democracy Project"). Scholte argued in the 1990s for redirecting attention away from the state per se to multiple, often nonstate actors, and toward a multidimensional concept of the relationship between social relations and global politics. Such an understanding of the implications of extreme inequality in a globalized world calls, he claimed, for breaking down the disciplinary walls between IR, Sociology, History, Economics, Anthropology, and Political Science (Scholte, 1993, 143–4).

A growing variety of international organizations, most of a nonpartisan nature, function as quasi-charitable organizations to facilitate development and encourage understanding, peace, and justice—though some highly visible NGOs embrace confrontation, and depend on the power of publicity and "world opinion" in an internet and satellite TV connected world. The realm of supranational activism extends beyond relations with governing bodies, though many NGOs have consultative status with, for instance, the UN Economic and Social Council (ECOSOC), the Council of Europe, or the Organization of American States. Amnesty International (1961), a London-based human rights group dedicated to bringing international law to bear on rights abusers, has sections in 41 countries and an international secretariat with a staff of 120 and 50 researchers; Greenpeace (1971), founded in Canada with its headquarters in Amsterdam, the Netherlands, is dedicated to worldwide environmentalism and peace; Human Rights Watch (1978), founded following the Helsinki Accords of 1975 to name and shame rights abusers (especially in the Soviet bloc), is a well-funded research organization with a global remit; and *Médecins Sans Frontières* (1971), founded in Geneva, Switzerland, after the humanitarian crisis in Biafra, asserts that all peoples have a right to health care, and is especially active in refugee camps and areas of civil strife. It called for military intervention during the Rwanda massacre.

Such international but non-governmental bodies represent an area largely ignored in much IR scholarship because it is not the hard stuff of Realpolitik and power politics, though activist NGOs have come to figure more largely in what might be called the "alternative" IR of human rights scholars, feminists, and ecologists who emphasize the way the mainstream discipline reflects masculinist and Western assumptions about power generally and the exploitative relationship especially of the developed to the underdeveloped world. Ann Tickner, for example, queried the "autonomy of the political" in much IR scholarship and called for it to pay more attention to the idea of the *collective empowerment of people* rather than being obsessed with the state, its sovereignty, and its coercive power of domination (Tickner, 1995, 67).

The UN's practical work at the ground level has evolved from a charter that was much more explicit than the League's had been in giving the international organization a broad role, not only in matters of collective security, but in economic, social, and cultural affairs, reflecting no doubt the fact that many of the new member states were postcolonial societies more acutely interested in accelerated state-directed economic development than in security or in Western-defined human rights. Nevertheless, some would argue that membership in the UN and participation in a plethora of international organizations advancing social welfare, the protection of women and children, and at least a gesture toward the goals of a global human rights regime has been instrumental in shaping what it is to *be* a state. As some Constructivists would argue, these facts have shifted the understanding of how sovereignty works and what its limits may be for polities inhabiting, if not exactly a global civic sphere, at least a world of much rhetoric and some practice.

The United States and human rights "norms" in world society

For its part, the United States has generally been reluctant to acknowledge the validity of the UN and NGO-inspired global human rights regime. Since 9/11, the United States, though eager for foreign "war criminals" to be brought to international justice, refuses itself to accept the jurisdiction of the International Court of Justice (out of fear that its own abuses at Abu Graib or Guantanamo will result in "political" prosecutions of US military personnel). George W. Bush declared a "war on terror" and argued that this was a real war, but in the absence of a formal declaration of war or indeed a state adversary, and invoked the United States' right to hold enemy combatants without trial for the duration (whatever that might be—some prisoners at Guantanamo have been there for more than a decade)—but at the same time resisted the logical corollary of war combatant status by refusing to accept the applicability of the Geneva Conventions with regard to the treatment of prisoners of war.

Rendition (the abduction and secret transportation of suspected enemies of the United States) and torture (waterboarding, sleep deprivation, solitary confinement, use of loud, disorienting noise, etc.) violate the "norms" of both international law and a supposed global human rights regime—which nevertheless the United States is ready to invoke when it is a matter of an enemy's abuses (as with Saddam Hussein) but rationalize as necessary to protect American citizens in the war on terror. These contradictions stem in part from the familiar sense of American exceptionalism that has long served to justify America to itself, in part from the fact that a great superpower might be expected to pick and choose whatever argument best serves its interests (the powerful do what they will, the weak what they must). The result, however, is that—as human rights culture and juridical processes have gained ground globally—the largest power (if a defensive one and perhaps a declining one) increasingly seemed to be itself a "rogue state."

Of course, the contradictions in much US rhetoric and policy since 9/11 have reflected the conundrum of how states are to deal with the security threats posed by nonstate actors like Al-Qaeda, a relatively minor theme in the long historical narrative of diplomacy, war, and peace. Facilitated by the diasporic, globalized character of the modern world and modern communications, this threat is untheorized, perhaps untheorizable, by a mainstream IR scholarship preoccupied with the concepts of sovereignty, state power, rational choice, and system logic. No one would claim that Al-Qaeda violence can be simply dealt with by improving social conditions in the underdeveloped world, but as Paul Kennedy, echoing many others, has observed, in 1947 the differential in average income between the West and the developing world was about 13 to 1; by the end of the century this had become 60 to 1 (Kennedy, 2006, 122). Some would argue that putting resources into improving life in places that have proved to be refuges and breeding grounds for extremism would be at least as constructive a way of meeting the apparently intractable security problem of terrorism as drones dropping bombs on villages in Helmand province.

The democratic peace

The neo-Wilsonianism that surfaced in American foreign policy in the aftermath of the Cold War—the hope that the sole remaining superpower might reform the world order in its own image through a general, perhaps enforced, democratization of nonliberal, generally non-Western states—resonated strongly with, and selectively drew from, the revival in IR of a sustained debate over the theory of the "democratic peace," however much, as one critic has put it, "hitching the zone of democratic peace to the calculations of a hegemon is to mix Kant with Hobbes" (Smith, 2011, 152–3).

The assault by Neoliberals and human rights advocates on the concept of a traditional IR of competitive sovereign states pursuing security and power within an anarchic system was accompanied by a revival of the Kantian idea of a democratic peace. This debate has challenged Realist and Neorealist assumptions by questioning the notion of "like units" (of undifferentiated unitary sovereign states) in IR theory and focusing on ideology (democratic values), (re)constructed identity (as in the European Union), and structure (state constitutions) in search for the differences that make some states less likely to war against each other. The democratic peace anticipated a post-Cold War transition to a world that is more democratic, less security-competitive (at least among liberal states), and less distinguished by the sovereignty of the Westphalian past.

Following the seminal work of Michael Doyle in the 1980s, there was a spate of research in the 1990s and early twenty-first century into issues inspired by Kant's conception of "cosmopolitan law" and, more specifically, his argument (in *Perpetual Peace*, 1795) that Republics (democracies in modern parlance) would be less prone to conflict than autocracies. Neo-Kantian analysis and predictions have been subjected to research by a number of political scientists and historians—often using (or contesting the use of) historical case studies. Though Spencer R. Weart's historical "proof" (in *Never at War*, 1998) has been challenged, examination of the historical record seems cautiously to confirm that while democracies are not necessarily less likely to engage in conflict, such conflict has mostly been with other regime types, not with other democracies. It may be argued that as a result of the spread of liberal democracies the system itself is much less prone to the kind of warfare that characterized the Westphalian system. This is a world in which regulating war among sovereign nations (as in the eighteenth century) is no longer the central purpose of international law because formal, declared state-to-state war has largely ceased to be endemic in the system. There is also some indication that the democratic peace can be regarded as an evolutionary "learning process" and that democracies seem to be faster learners in this regard.

Others question the definition of "democracy" in many studies (how should we regard the 1914 German Empire, with its universal manhood suffrage and parliamentary politics?), while some stress structural rather than ideological factors (it is simply easier for autocratic regimes to go to war than for democracies to mobilize and sustain political support), or have argued that the pacifism of liberal democracies derives less from political values than from their participation in the global marketplace and the norms of "market democracy" (free trade, contractual equality, trust, etc.). Somewhat narrowing the debate, the historian James Sheehan has argued (in *The Monopoly of Violence*, 2007) that the democratic peace of the European Union is a specifically European response to the trauma of twentieth-century warfare, a particular, perhaps uniquely, learned response, rather than a global phenomenon. He cites, for example, a 2003 poll that while 55 percent of Americans strongly agree that war may be necessary to obtain justice, only 12 percent of French and Germans do.

Generally, the greatest challenge to the idea of a liberal democratic peace has not been that of Realists (though many have heaped scorn on the concept) but the events of the past decade, including the manifest failure of hegemonic America to impose a democratic world order. Moreover, the violence and instability of the new century seems to provide ample evidence that the different character of states may be of less significance than resurgent idealisms (including fundamentalist religion) and recurring economic crises. As one journalist put it not long ago, those liberal internationalists who shared a certain euphoria in the 1990s face a world where the "script has gone awry" and there is a need to "scale down" expectations of shared norms of international order (Timothy Garton Ash, the *Guardian*, January 26, 2011).

***

In the end, some, like Krasner, would argue that the view of a contemporary erosion of sovereignty is "historically myopic," that there has never been a "golden age" for sovereignty: "the sovereign state model has always been a cognitive script; its basic rules are widely understood but also frequently violated" (Krasner, 2001, 17). On the one hand, such a view is congenial to those historians who have argued that the Westphalian model of sovereignty has hardly ever adequately defined historical practice and thus cannot be a reliable building block for IR theory. But it also suggests an ahistoricity of its own ("has always been"?) that downplays modern and postmodern changes that have arguably made the gap between concept and practice progressively larger and less exceptional—whether due to capitalist globalization; communications technologies that enhance communities of nonstate actors; diasporas and their mixed loyalties and conflicted subjectivities; a spreading global human rights regime; or the growth of international, supranational, and nongovernmental institutions.

The nineteenth-century art of international relations, and its assumptions about the nation-state (no doubt to some extent grounded psychologically in the sovereign-self of bourgeois individualism) can hardly be a guide to the international—perhaps that term itself is no longer adequate—relations of the future. The nation-state per se may not be obsolete, may even be reborn as an atavism nostalgically reimagined, but the river of history flows. The state's global contexts and its internal character today can hardly be compared with those known by Bismarck or even John Foster Dulles. As the "realist" E. H. Carr, somewhat surprisingly perhaps, put it in *The Twenty Years' Crisis*,

> One prediction may be made with some confidence. The concept of sovereignty is likely to become in the future even more blurred and indistinct than it is at present.... It was never more than a convenient label.... (230)

Recommended reading

For some observations on the return to history in IR scholarship, emphasizing its contribution to the agency-structure debate, see Geoffrey Roberts, "History, Theory and the Narrative Turn in IR," *Review of International Studies* 32 (2006), 703–14.

Some early responses to Huntington's thesis can be found in Huntington et al., *The Clash of Civilizations? The Debate* (1996). For a less essentialized treatment of civilizations, see Robert W. Cox, "Thinking About Civilizations," *Review of International Studies* 26 (2000), 217–34. The preoccupation with "civilizations" in IR can be traced in publications such as Mark B. Slater, *Barbarians and Civilization in International Relations* (2002), who is concerned with strategies of differentiation as exercises in power; Johann P. Arnason, *Civilizations in Dispute: Historical Questions and Theoretical Traditions* (2003); the 2005 ISA workshop papers presented in Martin Hall and Patrick Thaddeus (eds.), *Civilizational Identity: The Production and Reproduction of "Civilizations" in International Relations* (2007); Peter J. Katzenstein (ed.), *Civilizations in World Politics* (2009), who offered his own rebuttal of Huntington's thesis; or M. Michalis and F. Petito (eds.), *Civilisational Dialogue and World Order: The Other Politics of Cultures, Religions and Civilizations in International Relations* (2009).

F. H. Hinsley's *Sovereignty* (1966) has long offered the standard view of this central (Western) concept, though students will find a more contemporary summation in Robert H. Jackson's *Sovereignty: Evolution of an Idea* (2007); also see the essays in Jackson (ed.), *Sovereignty at the Millennium* (1999). For a social Constructivist view emphasizing "the mutability of political discourse," see Onuf's "Sovereignty: Outline of a Conceptual History," *Alternatives* 16 (1991), 425–46. The role of the concept beyond the West has been marginal to much of this debate, but see Christopher Clapham, "Sovereignty and the Third World States," *Sovereignty at the Millennium*, 100–15, and Jackson's *Quasi-States: Sovereignty, International Relations, and the Third World* (1990), where he employs the concept of "negative sovereignty." For Africa especially, see William Reno, *Warlord Politics and African States* (1998), which addresses the political economy of post-independence African "shadow states," receivers of Cold War patronage where a wide array of roles are contracted to outsiders, and Kevin C. Dunn and Timothy M. Shaw (eds.), *Africa's Challenge to International Relations Theory* (2001).

For examples of the use of globalization themes in addressing issues of state identity and sovereignty, see Ian Clark, *Globalization and Fragmentation: International Relations in the Twentieth Century* (1997), or Saskia Sassen, *Losing Control? Sovereignty in an Age of Globalization* (1996). For debate over imperialism and sovereignty sparked by Michael Hardt and Antonio Negri, *Empire* (2000), see a special issue of the *Review of International Studies* on "Empires, Systems and States," 27 (2001). The influence of diasporas on IR thinking and as independent actors is addressed in Yossi Shain and Aharon Barth, "Diasporas and International Relations Theory," *International Organization* 57 (2003), 449–79.

For contemporary debate over the European Union as a transnational phenomenon, a superstate in the making, or a "normative power," see Alan S. Milward, *The European Rescue of the Nation State* (2nd edn., 2002); Ian Manners, *Normative Power Europe: A Contradiction in Terms?* (2000); Etienne Balibar, *We the People? Reflections on Transnational Citizenship* (2002); or, in another direction, Mai'a K. Davis Cross, *Security Integration in Europe: How Knowledge-Based Networks are Transforming the European Union* (2011). For the concept generally of a "new medievalism" of overlapping authorities and multiple loyalties, and what it might mean for IR theory, see Jörg Friedrichs, "The Meaning of New Medievalism," *European Journal of International Relations* 7 (2001), 475–501. Andrew Moravcsik, "The Origins of Human Rights Regimes: Democratic Delegation in Postwar Europe," *International Organization* 54 (2000), 217–52, and "Explaining International Human Rights Regimes: Liberal Theory and Western Europe," *European Journal of International Relations* 1 (1995), 157–89, focuses on the European Convention on Human Rights.

Ways in which the expanding global human rights regime has impacted the concept of sovereignty have been explored by Christian Reus-Smit, from a Constructivist perspective, in "Human Rights and the Social Construction of Sovereignty," *Review of International Studies* 27 (2001), 519–38. There is a substantial general literature on human rights and interventionism. Paul Sieghart's *The Lawful Rights of Mankind: An Introduction to the International Legal Code of Human Rights* (1985) is useful, as is John Vincent, *Human Rights and International Relations* (1986); more recent scholarship would include Tim Dunne and Nicholas J. Wheeler (eds.), *Human Rights in Global Politics* (1999); David P. Forsythe (ed.), *Human Rights and Comparative Foreign Policy* (2000); Jack Donnelly, *Universal Human Rights in Theory and Practice* (2nd edn., 2003); Micheline R. Ishay, *The History of Human Rights: From Ancient Times to the Globalization Era* (2004); and Alice Bullard (ed.), *Human Rights in Crisis* (2008). Also see Paul Gordon Lauren, *The Evolution of International Human Rights: Visions Seen* (2nd edn., 2003), and Michael Barnett, *Empire of Humanity: A History of Humanitarianism* (2011). Aspects of Eurocentrism are explored in Lynda Bell, Andrew J. Nathan, and Ilan Peleg (eds.), *Negotiating Culture and Human Rights* (2001); John M. Headley, *The Europeanization of the World: On the Origins of Human Rights and Democracy* (2007); and Samuel Moyne's *The Last Utopia: Human Rights in History* (2010). Terry Nardin's *Law, Morality, and the Relations of States* (1983) offered a useful general exploration of the concepts of international society and the "common rules" of international law.

The current fashion for "transnational history" is addressed in a special issue of *International History Review* (Vol. 33, 2011). Also see Thomas Risse-Kappen (ed.), *Bringing Transnational Relations Back In: Non-State Actors, Domestic Structures, and International Institutions* (1995). On NGOs see John Boli and George M. Thomas (eds.), *Constructing World Culture: International Nongovernmental Organizations Since 1875* (1999).

Scholarly work on the "democratic peace" has been a growth industry since the turn of the century. A scholarly overview and assessment (as of 2005) can be found in Karen Rasler and William R. Thompson, *Puzzles of the Democratic Peace: Theory, Geopolitics, and the Transformation of World Politics* (2005). A number of critical responses to Weart can be found in an issue of the *International History Review* 23, 4 (2001). More recently, see the special issue of *Millennium* 37, 3 (2009), "Interrogating Democracy in International Relations," and a "roundtable" discussion of the theory and practice of democratic peace in *International Relations* 25, 2 (2011). On the somewhat controversial issue of international "learning" and democratic states, see George Modelski, "Is World Politics Evolutionary Learning?" *International Organization* 44 (1990), 1–24, and, more recently, Lars-Erik Cederman, "Back to Kant: Reinterpreting the Democratic Peace as a Macrohistorical Learning Process," *American Political Science Review* 95 (2001), 15–31. For strongly skeptical responses to the idea of the democratic peace, see articles by Christopher Layne ("Kant or Cant: The Myth of the Democratic Peace") and David E. Spiro ("The Insignificance of the Liberal Peace") in a special issue of *International Security* 19 (1994), as well as Layne's robust attack, "Shell Games, Shallow Gains, and the Democratic Peace," *International History Review* 23 (2001), 799–813.

AFTERWORD: DESCRIPTION, PREDICTION, POLICY—DOES HISTORY MATTER?

A much-discussed and debated issue, one that brought into question the use of history in establishing a basic predictive tenet of IR theory, arose with the peacetime disintegration of the Soviet Union. Would a world defined by a historically unprecedented "unipolarity"—by a single land, sea, and air global superpower—herald the end of the logic of balance of power? Would such a system prove stable or unstable? European history, which had been used to establish balancing as a law of political behavior, did not at first appear to provide much of a guide to a unipolar system, unless one regarded America as a kind of new Rome, and the "order" it enforces as an imperial *pax Americana*—and such analogic flights seem largely rhetorical. What could the social science of IR predict? The debate stretches beyond the heady era of triumphalism and confidence into a present marked by the tenacity of nonstate terrorism, economic crisis, and the rise of regional—but not yet global—power competitors pressing against if not exactly challenging the American dominium.

The "unipolar moment" has generated a great deal of heat within IR but little resolution. Realists rushed to argue that such a state of global affairs was "unnatural," contravening the dictates of an anarchic sovereign state system that would surely see the emergence sooner or later of balancing against American hegemony. The concept of universal empire had been largely relegated to an Asiatic past in most IR texts. By the end of the first decade of the twenty-first century, however, a number of scholars attempted to come to grips with the continued absence of significant balancing against American hegemony. Against the certainty expressed by Waltz and others in the early 1990s that it was "just a matter of time" before balancing—that is, before some version of historically familiar multipolarity—would reassert itself, there is now an arrayed spectrum of opinion. Some would argue, following the distinction Stephen Walt had drawn between "balance of power" and "balance of threat" (Walt, 1985), that the absence of balancing against the United States can be explained by America's "benign" character—that, while the United States has a global reach, it did not represent a security threat to most other powers. Others observe that the United States is not a *contiguous* threat to most states, being isolated geographically from continental powers beyond the Western Hemisphere. Still others have attempted to draw a distinction between "hard" balancing, involving military alliances and the threat of war, and "soft" balancing, involving opposition—like that of France and Germany over the US decision to invade Iraq in 2003—that is well short of formal offensive or defensive alliance. Mearsheimer based his own explanation on a resources argument: though the United States may seem to be a global hegemon, in fact no state has the power necessary to dominate the global, as opposed to a regional, system (Mearsheimer, 2001b).

To the extent this issue has developed as an exploration of the limitation of IR theory and prediction, much of the debate has pitted Realist against Realist. Perhaps the most interesting revisionist argument has been offered by Stephen Brooks and William Wohlforth (*World Out of Balance: International Relations and the Challenge of American Primacy*, 2008). Balance of power theory in fact predicts, they claim, that opposition would likely coalesce against a *rising* hegemon. The United States is not a rising threat, but rather has been confirmed in its global dominance since the Second World War. It thus presents a quite different case, as overt opposition to an *established* hegemon would expose balancers to unacceptable risks.

History, which seemed not to have much to offer beyond confirming balancing in the (European) past, has however been brought back into this debate by Jack Levy and William R. Thompson who argue that the best historical parallel with contemporary America is not that of expansionist land-based powers familiar to European history, but the unprecedented global *maritime* dominance of nineteenth-century Britain. Britain, a famous advocate of balancing on the European continent, was historically not at all interested in a doctrine of balance *at sea*. Nor, as the dominant naval power, did it in fact inspire the same kind of fearful balancing behavior against its domination that might be predicted against a hegemon on land. Alliance behavior, Levy and Thompson claim, works differently according to the kind of power (territorial, economic, or maritime) expressed, whether its field is a region or the world at large, and the purposes for which it is employed: "Unlike land-based empires, dominance in markets and on the seas does not generally involve infringements on territorial sovereignty of other leading powers in more developed areas" (Levy and Thompson, 2010, 17). Though one might note that such a generalization seems to fly in the face of the history of aggressive thalassocracies (sea powers) from ancient Athens to imperial Japan, they would argue that the global "order" advanced by Britain in the nineteenth and America in the twentieth and early twenty-first centuries provided real benefits to other states that generally counterbalanced any threat they may have posed to those states' sovereignty.

Levy and Thompson invoke history, but their contribution reminds us that there is not "a" history, but many possible, perhaps parallel narratives. To make use of the history of Great Britain—both a European and a global maritime power—is to invoke Janus, the Roman god of beginnings and endings, of war and peace. One face looks toward the horror of the Somme as an end result of the European doctrine of balance of power; the other, toward the way in which the Royal Navy and the Empire-Commonwealth can be made to point toward the contemporary globalization admired by Niall Ferguson. Shift the location and perspective, of course, and other lessons come into focus. "Benign" drops away and darker postcolonial readings assert themselves. And China, from its own millennia-informed perspective may draw from a yet deeper trove of historical evidence and reasoning.

***

All schools of IR "use" history—historical evidence if not historicist understanding or historical methodology—in one way or another. At the most basic level, history offers them a reservoir of empirical data for constructing theory and vetting hypotheses, but it also offers narratives and chronologies that inevitably introduce the problem of change through time, of origins and endings, of emergence, evolution, and decay. Because Political Science, Sociology/Anthropology, and Economics are prone to building models of just how a state system, a social group, or a market works, and are not always interested in or able to accommodate an historical questioning of just how these structured institutions and regimes come about—or may cease to operate effectively—historians find themselves often cast in the role of skeptical critics of much IR theorizing. On the other hand, many world and international historians, like many historians generally, find social science formulations critical in determining which "facts" are necessary to narration as well as analysis. This antinomy—history versus theory—is, then, misleading.

The one issue that does seem to separate history from the other disciplines that contribute to IR is the way historians are generally concerned not to wrench an empirical fact out of its temporal and cultural context, its *moment et milieu*. This reluctance can significantly inhibit the historian's willingness to sign on to the view that IR can or should be a predictive social science, and yet most historians like to believe in the usefulness of history and are prone to quote some version of George Santayana's dictum that those who cannot remember the past are condemned to repeat it. At the minimum, most historians would caution IR scholars and those who seek to employ their work to inform contemporary policy to pay closer attention to the limitations and complications inherent in drawing parallels between the texts, actions, and mentalities of the past and our own present and future.

To judge the potential usefulness of history requires first that one consider the assumptions buried in any unexamined appropriation of the past—that "human nature" is a constant, that similar material conditions will produce similar opportunities, constraints, and outcomes, that past values and ambitions are comparable to those of our time. This is not only of course a problem for Realists; Liberals may also make ahistorical, universal assumptions about the continuity of ethical discourse across time when history suggests a plurality of discourses among different cultures in different times.

The uses to which history is put cannot be critiqued without paying some attention to the ultimate purpose of the discipline of IR (if it has one). Is it simply to enable states (especially our own) to secure themselves, as they have done throughout history, in a competitive and threatening world? If so, the history that is most useful indeed may be that of Realism's canon, of Machiavelli and Hobbes, the balance of power, and Clausewitz's observation that war is simply politics by other means. But if its goal is, as many of the discipline's founders believed, to encourage the rational pursuit of a more peaceful global society, then the history of most interest may lie elsewhere, in eras of peace as more than interregnums between conflict, in the traditions of international law and arbitration, in the development of transnational institutions, and in a perspective that regards the recourse of states to force as not dictated by human nature or a simple corollary to a competitive system, but as a breakdown, failure, or pathology and that peaceful relations rather than the armed search for state security is the categorical imperative and end object of democracies which can "learn" from history. History may of course serve to confirm yet other teleologies—that, say, international relations since the early modern era, if properly interrogated, can reveal the evolving interests of global capital, that the history of conflict between competing commercial and financial interests as well as the exploitative relationship between metropole and periphery, between haves and have-nots, have more to tell us than theories of *state* behavior, that beneath the hegemonic conflict of states or civilizations or religions lies the conflict of class.

***

What might History bring to the actual business of making and conducting foreign policy? E. H. Carr believed in *progress*, including "moral progress," leading one scholar to label his perspective "utopian realism" (Howe, 1994). But Carr also acknowledged that the lessons of history may be difficult to read because we ourselves are enmeshed in its processes, its progress is rarely linear, and one must be cautious of drawing lessons from apparent repetitions in the historical record—which brings to mind Marx's famous observation, with regard to Napoleon's coup of 18 Brumaire and Louis Napoleon's a half-century later, that history repeats itself, first as tragedy and then as farce. For Carr, history is continuous development, though exactly *whither* it is tending may be only obscurely apprehended.

Gordon Craig, though by no means opposed to the tendency of political scientists to construct predictive theories and hypotheses about the conduct of international relations, emphasized the need to remain sensitive, when using historical example, to the particulars of time and place. One of the likeliest pitfalls in formulating present policy is, then, the mistake of assuming that a well-known historical phenomenon is exactly applicable to the present: as in the "lessons" of Munich or Vietnam or the Cold War. In 1956, Anthony Eden, the British Prime Minister who had served as foreign secretary during the late 1930s until resigning over Neville Chamberlain's appeasement policies, convinced himself that Egypt's Gamal Abdel Nasser was another Adolf Hitler and that his nationalization of the Suez Canal had to be resisted by force (an example, surely, of tragedy repeated as farce). Lyndon B. Johnson's advisors used a similar rhetoric with regard to the communist leaders of North Vietnam, while General Curtis LeMay, who had helped formulate American aerial warfare strategies during and after the Second World War, claimed that the only way to win in Vietnam was to "bomb them back to the stone age."

History is littered with the misreading of the present through a lens crafted from past experience with little regard to specific historical contexts. Also, the reading of history, and of the "answers" or "lessons" it offers, always debatable, can shift from era to era. Take the Vietnam War itself: in the 1970s, the lesson to be learned was the limit of American power generally and specifically the way "containment" strategy and "domino theory" simply misread the populist nationalism of the communist struggle in Indochina. By the Reaganite 1980s, the lesson most talked of was the way in which the Americans supposedly lost their will to prevail—through domestic dissention and liberal misgiving about the goals of the war. The Muse of History is after all part sphinx (posing unanswerable questions), but also part prostitute (serving whatever may be the prevailing ideology).

Whither?

An article a few years ago in the *New York Times* (June 11, 2009) by Patricia Cohen noted that diplomatic history still seems to be in decline, with few job openings, low enrolments in courses, and the journal *Diplomatic History* proposing to change its name in order to survive.

It may be, she reported, that fewer than half of college history departments in the United States have even a single diplomatic historian. If true, this fact may simply conceal a redefinition of diplomatic history, no longer compartmentalized as the study of high politics and foreign service elites but incorporated into a larger view. One historian Cohen interviewed observed that a future history of the then current Iraq and Afghan wars would be concerned with a host of issues beyond the comparatively narrow questions of what Bush said to Blair at Camp David or whether "the surge" worked. At the same time, many courses in American universities, traditionally taught as enclosed national surveys, are now offered with a regional or global focus, as the history of, say, the United States and the Atlantic world or, more generally, "the United States in the world."

Some IR scholars, in rejecting the rigidities of structural Realism, have widened their own frame of reference, incorporating essentially historical issues of social and cultural conditioning and the evolution and play of normative values. There are two things history can bring most directly to the contemporary practice of foreign relations. In a narrow sense, a deeper understanding of the culture and mentality of others is of fundamental importance in successful strategies of both war and peace. When the State Department rooted out those "Old China hands" during the anticommunist witch hunt of the later 1940s and early 1950s, it not only got rid of what had come to be considered dangerous left-wing bias, but deprived American policymakers of access to a deeper, more sophisticated understanding of China, its revolution, and the probable course of its development. In a larger sense, as often promised by world historians, history can encourage a shifting of perspective, a seeing through the other's eyes, which can lead to clearer and more *self-critical* analysis of what *we* are and what we do in the world. Self-criticism is not something US policymakers seem to do very well, but in an ever-more interconnected world, American exceptionalism and hubris may bear long-term costs.

***

IR seems to thrive in the contemporary American academy. Many of these programs, though commonly grounded in politics, encourage students to sample courses in History, Economics, Sociology/Anthropology, and culture-and-language studies, ideally not only to broaden one's access to a variety of approaches and information that may be relevant to good foreign policy analysis but in a larger sense to encourage an interdisciplinary back-and-forth that might serve to contest a little the premises and practices of each of these constituent disciplines. One may question, though, whether such contestation actually happens. Such programs are rather more *multi*disciplinary (where each does whatever it does and thus contributes to a useful bag of tricks) than *inter*disciplinary (where the theory and methods of one inform, interrogate, and ultimately co-constitute the others), leaving the student to construct the bridges that may link them. Maybe that's as it should be. At the end of the day, students should not expect definitive answers or indeed definitive questions from one disciplinary approach, however much it may claim to be based in rigorous scientific practice. As the poet William Blake admonished,

May God us keep/From Single vision & Newtons sleep.

NOTES

Introduction

1   Journals of general interest in the discipline would include the *European Journal of International Relations, International Organization, International Politics, International Relations*, the *International Studies Quarterly, Millennium*, the *Review of International Studies*, and *World Politics*. Those focusing on international history and diplomacy include *Diplomacy & Statecraft, Diplomatic History, International History Review*, and the *Journal of World History*. *New Political Economy* and the *Review of International Political Economy* address the subfield of international political economy. There are many more specialized journals such as the *Journal of the History of International Law, Cold War History*, or *International Security*. The most inclusive professional organization in the United States is the International Studies Association (f. 1959) and in the United Kingdom, the British International Studies Association (f. 1975), though in both countries historians of diplomacy and international studies have their own specialist organizations like the Society of Historians of American Foreign Relations (SHAFR, f. 1967).

Chapter 1

1   In the nineteenth-century sense (believers in individualism, meritocracy, progress, rationality, free trade, and suasion rather than force), with, often, an admixture of progressive social reformism.

Chapter 4

1   Quotations are from the 1954 Rex Warner translation, Thucydides, *History of the Peloponnesian War*, intro. by M. I. Finley (Penguin, 1972).

Chapter 5

1   The text referenced here is the Penguin edition of 2003, translated by George Bull.

WORKS CITED

Alkopher, Tal Dingott (2005). "The Social (and Religious) Meanings That Constitute War: The Crusade as Realpolitik vs. Socialpolitik," *International Studies Quarterly*, vol. 49, 715–37.

Aron, Raymond (1966). *Peace and War: A Theory of International Relations*. Garden City, NY: Doubleday.

Barkawi, Tarak, and Mark Laffey (2002). "Retrieving the Imperial: Empire and International Relations," *Millennium*, vol. 31, 109–27.

Bartelson, Jens (1995). *The Genealogy of Sovereignty*. Cambridge: Cambridge University Press.

Benner, Erica (2009). *Machiavelli's Ethics*. Princeton, NJ: Princeton University Press.

Bickerton, Christopher, Philip Cunliffe, and Alexander Gourevitch (2007). *Politics without Sovereignty: A Critique of Contemporary International Relations*. Abingdon: University College London Press.

Biersteker, Thomas J., and Cynthia Weber (eds) (1996). *State Sovereignty as Social Construct*. Cambridge: Cambridge University Press.

Black, Jeremy (2002). *European International Relations 1648–1815*. Basingstoke: Palgrave.

Black, Jeremy (2010). *A History of Diplomacy*. London: Reaktion Books.

Black, Jeremy (2012). *War and the Cultural Turn*. Cambridge: Polity Press.

Bloom, William (1990). *Personal Identity, National Identity and International Relations*. Cambridge: Cambridge University Press.

Booth, Ken (1991). "Security in Anarchy: Utopian Realism in Theory and Practice," *International Affairs*, vol. 67, 527–45.

Brown, Chris (2001). *Understanding International Relations*. Basingstoke: Palgrave.

Brown, Chris (2007). "Situating Critical Realism," *Millennium*, vol. 35, 409–16.

Bull, Hedley (1966). "International Theory: The Case for a Classical Approach," *World Politics*, vol. 18, 361–77.

Bull, Hedley (1977). *The Anarchical Society: A Study of Order in World Politics*. New York: Columbia University Press.

Butterfield, Herbert (1966). "The Balance of Power," in Herbert Butterfield and Martin Wight (eds), *Diplomatic Investigations: Essays in the Theory of International Politics*, 132–75. Cambridge, MA: Harvard University Press.

Buzan, Barry, and Richard Little (2000). *International Systems in World History: Remaking the Study of International Relations*. Oxford: Oxford University Press.

Buzan, Barry, and Richard Little (2001). "Why International Relations Has Failed as an Intellectual Project and What to Do about It," *Millennium*, vol. 30, 19–39.

Buzan, Barry, and Mathias Albert (2010). "Differentiation: A Sociological Approach to International Relations Theory," *European Journal of International Relations*, vol. 16, 315–37.

Byman, Daniel L., and Kenneth M. Pollack (2001). "Let Us Now Praise Great Men: Bringing the Statesman Back In," *International Security*, vol. 25, 107–46.

Campbell, Brian (2001). "Diplomacy in the Roman World (c.500 BC-AD235)," *Diplomacy & Statecraft*, vol. 12, 1–22.

Cardwell, Curt (2011). *NSC 68 and the Political Economy of the Early Cold War*. Cambridge: Cambridge University Press.

Carr, Edward Hallett (1946). *The Twenty Years' Crisis 1919-1939: An Introduction to the Study of International Relations* (2nd edn.). London: Macmillan.

Carr, Edward Hallett (1961). *What Is History?* New York: Vintage.

Clausewitz, Carl von (1831). *On War*. Everyman, from the 1984 Princeton Press edition.

Cohen, Benjamin J. (2007). "The Transatlantic Divide: Why Are American and British IPE So Different?" *Review of International Political Economy*, vol. 14, 197–219.

Cohen, Raymond (2001). "The Great Tradition: The Spread of Diplomacy in the Ancient World," *Diplomacy & Statecraft*, vol. 12, 23–38.

Condren, Conal (1997). "Political Theory and the Problem of Anachronism," in Andrew Vincent (ed.), *Political Theory: Tradition, Diversity, and Ideology*, 45–66. Cambridge: Cambridge University Press.

Cox, Robert W. (1981). "Social Forces, States and World Orders: Beyond International Relations Theory," *Millennium*, vol. 10, 126–55.

Cox, Robert W. (2000). "Thinking about Civilizations," *Review of International Studies*, vol. 26, 217–34.

Cox, Robert W. (2009). "The 'British School' in the Global Context," *New Political Economy*, vol. 14, 315–28.

Craig, Gordon A. (1979). "On the Nature of Diplomatic History: The Relevance of Some Old Books," in Paul Gordon Lauren (ed.), *Diplomacy: New Approaches in History, Theory, and Policy*, 21–42. New York: The Free Press.

Craig, Gordon A. (1983). "The Historian and the Study of International Relations," *American Historical Review*, vol. 88, 1–11.

Craig, Gordon A., and Alexander L. George (1990). *Force and Statecraft: Diplomatic Problems of Our Time* (2nd edn.). Oxford: Oxford University Press.

Curtis, Simon, and Marjo Koivisto (2010). "Towards a Second 'Second Debate'? Rethinking the Relationship between Science and History in International Theory," *International Relations*, vol. 24, 433–55.

Der Derian, James (1995). "A Reinterpretation of Realism: Genealogy, Semiology, Dromology," in Der Derian (ed.), *International Theory: Critical Investigations*, 363–96. London: Macmillan.

Deudney, Daniel (1995). "Nuclear Weapons and the Waning of the Real-State," *Daedalus*, vol. 124, 209–31.

Donnelly, Jack (1999). "The Social Construction of International Human Rights," in Tim Dunne and Nicholas J. Wheeler (eds), *Human Rights in Global Politics*, 71–102. Cambridge: Cambridge University Press.

Donnelly, Jack (2003). *Universal Human Rights in Theory and Practice* (2nd edn.). Ithaca, NY: Cornell University Press.

Dunne, Tim (1998). "International Theory and the Mirror of History [rev. art.]," *European Journal of International Relations*, vol. 4, 347–62.

Eckstein, Arthur M. (2003). "Thucydides, the Outbreak of the Peloponnesian War, and the Foundation of International Systems Theory," *International History Review*, vol. 25, 757–74.

Eckstein, Arthur M. (2010). "The Character of Pre-Modern Interstate Diplomacy," *International History Review*, vol. 32, 319–28.

Elshtain, Jean Bethke (1995). "Feminist Themes and International Relations," in James Der Derian (ed.), *International Theory: Critical Investigations*, 340–60. London: Macmillan.

Ferguson, Niall (2010). "Realism and Risk in 1938: German Foreign Policy and the Munich Crisis," in Rosecrance May, and Zara Steiner (eds), *History and Realism*, 155–84. Cambridge: Cambridge University Press.

Ferguson, Yale H., and Richard W. Mansbach (1988). *The Elusive Quest: Theory and International Politics*. Columbia, SC: University of South Carolina Press.

Works Cited

Ferguson, Yale H., and Richard W. Mansbach (2007). "Post-Internationalism and IR Theory," *Millennium*, vol. 35, 529–49.

Finley, M. I. (1972). "Introduction" to Thucydides *History of the Peloponnesian War*. London: Penguin Press.

Finley, M. I. (1977). *The Greek Historians* (first pub. 1959). London: Penguin Press.

Finnemore, Martha (1996). *National Interests in International Society*. Ithaca, NY: Cornell University Press.

Fox, William T. R. (1985). "E. H. Carr and Political Realism: Vision and Revision," *Review of International Studies*, vol. 11, 1–16.

Gaddis, John Lewis (1992/1993). "International Relations and the End of the Cold War," *International Security*, vol. 17, 5–58.

Gaddis, John Lewis (2001). "In Defense of Particular Generalization: Rewriting Cold War History, Rethinking International Relations Theory," in Colin Elman and Miriam Findius Elman (eds), *Bridges and Boundaries*, 301–26. Cambridge, MA: MIT Press.

Gaddis, John Lewis (2005). *The Cold War: A New History*. New York: Penguin Press.

Garst, Daniel (1989). "Thucydides and Neorealism," *International Studies Quarterly*, vol. 33, 3–28.

Gilbert, Alan (1999). *Must Global Politics Constrain Democracy? Great-Power Realism, Democratic Peace, and Democratic Internationalism*. Princeton, NJ: Princeton University Press.

Gilpin, Robert G. (1984). "The Richness of the Tradition of Political Realism," *International Organization*, vol. 38, 287–304.

Gilpin, Robert G. (1987). *The Political Economy of International Relations*. Princeton, NJ: Princeton University Press.

Gilpin, Robert G. (2005). "Conversations in *International Relations*: Interview with Robert Gilpin," *International Relations*, vol. 91, 361–72.

Goldstein, Erik (1991). *Winning the Peace: British Diplomatic Strategy, Peace Planning, and the Paris Peace Conference 1916–1920*. Oxford: Clarendon Press.

Gorman, Daniel (2012). *The Emergence of International Society in the 1920s*. Cambridge: Cambridge University Press.

Halliday, Fred (1999). *Revolution and World Politics: The Rise and Fall of the Sixth Great Power*. Durham, NC: Duke University Press.

Hamilton, Keith, and Richard Langhorne (1995). *The Practice of Diplomacy: Its Evolution, Theory and Administration*. London: Routledge.

Hobden, Stephen (1998). *International Relations and Historical Sociology: Breaking Down Boundaries*. London: Routledge.

Hobson, John M., and Leonard Seabrooke (2001). "Reimagining Weber: Constructing International Society and the Social Balance of Power," *European Journal of International Relations*, vol. 7, 239–74.

Hoffman, Mark (1987). "Critical Theory and the Inter-Paradigm Debate," *Millennium*, vol. 16, 231–49.

Hoffmann, Stanley (1959). "International Relations: The Long Road to Theory," *World Politics*, vol. 11, 346–77.

Hoffmann, Stanley (1977). "An American Social Science: International Relations," in *Daedalus*. Reprinted in *Janus and Minerva: Essays in the Theory and Practice of International Politics* (1987), 3–24. Boulder, CO: Westview Press.

Horowitz, Michael C. (2009). "Long Time Going: Religion and the Duration of Crusading," *International Security*, vol. 34, 162–93.

Howe, Paul (1994). "The Utopian Realism of E. H. Carr," *Review of International Studies*, vol. 20, 277–97.

Iriye, Akira (1997). *Cultural Internationalism and World Order*. Baltimore, MD: Johns Hopkins University Press.

Jervis, Robert (1976). *Perception and Misperception in International Politics*. Princeton, NJ: Princeton University Press.

John, Ieuan, Moorhead Wright, and John Garnett (1972). "International Politics at Aberystwyth 1919–1969," in Brian Porter (ed.), *The Aberystwyth Papers: International Politics 1919–1969*. London: Oxford University Press.

Kaiser, David (1990). *Politics and War: European Conflict from Phillip II to Hitler*. Cambridge, MA: Harvard University Press.

Kang, David C. (2007). "Stability and Hierarchy in East Asian International Relations, 1300–1900 CE," in Stuart J. Kaufman, Richard Little, and William C. Wohlforth (eds), *The Balance of Power in World History*, 199–227. London: Palgrave Macmillan.

Kaplan, Morton A. (1957). *System and Process in International Politics*. New York: John Wiley & Sons.

Katzenstein, Peter J. (1996a). *Cultural Norms and National Security: Police and Military in Postwar Japan*. Ithaca, NY: Cornell University Press.

Katzenstein, Peter J. (ed.) (1996b). *The Culture of National Security: Norms and Identity in World Politics*. New York: Columbia University Press.

Kaufman, Stuart J., and William C. Wohlforth (2007). "Balancing and Balancing Failure in Biblical Times: Assyria and the Ancient Middle Eastern System, 900–600 BCE," in Stuart J. Kaufman, Richard Little, and William C. Wohlforth (eds), *The Balance of Power in World History*, 22–46. London: Palgrave Macmillan.

Keck, Margaret E., and Kathryn Sikkink (1998). *Activists Beyond Borders: Advocacy Networks in International Politics*. Ithaca, NY: Cornell University Press.

Kegley, Charles R. (1993). "The Neoidealist Moment in International Studies? Realist Myths and the New International Realities," *International Studies Quarterly*, vol. 37, 131–46.

Kennedy, Paul (2006). *The Parliament of Man: The United Nations and the Quest for World Government*. London: Allen Lane.

Keohane, Robert O. (2009). "The Old IPE and the New," *Review of International Political Economy*, vol. 16, 34–46.

Keohane, Robert O., and Joseph S. Nye, Jr. (eds) (1972). *Transnational Relations and World Politics*. Cambridge, MA: Harvard University Press.

Kissinger, Henry (1994). *Diplomacy*. New York: Simon & Schuster.

Klusmeyer, Douglas B. (2011). "Contesting Thucydides' Legacy: Comparing Hannah Arendt and Hans Morgenthau on Imperialism, History and Theory," *International History Review*, vol. 33, 1–25.

Knutsen, Torbjörn L. (1997). *A History of International Relations Theory* (2nd edn. [1st edn. 1992]). Manchester: Manchester University Press.

Kokaz, Nancy (2001). "Between Anarchy and Tyranny: Excellence and the Pursuit of Power and Peace in Ancient Greece," *Review of International Studies*, vol. 27, 91–118.

Krasner, Stephen D. (1993). "Westphalia and All That," in Judith Goldstein and Robert O. Keohane (eds), *Ideas and Foreign Policy*, 235–64. Ithaca, NY: Cornell University Press.

Krasner, Stephen D. (1999). *Sovereignty: Organized Hypocrisy*. Princeton, NJ: Princeton University Press.

Krasner, Stephen D. (2001). "Rethinking the Sovereign State Model," *Review of International Studies*, vol. 27, 17–42.

Krasner, Stephen D. (2004). "Sharing Sovereignty: New Institutions for Collapsed and Failing States," *International Security*, vol. 29, 85–120.

Kuhn, Thomas S. (1962). *The Structure of Scientific Revolutions*. Chicago, IL: University of Chicago Press.

LaFeber, Walter (1994). *The American Age: United States Foreign Policy at Home and Abroad, 1750 to the Present* (2nd edn.). New York: Norton.

Lafont, Bertrand (2001). "International Relations in the Ancient Near East: The Birth of a Complete Diplomatic System," *Diplomacy & Statecraft*, vol. 12, 39–60.

Lake, David (2003). "The New Sovereignty in International Relations," *International Studies Review*, vol. 5, 303–23.

Lake, David (2007). "Escape from the State of Nature: Authority and Hierarchy in World Politics," *International Society*, vol. 32, 47–79.

Lapid, Yosef (1996). "Nationalism and Realist Discourses of International Relations," in Francis A. Beer, and Robert Hariman (eds), *Post-Realism: The Rhetorical Turn in International Relations*, 239–56. East Lansing, MI: Michigan State University Press.

Latham, Andrew A. (2011). "Theorizing the Crusades: Identity, Institutions, and Religious War in Medieval Latin Christendom," *International Studies Quarterly*, vol. 55, 223–43.

Lebow, Richard Ned (1994). "The Long Peace, the End of the Cold War, and the Failure of Realism," *International Organization*, vol. 48, 249–77.

Lebow, Richard Ned (2005). "Power, Persuasion and Justice," *Millennium*, vol. 33, 551–81.

Lévesque, Jaques (1997). *The Enigma of 1989: The USSR and the Liberation of Eastern Europe*. Berkeley, CA: University of California Press.

Levy, Jack S. (2001). "Explaining Events and Developing Theories: History, Political Science, and the Analysis of International Relations," in Colin Elman and Miriam Findius Elman (eds), *Bridges and Boundaries*, 39–83. Cambridge, MA: MIT Press.

Linklater, Andrew (1992). "The Question of the Next Stage in International Relations Theory: A Critical-Theoretical Point of View," *Millennium* 21, 77–100.

Linklater, Andrew (1996). "Citizenship and Sovereignty in the Post-Westphalian State," *European Journal of International Relations*, vol. 2, 77–103.

Lobell, Steven E., Norrin M. Ripsman, and Jeffrey W. Taliaferro (eds) (2009). *Neoclassical Realism, the State, and Foreign Policy*. Cambridge: Cambridge University Press.

Loughlin, Martin (2003). "Ten Tenets about Sovereignty," in Neil Walker (ed.), *Sovereignty in Transition*, 55–86. Portland, OR: Hart.

Lynch, Marc (2000). "The Dialogue of Civilisations and International Public Spheres," *Millennium*, vol. 29, 307–30.

Mackinder, Halford John (1902). *Britain and Her Seas*. New York: D. Appleton.

Maliniak, Daniel, et al. (2011). "International Relations in the US Academy," *International Studies Quarterly*, vol. 55, 437–64.

Mallett, Michael (2001). "Italian Renaissance Diplomacy," *Diplomacy & Statecraft*, vol. 12, 61–70.

Mann, Michael (1986). *The Sources of Social Power*, vol. i: *A History of Power from the Beginning to A.D. 1760*. Cambridge: Cambridge University Press.

Mansfield, H. C., and N. Tarcov (1996). "Introduction" to Machiavelli's *Discourses on Livy*, xvii–xlvii. Chicago, IL: University of Chicago Press.

Mattingly, Garrett (1955). *Renaissance Diplomacy*. Boston, MA: Houghton Mifflin.

Mazower, Mark (2012). *Governing the World: The History of an Idea*. New York: Penguin Press.

Mearsheimer, John J. (1990). "Back to the Future: Instability in Europe after the Cold War," *International Security*, vol. 15, 5–56.

Mearsheimer, John J. (2001a). *The Tragedy of Great Power Politics*. New York: W. W. Norton.

Mearsheimer, John J. (2001b). "The Future of the American Pacific," *Foreign Affairs*, vol. 80, 46–61.

Morgenthau, Hans (1948). *Politics Among Nations: The Struggle for Power and Peace*. New York: A. A. Knopf.

Morgenthau, Hans (1970). "The Intellectual and Political Functions of Theory," in *Truth and Power* [reprinted in James Der Derian (ed.), *International Theory: Critical Investigations* (1995), 36–52]. London: Macmillan.

Mueller, John (1995). *Quiet Cataclysm: Reflections on the Recent Transformation of World Politics*. New York: Harper Collins.

Nehring, Holger (2012). "What Was the Cold War?" *English Historical Review*, vol. 127, 920–49.

Nye, Joseph (1988). "Neorealism and Neoliberalism," *World Politics*, vol. 40, 235–51.

Obolensky, Dimitri (1971). *The Byzantine Commonwealth: Eastern Europe, 500–1453*. London: Weidenfeld & Nicolson.

Olson, William, and Nicholas Onuf (1985). "The Growth of a Discipline: Reviewed," in Steve Smith (ed.), *International Relations: British and American Perspectives*, 1–28. Oxford: Basil Blackwell.

Onuf, Nicholas Greenwood (1989). *World of Our Making: Rules and Rule in Social Theory and International Relations*. London: Routledge.

Osiander, Andreas (2001a). "Before Sovereignty: Society and Politics in *Ancient Régime* Europe," *Review of International Studies*, vol. 27, 119–45.

Osiander, Andreas (2001b). "Sovereignty, International Relations, and the Westphalian Myth," *International Organization*, vol. 55, 251–87.

Parker, Geoffrey (1988). *The Military Revolution: Military Innovation and the Rise of the West, 1500–1800*. Cambridge: Cambridge University Press.

Philpott, Daniel (2001). *Revolutions in Sovereignty: How Ideas Shaped Modern International Relations*. Princeton, NJ: Princeton University Press.

Pitkin, Hannah Fenichel (1984). *Fortune Is a Woman: Gender and Politics in the Thought of Niccolo Machiavelli*. Berkeley, CA: University of California Press.

Prokhovnik, Raia (2008). *Sovereignty: History and Theory*. Exeter: Imprint Academic.

Rasmusen, Mikkel Vedby (2003). "The History of a Lesson: Versailles, Munich and the Social Construction of the Past," *Review of International Studies*, vol. 29, 499–519.

Rendall, Matthew (2006). "Defensive Realism and the Concert of Europe," *Review of International Studies*, vol. 32, 523–40.

Reus-Smit, Christian (2001). "Human Rights and the Social Construction of Sovereignty," *Review of International Studies*, vol. 27, 519–38.

Ridolfi, Roberto (1967). *The Life of Francesco Guicciardini* [trans. Cecil Grayson]. London: Routledge & Kegan Paul.

Roberts, Geoffrey (2007). "Stalin at the Tehran, Yalta, and Potsdam Conferences," *Journal of Cold War Studies*, vol. 9, 6–40.

Roberts, Michael (1956). *The Military Revolution, 1560–1660*. Belfast: Marjory Boyd.

Ruggie, John Gerard (1983). "International Regimes, Transactions, and Change: Embedded Liberalism in the Postwar Economic Order," in Stephen Krasner (ed.), *International Regimes*, 195–231. Ithaca, NY: Cornell University Press.

Ruggie, John Gerard (1993). "Territoriality and Beyond: Problematizing Modernity in International Relations," *International Organization*, vol. 47, 139–74.

Ruggie, John Gerard (1998). "What Makes the World Hang Together? Neo-Utilitarianism and the Social Constructivist Challenge," *International Organization*, vol. 52, 855–85.

Russell, Greg (2005). "Machiavelli's Science of Statecraft: The Diplomacy and Politics of Disorder," *Diplomacy & Statecraft*, vol. 16, 227–50.

Sassen, Saskia (2003). "Globalization or Denationalization?" *Review of International Political Economy*, vol. 10, 1–22.

Schmidt, Brian C. (1998). *The Political Discourse of Anarchy: A Disciplinary History of International Relations*. Albany, NY: State University of New York Press.

Schmidt, Brian C. (2005). "Competing Realist Conceptions of Power," *Millennium*, vol. 33, 523–49.

Schroeder, Paul W. (1989). "The Nineteenth Century System: Balance of Power or Political Equilibrium?" *Review of International Studies*, vol. 15, 135–54.

Schroeder, Paul W. (1994). *Transformation of European Politics 1763–1848*. Oxford: Oxford University Press.

Works Cited

Schroeder, Paul W. (1997). "History and International Relations Theory: Not Use or Abuse, but Fit or Misfit," *International Security*, vol. 22, 64–74.

Schroeder, Paul W. (2001). "A. J. P. Taylor's International System," *International History Review*, vol. 23, 3–27.

Sheehan, James J. (2006). "The Problem of Sovereignty in European History," *American Historical Review*, vol. 111, 1–15.

Sked, Alan (1989). *The Decline and Fall of the Habsburg Empire 1815–1918*. New York: Longman.

Skocpol, Theda (1979). *States and Social Revolutions: A Comparative Analysis of France, Russia, and China*. Cambridge: Cambridge University Press.

Smith, Thomas (1999). *History and International Relations*. London: Routledge.

Smith, Tony (2011). "Democratic Peace Theory: From Promising Theory to Dangerous Practice," *International Relations*, vol. 25, 151–7.

Snyder, Glenn H. (2002). "Mearsheimer's World—Offensive Realism and the Struggle for Security: A Review Essay," *International Security*, vol. 27, 149–73.

Snyder, Jack (2002). "Anarchy and Culture: Insights from the Anthropology of War," *International Organization*, vol. 56, 7–45.

Spruyt, Hendrik (1994). *The Sovereign State and Its Competitors: An Analysis of Systems Change*. Princeton, NJ: Princeton University Press.

Steiner, Zara (2001). "The Treaty of Versailles Revisited," in Michael Dockrill and John Fisher (eds), *The Paris Peace Conference, 1919: Peace without Victory?* 13–34. New York: Palgrave.

Steiner, Zara (2010). "British Decisions for Peace and War 1938-1939: The Rise and Fall of Realism," in Ernest R. May, Richard Rosecrance, and Zara Steiner (eds), *History and Neorealism*, 129–54. Cambridge: Cambridge University Press.

Strayer, Joseph R. (1970). *On the Medieval Origins of the Modern State*. Princeton, NJ: Princeton University Press.

Struck, Bernhard (2011). "Space and Scale in International History," *International History Review*, vol. 33, 573–84.

Sullivan, Vickie B. (2004). *Machiavelli, Hobbes, and the Formation of a Liberal Republicanism in England*. Cambridge: Cambridge University Press.

Tadjbakhsh, Shahrbanou (2010). "International Relations Theory and the Islamic Worldview," in Amitav Acharya and Barry Buzan (eds), *Non-Western International Relations Theory*, 174–96. London: Routledge.

Tannenwald, Nina (2007). *The Nuclear Taboo: The United States and the Non-Use of Nuclear Weapons since 1945*. Cambridge: Cambridge University Press.

Taylor, A. J. P. (1954). *The Struggle for Mastery in Europe, 1848–1918*. Oxford: Clarendon Press.

Teschke, Benno (1998). "Geopolitical Relations in the European Middle Ages: History and Theory," *International Organization*, vol. 52, 325–58.

Tickner, J. Ann (1994). "A Feminist Critique of Political Realism," in Peter R. Beckman and Francine D'Amico (eds), *Women, Gender, and World Politics: Perspectives, Policies and Prospects*, 29–40. Westport, CT: Bergin & Garvey.

Tickner, J. Ann (1995). "Hans Morgenthau's Principles of Political Realism: A Feminist Reformulation," in James Der Derian (ed.), *International Theory* (1995), 53–71 [orig. pub. *Millennium*, vol. 17 (1988)].

Tilly, Charles (1992). *Coercion, Capital, and European States, AD 990–1992*. Oxford: Basil Blackwell (rev. edn.; first pub. 1990).

Trachtenberg, Marc (2001). "New Light on the Cold War?" *Diplomacy & Statecraft*, vol. 12, 10–17.

Trachtenberg, Marc (2006). *The Craft of International History: A Guide to Method*. Princeton, NJ: Princeton University Press.

Waever, Ole (1998). "The Sociology of a Not So International Discipline: American and European Developments in International Relations," *International Organization*, vol. 52, 687–727.

Walker, R. B. J. (1989). "History and Structure in the Theory of International Relations," *Millennium*, vol. 18 [reprinted in James Der Derian (ed.), *International Theory: Critical Investigations* (1995), 308–39].

Walker, R. B. J. (1993). *Inside/Outside: International Relations as Political Theory*. Cambridge: Cambridge University Press.

Walt, Stephen M. (1985). "Alliance Formation and the Balance of World Power," *International Security*, vol. 9, 3–43.

Waltz, Kenneth N. (1959). *Man, the State, and War: A Theoretical Analysis*. New York: Columbia University Press.

Waltz, Kenneth N. (1979). *Theory of International Politics*. Reading, MA: Addison-Wesley.

Waltz, Kenneth N. (2000). "Structural Realism after the Cold War," *International Security*, vol. 25, 5–41.

Watson, Adam (1992). *The Evolution of International Society: A Comparative Historical Analysis*. London: Routledge.

Weber, Max (1958). "Structures of Power," in H. H. Gerth and C. Wright Mills (eds), *From Max Weber: Essays in Sociology*. New York: Oxford University Press.

Weiler, Björn (2003). "The *Negotium Terrae Sanctae* in the Political Discourse of Latin Christendom," *International History Review*, vol. 25, 1–36.

Welch, David A. (2003). "Why International Relations Theorists Should Stop Reading Thucydides," *Review of International Studies*, vol. 29, 301–19.

Weltman, John J. (1995). *World Politics and the Evolution of War*. Baltimore, MD: Johns Hopkins University Press.

Wendt, Alexander (1992). "Anarchy Is What States Make of It: The Social Construction of Power Politics," *International Organization*, vol. 46, 391–425.

Wight, Martin (1966). "Why Is There No International Theory?" [reprinted in James Der Derian and Adam Watson (eds), *International Theory: Critical Investigations* (1995), 15–35].

Wohlforth, William C. (1994/1995). "Realism and the End of the Cold War," *International Security*, vol. 19, 91–129.

Wolpert, Andrew (2001). "The Genealogy of Diplomacy in Classical Greece," *Diplomacy & Statecraft*, vol. 12, 71–88.

Wright, Quincy (1942). *A Study of War*. Chicago, IL: University of Chicago Press.

Wright, Quincy (1955). *The Study of International Relations*. New York: Appleton-Century-Crofts.

INDEX

Locators following "n" refer to notes.

Index

Index

Index

Index

Index

Index